BASE
HALL OF FAME
OR HALL OF SHAME?

BASEBALL'S HALL OF FAME

OR HALL OF SHAME?

ROBERT W. COHEN

CARDOZA PUBLISHING

Cardoza Publishing has a library of more than 200 up-to-date and easy-to-read books on gaming and sports information. With more than 10,000,000 books in print, these titles represent the best-selling and most popular gaming books anywhere.

First Edition

Library of Congress Catalog No: 2008940737
ISBN: 1-58042-232-2

Visit the Cardoza Publsihing website or write us for a full list of our more than 200 titles.

CARDOZA PUBLISHING
P.O. Box 98115, Las Vegas, NV 89193
Phone (800)577-WINS
email: cardozabooks@aol.com
www.cardozabooks.com

TABLE OF CONTENTS

Acknowledgments

I wish to express my appreciation to Bill Deane, whose "Awards and Honors" chapter in *Total Baseball* proved to be an invaluable source of information to me during my research. Mr. Dean's material included all the voting results from the Hall of Fame balloting through 1992.

In loving memory of my dad, who instilled in me
a love of the game of baseball and a
great appreciation of the history of the sport.
May you rest in peace, Dad.

THE EARLY YEARS AND THE FIRST SIGNS OF FAVORITISM

The National Baseball Hall of Fame in Cooperstown, New York is unquestionably the most famous and prestigious sports Hall of Fame in existence. The odds against election are about 1,500 to 1 for the typical major leaguer, and enshrinement is considered to be the highest honor accorded to any player. The annual elections that are held to announce the latest inductees are followed very closely by fans of the game and, in some instances, inspire a great deal of controversy and debate. Baseball fans are very passionate about their favorite players, and are equally passionate about which ones should be inducted into Cooperstown.

There are those baseball purists who feel that only the greatest of the great should be enshrined, while many others have adopted a far more liberal philosophy. They feel that any player who was either a good, solid player for a very long period of time, or a very good player for a short period of time should be deemed worthy of election. There are even people who feel that a good player who truly excelled at only one aspect of the game should merit serious consideration.

Thus, in spite of the seemingly overwhelming odds against election, many of the selections that have been made over the years have inspired a great deal of controversy and second-guessing. The primary focus of this book will be on the validity of all the selections made, and, in some of the more questionable cases, providing a possible explanation as to the reasons behind the selections.

In the early years of the Hall's existence, it was never thought that the selection process would eventually prove to be such a point of contention. In fact, the Hall had two much more simplistic purposes behind its creation. The first of these was to assemble a collection of baseball artifacts that might serve as a tourist attraction to the village of Cooperstown, considered by many to be the game's birthplace. The second was to attempt to rekindle fan interest in the sport in the midst of the *Great Depression*. An earlier attempt had been made to accomplish the very same thing just a few years earlier when the All-Star game was played for the first time. Fans were encouraged to vote for the players they most wanted to see, briefly creating a positive reaction among patrons of the game. However, it was difficult for fans to attend games since the hot dog and soda they purchased at the ballpark was, in most cases, the only meal they could afford all day.

Nevertheless, fans gradually started returning to the game, and, in preparation for the opening of the Hall, two elections were held in 1936. The first was by the 226 members of the Baseball Writers Association of America (BBWAA), and the other was by a special 78-member Veterans Committee. The BBWAA was to select five "modern" players from the twentieth century, while the Veterans Committee was to select five old-timers from the nineteenth century. Both elections required that any player chosen must be named on at least 75 percent of the ballots. The five "moderns" chosen were Ty Cobb (named on 222 of the ballots), Babe Ruth and Honus Wagner (both named on 215), Christy Mathewson (named on 205), and Walter Johnson (named on 189). Unfortunately, the Veterans Committee was unable to agree on who their five players should be. As a result, no old-timers were elected. For that election, 59 votes were needed to meet the minimum 75 percent requirement, but only Cap Anson and Buck Ewing were able to accumulate as many as 40 votes.

Therefore, only the five aforementioned all-time greats were initially selected for induction. However, annual elections were held in each of the next three years, in which the BBWAA voted in eight more worthy players:

Napoleon Lajoie	(1937)
Tris Speaker	(1937)
Cy Young	(1937)

Grover Cleveland Alexander	(1938)
George Sisler	(1939)
Eddie Collins	(1939)
Willie Keeler	(1939)
Lou Gehrig	(1939)

During this same period, the original Veterans Committee was replaced by a smaller, more agreeable committee of Judge Landis, Ford Frick, Will Harridge, John Heydler, William Branham, and George Trautman. Thus, in essence, this committee was comprised of a commissioner, two league presidents, a retired league president, and the head of the National Association—all the men who held the power in baseball at the time. They appointed themselves the "Centennial Commission," and, from 1937 to 1938, took it upon themselves to elect George Wright, Morgan Bulkeley, Ban Johnson, John McGraw, Connie Mack, Alexander Cartwright and Henry Chadwick to the Hall. None of these men had distinguished themselves as ballplayers—they were either managers, developers, or off-the-field powers—and, in certain instances, represented the people who had selected the members on the committee to office. While McGraw and Mack were long-time managers who were deserving of a place in Cooperstown, the other selections represent the first instances of favoritism shown in the selection process.

When old-timers complained that no players whose careers ended prior to the turn of the century were being elected, this Centennial Commission streamlined itself down to just Landis, Frick, and Harridge, re-named itself the Old-Timers Committee, and made six more selections in 1939. The six players they named were Cap Anson, Buck Ewing, Candy Cummings, Old Hoss Radbourne, Albert Spalding, and Charles Comiskey. While the other five choices were all legitimate, Comiskey clearly reflected the bias of the members on the selection committee. A mediocre first baseman for three different major league teams, Comiskey was far more noteworthy as a baseball pioneer and the long-time owner of the Chicago White Sox. However, as owner of the Sox, he was well renowned for being a cheapskate and for mistreating his players. In fact, as we will see later, he was largely responsible for the Black Sox scandal of 1919.

By the time the Hall of Fame opened on June 12, 1939, in Cooperstown, it had 26 members—13 "modern" players elected by the BBWAA, six nineteenth century players selected by the Old-Timers Committee, and seven managers/executives/baseball pioneers selected by the Centennial Commission.

Some three years later, at the winter meetings held in Cincinnati in December of 1939, the writers decided to conduct an election every three years in the future, rather than on an annual basis. This ruling negatively impacted the Hall of Fame in two ways. Firstly, with elections being held more infrequently, attention was drawn away from the Hall. Fans eagerly anticipated the announcement of the annual selections, and their interest began to wane when they had to wait significantly longer for the elections to be held. Furthermore, a backlog of worthy candidates was created, making it more difficult for retired standouts to get elected.

With the names of so many outstanding players appearing on the ballot, it became more difficult for the voters to focus on the most worthy candidates, and for the players to meet the minimum 75 percent requirement for election. Thus, no new members were inducted in either 1940 or 1941, and, when the writers finally voted again in 1942, the only player they were able to agree on was Rogers Hornsby.

When the next election was held in 1945, no player was able to accumulate enough votes to be elected, despite the presence on the ballot of several all-time greats such as Lefty Grove and Jimmie Foxx. Fortunately, in 1945, a decision was reached to once again have the BBWAA vote every year.

Meanwhile, the composition of the Old-Timers Committee had been altered since its last set of selections in 1939. From 1939 through 1944, it consisted of Ed Barrow, president of the Yankees, Bob Quinn, president of the Braves, Sid Mercer, an old baseball writer, and Connie Mack. During this period, the Committee chose not to select anyone to the Hall. As a result, Rogers Hornsby was the only player inducted from 1940 through much of 1944. Then, in August of 1944, with Commissioner Landis suffering from ill health, he expanded the Old-Timers Committee to six members, adding Stephen C. Clark and Mel Webb. Clark was one of the Hall's founders, and Webb was a disagreeable old sportswriter from Boston who cost Ted Williams the MVP Award one year by leaving him completely off his ballot. Landis also gave the committee more power by appointing its members to be the trustees of the institution, and by establishing its existence through perpetuity. He further authorized its members to select players who played before 1900, and to dictate the rules and policies of the entire Hall of Fame selection process.

The first official act of this new "Permanent Committee" after meeting for the first time at Landis' funeral in November of 1944 was to elect him to the Hall of Fame. The validity of this selection will be discussed in a later chapter, but this was only the first of several rather questionable decisions the group would eventually make. Over the next two years, 1945 and 1946, the committee elected no fewer than 21 players from the nineteenth century and first few years of the twentieth. Approximately one-half of these selections were valid ones, but the others were all questionable. These players were:

Roger Bresnahan	(1945)
Dan Brouthers	(1945)
Fred Clarke	(1945)
Jimmy Collins	(1945)
Ed Delahanty	(1945)
Hugh Duffy	(1945)
Hughie Jennings	(1945)
Mike "King" Kelly	(1945)
Jim O'Rourke	(1945)
Wilbert Robinson*	(1945)
Jesse Burkett	(1946)
Frank Chance	(1946)
Johnny Evers	(1946)
Joe Tinker	(1946)

* Wilbert Robinson was elected as a player/manager/baseball pioneer.

Jack Chesbro	(1946)
Clark Griffith	(1946)
Tom McCarthy	(1946)
Joe McGinnity	(1946)
Eddie Plank	(1946)
Rube Waddell	(1946)
Ed Walsh	(1946)

Brouthers, Clarke, Collins, Delahanty, Duffy, Kelly, Griffith, McGinnity, Plank, and Walsh were all good choices, but the others were highly debatable, and, in some instances, unjustifiable. Each of these selections will be discussed in detail later in this book, but, for the first time, players were elected who clearly did not belong. The saddest part of this is that irreparable damage was done to the Hall, since its standards were lowered considerably. No longer could it be said that only great players resided in the Hall of Fame because several others of lesser ability had now been inducted as well. This created a gray area for voters in future elections, one that, unfortunately, still exists to this day.

SELECTION PROCESS AND ELIGIBILITY

There are several flaws in the selection process employed over the years to determine which players are most deserving of enshrinement at Cooperstown. Many of these defects will be touched on in later chapters. The one that will be mentioned here, though, is baseball's inability to change with the times. The BBWAA's initial assignment of conducting the elections back in 1936 seemed quite reasonable at the time. There was no television, most games were not broadcast over the radio, and the number of baseball publications and magazines were few and far between. Aside from former players, managers, and coaches, the baseball writers seemed to be the most knowledgeable people, and the most logical ones to be entrusted with making the selections. They represented the only true form of sports media in this country at that time.

However, as we all know, radio and television broadcasting of baseball games has grown dramatically over the past several decades. Specialized TV stations such as ESPN, that not only broadcast games, but show highlights on a nightly basis, and publications such as *The Sporting News* and *Sports Illustrated*, have become commonplace. Clearly, the baseball writers no longer hold a monopoly on the media frenzy surrounding the sport, and they are no longer the only people who are qualified to vote in the Hall of Fame elections. Yet they continue to be the only ones involved in the process. This system excludes others who are not only qualified to take part in the elections, but who, in many instances, are more qualified than the writers. It also works under the incorrect assumption that the writers, who usually come into closer contact with the players over the course of the season than do other members of the media, can put aside their own personal feelings and biases towards the players and base their selections strictly on performance and on-the-field achievements. As we have seen over the years, that is not always the case.

There are several examples of this. One would be Juan Marichal, who, with the exception of Sandy Koufax, was as great a pitcher as anyone during the 1960s. Yet, due to an unfortunate incident that occurred in a 1965 game between his San Francisco Giants and the archrival Los Angeles Dodgers in which he hit Dodger catcher John Roseboro over the head with a bat, Marichal had to wait until his third year of eligibility to be voted into Cooperstown. Meanwhile, contemporaries Bob Gibson, Tom Seaver, Jim Palmer, and later, Nolan Ryan, none of whom, with the possible exception of Gibson, was a better pitcher than Marichal, all made it in on the first try.

Another example would be Jim Rice. The former Boston Red Sox outfielder was far more of a borderline Hall of Fame candidate than Marichal, but his credentials were actually quite similar to those of media favorite Kirby Puckett, who was elected the first time his name appeared on the ballot. Rice, who shared a somewhat contentious relationship with the writers throughout his career, finally gained admittance in his last year of eligibility.

In addition, although his case could not be directly related to the Hall of Fame voting, Ted Williams' lack of popularity with the press would be another prime example of bias on the part of writers. The Red Sox great once lost an MVP vote by one point because one of the Boston sportswriters (the aforementioned Mel Webb) didn't give him as much as a tenth-place vote on his ballot.

It, therefore, seems quite clear that granting sole responsibility to one body of people during the selection process can be a dangerous thing, and that it can often lead to inaccuracies and injustices. Nevertheless, a system has evolved through the years that provides players with two means of getting into the Hall of Fame. Essentially, that system is the following:

- A player can be elected by either the Baseball Writers Association of America or by the Hall of Fame Veterans Committee.

- A player becomes eligible five years after he retires, if he plays at least ten seasons in the Major Leagues.
- To be selected for the Hall of Fame, a player must be named on at least 75 percent of the BBWAA ballots.
- A player becomes ineligible for election by the BBWAA if he has not been selected in the first fifteen years that his name has been on the ballot.
- Those who are not selected in their fifteen years of BBWAA eligibility are ineligible for five years following.
- After five years, those players rejected by the BBWAA become eligible to be elected by the Hall of Fame Veterans Committee.
- The old 15-member Veterans Committee, which was comprised of veteran players, managers, and/or baseball executives, was replaced in 2003 by a group comprised of the living members of the Baseball Hall of Fame (60), living recipients of the J.G. Taylor Spink Award (12), living recipients of the Ford C. Frick Award (13), and the old Veterans Committee members whose terms had yet to expire (3). This group of 90 increased the size of the old committee six-fold.
- The Hall of Fame Veterans Committee also requires a 75 percent vote to elect anyone.
- Beginning in 2003, the Veterans Committee began holding its election of players every other year. Also beginning in 2003, the election of managers, umpires, and executives by the Veterans Committee now occurs every four years.

The rules governing the elections state that, "Candidates shall be chosen on the basis of playing ability, integrity, sportsmanship, character, and their contribution to the team, or teams, on which they played—as well as to baseball in general."

As we shall see later, these rules have not always been strictly adhered to, and much liberty has been taken in their interpretation.

SPECIAL SELECTION COMMITTEES

There has always been at least one other selection committee involved in the Hall of Fame election process to augment the selections made by the BBWAA. Over the years, the composition and function of this committee has changed, but it has always managed to make its presence felt.

First, there was the original Old-Timers Committee, which couldn't agree on anything, never elected anyone to the Hall, and was disassembled prior to 1937. Then, there was the Centennial Commission of 1937 and 1938, headed by Judge Landis. As we saw earlier, this group chose not to elect any nineteenth century players, but, rather, the people who were most influential in getting them elected to office.

After this Centennial Commission was pared down and retooled, its name was changed back to the Old-Timers Committee in 1939, and, for more than a dozen years, this group's primary function was selecting players whose careers spanned parts of the nineteenth century, or the first decade of the twentieth. Unfortunately, as we also saw, this committee did irreparable damage to the Hall by electing many players with questionable credentials, permanently lowering its standards. This committee was replaced by the first Veterans Committee in 1953, whose responsibility was to select the old-time players previously passed on by the BBWAA and no longer eligible to be voted in by them. Its members were also to elect any former managers, umpires, or executives who they deemed worthy of induction. This group was comprised of former players, managers, executives and members of the media who had been around the game for many, many years. Although the members of this committee periodically changed, it is particularly noteworthy because this Veterans Committee continued to function for the next 50 years.

We will go into more detail about this group shortly, after we discuss the final special selection committee empowered with inducting players into the Hall of Fame.

That final group was the Negro Leagues Committee of 1971-1977. Appointed by then-commissioner Bowie Kuhn to evaluate Negro League stars, this group was comprised of five former players (Eppie Barnes, Roy Campanella, Monte Irvin, Judy Johnson, Bill Yancey), three former executives or promoters (Frank Forbes, Ed Gottlieb, and Alex Pompez), and two writers (Sam Lacy and Wendell Smith). After it was announced early in 1971 that former pitching great Satchel Paige was the first former Negro League star to be inducted into the Hall of Fame, this committee met annually for the next seven years and elected eight other former Negro League players to the Hall: Josh Gibson and Buck Leonard in 1972, Monte Irvin in 1973, Cool Papa Bell in 1974, Judy Johnson in 1975, Oscar Charleston in 1976, and John Henry "Pop" Lloyd and Martin Dihigo in 1977. After their 1977 meeting, the committee voted to disband, informing the Hall of Fame that their assignment was completed. The committee was discontinued, and the power to select Negro League players was transferred to the "Veterans Committee." Several more players from the Negro Leagues were eventually inducted, more than doubling the total number of former Negro League stars in the Hall of Fame.

Now, back to the Veterans Committee, which had its roots in the original Old-Timers Committee. In all fairness, the members of the Old-Timers Committee cannot be faulted *too* heavily for their selection of several turn-of-the century players who were not truly worthy of induction, because they did not have available to them the plethora of statistics that have since been uncovered. In the early years, organized baseball did not maintain career records. There was no *Baseball Encyclopedia* or *Total Baseball* that these men could use as a point of reference. They had to base their opinions mostly on what they had either seen for themselves, read in the newspapers, or been told by other people. Until men like

Ernest Lanigan came along, the outstanding baseball statistician of his time who was hired as the Historian of the Hall of Fame in 1948, baseball statistics were hard to come by. Lanigan collected box scores and accounts of games, studied and analyzed them, and wrote articles about them. Before Lanigan came along, career records were practically non-existent.

When Lanigan retired in November of 1958, he was replaced in early 1959 as the Hall of Fame's Historian by Lee Allen. Allen, like Lanigan, was fascinated with statistics and began looking into all the research materials that the Hall had accumulated over the years, putting it into the form of a library. He was perhaps the game's first true historian. Eventually, Allen came to serve as an advisor to the members of the Veterans Committee, preparing background material on the players being considered for election—clippings, statistics, and other personal material. With this background information now available to them, the committee members were able to make more informed decisions and, for the most part, do a better job of electing the most-deserving players. There are, however, always exceptions, and these exceptions are all too often rooted in favoritism.

Frankie Frisch was a Hall of Fame second baseman who played for the New York Giants from 1920 to 1926, and for the St. Louis Cardinals from 1927 to 1937. He was also a player-manager for the Cardinals for several years, and was known for being a team leader, having a fiery personality, being somewhat intimidating, and yet also being well liked. Frisch felt that the players of his day were superior to the more modern players, and he made no attempt to conceal that opinion to others. He was named to the Veterans Committee in 1967 and was joined four years later by his former Giants teammate Bill Terry, also a former player-manager, and another man known for being a leader. Over the next few seasons, Frisch and Terry embarked on getting as many of their former teammates elected as possible. This would not have been a bad thing if they were truly deserving of induction, but, in most instances, that was not the case. Enshrined in Cooperstown, largely as a result of Frisch's and Terry's prodding, were:

Jesse Haines—a good pitcher on Frisch's Cardinals teams.

Dave Bancroft—the Giants' shortstop and Frisch's double play partner for four years.

Chick Hafey—a hard-hitting outfielder and Frisch's teammate on the Cardinals for five seasons.

Ross Youngs—a good-hitting outfielder with little power who played with Frisch on the Giants for seven seasons.

George "High-Pockets" Kelly—a power-hitting, good-fielding first baseman who played alongside Frisch in the Giants' infield for seven seasons.

Jim Bottomley—St. Louis Cardinals first baseman from 1922 to 1932 and Frisch's teammate for six seasons.

Fred Lindstrom—Giants third baseman from 1924 to 1932, a teammate of Frisch for three seasons, and of Terry for all nine of those years.

Of these seven players, only Bottomley was a legitimate Hall of Famer. Lindstrom and, perhaps, Bancroft could be described as marginal candidates, but the other four men were undeserving. The careers of Kelly, Youngs, and Hafey were all too short and not productive enough, and Haines simply wasn't good enough. We will take a closer look at each of these players later, but it seems clear that the selections of the members on the Veterans Committee have often been based on more than just playing ability.

This revised Veterans Committee served for 50 years, from 1953 to 2002 and in 2003, it was replaced by a group comprised of the living members of the Baseball Hall of Fame, the living recipients of the J.G. Taylor Spink Award, the living recipients of the Ford C. Frick Award, and the remaining Veterans Committee members whose terms had not yet expired. This realignment should help to minimize the number of elections based on bias and eliminate some of the peer pressure that previously existed whenever the committee got together. This reconfiguration was most likely prompted by the general feeling that the Hall of Fame standards had become too low, and that too many players had already been elected who were not truly deserving. In particular, there were many who objected to the election of former Pirates second baseman Bill Mazeroski in 2001, one of the worst choices in the history of the Hall of Fame voting. Hopefully, this revamped committee will do a better job.

DEFINITION OF A HALL OF FAMER

One of the major problems that has always made voting for potential Hall of Famers so difficult is that it has never been clearly defined what constitutes a legitimate Hall of Famer. While certain statistical standards have been used to attempt to identify qualified candidates, much of the selection process is subjective, since each person looks for different things and has a different idea of what qualifies a player to be elected. Certain benchmarks have been used to identify worthy candidates. Thus far, all eligible players who accumulated either 500 home runs (with the exception of Mark McGwire) or 3,000 hits during their careers have made it into Cooperstown. So, too, have all pitchers with 300 or more wins. But the majority of players who have been elected did not reach any of these milestones, so, obviously, other criteria are being used as well

The first question that needs to be asked is this: Should 500 home runs, 3,000 hits, or 300 victories guarantee election? While most people would most likely answer in the affirmative, I am somewhat hesitant to do so. While accumulating 3,000 hits or 300 wins is certainly an outstanding achievement that signifies a certain level of consistency that few have attained, it is possible to reach either plateau more because of longevity than because of greatness. In particular, this applies to the attainment of 300 victories. All one needs to do is look at the careers of pitchers such as Don Sutton and Phil Niekro. Both men were fine pitchers who had long and successful careers. But neither man was ever thought of as being a *great* pitcher, even at his very best. It is also possible to win in excess of 300 games, but also to lose close to 300 games, as both Niekro and Nolan Ryan did. Thus, while reaching such milestones certainly goes a long way towards qualifying a player for Hall of Fame election, one still needs to examine the player's entire career before blindly admitting him.

In the case of 500 career home runs, that is a benchmark that may have to reevaluated going forward since it no longer carries the same significance it once did. Prior to 1990, it was commonplace for a player to lead his league in home runs with a total that approximated 40. Hitting 50 homers in a season was considered to be quite an achievement. However, players have compiled more than 40 home runs in a season with great regularity over the past two decades. Furthermore, it was not at all uncommon during the Steroid Era that lasted from the 1990s to the turn of the century for the league leader to finish with a total somewhere between 50 and 60 long balls. It follows that, in future seasons, more players will likely be reaching the 500 home run plateau. It may well be that the bar needs to be raised to 600 homers when considering future generations of sluggers for Hall of Fame induction. After all, the Hall is supposed to be reserved only for those players who exhibited exceptional performance during their careers. If the attainment of 500 home runs becomes a more common occurrence, can it honestly be said that any player who reaches that milestone accomplished something truly exceptional? A player must be judged within the context of the era in which he played, and his numbers must stand out among those of the other players of his era.

Along those lines, what seems like a very high career batting average should not automatically guarantee induction either. During the 1920s and 1930s, known for being a hitter's era, it was not at all uncommon for players to lead the league in batting with marks approaching, or even exceeding .400. In fact, in every season from 1920 to 1925, at least one player in the major leagues surpassed the .400 mark. Team batting averages routinely approached .300, particularly during the '20s and early '30s. More players during this period finished with career batting averages well above the .300 mark than in any other era in baseball history.

Were the players of this period better, or did the rules of the game employed at that particular time simply favor the hitters?

One would tend to think the latter. Yet more hitters who played during this period were inducted into the Hall of Fame than from any other era. While players such as Earle Combs, Heinie Manush, Chick Hafey, Fred Lindstrom, and Ross Youngs were all good players who finished with career batting averages well above .300, were they truly exceptional enough to be deserving of Hall of Fame status? That is something this book will attempt to ascertain by judging these men within the context of the era in which they played.

The question then follows: If statistics by themselves are not the determining factor, how can you truly tell if a player excelled enough during his respective era to be worthy of induction into the Hall? To answer that question, I came up with a list of eight other questions. Some of these questions are actually quite similar in nature to those asked by Bill James in his book, *Whatever Happened To The Hall Of Fame? Baseball, Cooperstown, and the Politics of Glory*, a work that will be referred to more than once throughout this book. At the root of each question is an attempt to uncover just how dominant a player was during the time in which he played, since the feeling here is that a certain level of dominance must have been achieved in order for a player to be Hall of Fame worthy.

The chart indicates the questions that need to be asked:

Hall of Fame Questions

1. In his prime, was the player ever considered to be, for at least three years, either the best player in baseball or the best player in his league?
2. For the better part of a decade, was the player considered to be among the five or six best players in baseball?
3. Could a valid case be made for the player being one of the ten best players at his position in baseball history?
4. For the better part of a decade, was the player considered to be the best player in the game at his position? In his league?

5. How did the player fare in the annual voting for the MVP or Cy Young Award? Did he ever win either award? If not, how often did he finish in the top 10?
6. How often was the player selected to the All-Star team?
7. How often did the player lead his league in some major offensive or pitching statistical category?
8. Was the player a major contributor to his team's success? Did he do the little things to help his team win? Did he play mostly on winning teams? Was he a team leader? Was he a good defensive player? Is there any evidence to suggest that the player was significantly better or worse than is suggested by his statistics?

The answers to these questions will go a long way in determining a player's Hall of Fame legitimacy, and some will carry more weight than others. For example, if the answer to the third question is "yes," and a legitimate case could be made for the player being one of the greatest ever at his position, this by itself should be enough to legitimize his place in Cooperstown. If questions one, two, and four can be answered in the affirmative, the chances are pretty good that the player deserves to be in the Hall of Fame. There are, however, exceptions. One can look at players such as Don Mattingly and Dave Parker for examples. Both Mattingly and Parker were thought of as being arguably the best player in the game at one point. For five or six years, each man was considered to be among the top five players in the game, and, quite possibly, the best player at his respective position (Parker, from 1975 to 1979; and Mattingly, from 1984 to 1988). Each player also did relatively well in the other areas. Each won an MVP Award; each made the All-Star team several times; each led his league in various hitting categories. But, in each case, the player's dominant level of play lasted only a few years (in Mattingly's case, because of back problems; in Parker's case, because of drug and weight-related problems) and, as a result, neither man is in the Hall of

Fame. Therefore, other things need to be considered, along with the answers to these questions.

If questions five through eight can be answered in the affirmative, the player is doing well. However, he probably needs to get a positive response to at least one of the other four questions to legitimize his place in Cooperstown.

Of course, the concept of using these questions as the primary criterion is not without its flaws. For one thing, prior to 1932, there were many seasons in which one or both major leagues did not present an award for its Most Valuable Player. Also, prior to 1956, no Cy Young Award was presented annually, and from 1956 to 1966, only one was given out to the best pitcher in both leagues combined. In addition, the first All-Star game was played in 1933, so All-Star appearances cannot be used as a reference prior to that.

Finally, there is the case of the stars from the old Negro Leagues. Due to the limited availability of statistical data and information in general surrounding their careers, the answers to many of the above questions are unattainable. With these players, most of what is known about them comes from the things others who saw them play have said. We will have to assume that the panel of experts on the Negro Leagues Committee of 1971-1977, as well as the members of the Veterans Committee who later elected several other stars from these leagues, knew what they were doing. The pieces of information that I have been able to uncover about these players through research seem to indicate that the committee members did a good job. This will be discussed at greater length in future chapters.

Keeping all this in mind, we are now ready to take a look at each member of the Hall of Fame, examine his credentials, and determine whether or not he truly belongs in Cooperstown. The format that will be used is a relatively simple one:

1. The players at each position who have been elected to the Hall of Fame will be listed in chronological order based on the years that they played.

2. The years that the players' careers spanned, the manner in which they were elected, and the year in which they were elected will also be listed.
3. A summary of each player's credentials will be provided, as well as a discussion of the legitimacy of his selection, or lack thereof. The player summaries for each position will start with the most valid selections, and end with the most questionable.

FIRST BASEMEN (21)

PLAYER	YEARS	ELECTED BY	YEAR ELECTED
Cap Anson	1876-1897	Old-Timers Committee	1939
Dan Brouthers	1879-1896	Old-Timers Committee	1945
Roger Connor	1880-1897	Veterans Committee	1976
Jake Beckley	1888-1907	Veterans Committee	1971
Frank Chance	1898-1914	Old-Timers Committee	1946
Ben Taylor	1910-1929	Veterans Committee	2006
George Sisler	1915-1930	BBWAA	1939
George Kelly	1915-1930	Veterans Committee	1973
Jim Bottomley	1922-1937	Veterans Committee	1974
Lou Gehrig	1923-1939	BBWAA	1939
Bill Terry	1923-1936	BBWAA	1954
Mule Suttles	1923-1944	Veterans Committee	2006
Jimmie Foxx	1925-1945	BBWAA	1951
Hank Greenberg	1933-41,45-47	BBWAA	1956
Buck Leonard	1933-1950	Negro Leagues Committee	1972
Johnny Mize	1936-42,46-53	Veterans Committee	1981
Harmon Killebrew	1954-1975	BBWAA	1984
Orlando Cepeda	1958-1974	Veterans Committee	1999
Willie McCovey	1959-1980	BWAA	1986
Tony Perez	1964-1986	BWAA	2000
Eddie Murray	1977-1997	BWAA	2003

Lou Gehrig/Jimmie Foxx

As the two greatest first basemen in baseball history, both Gehrig and Foxx are most deserving of their places in Cooperstown.

Lou Gehrig's 493 home runs, 1,995 runs batted in, .340 career batting average, 1,888 runs scored, .447 career on-base percentage, and .632 slugging percentage all place him high on the all-time lists. He is also the career leader in grand-slams (23), and he led his league in home runs three times, RBIs five times, and batting average once, winning the American League triple crown in 1934 (49 HR, 165 RBIs, .363 AVG), and the league's MVP Award twice. He was selected to six American League All-Star teams, even though the game was not played until his eighth full season in the league. Gehrig was also selected to *The Sporting News*' All-Star team six times, and was the best first baseman in baseball for much of his career. He was clearly the best in the major leagues at his position in 1927, 1928, 1931, 1934, and 1936 (he hit more than 45 home runs, knocked in more than 150 runs, and batted over .350 in four of those seasons). He also vied with the National League's Bill Terry for that honor in 1930 (41 HR, 174 RBIs, .379 AVG), and with the American League's Hank Greenberg in 1937 (37 HR, 159 RBIs, .351 AVG). Gehrig was among the top five players in the game from 1927 to 1937, and was arguably its best player in 1927, 1931, 1934, and 1936. In most opinion polls, he has been selected as the game's greatest all-time first baseman, and he is generally considered to be one of the five or ten greatest players in the history of the game.

Jimmie Foxx's resume is almost as impressive as Gehrig's. He had 534 home runs, 1,922 RBIs, a .325 career batting average, 1,751 runs scored, a .428 on-base percentage, and a .609 slugging percentage. He won four home run crowns, three RBI titles, and led the league in batting twice. Like Gehrig, he won a triple crown, capturing his in 1933, when he hit 48 home runs, drove in 163 runs, and batted .356 for the Philadelphia Athletics. Foxx was the first player in either league to win the MVP Award three times, and was also the first player to hit more than 50 home runs with two different teams, slugging 58 for the Athletics in 1932, and smashing another 50 for the Boston Red Sox in 1938. Foxx was the best first baseman in baseball in 1932, 1933, 1938, and 1939, and was selected to the American League All-Star team in each season, from 1933 to 1940. He was among the top five players in the game from 1929 to 1940, surpassing 30 home runs and 100 RBIs in each of those 12 seasons. He was also the very best player in the game in each of his three MVP seasons—1932, 1933, and 1938. Although he is not as well-remembered as Gehrig, Foxx was one of the most prolific sluggers the game has ever seen, and deserves to be ranked somewhere in the top ten players of all-time.

George Sisler/Hank Greenberg

Although neither Sisler nor Greenberg was quite on the same level as Gehrig and Foxx, they were both great players who clearly earned their places in Cooperstown.

George Sisler was generally considered to be one of the finest all-around players of his era. An excellent baserunner and the finest fielding first baseman of his day, he finished his career with a .340 batting average and 375 stolen bases. Sisler won two batting titles, hitting .407 in 1920, and compiling a .420 batting average in 1922, while capturing league MVP honors. His 257 hits in 1920 stood as the major league record for 84 years, until Ichiro Suzuki collected 262 safeties in 2004. From 1920 to 1922, Sisler was one of the two or three best players in the game, and, from 1917 to 1922, he was clearly the best first baseman in baseball. Over that six-year stretch, he batted no lower than .341, surpassed the century mark in both RBIs and runs scored three times each, and stole at least 35 bases five times. Sisler was arguably one of the five greatest players at his position in baseball history, and many who saw him play, including Ty Cobb, considered him to be as fine an all-around player as they ever saw.

Hank Greenberg missed almost five full seasons in the prime of his career to military service, yet still managed to hit 331 home runs, drive in 1,276 runs, win two MVP Awards, and help lead his Detroit Tigers to four pennants and two world championships. He led the American League in home runs and runs batted in four times each, once hitting 58 homers, challenging Babe Ruth's record of 60, and once driving in 183 runs, challenging Lou Gehrig's A.L. single-season record of 184. He is also tied with Gehrig for the highest RBI per-game ratio since 1900, with a mark of .92.

Greenberg was one of the five or six best players in the game from 1935 to 1940, during which time he vied with Lou Gehrig and Jimmie Foxx for first base supremacy in the major leagues. He was arguably the very best player in the game in 1935, 1937, and 1940. In the first of those seasons, Greenberg led the majors in home runs (36) and runs batted in (170), while batting .328, scoring 121 runs, and finishing with 16 triples, 46 doubles, and 203 hits in winning A.L. MVP honors. In 1937, he hit 40 homers, led the majors with 183 runs batted in, batted .337, scored 137 runs, and collected 14 triples, 49 doubles, and 200 base hits. In 1940, Greenberg won his second MVP Award by leading the league in home runs (41) and runs batted in (150), batting .340, and scoring 129 runs. In just nine full major league seasons, Greenberg finished in the top ten in the league MVP balloting six times. Despite the relative brevity of his career, Greenberg may well have been one of the five greatest first basemen in baseball history.

Eddie Murray

Although he has never fully received the credit he deserves for having been one of the greatest first basemen ever to play the game, Eddie Murray was just that. In fact, while Mark McGwire was more popular with the press and the fans, Murray was arguably the finest all-around first baseman of the last half of the 20th century. McGwire, Harmon Killebrew, and Willie McCovey all hit more home runs over the course of their careers, but none was as consistent as Murray as a run-producer, hit for as high an average, or was as good defensively. Rafael Palmeiro also hit more home runs than Murray, was extremely consistent, and hit for a comparable average. However, his numbers were inflated by both the era and the ballparks in which he played, and a huge cloud hangs over his accomplishments due to his involvement with steroids.

Murray ended his career with 504 home runs, 1,917 runs batted in, 1,627 runs scored, a .287 batting average, and 19 grand slams—good enough for third on the all-time list. He also won three Gold Glove Awards.

Murray was a model of consistency, averaging 28 home runs and 99 runs batted in a year from 1977 to 1988. During that period, he hit more than 30 homers, knocked in more than 100 runs, and batted over .300 five times each. His best years were 1980 to 1985, a period during which he hit at least 29 home runs and bettered the 100-RBI mark in all but the strike-shortened 1981 season. He also batted over .300 four times during that stretch, with his finest seasons coming in 1983 and 1985. In the first of those years, Murray hit 33 home runs, knocked in 111 runs, batted .306, and finished runner-up to teammate Cal Ripken Jr. in the league MVP voting. Two years later, he hit 31 homers, knocked in a career-high 124 runs, and batted .297. For those six seasons, Murray was one of the top two or three players in the American League, and one of the five best in baseball. He was clearly the best first baseman in the game from 1980 to 1983, and vied with Don Mattingly for that title in 1984.

During his career, Murray finished in the top ten in the MVP voting ten times, making it into the top five on five separate occasions. He was selected to the All-Star team eight times and led the American League in home runs and runs batted in once each. In addition, although Murray's contributions off the field have never been well publicized, he contributed to his team's success with more than just his playing ability. Cal Ripken Jr. has identified Murray as being the player who, perhaps more than anyone else, influenced him in a positive way early in his career. A valid case could also be made for Murray having been one of the five greatest first basemen in baseball history. That, in itself, justifies his place in Cooperstown.

Buck Leonard

As one of the very first Negro League players selected by the Negro Leagues Committee for induction into the Hall of Fame,

Buck Leonard was clearly held in high esteem by those who were fortunate enough to have seen him play. The greatest first baseman in Negro League history, the lefthanded hitting Leonard was often compared to Lou Gehrig as a hitter, and to George Sisler as a fielder. Playing for the Homestead Grays team that won nine consecutive Negro National League titles from 1937 to 1945, Leonard was a two-time NNL home run champion and a three-time batting champion, twice topping the .395-mark. He usually hit fourth for the Grays, providing protection in the batting order for Josh Gibson, who batted third. The powerfully built Leonard was one of the Negro Leagues' most feared hitters. Roy Campanella, who competed against him during the second half of Leonard's career, discussed the first baseman's hitting prowess: "He (Leonard) had a real quick bat, and you couldn't get a fastball by him. He was strictly a pull hitter with tremendous power." Leonard is looked upon by most black baseball experts as having been one of the five greatest players in Negro League history.

Bill Terry

Bill Terry was the finest first baseman in the National League from 1929 to 1934, and, perhaps, the best in baseball in both 1929 and 1930. In the first of those seasons, he hit 14 home runs, knocked in 117 runs, batted .372, scored 103 runs, and collected 226 hits. The following season, Terry became the last N.L. player to hit .400 when he batted .401, hit 23 homers, drove in 129 runs, scored 139 others, and set a league record by collecting 254 base hits. He had another great year in 1932, when he hit 28 home runs, knocked in 117 runs, batted .350, scored 124 runs, and finished with 225 hits. From 1929 to 1934, Terry was also among the five best players in the National League, topping the .340-mark, scoring more than 100 runs, and collecting more than 200 hits each in five of those seasons. During his career, Terry knocked in more than 100 runs six times, scored more than 100 runs seven times, and finished with more than 200 hits six times. His .341 career average ranks among the all-time best, and he was considered to be the finest defensive first baseman in the National League during the time in which he played. Terry was arguably one of the ten best first basemen in baseball history, and one of the two or three best ever to play in the National League.

Dan Brouthers/Roger Connor/Cap Anson

These three men were, by far, the greatest first basemen of the 19th century.

Dan Brouthers was probably the game's greatest all-around hitter of his time. He led the league in batting five times, finishing his career with a mark of .342, and was a league leader in every major batting department at one time or another. In a day when knocking in 100 runs was considered to be quite an achievement, Brouthers accomplished the feat five times, twice driving in more than 120 runs. He also scored more than 100 runs eight times, reaching a career-high 153 runs scored in 1887 for the Detroit Wolverines, and topping 130 on two other occasions. Brouthers batted .350 or better six times during his career, finished in double-digits in home runs three times, finished with more than 10 triples eleven times, and stole more than 20 bases eight times. In virtually every season from 1882 to 1892, he was among the two or three best players in the game, and the sport's top first baseman.

Although most people are probably not aware of it, it was Roger Connor's career home run record that Babe Ruth shattered when he became the game's dominant slugger during the 1920s. Prior to the Babe bursting onto the scene, Connor's career mark of 138 home runs had stood for almost 25 years. Six times, Connor finished in double-digits in homers, hitting as many as 17 for the New York Giants in 1887. However, Connor did more than just hit home runs. He finished his career with 233 triples, a .317 batting average, and was the only player before 1900 to collect more than 1,000 walks. Connor knocked in more than 100 runs four times, scored more than 100 runs eight times, batted over .300 eleven times, topping the .350-mark three times, and finished in double-digits in triples eleven times, three times tallying more than 20 three-baggers.

Cap Anson was the first player to accumulate 3,000 hits, totaling 3,418 safeties in over 10,000 at-bats during his long and illustrious career, spent mostly with the Chicago Cubs. He led the league in runs batted in a record nine times, topping 100 RBIs seven times, and also won two batting titles, hitting over .350 seven different times and finishing his career with a .333 average. He also scored more than 100 runs six times. Anson had perhaps his finest all-around season for the Cubs in 1886. That year, he hit 10 home runs, knocked in 147 runs, batted .371, and scored 117 runs.

Unfortunately, Anson's character did not match his playing ability, since he was known to have had a major influence on the barring of black players from major league baseball. Prior to a game during the 1885 season in which the opposing team intended to field a black player, Anson threatened to organize a players' strike to bar black players from competing in the major leagues. His threat achieved its desired result and succeeded in clandestinely barring blacks from the majors, albeit unofficially, until 1947. His induction into the Hall of Fame is a prime example of the manner in which the institution's rules regarding the judging of candidates based on "integrity and sportsmanship," among other things, have often been ignored. It also symbolizes one of the great hypocrisies that the Hall of Fame, as well as baseball in general, has come to represent.

Willie McCovey/Harmon Killebrew

Neither Willie McCovey nor Harmon Killebrew could be included among the very greatest first basemen of all time. They were both slow afoot, below average defensively, and were somewhat one-dimensional on offense, failing to hit for a particularly high batting average over the course of their respective careers. However, both men were big run producers who possessed awesome power. During their careers, both McCovey and Killebrew surpassed the 500 home run mark, and also drove in well over 1,500 runs. Those figures were enough to justify their selections to the Hall of Fame.

Willie McCovey hit 521 homers and drove in 1,555 runs during his 22-year career. He led the National League in home runs three times, and in runs batted in twice, leading the league in both categories in two straight seasons (1968 and 1969). McCovey was named the National League's Most Valuable Player in 1969 when he hit 45 homers, knocked in 126 runs, and batted .320. He also finished in the top ten in the voting three other times. McCovey was a six-time All-Star, and was probably the most feared hitter in baseball for much of the pitching-dominated 1960s. During his career, McCovey topped the 30-homer mark seven times, surpassing 40 on two separate occasions. He also knocked in more than 100 runs four times, scored more than 100 runs twice, and batted over .300 twice. Although he faced stiff competition from Harmon Killebrew and Orlando Cepeda, McCovey was arguably the best first baseman in baseball for much of the period extending from 1963 to 1970. He was certainly the sport's top first baseman in 1963 (44 HR, 102 RBIs, 103 RUNS, .280 AVG), 1966 (36 HR, 96 RBIs, .295 AVG), and from 1968 to 1970, when he averaged 40 home runs and 119 runs batted in per season.

Harmon Killebrew, in almost the same number of at-bats as McCovey, hit even more home runs (573) and drove in even more runs (1,584). Those numbers more than make up for the fact that his lifetime batting average was only .256. He has the fourth highest home run-to-at-bat ratio in the history of the game (behind only Mark McGwire, Babe Ruth and Ralph Kiner), and he hit more home runs than any other righthanded batter in American League history. Killebrew led the league in home runs six times, runs batted in three times, walks four times, and slugging once. He topped the 40-homer mark eight times, knocked in more than 100 runs nine times, and drew over 100 walks seven times. Like McCovey, he won his league's MVP Award in 1969. That year, he led the A.L. with 49 home runs, 140 runs batted in, and 145 walks, while batting .276. Killebrew was an 11-time All-Star and, although he split time at other positions during his career, was the top first baseman in the American League for most of the 1960s. It could also be argued that he was one of the five or six best players in the league from 1959 to 1970.

Johnny Mize/Jim Bottomley

Although neither man should be viewed as a clear-cut choice, both Johnny Mize and Jim Bottomley are deserving of their places in Cooperstown because they were very, very good players who were each the best first baseman in the National League for extended periods of time.

Johnny Mize hit 359 home runs, drove in 1,337 runs, and batted .312 during an abbreviated career in which he lost three years due to time spent in the military. He led the N.L. in home runs four times, hitting 51 for the Giants in 1947. He also led the league in runs batted in three times, batting average once, and slugging percentage four times. Playing from the mid-1930s to the early 1950s, during a fairly good era for hitters, Mize knocked in more than 100 runs eight times, scored over 100 runs five times, and batted over .300 nine times, topping the .340 mark twice. He was a 10-time All-Star, and he fared well in the MVP voting as well, finishing second twice, third once, and in the top 10 on three other occasions. Mize was the best first baseman in the National League from 1937 to 1948, with the exception of the three years he was in the military, and also 1941, when Dolph Camilli of the Dodgers won the league's Most Valuable Player Award. He was arguably the best first baseman in the game in 1940 (43 HR, 137 RBIs, 111 RUNS, .314 AVG), 1942 (26 HR, 110 RBIs, .305 AVG), 1946 (22 HR, 70 RBIs, .337 AVG, in only 101 games), and 1947 (51 HR, 138 RBIs, 137 RUNS, .302 AVG).

In his book, *Whatever Happened to the Hall of Fame?*, Bill James describes Jim Bottomley as a "good ballplayer" and as a "marginal Hall of Famer at best." While James' book is informative insightful, and makes some very interesting points, he also makes mistakes and, in my opinion, errors in judgment. This is a prime example. While not a great player, Bottomley was a very good one and a worthy Hall of Famer. (James lost a great deal of credibility when he predicted in his book, published in 1994, that future

Hall of Famers included the likes of Ruben Sierra, Lou Whitaker, Brett Butler, Joe Carter, Al Oliver, and Alan Trammell—all good players, but none, with the possible exceptions of Oliver and Trammell, even close to being Hall of Fame caliber). Anyway, back to Bottomley.

During an era in which a lot of runs were scored, Jim Bottomley was one of the game's best run-producers. Playing for the St. Louis Cardinals, in the six seasons from 1924 to 1929 he drove in 756 runs, averaging 126 RBIs per year over that stretch. Bottomley led the National League in that department twice, and also topped the circuit in home runs once. During his career, Bottomley batted over .300 nine times, topping the .340-mark three times, and hitting as high as .371 in 1923. He also had more than 10 triples in a season nine times, reaching the 20-mark once, in 1928. In fact, in that 1928 season Bottomley was named the league's Most Valuable Player for hitting 31 home runs, knocking in 136 runs, scoring 123 others, batting .325, and collecting 42 doubles. His feat that season of hitting more than 20 homers, 20 triples and 20 doubles makes him one of only six players in baseball history to reach the 20-mark in each category in the same season. Bottomley was clearly the National League's best first baseman from 1925 to 1928, and he also rivaled the Giants' George Kelly and Bill Terry in 1924 and 1929, respectively. He was the best first baseman in baseball in 1925, when he finished with 21 homers, 128 runs batted in, a batting average of .367, 227 hits, 12 triples, and 44 doubles.

Jake Beckley

Jake Beckley is an interesting case because his career actually spanned three different eras. During his first five seasons (1888-1892), the pitcher's mound was only 50 feet from home plate. Needless to say, pitchers dominated the sport during that period, with most hitters posting below normal batting averages. However, after the mound was moved back to 60 feet, 6 inches prior to the 1893 season, batting averages began to soar. In 1892, the league average was a paltry .245, but it rose to an all-time high of .309 by 1894. Thus, from 1893 to 1900, Beckley was the beneficiary of the rules changes that went into effect at the beginning of that period. However, the rules of the game were altered once more at the turn of the century, once again shifting the balance of power back to the pitchers. Included in these rules changes were an increase in the size of the strike zone and the further deadening of the ball. As a result, Beckley's last seven seasons were spent hitting in a pitcher's era once again. It seems, therefore, that his numbers can basically be taken at face value. Doing so causes one to think that the Veterans Committee did not make a bad choice when it voted him into the Hall of Fame in 1971.

Beckley played more games at first base than any player in history, except for Eddie Murray. Along the way, he compiled a lifetime .308 batting average, totaling 2,931 hits in 9,527 at-bats, scoring 1,600 runs, and driving in 1,575 others. He also accumulated 243 triples and stole 315 bases. Beckley drove in more than 100 runs four times, scored more than 100 runs five times, batted over .300 fourteen times, surpassing the .330-mark on six separate occasions, and finished with at least 10 triples thirteen times. He had his most productive season for the Pittsburgh Pirates in 1894, when he knocked in 120 runs, scored 121 others, and batted .343. Beckley was arguably the best first baseman in the game from 1893 to 1895, and then again, from 1899 to 1903. While he may not have been a great player, Beckley was a very good one and, at the very least, a marginal Hall of Famer.

Mule Suttles/Ben Taylor

Although they were polar opposites as players, Suttles and Taylor have been grouped together here because they are generally considered to be, with the exception of Buck Leonard, the two greatest first basemen in Negro League history. As such, it would seem that they were both worthy of their 2006 Hall of Fame inductions.

George "Mule" Suttles played for nine different teams during a 22-year Negro League career that began with the Birmingham Black Barons in 1923. Suttles was a tremendous righthanded power hitter who, using a 50-ounce bat, generated as much power as anyone in black baseball. He was a free-swinging low-ball hitter who was known for hitting towering, tape measure home runs. It is said that he once hit a ball completely out of Havana's Tropical Park that was later measured at close to 600 feet. Suttles' prodigious power enabled him to lead the Negro National League in home runs twice. Suttles, though, was more than just a slugger. Although he struck out frequently, the six-foot three-inch, 215-pound first baseman maintained a consistently high batting average throughout his career, finishing with a mark of either .321, .329, or .338, depending on the source. He is also credited with a lifetime batting average of .374, with five home runs, in 26 exhibition games against white major leaguers. Suttles was elected five times to represent his team in the East-West All-Star Game, and played for three championship teams during his Negro League career.

On the flip side, Suttles' limited mobility made him a below-average fielder. Yet, it is said that the hulking first baseman handled almost everything he could reach, and his hitting prowess more than compensated for his defensive deficiencies. The late Chico Renfroe, former Kansas City Monarchs infielder and longtime sports editor of the *Atlanta Daily World*, referred to Suttles as the hitter who "had the most raw power of any player I've ever seen. He went after the ball viciously! He wasn't a finesse player at all. He just overpowered the opposition."

While Mule Suttles was a pure slugger, Ben Taylor was a scientific hitter, known for his ability to hit line drives to all fields, and for his proficiency at executing the hit-and-run play. Generally considered to be the premier Negro League first baseman of the first quarter of the twentieth century, Taylor spent 20 years in black baseball, splitting time between 11 different teams. An extremely productive offensive player, Taylor posted a .334 lifetime batting average. He is credited with having batted over .300 in fifteen of his first sixteen seasons in baseball.

In addition to being an outstanding lefthanded batter, Taylor was a smooth defensive first baseman who made difficult plays look easy. An excellent teacher as well, it was Taylor who helped Buck Leonard refine his skills as a first baseman.

Orlando Cepeda/Tony Perez

Now we are getting into a very gray area. Neither Orlando Cepeda nor Tony Perez was a great player, but both were very good. At their peaks, Cepeda was probably a little better, but Perez was a good player for a longer period of time. As a result, his career numbers compare favorably to those of Cepeda in most categories. Let's take a look at the statistics compiled by both men, alongside those of Willie McCovey, a contemporary of both players who we have already identified as a legitimate Hall of Famer:

PLAYER	AB	HITS	RUNS	2B	3B	HR	RBI	AVG	SB	OBP	SLG PCT
Willie McCovey	8,197	2,211	1,229	353	46	521	1,555	.270	26	.377	.515
Orlando Cepeda	7,927	2,351	1,131	417	27	379	1,365	.297	142	.353	.499
Tony Perez	9,778	2,732	1,272	505	79	379	1,652	.279	49	.344	.463

The numbers would seem to indicate that, with the exception of home runs, both Cepeda and Perez were very comparable players to McCovey. The latter had a couple of truly dominant seasons that separated him somewhat from Cepeda and Perez. He also won a Most Valuable Player Award, something Cepeda accomplished as well, but Perez failed to do. However, both Cepeda and Perez were actually a bit more consistent than McCovey, and had more quality seasons over the course of their respective careers.

A look at the career of McCovey reveals that he had only seven truly outstanding seasons; those in which he hit over 30 home runs and drove in close to, or more than, 100 runs. As was mentioned earlier, he was selected to the N.L. All-Star team six times. Cepeda, however, actually had nine *All-Star type* seasons, even though he was selected to the team only seven times. In nine different seasons, he hit close to, or more than, 30 home runs, drove in approximately 100 runs, and batted over .300. Perez was perhaps the most consistent RBI-man in the game from 1967 to 1977. In each of those 11 seasons he knocked in more than 90 runs while hitting more than 20 homers and batting above .280

on most occasions. Perez was also selected to the All-Star team seven times.

Let's take a look at how both Cepeda and Perez stack up when evaluating their careers based on the selection criteria we are using to define a Hall of Famer:

Neither Cepeda nor Perez was ever the best player in the game at any point during his career. Nor was either man among the five or six best players in baseball for an extended period of time, or one of the greatest first basemen in the history of the game. However, it could be argued that each man was the top player at his position for an extended period of time. From 1959 to 1962, then again in 1967, Cepeda was arguably the best first baseman in baseball. From 1959 to 1962, he averaged 33 home runs and 114 runs batted in, while batting near or above .300 each season. In 1961, he led the N.L. with 46 home runs and 142 RBIs, while batting .311 for the San Francisco Giants. In 1967, he was named the league's Most Valuable Player when he helped lead the St. Louis Cardinals to the pennant and world championship by hitting 25 homers, leading the league with 111 runs batted in, and batting .325.

Perez vied with Ron Santo of the Cubs for the honor of being the best National League third baseman from 1967 to 1970. After being shifted to first base at the conclusion of the 1971 campaign, he was the league's top first baseman in both 1972 and 1973.

In the MVP voting, both players received a reasonable amount of support. As we saw earlier, Cepeda won the award in 1967. He also finished second once (in 1961), and in the top 10 one other time. Perez finished in the top 10 in the balloting four times. Both players were selected to the All-Star team seven times. Cepeda was a league-leader in a major statistical category only three times, topping the N.L. in home runs once, and in runs batted in twice. Despite knocking in more than 100 runs seven times, Perez never led the league in any offensive category.

Neither player was particularly strong defensively, but it would appear that Perez had some intangible qualities that Cepeda may have lacked. In 1961, when Cepeda led the National League in home runs and runs batted in, Giants manager Alvin Dark was quoted as saying, "I'm sick and tired of players on this team leading the league in home runs and RBIs and not doing anything to help us win!" It is true that Dark's opinion of Cepeda may have been somewhat jaded since, later in his managerial career, he was quoted as having made some racist remarks. Nevertheless, the big first baseman—at least in Dark's eyes—did not do the little things to help his team win. Perez, on the other hand, was a great team leader who helped lead the Cincinnati Reds to four pennants and two world championships. His manager with the Reds, Sparky Anderson, once said that all the other leaders on the Big Red Machine (i.e. Johnny Bench, Joe Morgan and Pete Rose) deferred to *the Big Dawg*, as Perez was known to his teammates. He was the leader on that team.

In evaluating the credentials of Cepeda and Perez, we discover that we have two very good players who meet about half of our Hall of Fame criteria. The feeling here is that both men should be viewed as borderline candidates who were not the greatest of choices, but who were far from the worst. They were both much better players than many of the other men who have been elected to Cooperstown.

Frank Chance/George Kelly

This brings us to the final two first basemen in the Hall of Fame: Frank Chance and George "High-Pockets" Kelly.

Frank Chance played first base for the Chicago Cubs from 1898 to 1914. He also managed the team for several of those seasons. Chance was fortunate enough to have played on the great Cubs teams that dominated the National League for much of the first decade of the 20th century. Playing mostly during the dead-ball era, one would not expect Chance's offensive numbers to be on a par with some of the other great first basemen who have been elected to Cooperstown. However, one would have to look long and hard to be able to justify his selection.

During Chance's career, he led the National League in stolen bases and on-base percentage twice each, and in runs scored once.

However, he was never a league-leader in any other offensive category. A look at the statistics compiled by Chance over the course of his 17 major league seasons indicates that he neither had a sufficient number of plate appearances nor the necessary numbers to be deemed a worthy Hall of Famer. Let's take a look at his numbers alongside those of Jake Beckley, whose career overlapped with Chance's:

PLAYER	AB	HITS	RUNS	2B	3B	HR	RBI	AVG	SB	OBP	SLG PCT
Jake Beckley	9,526	2,930	1,600	473	243	86	1,575	.308	315	.361	.435
Frank Chance	4,297	1,273	797	200	79	20	596	.296	401	.394	.394

Certainly, a large part of the discrepancy in the numbers posted by the two men can be attributed to the fact that Beckley had more than twice as many plate appearances as Chance. However, Beckly was also the far more productive hitter of the two. He had a huge edge over Chance in every statistical category except stolen bases and on-base percentage. Beckley, already described here as a somewhat marginal Hall of Famer, had three times as many triples, more than four times as many homers, and almost three times as many runs batted in as Chance. Regardless of the era in which he played, 20 career home runs, 596 runs batted in, and 797 runs scored should not be enough to get a player elected into the Hall of Fame.

The only reasonable explanation as to why Chance was elected comes from a poem that was written by a New York sportswriter during the first decade of the 20th century. Frustrated that his beloved Giants were repeatedly victimized by the powerful Cubs teams of those years, this writer composed a poem extolling the virtues of Chicago's double-play combination of shortstop Joe Tinker, second baseman Johnny Evers, and first baseman Chance. The poem became quite famous and ended up immortalizing the trio, and the phrase "Tinker-to-Evers-to-Chance." As a result, the three men were elected *en masse* to the Hall of Fame by the Old-Timers Committee in 1946, in one of the many blunders it committed during this period. None of the three players truly deserved to be admitted to Cooperstown.

George Kelly was the regular first baseman for the New York Giants for much of the 1920s, prior to being displaced by Bill Terry. During his career, he surpassed the 100-RBI mark five times and led the N.L. in home runs once and in runs batted in twice. He never led the league in any other offensive category, and he never scored as many 100 runs in a season. Let's take a look at his numbers alongside those of Jim Bottomley, who we have categorized as a legitimate Hall of Famer, and Dolph Camilli, the slugging first baseman for the Phillies and Dodgers from 1933 to 1945, who never made it into the Hall:

PLAYER	AB	HITS	RUNS	2B	3B	HR	RBI	AVG	SB	OBP	SLG PCT
Jim Bottomley	7,471	2,313	1,177	465	151	219	1,422	.310	58	.369	.500
George Kelly	5,993	1,778	819	337	76	148	1,020	.297	65	.342	.452
Dolph Camilli	5,353	1,482	936	261	86	239	950	.277	60	.388	.492

Clearly, Kelly's numbers fall far short of those compiled by Bottomley, who played during the same period. Meanwhile, Camilli, playing in an era less dominated by hitting, posted numbers that compare quite favorably to Kelly's. In approximately 600 fewer at-bats than Kelly, he hit almost 100 more home runs, knocked in only 70 fewer runs, accumulated more triples, scored more runs, and posted much higher on-base and slugging percentages. The logical question then is this: Why is Kelly in the Hall of Fame while Camilli is not? The answer is a simple one: Frankie Frisch. As we saw earlier, Frisch's strong personality and leadership skills enabled him to exert a great deal of influence over the other members in his years on the Veterans Committee. He argued extensively for his former Giants and Cardinals teammates, and was successful in getting many of them elected. However, Kelly, while a very solid player, really did not deserve to be inducted into the Hall of Fame any more than Camilli, Hal Trosky, Ted Kluszewski, Gil Hodges, Steve Garvey, Don Mattingly, Keith Hernandez, or about a half dozen other first basemen.

Speaking of Hodges, over the years there has been much clamoring for his election to the Hall of Fame. His supporters point to his 370 home runs, 1,274 runs batted in, six seasons with more than 30 homers, two 40-homer campaigns, seven seasons with more than 100 RBIs, eight All-Star game appearances, and integral role on those great Dodger teams of the 1950s, and wonder why he has yet to be elected. The fact is, while Hodges was a fine player and a good man, he simply does not deserve to be enshrined into Cooperstown.

Hodges never led the league in any major offensive category. In spite of the fact that the Dodger teams for which he played were always in contention, winning six pennants in his years with the team, he never finished any higher than eighth in the league MVP voting, placing in the top 10 only three times. While Hodges had seasons in which he was the National League's top first baseman, he was not generally regarded as the league's dominant player at his position during his era (Ted Kluszewski, Joe Adcock, and, later, after he was shifted from leftfield, Stan Musial were all perceived as being on his level). More importantly, Hodges was generally considered to be only the fifth, or sixth, best player on his own team, behind Roy Campanella, Duke Snider, Jackie Robinson, Pee Wee Reese, and, perhaps, Don Newcombe. A look at Hodges' career numbers, compared to two other first basemen not in the Hall of Fame, seems to support the theory that he wasn't quite good enough to be included among the game's elite:

PLAYER	AB	HITS	RUNS	2B	3B	HR	RBI	AVG	SB	OBP	SLG PCT
Gil Hodges	7,030	1,921	1,105	295	48	370	1,274	.273	63	.361	.487
Norm Cash	6,705	1,820	1,046	241	41	377	1,103	.271	43	.377	.488
Joe Adcock	6,606	1,832	823	295	35	336	1,122	.277	20	.339	.485

Joe Adcock was a contemporary of Hodges who spent most of his career with the Milwaukee Braves. Although Hodges' numbers were slightly better, the two players were actually quite comparable. Yet there has been virtually no support for Adcock's election to the Hall of Fame.

The same could be said for Norm Cash, who played for the Detroit Tigers during the 1960s and early 1970s, in much more of a pitcher's era than when Hodges played. In slightly fewer at-bats, Cash put up virtually the same numbers as Hodges. While it could be said that Tiger Stadium was a great ballpark for hitters, the same was true of Ebbetts Field, Hodges' home ballpark.

It is quite possible, especially with the politics that always seem to surround these elections, that Gil Hodges will be elected to the Hall of Fame at some point in the future. Why not? He was better than 20 or 30 other players already in. But, in all honesty, he should not be voted in.

SECOND BASEMEN (20)

PLAYER	YEARS	ELECTED BY	YEAR ELECTED
Bid McPhee	1882-1899	Veterans Committee	2000
Frank Grant	1886-1903	Veterans Committee	2006
Napoleon Lajoie	1896-1916	BBWAA	1937
Johnny Evers	1902-1917	Old-Timers Committee	1946
Eddie Collins	1906-1930	BBWAA	1939
Rogers Hornsby	1915-1937	BBWAA	1942
Frankie Frisch	1919-1937	BBWAA	1947
Charlie Gehringer	1924-1942	BBWAA	1949
Tony Lazzeri	1926-1939	Veterans Committee	1991
Billy Herman	1931-43, 46-47	Veterans Committee	1975
Bobby Doerr	1937-44, 46-51	Veterans Committee	1986
Joe Gordon	1938-43, 46-50	Veterans Committee	2009
Red Schoendist	1945-1963	Veterans Committee	1989
Jackie Robinson	1947-1956	BBWAA	1962
Nellie Fox	1947-1965	Veterans Committee	1997
Bill Mazeroski	1956-1972	Veterans Committee	2001
Joe Morgan	1963-1984	BBWAA	1990
Rod Carew	1967-1985	BBWAA	1991
Paul Molitor	1978-1998	BBWAA	2004
Ryne Sandberg	1981-1997	BBWAA	2005

Rogers Hornsby/Charlie Gehringer/Napoleon Lajoie/ Eddie Collins/Joe Morgan

These five men have been grouped together because they were not only the finest second basemen of their respective eras, but were also among the very greatest players of their time. They are clearly deserving of their places in Cooperstown.

Rogers Hornsby is considered by many to have been the greatest righthanded hitter in baseball history. His .358 lifetime batting average is second only to Ty Cobb's mark of .367, and he was the National League's most dominant player, and among the two or three best players in the game, for much of the 1920s. During that decade, he won seven batting titles, including six consecutively from 1920 to 1925. Over that six-year stretch, Hornsby batted .400 or better three times, reaching a career-best .424 in 1924. From 1921 to 1925, his *combined* average was over .400.

Hornsby was the best player in the game in at least three seasons. In 1922, he won the first of his two triple crowns for the Cardinals by leading the league with 42 home runs, 152 runs batted in, and a batting average of .401, while scoring 141 runs and collecting 250 hits. In 1925, Hornsby won his second triple crown and first Most Valuable Player Award by hitting 39 home runs, driving in 143 runs, and batting .403, while scoring 133 runs and tallying 203 hits. In 1929, with the Cubs, he won his second MVP Award by hitting 39 homers, knocking in 149 runs, batting .380, scoring 156 runs, and collecting 229 hits. During his career, Hornsby led the league in home runs twice, runs batted in, doubles and hits four times each, runs scored five times, on-base percentage eight times, and slugging percentage ten times. He finished his career with 301 home runs (second only to Jeff Kent all-time among second basemen), and an on-base percentage of .434, along with a slugging percentage of .577—both records for second basemen.

Charlie Gehringer was the finest second baseman in the American League from 1927 to 1938, and the best second baseman in the game for virtually all of the 1930s. In fact, he was one of the five or six best all-around players in baseball for much of that decade. Combining superb hitting and run-production with excellent defense, Gehringer was one of the most complete players of his era. Seven times during his career he drove in more than 100 runs, and 12 times he crossed the plate more than 100 times himself. He also had 200 or more hits in a season seven times, and hit .300 or better 14 times. At different times, he led the league in batting average, triples, doubles, stolen bases, hits, runs scored, putouts and fielding. Gehringer also won the league's Most Valuable Player Award in 1937 and finished in the top five in the voting on two other occasions. He ended his career with a .320 batting average, and finished second all-time among second basemen with 1,774 runs scored and a .480 slugging percentage.

Napoleon Lajoie was the finest second baseman in baseball, and the best player in the American League, for the first decade of the twentieth century. During that ten-year period, Lajoie led the league in runs batted in three times, batting average four times, home runs once, doubles five times, hits four times, runs scored once, and slugging percentage four times. In 1901, he won the league's triple crown by hitting 14 home runs, knocking in 125 runs and batting .426, the highest single-season batting average attained since 1900. He was also a fine fielder, having led league second basemen in fielding six times. Over the course of his career, Lajoie accumulated 1,599 runs batted in and 657 doubles, both records for a second baseman. In addition, his .338 career average and 3,242 hits place him second all-time among second basemen (behind only Hornsby in batting average and Eddie Collins in hits).

Eddie Collins bridged the gap between Nap Lajoie and Charlie Gehringer as the best second baseman in the American League, holding that distinction from 1911 to 1925. In fact, prior to Rogers Hornsby establishing himself as the National League's best player in 1920, Collins was the best second baseman in baseball over a nine-year stretch. During his career, he led the A.L. in batting and on-base percentage once each, runs scored three times, and stolen bases four times. He finished his career with more hits (3,312), runs scored (1,821), stolen bases (744), and triples (186) than any other second baseman in history. His .333 lifetime batting average and .424 on-base percentage also rank with the best. Even though the American League did not present a Most Valuable Player Award for any of the seasons from 1915 to 1921—some of Collins' peak years—he still managed to finish in the top five in the MVP voting five times during his career. He won the award in 1914, when he helped lead the Philadelphia Athletics to the pennant. He also won two more pennants with the Chicago White Sox in 1917 and 1919, so it could definitely be said that he possessed many of the intangibles one would look for in a Hall of Famer.

Joe Morgan was a good player with the Houston Astros from 1965 to 1971, but a great one with the Cincinnati Reds from 1972 to 1977. After Morgan was traded to Cincinnati in a multi-player deal following the 1971 season, Reds' manager Sparky Anderson quickly recognized the intelligence with which he played the game and gave his new second baseman total freedom both at the plate and on the basepaths. The result was the maturation of Morgan into the best second baseman in baseball, and one of the finest players in the game, distinctions he held for the next six seasons. In fact, Morgan was named the National League's Most Valuable Player in both 1975 and 1976, and, for those two seasons, was the finest all-around player in the game, leading his team to consecutive world championships. In 1975, Morgan hit 17 home runs, knocked in 94 runs, batted .327, stole 67 bases, and led the league in both walks (132) and on-base percentage (.471). The following season, he was even better, finishing the campaign with 27 homers, 111 runs batted in, and an average of .320, while leading the league in both on-base (.453) and slugging percentage (.576). Morgan finished his career with 1,650 runs scored, 268 home runs, 689 stolen bases, and an on-base percentage of .395.

Frankie Frisch/Jackie Robinson/Rod Carew

These three men form the next tier of outstanding second basemen who clearly earned their places in Cooperstown.

Only Rogers Hornsby kept Frankie Frisch from being the National League's best second baseman for virtually all of the 1920s.

Still, Frisch was the league's top player at that position in 1927, and from 1930 to 1934. In fact, he was the best second baseman in baseball in both 1927 and 1931, finishing second to Paul Waner in the N.L. MVP voting in 1927, and winning the award in 1931. In the first of those two years, Frisch had probably his finest all-around season after being traded to the Cardinals from the Giants during the off-season for Hornsby. That year, Frisch hit .337, led the league in steals, and handled a record 1,059 chances (including a record 641 assists). During his career, Frisch topped the .300 mark 13 times, including 11 straight seasons from 1921 to 1931. He also surpassed the 100 RBI-mark three times and scored more than 100 runs seven times. He led the league in hits and runs scored once each, and also topped the circuit in stolen bases three times. Frisch ended his career with a batting average of .316, 2,880 hits, and 419 stolen bases.

The historical significance that Jackie Robinson had on the game of baseball, in itself, probably earned him his place in Cooperstown. The strength and courage he showed in the face of the taunts and abuse he had to endure from fans, opposing players, and even his own teammates in some instances were the embodiment of the best the human spirit has to offer. However, Robinson was also a superb baseball player who, had he not had to deal with the overwhelming pressure of being the first black player to play in the major leagues, would undoubtedly have been even better. As it is, he was the best second baseman in the game from 1949 to 1953, hitting well over .300 each season and scoring more than 100 runs in four of those years. Robinson had his finest season in 1949, when he hit 16 home runs, knocked in 124 runs, scored 122 others, had 203 hits, and led the league with a .342 batting average en route to winning the Most Valuable Player Award. His competitive spirit and desire to win were recognized as one of the driving forces behind the Dodgers' success during his years in Brooklyn, since the writers who voted annually for the league's MVP placed him in the top 10 in the balloting in four of his ten seasons in the league.

Although Rod Carew spent the second half of his career playing first base, he was the best second baseman in the American League from 1967 to 1975, and the best in baseball in at least two or three of those seasons. During his career, Carew won seven batting titles, leading the league each year from 1972 to 1975. He also led the league in hits three times, runs scored once, triples twice, and on-base percentage four times.. He had more than 200 hits four times, stole more than 30 bases four times, and hit over .300 fifteen years in a row, from 1969 to 1983, including five seasons of .350 or better. His career batting average of .328 was, at the time of his retirement, the highest career average of any player who played in at least 1,000 games since Ted Williams retired in 1960. Carew also was voted the American League's Most Valuable Player in 1977 when he reached career highs in batting (.388), home runs (14), runs batted in (100), slugging percentage (.570), triples (16), hits (239), and runs scored (128), and led the league in five different offensive categories. In addition, he was selected to the All-Star team on 18 different occasions.

Ryne Sandberg

As one of the finest all-around second baseman ever to play the game, Ryne Sandberg was clearly deserving of his 2005 election to Cooperstown. For a nine-year period, beginning in 1984 and ending in 1992, Sandberg was the best second baseman in baseball. Over that stretch, he hit more than 25 homers five times, knocked in 100 runs twice, scored more than 100 runs six times, and batted over .300 four times. Sandberg was voted the National League's Most Valuable Player in 1984 when he hit 19 home runs, knocked in 84 runs, batted .314, collected 200 hits, and led the league with 19 triples and 114 runs scored in leading the Chicago Cubs to the N.L. East title. The following year, he stole a career-high 54 bases, and, in 1990, he became only the third second baseman in major league history to hit 40 home runs in a season (Rogers Hornsby and Davey Johnson were the others). In so doing, Sandberg also became the only player ever to have seasons in which he hit 40 home runs, stole 50 bases, and compiled 200 hits. In all, he hit more than 25 homers six times, stole more than 30 bases five times, and scored more than 100 runs seven times. Sandberg led the National League in runs scored three times, and in home runs, triples, and total bases once each.

As good an offensive player as Sandberg was, he was even better in the field. His defensive resume is as impressive as that of any second baseman who ever played the game. In addition to winning nine Gold Gloves, he is the all-time leader in fielding average among major league second basemen, with a mark of .990. From June 21, 1989 to May 17, 1990, he played 123 consecutive games and accepted 582 chances without making an error, both records for National League second basemen.. During his career, he put together streaks of 30 or more errorless games 15 times.

Sandberg also fared extremely well in our other selection criteria. In his 15 seasons as a full-time player, he was selected to 10 All-Star teams and also finished in the top five in the league MVP voting on three occasions.

Paul Molitor

Whether viewed as a second baseman, third baseman, outfielder, or designated hitter, Paul Molitor was one of the finest players of his time. Over 21 major league seasons, with three different teams, Molitor compiled a lifetime batting average of .306, with 3,319 hits and 1,782 runs scored. He batted over .300 twelve times, scored more than 100 runs five times, compiled more than 200 hits four times, knocked in more than 100 runs twice, and stole more than 30 bases eight times. Molitor led the American League in runs scored three times, and in base hits, doubles, and triples once each.

Although never considered to be more than a mediocre fielder, Molitor had several seasons in which he was among the best all-around offensive players in baseball. Perhaps his two best years came in 1987 and 1993. Playing for the Milwaukee Brewers in 1987, Molitor hit a career-high .353, while scoring 114 runs and stealing 45 bases. With the Toronto Blue Jays in 1993, he batted

.332, while hitting 22 homers, knocking in 111 runs, scoring 121 others, and compiling 211 base hits.

Since he was not a particularly strong defensive player who served primarily as a designated hitter for a good portion of his career, it would be difficult to classify Molitor as an exceptional all-around player. However, he was a terrific offensive player who clearly earned his place in Cooperstown.

Bid McPhee

As arguably the finest second baseman of the 19th century, Bid McPhee would have to be considered a legitimate Hall of Famer. McPhee's career with the Cincinnati Reds began in 1882 and ended in 1899. He, therefore, spent most of his time facing pitchers who stood less than 60 feet, 6 inches from home plate. As a result, McPhee's lifetime batting average was a decidedly mediocre .271. However, even though he batted over .300 only three times, McPhee still managed to compile a career .355 on-base percentage, finish in double-digits in triples nine times, score more than 100 runs in a season ten different times, and steal more than 40 bases seven times, compiling a career-best 95 thefts in 1887. During his career, McPhee scored a total of 1,678 runs and finished with 188 triples and 2,250 base hits. In addition, he led the league's second basemen in fielding on eight different occasions.

Frank Grant

Rivaling Bid McPhee as the 19th century's best second baseman was Ulysses "Frank" Grant, who played for numerous teams during his 18 years in baseball. The 5'7", 155-pound Grant began his career with Buffalo of the International League in 1886. Grant remained with Buffalo until the conclusion of the 1888 campaign, thereby becoming the first black man to play on the same team in organized ball, albeit at the minor league level, for three consecutive seasons. However, prior to the start of the 1889 season, organized ball instituted its ban on black players, relegating Grant to a nomadic existence for the remainder of his career. He spent the next decade playing with some of the top black clubs of the era, including the Cuban Giants, New York Gorhams, and Philadelphia Giants.

Grant was a consistent .300 hitter with power, an excellent baserunner, and an outstanding fielder. His strong arm and quickness in the field prompted others to compare him favorably to Fred Dunlap, the best-fielding white second baseman of the 1880s. During Grant's days in the International League, one Buffalo writer called him the best all-around player ever to take the field for the team, even though four future Hall of Famers previously played for Buffalo.

Thus, it would seem that Grant's 2006 induction into the Hall of Fame by the Veteran's Committee was long overdue. However, it must be considered that he played prior to the formation of the Negro Leagues at the beginning of the 20th century. Therefore, even though Grant played for some of the top black teams of the era, he competed in leagues that were not very well organized, and whose level of competition is a mystery to even the most knowledgeable baseball historians. Furthermore, the paucity of available statistics surrounding his career makes it extremely difficult to determine just how good Grant truly was

Nevertheless, Grant is generally considered to have been the most accomplished black baseball player of the 19th century, and he certainly cannot be penalized for not being allowed to compete against the white major leaguers of the day.

Tony Lazzeri/Billy Herman/Bobby Doerr/Joe Gordon/ Red Schoendist/Nellie Fox

These six second basemen have been grouped together, even though each had a unique skill-set, because they all fit into the same category of being very good players who were questionable Hall of Fame selections. Let's take a look at each one individually:

Tony Lazzeri was the Yankees' regular second baseman from 1926 to 1937. He was a righthanded power hitter who, despite playing his home games in Yankee Stadium with its unfavorable dimensions for righthanded batters, managed to hit 18 home runs four times and drive in more than 100 runs on seven occasions. He also batted over .300 five times, hitting a career-high .354 in

1929. Lazzeri scored more than 100 runs twice, finished his career with a .380 on-base percentage, and was a solid fielder.

However, it must be remembered that Lazzeri played during a hitter's era and never even came close to leading the league in any major offensive category. In addition, he was never considered to be the best second baseman in the game, and, with the possible exception of the 1926 and 1929 seasons, was rated well behind Charlie Gehringer in the American League. Furthermore, while it is true that he knocked in more than 100 runs seven times, it should be noted that Lazzeri spent much of his career batting sixth in the Yankee lineup behind Babe Ruth, Lou Gehrig, and Bob Meusel. While it is also true that Ruth and Gehrig hit a lot of home runs, thereby clearing the bases and cutting down on Lazzeri's RBI opportunities, Ruth's career on-base percentage was .474, Gehrig's was .447, and Meusel was a lifetime .300 hitter. Therefore, Lazzeri clearly came to the plate with a lot of men on base. In the MVP voting, he finished as high as fourth one year, and finished in the top 10 two other times.

Billy Herman was the National League's best second baseman from 1935 to 1943. During that period, he led the league in hits, doubles, and triples once each, knocked in 100 runs once, scored more than 100 runs five times, and finished in the top 10 in the MVP voting five times. He was selected to the All-Star team nine times and was a good fielder as well, having led league second basemen in fielding three times. He finished with a .304 career batting average and an on-base percentage of .367. In addition, in his years with the Chicago Cubs and Brooklyn Dodgers, he helped lead his team to four pennants.

However, during his prime, Herman was never considered to be the best second baseman in baseball. From 1935 to 1938, that distinction was held by Charlie Gehringer, and from 1939 to 1943, Joe Gordon was thought to be his superior. In addition, his run production was not on the same level as most of the other Hall of Fame second basemen. For his career, Herman totaled 839 RBIs and 1,163 runs scored. Those totals place him ahead of only Red Schoendist, Nellie Fox and Johnny Evers in runs batted in, and Tony Lazzeri, Bobby Doerr, Joe Gordon, Johnny Evers and Bill Mazeroski in runs scored—all men whose Hall of Fame credentials are certainly open to debate.

Bobby Doerr had good power for a middle infielder, hitting more than 20 homers three times and driving in more than 100 runs six times during his 14-year career with the Boston Red Sox. He also batted over .300 three times and led the American League in triples once and slugging percentage once. He was also an outstanding defensive player, leading league second basemen in fielding four times. Doerr was selected to the All-Star team nine times and finished in the top 10 in the MVP voting twice.

However, Doerr's offensive numbers were inflated by the fact that he was a righthanded hitter playing all his home games in Fenway Park. All one needs to do to see just how much he benefited from playing in Fenway is to take a look at the home and away numbers he posted throughout his career:

	AB	HITS	RUNS	2B	3B	HR	RBI	AVG	OBP	SLG PCT
HOME	3,554	1,119	634	246	46	145	743	.315	.395	.532
AWAY	3,539	923	460	135	43	78	504	.261	.327	.389

From this graphic, it becomes apparent that Doerr was a Hall of Famer when he played at Fenway but just a pretty good player when he performed elsewhere. In addition, Joe Gordon, the Yankees second baseman of the same period, was selected ahead of Doerr by *The Sporting News* for its major league All-Star team from 1939 to 1942, and again in 1947 and 1948. Gordon also fared better than his rival in the annual MVP voting, winning the award in 1942 and finishing in the top 10 four other times. Factoring into the equation the ballparks in which they played their home games, a look at the career numbers posted by Doerr and Gordon reveals that the latter may well have been the better player:

PLAYER	AB	HITS	RUNS	2B	3B	HR	RBI	AVG	SB	OBP	SLG PCT
Bobby Doerr	7,093	2,042	1,094	381	89	223	1,247	.288	54	.362	.461
Joe Gordon	5,707	1,530	914	264	52	253	975	.268	89	.357	.466

Yet, Doerr was elected to the Hall of Fame in 1986, while Gordon wasn't voted in until 2009. That last fact can most likely be explained by the presence of Ted Williams on the Veterans Committee when Doerr was selected. Williams, an extremely influential and imposing speaker, was Doerr's teammate in Boston for ten seasons. He always spoke very highly of Doerr's playing ability, and undoubtedly made a strong impression on the other Committee members.

Joe Gordon was one of the most prolific offensive second basemen in baseball history. A righthanded batter who spent the better part of his career playing in spacious Yankee Stadium, Gordon managed to hit 253 home runs in fewer than 6,000 at-bats in his 11 big-league seasons. He topped 20 homers in seven of those years, surpassing the 30-homer mark on two separate occasions. He also knocked in more than 100 runs four times and scored more than 100 runs twice. Gordon had his two best years in New York in 1940 and 1942. In the first of those campaigns, he hit 30 home runs, drove in 103 runs, batted .281, and scored a career-high 112 runs. In 1942, he hit 18 homers, knocked in 103 runs, and batted a career-best .322 en route to being named the American League's Most Valuable Player. Gordon also had an exceptional year for the Cleveland Indians in 1948, establishing career-highs with 32 home runs and 124 runs batted in, scoring 96 times, and batting .280. A perennial All-Star, Gordon was named to the American League All-Star team in nine of his eleven seasons, and also finished in the top ten of the league MVP balloting a total of five times.

Still, several legitimate arguments can be waged against Gordon's 2009 selection by the Veterans Committee. Missing two full seasons to time spent in the military during World War II, Gordon's career was relatively short. Not only did he play just 11 years, but Gordon compiled barely over 5,700 at-bats. As a result, he finished with fairly modest career numbers, failing to surpass either 1,000 runs batted in or 1,000 runs scored. In addition, Gordon never finished higher than third in the league in any major offensive category. Furthermore, Gordon's .268 career batting average was not particularly impressive, although he posted a solid .357 on-base percentage and a .466 slugging percentage, unusually high for a second baseman. Gordon was generally considered to be one of the more acrobatic middle infielders of his era. Yet he committed as many as 28 errors in a season five different times, topping 30 miscues on two separate occasions. And his career fielding percentage of .970 was ten percentage points lower than the mark of .980 compiled by his contemporary Bobby Doerr.

Red Schoendist teamed with shortstop Marty Marion from the mid-1940s to the early 1950s to give the St. Louis Cardinals probably the finest double-play combination of that period. Schoendist was an excellent fielder, having led National League second basemen in fielding six times. He was also a solid hitter, leading the league in hits and doubles once, and finishing second in batting once, in 1953. That season was Schoendist's best as he hit 15 home runs, knocked in 79 runs and batted .342. He finished in the top 10 in the MVP voting four times and was selected to the All-Star team nine times.

The thing about Schoendist, though, is that, while he may have had three or four seasons in which he was considered to be the best second baseman in the National League, with the possible exception of that 1953 season, he was never considered to be the best major league player at his position. During the 1940s, both Doerr and Gordon were rated above him, during the early 1950s, Jackie Robinson was considered to be his superior, and, later in the decade, Nellie Fox was rated ahead of him. Thus, what we have is someone who was a very solid and dependable player, but not someone who truly stood out among his peers. It should be mentioned that Schoendist may well have been elected to the Hall partly because of the success he had as the Cardinals manager after his playing career was over. However, the feeling here is that a man should be elected on the strength of either his playing career or his managerial career, but not both. When selections are made using both as the basis, the Hall of Fame standards will invariably suffer.

Nellie Fox was the best second baseman in the American League for a decade. From 1951 to 1960, there was no better second sacker in the league and, in at least three or four of those seasons, he was the best player at his position in baseball. He led the league in hits four times, batted over .300 six times, scored more than 100 runs four times, and was an outstanding fielder, leading the league six times. He was selected to the All-Star team 12 times, won the league MVP Award in 1959, and finished in the top ten in the voting five other times. A look at his numbers reveals that Fox was actually quite comparable to Schoendist offensively:

PLAYER	AB	HITS	RUNS	2B	3B	HR	RBI	AVG	SB	OBP	SLG PCT
Red Schoendist	8,479	2,449	1,223	427	78	84	773	.289	89	.338	.387
Nellie Fox	9,232	2,663	1,279	355	112	36	790	.288	76	.349	.363

Why, then, does his resume seem to be so much more impressive than that of Schoendist? The reason lies in the fact that the two men played during an era in which the National League (Schoendist's) was becoming the more dominant of the two. Due to the senior circuit's greater willingness to adapt to the changing times and accept into its ranks the top black and Hispanic talent that was available, the N.L. became the stronger of the two leagues during the 1950s. Therefore, Schoendist had a more difficult time finishing among the league leaders in the various hitting categories and receiving support in the MVP voting. But, in actuality, both players were very similar.

So, what does all this mean? How should these players be viewed, and which, if any of the six belong in Cooperstown?

The feeling here is that the answer lies in the standards one sets for legitimate Hall of Famers. None of the six men—Lazzeri, Herman, Doerr, Gordon, Schoendist, or Fox—was a truly great player who should be thought of as an obvious Hall of Famer. But all six were very good players whose presence in Cooperstown is not an embarrassment to the Hall.

Johnny Evers

We saw earlier that Frank Chance was not truly deserving of a spot in Cooperstown. The same could be said for his infield mate Johnny Evers. A look at his career numbers makes one search for a plausible explanation for his election:

AB	HITS	RUNS	2B	3B	HR	RBI	AVG	SB	OBP	SLG PCT
6,137	1,659	919	216	70	12	538	.270	324	.356	.334

In spite of the fact that Evers played during the Deadball Era, 12 home runs, 538 runs batted in, 919 runs scored, a .270 career batting average, and a slugging percentage of .334 are not very impressive numbers. He never led the league in any major offensive category, coming the closest by finishing second in stolen bases in 1907, and second in on-base percentage in both 1908 and 1912. Evers did manage to hit .300 twice, but never knocked in more than 63 runs or scored more than 88 runs in any season. Somehow, he managed to win the National League Most Valuable Player Award in 1914 despite hitting just one home run, driving in only 40 runs, batting only .279, accumulating just 137 hits, and stealing only 12 bases for the pennant-winning Boston Braves.

One would think that the explanation for Evers' election must be rooted in the fact that he was such a great defensive player. Yet, during his career, he led National League second basemen in fielding just once, and the "great" double-play combination of *Tinker-to-Evers-to-Chance* led the league in double-plays just once. It is quite apparent, then, that just as his teammate Frank Chance made it in on the heals of the effusive praise doled out by that frustrated New York sportswriter, Evers' election too was based more on rhetoric than on performance.

Bill Mazeroski

In a letter to *The Sporting News*, which appeared in the July 21, 1986 issue, Thomas A. Morgan of Oakville, Connecticut wrote: "It is already absurd the number of less-than-fantastic players who have gone to Cooperstown. Let's not get totally ridiculous over players who excelled in one or two areas and were less than mediocre in all others..."

One would think that Mr. Morgan had Bill Mazeroski in mind when he wrote this letter. Mazeroski turned two on the double-play better than any other second baseman in baseball history, but, other than that, he was a very mediocre player. Putting him in the Hall of Fame is equivalent to admitting Carl Furillo because he had perhaps the strongest throwing arm of any outfielder in baseball history, or Jim Sundberg because he was as good behind the plate as any catcher has been, or Vince Coleman because he was a great base-stealer.

No player should be elected to the Hall of Fame because he excelled in one area, if he was mediocre in all others.

Some might argue that Lou Brock and Rickey Henderson were elected primarily on the strength of their abilities as base-stealers. However, both men were far more than just base-stealers, excelling in other areas as well. Brock was a .293 lifetime hitter who finished his career with more than 3,000 hits and 1,600 runs scored. In addition, he helped change the way the game was played with his thievery on the base-paths. Henderson was the greatest leadoff hitter the game has ever seen. In addition to being the all-time base-stealing king, he is the all-time leader in runs scored, and he compiled a lifetime .401 on-base percentage and more than 3,000 hits.

Bill Mazeroski, on the other hand, was a below-average offensive player, even for a second baseman. Here are his career numbers:

AB	HITS	RUNS	2B	3B	HR	RBI	AVG	SB	OBP	SLG PCT
7,755	2,016	769	294	62	138	853	.260	27	.302	.367

Mazeroski never came close to leading the league in any offensive category. The best he could do was finish in the top 10 three times in triples. In 17 seasons, he scored only 769 runs and batted .260, and his career on-base percentage was a poor .302. That last mark was the result of his lack of patience at the plate, since he never walked more than 40 times in any season. Mazeroski never hit any higher than .283, and he never scored more than 71 runs in a season. In addition, he did not fare particularly well in the MVP balloting, placing in the top 10 only once, in 1958, when he finished in eighth place.

Mazeroski was selected to the N.L. All-Star team seven times—from 1958 to 1960, from 1962 to 1964, and again in 1967. However, in only one of those seasons, 1958, could he have been legitimately referred to as the best second baseman in baseball. Nellie Fox was the top second baseman in 1959-60, Bobby Richardson was number one from 1962-64, and Rod Carew was tops in 1967.

There are some who would argue that Brooks Robinson and Ozzie Smith were elected to the Hall of Fame primarily for their defense. While this is true, both players were also above-average offensive players, and they fared much better than Mazeroski in the annual MVP and All-Star voting.

Robinson hit 268 career home runs, accumulated more than 2,800 hits, and scored more than 1,200 runs. He was also an excellent clutch performer, with 1,357 career runs batted in and a .303 lifetime postseason batting average. In addition, he was voted the American League's Most Valuable Player in 1964, finished in the top five on four other occasions, and was selected to the All-Star Team 15 straight seasons at one point.

While Smith struggled at the plate in his first few seasons, he eventually turned himself into a solid offensive player, finishing his career with 2,460 hits, 1,257 runs scored, and 580 stolen bases. Like Robinson, he was a perennial All-Star.

In addition, both Robinson and Smith were clearly the greatest defensive players at their positions in baseball history. While many have said the same thing about Mazeroski, that is actually quite debatable. Though he is undoubtedly somewhat prejudiced, Tim McCarver has said that, as good a defensive player as Mazeroski was, his former Cardinals teammate Julian Javier was the best fielding second baseman he ever saw. While he may have been the best at turning the double-play, it is also difficult to imagine Mazeroski being a better all-around second baseman than either Roberto Alomar, Ryne Sandberg or Bobby Grich. Alomar was more acrobatic and had more range than Mazeroski. Sandberg is the all-time leader in fielding average among major league second basemen, with a mark of .990 (seven points higher than Mazeroski), and also holds N.L. records for second basemen by playing 123 consecutive games and accepting 582 chances without making an error. In two different seasons, Mazeroski made as many as 23 errors, quite a substantial number for a second baseman. Grich was also an exceptional fielder who finished his career with the same fielding average as Mazeroski.

Aside from being outstanding fielders, another thing that Alomar, Sandberg and Grich had in common was that they were all much, much better offensive players than Mazeroski. Having played from 1970 to 1986, Grich was the closest contemporary of the three to Mazeroski. Let's take a look at the career numbers of both players alongside one another:

PLAYER	AB	HITS	RUNS	2B	3B	HR	RBI	AVG	SB	OBP	SLG PCT
Bill Mazeroski	7,755	2,016	769	294	62	138	853	.260	27	.302	.367
Bobby Grich	6,890	1,833	1,033	320	47	224	864	.266	104	.373	.424

Note that, in almost 1,000 fewer at-bats, Grich finished well ahead of Mazeroski in almost every offensive category. In particular, notice the difference in the number of runs scored and home runs, and the discrepancy in their on-base and slugging percentages. In addition, Grich once led the American League in home runs and, in another season, hit 30 homers, knocked in 101 runs, and batted .294. Even if a slight edge on defense is conceded to Mazeroski, it is quite apparent that Bobby Grich was a far better all-around player. Yet, Mazeroski is in the Hall of Fame and Grich is not.

Why?

The answer lies in the fact that the former had friends on the Veterans Committee that elected him in 2001. One of the members of the Committee, in particular, had strong ties to Mazeroski. That would be Joe Brown, former Pirates executive during Mazeroski's playing career in Pittsburgh.

In his book on the Hall of Fame, published in 1994, before Mazeroski's election, Bill James writes: "I'd like to see Mazeroski in the Hall of Fame because I'm a Royals fan and the selection of Mazeroski would greatly strengthen the argument for Frank White…" He then goes on to compare both the offensive and defensive career statistics for both players to provide evidence of what truly comparable players they were. He is right; they *were* truly comparable players. However, his argument is a perfect illustration of why players like Bill Mazeroski should never be elected to the

Hall of Fame. They lower the standards for all the other players, and lessen the credibility of those making the selections.

Everyone who thinks like James, and has a favorite player of his own, will say: *"If he's in, why not him?"* The problem is Bill Mazeroski does not belong in the Hall of Fame any more than Frank White does, or, for that matter, any more than 100 other players of comparable, or even greater, ability. While Mazeroski may not be the worst player ever elected to Cooperstown, his selection was one of the biggest mistakes the voters have ever made, and one of the Hall's darkest hours.

THIRD BASEMEN (13)

PLAYER	YEARS	ELECTED BY	YEAR ELECTED
Jimmy Collins	1895-1908	Veterans Committee	1945
Frank Baker	1908-14, 16-22	Veterans Committee	1955
Judy Johnson	1919-1938	Negro Leagues Committee	1975
Pie Traynor	1920-1935	BBWAA	1948
Jud Wilson	1922-1945	Veterans Committee	2006
Fred Lindstrom	1924-1936	Veterans Committee	1976
Ray Dandridge	1933-1948	Veterans Committee	1987
George Kell	1943-1957	Veterans Committee	1983
Eddie Mathews	1952-1968	BBWAA	1978
Brooks Robinson	1955-1977	BBWAA	1983
Mike Schmidt	1972-1989	BBWAA	1995
George Brett	1973-1993	BBWAA	1999
Wade Boggs	1982-1999	BBWAA	2005

Mike Schmidt/George Brett

Their status as the two greatest third basemen in baseball history clearly establishes Schmidt and Brett as legitimate Hall of Famers.

Mike Schmidt is generally thought to have been the greatest all-around third baseman in major league history. His 548 career home runs are not only a record for third basemen, but place him among the all-time leaders. His 1,595 runs batted in tie him with Brett for the most by a third baseman, and his .527 slugging percentage is a record for players at the position. Schmidt led the National League in home runs a record eight times, runs batted in four times, on-base percentage three times, slugging percentage five times, and walks four times. His 10 Gold Gloves are a record for National League third basemen. In addition, he won three N.L. Most Valuable Player Awards and, from 1980 to 1986, was considered to be not only the best third baseman in the game, but one of the five best players in baseball. Schmidt was arguably the very best player in the game in both 1980 and 1981. In the first of those seasons, he won the first of his three MVP Awards by leading the Phillies to the N.L. pennant and world championship. That year, he led the league with 48 home runs and 121 runs batted in, while batting .286 and scoring 104 runs. In the following strike-shortened season, Schmidt once again led the league in both homers (31) and RBIs (91), while batting .316 and winning his second consecutive MVP Award.

George Brett may well have been the greatest hitting third baseman of all-time. He certainly was one of the two or three best hitters, and one of the five best players in the American League from 1976 to 1990. He is the only player to win batting titles in three different decades, having accomplished the feat in 1976, 1980 and 1990. His mark of .390 in 1980 stands as the highest average of any player since Ted Williams hit .406 in 1941. He finished his career with 317 home runs, 1,595 runs batted in, a .305 batting average, 137 triples, and 201 stolen bases, and his 665 doubles and 3,154 hits are both records for third basemen. In addition to being a three-time batting champion, Brett led the league in hits, triples, and slugging three times each, doubles twice, and on-base percentage once. He batted over .300 eleven times, hit more than 20 homers eight times, and drove in more than 100 runs four times. Brett had his finest season in 1980 when he was named the A.L.'s Most Valuable Player for leading the Royals to the pennant with a .390 batting average, 24 home runs, and 118 runs batted in.

With the possible exception of Mike Schmidt, Brett was the finest player in the game that season. Brett was also among the top two or three players in the game in both 1979 and 1985. In 1979, he hit 23 homers, knocked in 107 runs, batted .329, and finished with 20 triples, 212 hits, and 119 runs scored. In 1985, Brett hit 30 homers, knocked in 112 runs, batted .335, scored 108 runs, and finished second to Don Mattingly in the MVP voting. In all, Brett finished in the top five of the balloting four times during his career.

Eddie Mathews/Brooks Robinson/ Pie Traynor/Wade Boggs

These four men are the other third basemen whose Hall of Fame credentials would not be questioned by anyone.

Although not necessarily regarded as such, at the time of his retirement in 1968, Eddie Mathews was the greatest third baseman to have ever played in the major leagues. His 512 career home runs (later surpassed by Schmidt), and his 1,453 runs batted in (also surpassed by Schmidt as well as Brett) were both records for third basemen at that time. He also finished his career with 1,509 runs scored and an on-base percentage of .378 (both third all-time among third basemen), and a slugging percentage of .509 (second only to Schmidt). Primarily because he played on the same team as the great Hank Aaron for most of his career, Mathews is perhaps the most overlooked superstar in the history of the game. There is little doubt, though, that he was the best third baseman in the National League from 1953 to 1961, when he hit more than 30 home runs in each season. In fact, in most of those seasons, he was the best third baseman in baseball, and one of the five or six best players in the National League. He led the league in home runs twice, hitting over 40 four times, and in walks four times, drawing more than 100 bases on balls in five different seasons. He also knocked in more than 100 runs five times and batted over .300 three times. A perennial All-Star, twice during his career Mathews finished runner-up in the league MVP voting.

Brooks Robinson was the greatest fielding third baseman in baseball history. Although he did not possess a particularly strong throwing arm, and was a very slow runner, Robinson's quickness and superb reflexes helped him to revolutionize third base play. He holds major league records for third basemen with highest fielding average (.971), most putouts (2,697), most assists (6,205), and most double plays (618). He led American League third basemen in fielding 11 times, and in putouts and assists eight times each.

In addition, Robinson was a solid hitter, hitting over 20 homers six times, driving in more than 100 runs twice, and batting over .300 twice. He finished his career with 268 home runs, 1,357 runs batted in, and 2,848 hits. A 15-time All-Star and 16-time Gold Glove winner, Robinson also fared well in the league MVP voting, winning the award in 1964 and finishing in the top five four other times. In that 1964 season, Robinson hit 28 homers, knocked in a league-leading 118 runs, and batted a career-high .317. From 1960 to 1972, with the exception of the 1961, 1969, and 1970 seasons, when Harmon Killebrew played mostly third base and had some of his finest seasons for the Twins, Robinson was clearly the best third baseman in the American League. In some of those seasons (although he faced stiff competition from National Leaguers such as Eddie Mathews, Ken Boyer, and Ron Santo), he was rated the best third baseman in the game.

Although he is not as highly regarded as he once was, Pie Traynor is generally considered to have been the greatest third baseman of the first half of the twentieth century. Therefore, even though he never led the National League in any major offensive category, he has to be considered a legitimate Hall of Famer. Traynor's .320 career batting average, 1,273 runs batted in, and 164 triples top all other major league third basemen who played during the first half of the century. Although he hit only 58 home runs during his career, Traynor was a productive hitter, knocking in more than 100 runs seven times and batting over .300 ten times. He also stole more than 20 bases twice and struck out only 278 times in more than 7,500 career at-bats.

Traynor was also a good fielder. He led National League third basemen in putouts seven times, in chances five times, and in double plays four times.

Wade Boggs was not your prototypical Hall of Fame third baseman, in the mold of some of the other great players at that position. He wasn't the home run hitter that Mike Schmidt or Eddie Mathews was. He didn't drive in runs the way Schmidt, Mathews, or George Brett did. He wasn't the great fielder that Brooks Robinson, Ray Dandridge, or Schmidt was. However, he could hit for average and get on base, two things he did better than any other third baseman in baseball history.

Boggs' 18-year major league career included stints with the Boston Red Sox, New York Yankees, and Tampa Bay Devil Rays, and ended with him leading all other third basemen in career batting average (.328) and on-base percentage (.415). He also collected 3,010 base hits, the second highest total of any third baseman, next to Brett's 3,154, and finished with 1,513 runs scored and 578 doubles, also second to Brett among third basemen.

Boggs led the American League in batting five times, including four straight seasons, from 1985 to 1988. He compiled batting averages over .350 five times during his career, hitting as high as .368 in 1985. He also led the league in runs scored, doubles, and walks twice each, and in on-base percentage six times. Although he never knocked in more than 89 runs in any season, Boggs scored more than 100 seven times. This was the direct result of his propensity for getting on base via either the base hit or base on balls. Seven times during his career Boggs collected more than 200 hits, and four times he drew more than 100 walks.

Boggs' two finest seasons came in 1985 and 1987. In the first of those years, in addition to batting .368, he collected a career-high 240 base hits, scored 107 runs, and drove in 78 others. Boggs' most productive season came in 1987, though, when he set career highs in home runs (24) and runs batted in (89), while batting .363 and scoring 108 runs.

Although never considered to be either the best player in baseball or the best in his own league, Boggs was the game's top third baseman in virtually every season, from 1983 to 1991. He was also among the five best players in the game in 1983, and from 1985 to 1988, never batting below .357 in any of those seasons. Boggs was selected to the A.L. All-Star Team 12 straight times between 1985 and 1996, and also placed in the top ten in the league MVP voting in each of the four seasons he won the batting title between 1985 and 1988. While he was a defensive liability early in his career, he worked hard on improving his fielding and turned himself into an above-average third baseman. A valid case could be made for him being among the five greatest third basemen in baseball history. If not, he was certainly in the top ten.

Frank "Home Run" Baker/Jimmy Collins

Neither Frank Baker nor Jimmy Collins was a truly great player or among the five or six best players of his time. In addition, even though each man spent 14 seasons in the big leagues, neither accumulated the number of at-bats that you might expect from a typical Hall of Famer (Baker had just under 6,000 and Collins had just under 6,800). However, each man was clearly the best third baseman of his era, and they were the two best players at their position over the first fifty years of major league baseball.

Although Frank "Home Run" Baker hit only 96 home runs during his career, he may well have been the finest long-ball hitter of the Deadball Era. Playing for Connie Mack's Philadelphia Athletics, Baker led the American League in home runs four straight years, from 1911 to 1914. He also led the league twice in runs batted in and once in triples, and he still holds the A.L. record for most triples by a rookie with his total of 19 in 1909. Baker finished his career with a .307 batting average and 235 stolen bases, including a career-high 40 thefts in 1912. In fact, that 1912 season was Baker's best as he led the league in home runs and runs batted in (with a career-high of 130), and also batted .347, a record for A.L. third basemen that stood until 1980 when George Brett batted .390. Baker finished in double-digits in home runs five times (quite a lot for those days), knocked in over 100 runs three times, batted over .300 six times, scored more than 100 runs twice, and stole more than 20 bases five times.

After a contract dispute with team owner and manager Connie Mack caused Baker to sit out the 1915 season, he was never quite the same player. However, in the six seasons prior (1909-1914), Baker had already established himself as the finest third baseman to play major league ball up to that point, earning him a place in Cooperstown.

Jimmy Collins' position as a legitimate Hall of Famer is a bit more tenuous than that of Baker since his overall numbers were slightly less impressive. In 600 more career at-bats, he hit fewer home runs, drove in virtually the same number of runs, stole fewer bases, compiled a lower batting average (.294 to Baker's .307), and finished with considerably lower on-base and slugging percentages. In addition, his major league career started in 1895, which means his first six seasons were spent hitting under much more favorable conditions. He also didn't do as well as Baker in the various criteria being used here to evaluate Hall of Famers. He only led his league once in a major offensive category—to Baker's seven—and, while neither player was ever considered to be the best player in baseball, a case could be made for Baker having been among the game's five or six best players from 1909 to 1914. The same could not be said for Collins at any point during his career.

However, Collins' fielding ability, according to those who saw him play, was unparalleled by any of his time. He is said to have been the first to charge bunts and play them barehanded, and, in 1899 and 1900, he set records for chances (593) and putouts (251) by a third baseman (both of which were broken in later years). He was also a good hitter, having led the National League with 15 homers in 1898, and also having driven in more than 100 runs twice, and batted over .300 five times during his career. While those numbers may seem modest by modern standards, they were actually considered to be rather impressive during Collins' time. And, when taking into consideration his reputation as a fielder, they are probably just enough to justify Collins' selection to the Hall of Fame.

Ray Dandridge/Judy Johnson

Although the statistics that are available for both Dandridge and Johnson are extremely limited, the reputations of both men suggest that they were exceptional players. Also, seeing as how both were generally considered to have been among the ten greatest players in the history of the Negro Leagues, it would seem that Dandridge and Johnson are deserving of their places in Cooperstown.

Ray Dandridge is considered to be, by those who saw him play, one of the greatest fielding third basemen in baseball history. In fact, although he played during the 1930s and 1940s, his fielding has often been compared to that of Brooks Robinson, although, it is said, he had a better arm. Hall of Famer Monte Irvin, who played against Dandridge in the Negro Leagues, said of him, "He had the quickest reflexes and the surest hands of any infielder I've ever seen. In a season, he had a bad year if he made four errors."

Dandridge was also an excellent contact hitter, compiling a lifetime .335 batting average in Negro League competition, hitting a career-high .370 in 1944, and hitting .347 in exhibition games against major league pitching during the course of his career.

Speaking of the righthanded hitting Dandridge, Irvin said, "Most of his career, he batted in the number two position because he made real good contact and could hit the ball like a shot to rightfield on a hit-and-run situation."

All things considered, Dandridge probably deserves to be ranked among the ten greatest third basemen in baseball history, and possibly in the top five.

Judy Johnson, as Pittsburgh outfielder Ted Page said in *The Official Negro Leagues Book*, "...was a scientific ballplayer who did everything with grace and poise. You talk about playing third base, heck, he was better than anybody I saw—Brooks Robinson, Mike Schmidt, or Pie Traynor."

Although known more for his defense, Johnson was also a consistent .300 hitter who was renowned for his cerebral approach to the game. His baseball acumen eventually landed him a job as a major league scout, and he is credited with signing Richie (Dick)

Allen while scouting for the Phillies and outfielder Bill Bruton when he was a Milwaukee Braves scout.

While, in all probability, Johnson was a worthy Hall of Famer, he doesn't seem to have quite the credentials of Dandridge. Even with the limited availability of statistical data surrounding Negro League players, it appears that Dandridge was the better hitter, and he was probably at least the equal of Johnson defensively. Therefore, the logical question that follows is: Why was Johnson elected to the Hall of Fame by the original Negro Leagues Committee in 1975, while Dandridge had to wait until 1987 to be elected by the Veterans Committee? The most likely reason is that Johnson was a member of that Negro Leagues Committee and Dandridge was not.

Jud Wilson

Generally rated right behind Ray Dandridge and Judy Johnson among Negro League third basemen was Jud Wilson, who played for four teams over the course of his 24-year career. Though not as strong defensively as either Dandridge or Johnson, Wilson was the best hitting third baseman in the history of black baseball. Satchel Paige considered him to be one of the two best hitters he ever faced, and Josh Gibson felt that Wilson was at least his equal as a hitter.

The lefthanded swinging Wilson was a pure hitter who had excellent power and drove fierce line drives to all fields. He earned the nickname "Boojum" because of the sound his line drives made when they smashed up against outfield fences. Wilson was a multiple batting champion, who, with a career mark of .345, posted the third highest batting average in Negro League history. He also ranks tenth in lifetime home runs, and batted .356 in 26 games against white major leaguers. In addition, Wilson recorded the highest lifetime average in the Cuban Winter Leagues, hitting .372 over the course of six seasons, including batting titles of .403 in '25-'26 and .441 in '27-'28 playing for Havana.

Wilson played for 10 championship teams over the course of his career, winning a title with the Baltimore Black Sox in 1929, one with the Homestead Grays in 1931, one with the 1932 Pittsburgh Crawfords, one with the 1934 Philadelphia Stars, and another six with the Grays between 1940 and 1945.

In all likelihood, Wilson's mediocre fielding caused him to be elected to the Hall of Fame long after both Dandridge and Johnson. He was considered to be merely adequate at the hot corner, possessing neither the hands nor the quickness of the other two men. Wilson played third base by keeping everything in front of him, knocking the ball down with his chest, and then throwing the batter out. He was generally described as a "crude but effective workman" in the field.

Another possible reason for Wilson's late induction may have been his reputation for being a habitual brawler. His competitive spirit and dour disposition prompted numerous altercations with opposing players, umpires, and even teammates. But Wilson's playing ability clearly earned him a spot in Cooperstown.

Fred Lindstrom

As of 1975, only four third basemen had been elected to the Hall of Fame—Jimmy Collins, Frank Baker, Pie Traynor, and Judy Johnson. Many people began to complain that the number should be greater. In response, in 1976, the Veterans Committee elected Fred Lindstrom, who played for the New York Giants and Cincinnati Reds from 1924 to 1936. While Lindstrom was a good, solid player, it is debatable whether his selection was based more on merit or the popular opinion that the Hall was short of third basemen. Let's take a look at his qualifications.

Lindstrom finished his career with a .311 batting average. In 1928, he hit 14 home runs, drove in 107 runs, batted .358, and had 231 hits. In 1930, Lindstrom had his finest season. That year, he hit 22 home runs, drove in 106 runs, batted .379 (a record for National League third basemen), scored 127 runs, and once again finished with 231 hits.

However, those two seasons were the only two "Hall of Fame type" seasons Lindstrom had during his career. Playing in a hitter's era, when batting averages of .300 or better were commonplace, he never again hit higher than .319. Furthermore, his .379 average in 1930 was only the fifth best in the league.

Using our Hall of Fame criteria, Lindstrom was never considered to be among the game's elite players. A case could not be made for him being one of the ten best third basemen in history. For most of his career, Lindstrom was rated behind Pie Traynor among National League third basemen, perhaps surpassing him only in his two best seasons. He finished in the top 10 in the MVP voting only twice during his career and was a league-leader in a hitting category only once (231 hits in 1928). Perhaps even more significant is the fact that Lindstrom was a full-time player for only seven seasons. As a result, his career numbers were far from overwhelming, and were actually quite comparable to those of some other third basemen not in the Hall of Fame. One of those players was Stan Hack, the Cubs third baseman from 1932 to 1947. Let's take a look at the numbers of the two players, side-by-side:

PLAYER	AB	HITS	RUNS	2B	3B	HR	RBI	AVG	SB	OBP	SLG PCT
Fred Lindstrom	5,611	1,747	895	301	81	103	779	.311	84	.351	.449
Stan Hack	7,278	2,193	1,239	363	81	57	642	.301	165	.394	.397

Lindstrom's power numbers (i.e. home runs, runs batted in, and slugging percentage) were superior, but Hack had a decided edge in most other offensive categories. His on-base percentage was much higher than Lindstrom's, and he scored many more runs, both critical numbers for a leadoff hitter, which Hack was. In fact, he may very well have been the best leadoff hitter in the National League during the 1930s and 1940s. In addition, he was a regular for eleven seasons (as opposed to Lindstrom's seven), and he led the league in batting once and in hits twice. Hack also batted over .300 six times, scored more than 100 runs seven times, and was selected to the All-Star team four times. It would seem that Hack's credentials are every bit as impressive as Lindstrom's, if not more so. Why, then, is he not in the Hall of Fame, while Lindstrom is? Perhaps the explanation lies in the fact that Bill Terry, Lindstrom's former teammate with the Giants, was on the Veterans Committee that elected him in 1976.

More importantly, though, was Lindstrom's selection a good one? The evidence seems to indicate that Lindstrom was a good player who was among the best third basemen of the first half of the 20th century. Therefore, he was not a particularly bad choice. However, there were other third basemen who have yet to be elected who would have been better selections. We will soon see who some of those other players were.

George Kell

In 1983, the Veterans Committee elected George Kell to the Hall of Fame. Kell played mostly for the Detroit Tigers and Boston Red Sox from 1943 to 1957, a fairly decent era for hitters. During his career, Kell led the American League in batting once, doubles twice, and hits twice, and compiled a .306 batting average. He was also a good fielder, having led league third basemen in fielding seven times. He was selected to the All-Star Team seven times and finished in the top 10 in the MVP voting three times.

However, Kell had virtually no power. He never hit more than 12 home runs in a season, finishing his career with just 78 long balls. In addition, he knocked in and scored 100 runs only one time each during his career. Thus, it could not be said that Kell was a big run-producer, one of the more desirable qualities in a Hall of Fame third baseman. If his career numbers are compared to those of Bill Madlock, who played from 1973 to 1987, during more of a pitcher's era, one notices a remarkable similarity:

PLAYER	AB	HITS	RUNS	2B	3B	HR	RBI	AVG	SB	OBP	SLG PCT
George Kell	6,702	2,054	881	385	50	78	870	.306	51	.368	.414
Bill Madlock	6,594	2,008	920	348	34	163	860	.305	174	.369	.442

While Kell was a far better fielder than Madlock, on offense it appears that Madlock was Kell with more power and speed. In addition, Madlock won four batting titles, twice topping the .340 mark, was a three-time All-Star, and finished in the top 10 in the MVP voting twice. Therefore, Madlock's Hall of Fame credentials are quite comparable to those of Kell. Yet he has received virtually no support.

Far more disturbing, though, is the lack of support shown for both Ron Santo and Ken Boyer, two of the very best players not in the Hall of Fame. Let's take a look at their numbers, along with those of Graig Nettles and Buddy Bell, two other third basemen with credentials just as impressive as Kell's:

PLAYER	AB	HITS	RUNS	2B	3B	HR	RBI	AVG	SB	OBP	SLG PCT
Ron Santo	8,143	2,254	1,138	365	67	342	1,331	.277	35	.366	.464
Ken Boyer	7,455	2,143	1,104	318	68	282	1,141	.287	105	.351	.462
Graig Nettles	8,986	2,225	1,193	328	28	390	1,314	.248	32	.332	.421
Buddy Bell	8,995	2,514	1,151	425	56	201	1,106	.279	55	.343	.406

It is obvious that all four men had much more power than Kell, and were far superior to him as run-producers. Each player also had some other fairly impressive credentials:

Ron Santo played for the Cubs from 1960 to 1974, during a pitcher's era. In at least four of those seasons ('65-'67, '69), he was the top third baseman in the National League and, perhaps, in all of baseball. He led the league in walks four times, on-base percentage twice, and triples once. He hit more than 20 homers eleven times, surpassing the 30-mark four times, drove in more than 100 runs four times, topping 90 on four other occasions, and batted .300 four times. He was an outstanding fielder, winning five Gold Gloves and setting a major league record by leading third basemen in total chances the most times (9), and he shares National League records for leading the most times in putouts and assists (7), and double plays (6). Santo was also selected to the All-Star Team nine times, finished in the top 10 in the MVP voting four times, and, as captain of the Cubs, was an outstanding team-leader.

Ken Boyer spent most of his 15 big league seasons from 1955 to 1969 with the St. Louis Cardinals. He was the National League's top third baseman from 1962 to 1964, and vied for that honor with Eddie Mathews in both 1956 and 1961. He was the top player at his position in the major leagues in at least two of those seasons. Boyer led the league in runs batted in only once, but he knocked in more than 100 runs twice and surpassed the 90 RBI-mark six other times. Playing in a ballpark in St. Louis that was extremely difficult for righthanded power hitters, Boyer still managed to hit

30 homers once and hit more than 20 long balls eight other times. He also batted over .300 five times and scored more than 100 runs three times. Like Santo, he won five Gold Gloves, and he was selected to the All-Star Team seven times. In 1964, the Cardinals captain led his team to a victory over the Yankees in the World Series by turning the Series around with his grand-slam home run off Al Downing in Game Four. Boyer was selected N.L. MVP that season, one of four times he finished in the top 10 in the voting.

Probably the only thing keeping Graig Nettles out of the Hall of Fame is his career batting average of .248. His 390 career home runs are the third highest total ever by a third baseman, and the most ever by an American League player at that position. While he was rated behind George Brett among A.L. third basemen throughout much of his career, he was selected to *The Sporting News' All-Star Team* following each of the 1975, 1977, and 1978 seasons. He was also selected to the A.L. All-Star team six times and finished in the top 10 in the MVP voting twice. Although Nettles won only two Gold Gloves, he was one of the finest fielding third basemen in baseball history, shifting the momentum of the 1978 World Series with his great glove work in Game Three against the Dodgers.

Buddy Bell is one of the more underrated players at this position. He was not a dominant player, never having led the league in any major offensive category. He never scored 100 runs, and he knocked in 100 runs and hit as many as 20 home runs only one time each. However, Bell batted .300 twice, was selected to the All-Star Team five times, and finished in the top 10 in the MVP voting once, despite playing for mediocre teams in Cleveland and Texas throughout virtually his entire career. He was also the equal of Nettles, defensively, leading the league in fielding three times and winning six Gold Glove Awards.

Now, back to the subject at hand—George Kell. While Kell was a good player who was far from being the worst selection ever made by the Veterans Committee, he was not productive enough for a player at his position to legitimize his presence in Cooperstown. Santo and Boyer, both of whom were eligible for selection to the Hall of Fame when Kell was elected in 1983, would have been far better choices. Nettles and Bell, and perhaps even Madlock and former Cleveland Indian third baseman, Ken Keltner, have credentials equal to those of Kell.

SHORTSTOPS (22)

PLAYER	YEARS	ELECTED BY	YEAR ELECTED
George Davis	1890-1909	Veterans Committee	1998
Hughie Jennings	1891-1903	Veterans Committee	1945
Bobby Wallace	1894-1918	Veterans Committee	1953
Honus Wagner	1897-1917	BBWAA	1936
Joe Tinker	1902-1916	Veterans Committee	1946
John Henry Lloyd	1905-1932	Negro Leagues Committee	1977
Rabbit Maranville	1912-1935	BBWAA	1954
Dave Bancroft	1915-1930	Veterans Committee	1971
Joe Sewell	1920-1933	Veterans Committee	1977
Travis Jackson	1922-1936	Veterans Committee	1982
Willie Wells	1924-1948	Veterans Committee	1977
Joe Cronin	1926-1945	BBWAA	1956
Luke Appling	1930-1950	BBWAA	1964
Arky Vaughan	1932-43,47-48	Veterans Committee	1985
Lou Boudreau	1938-1952	BBWAA	1970
Pee Wee Reese	1940-42,46-58	Veterans Committee	1984
Phil Rizzuto	1941-42,46-56	Veterans Committee	1994
Ernie Banks	1953-1971	BBWAA	1977
Luis Aparicio	1956-1973	BBWAA	1984
Robin Yount	1974-1992	BBWAA	1999
Ozzie Smith	1978-1996	BBWAA	2002
Cal Ripken Jr.	1981-2001	BBWAA	2007

Honus Wagner/Ernie Banks

As two of the three greatest shortstops in major league history (Alex Rodriguez being the other), Honus Wagner and Ernie Banks have overwhelming Hall of Fame credentials.

Honus Wagner was not only the finest shortstop of his time, but was the game's greatest player during the first decade of the 20th century. From 1900 to 1909, Wagner won eight National League batting titles and led the league in runs batted in and stolen bases five times each, slugging percentage six times, and doubles seven times. When he retired, he had compiled more hits, runs, total bases, RBIs and stolen bases than any player in history, to that point. To this day, he still has more hits (3,415), doubles (640), triples (252), RBIs (1,732), and stolen bases (722) than any other shortstop who ever played, as well as the highest career batting average (.327). Many who saw him play considered him to be the greatest all-around player they ever saw. He is generally regarded as one of the 10 or 15 greatest players in baseball history.

Ernie Banks was the greatest shortstop of the second half of the 20th century, and one of the game's most dominant players during the 1950s and 1960s. From 1955 to 1960, he hit more home runs than any other player in baseball, and was one of the top five players in the game. He won back-to-back National League MVP Awards in 1958 and 1959, when, playing for the second-division Chicago Cubs, he averaged 46 home runs and 136 runs batted in, while batting over .300 each season. He also finished in the top five in the league MVP voting two other times and was a perennial All-Star. Banks led the league in both homers and RBIs twice, and in slugging percentage once. He hit over 40 homers five times, finishing his career with 512, and knocked in more than 100 runs eight times. Banks was clearly the best shortstop in baseball from 1955 to 1961 and, after being shifted to first base following the 1961 season, went on to become one of the top players at that position for the next eight seasons.

Cal Ripken Jr.

Equally deserving of a place in Cooperstown is Cal Ripken Jr., the man who, in many ways, revolutionized his position for future generations of players who aspired to play shortstop in the major leagues.

Although he will always be remembered as the man who broke Lou Gehrig's record for the most consecutive games played, Cal Ripken Jr. was an exceptional player whose list of accomplishments extends far beyond that revered mark.

In his 21 seasons with the Baltimore Orioles, Ripken hit 431 home runs, knocked in 1,695 runs, scored another 1,647, and compiled 3,184 hits and 603 doubles, to finish second all-time among major league shortstops in each offensive category. He hit more than 20 homers twelve times, knocked in more than 100 runs four times, scored more than 100 runs three times, and batted over .300 five times, while compiling a lifetime mark of .276.

Ripken is the only shortstop in American League history to win two Most Valuable Player Awards. He earned the honor for the first time in 1983 when he hit 27 home runs, knocked in 102 runs, batted .318, and led the league in runs scored (121), hits (211), and doubles (47), while leading the Orioles to the world championship. He won the award again in 1991, when he established career highs in homers (34), runs batted in (114), and batting average (.323). Ripken was the top shortstop in the American League in virtually every season from 1983 to 1994, with only Alan Trammell's superb 1987 season for Detroit breaking the string. He was also the best shortstop in baseball in many of those seasons.

Although he is remembered more for his offense, Ripken was also an excellent defensive player, having led A.L. shortstops in fielding twice. Even though he was not particularly quick or overly spectacular, Ripken had exceptional hands and was an expert at studying opposing hitters and positioning himself in the right spot on the field. He also set the mold for other big shortstops of future generations to follow, being credited by others such as Alex Rodriguez and Derek Jeter as having been a huge influence on their careers. Ripken is clearly among the four or five greatest shortstops in baseball history. As such, he is most deserving of his 2007 election into Cooperstown.

Ozzie Smith

Ozzie Smith was unquestionably the greatest fielding shortstop in baseball history. While there have been others such as Marty Marion, Luis Aparicio, and Omar Vizquel who have excelled at the position, no other player could quite match Smith's acrobatic play and wizardry in the field. As spectacular as he was, though, he was also extremely consistent, setting a record for National League shortstops in 1991 by committing only eight errors in 150 games. His 13 Gold Gloves are a record for shortstops.

Offensively, while Smith's numbers are not on a par with many of the other players in the Hall of Fame, he was able to turn himself into an above-average offensive player, totaling 2,460 hits, 1,257 runs, and 580 stolen bases during his career. Although, among major league shortstops, Cal Ripken Jr.'s hitting made him a better all-around player, Smith was clearly the National League's best shortstop during the 1980s. He was also unquestionably one of the ten greatest shortstops in baseball history, thereby justifying his place in Cooperstown.

John Henry "Pop" Lloyd/Willie Wells

As the two greatest shortstops in Negro League history, both Lloyd and Wells clearly earned their places in Cooperstown.

Although he was never given a chance to play in the major leagues because of the color of his skin, John Henry "Pop" Lloyd was clearly one of the greatest shortstops in baseball history. Generally considered to be the greatest Negro League player of the Deadball Era, Lloyd was regarded by some as the finest player in all of baseball during his playing days. Babe Ruth once stated that he believed Lloyd to be the greatest player he ever saw.

Lloyd spent more than a quarter of a century playing in the black professional leagues, for 12 different teams. He began to establish his reputation as one of the game's great players in 1910 when he joined Rube Foster's Chicago Leland Giants. That year, the Giants won 123 games and Lloyd hit .417. Also that season,

Lloyd spent some time playing in Cuba for the Havana Reds. While there, he played five exhibition games against Ty Cobb and his Detroit Tigers. Against Detroit, Lloyd batted .500, getting 11 hits in 22 at-bats, out-hitting Cobb by 131 points, and causing the latter to proclaim that he would never again play against black players.

Lloyd was a complete player who could hit, run, field, and throw. An exceptional lefthanded line-drive hitter, Lloyd usually batted fourth in his team's lineup. Different sources have him batting either .337 or .368 over the course of his career. In the field, Lloyd positioned himself wisely, got a good jump on the ball, and possessed both outstanding range and sure hands. Among Negro League shortstops, only Dick Lundy drew favorable comparisons to him as a fielder, and Lloyd was widely regarded as the greatest shortstop in the history of black baseball. Indeed, he was frequently referred to as "the black Honus Wagner" for his tremendous all-around ability. Aside from Wagner, no other major league shortstop of the first half of the 20th century was considered to be his peer by those who saw him play. Wagner, himself, after being told of the comparisons being made between himself and Lloyd, commented: "After I saw him play, I felt honored that they should name such a great ballplayer after me."

Long before Cal Ripken Jr. set the standards for major league shortstops by combining exceptional fielding with home-run power, Willie Wells was doing the same in the Negro Leagues. Besides having great range, soft hands, and an extremely accurate throwing arm, Wells also possessed outstanding power that enabled him to set a Negro Leagues single-season record for home runs by a shortstop, with 27. Over his 25-year career, he also batted .334.

Negro League legend Buck O'Neill said in his 1996 autobiography, "If I had to pick a shortstop for my team, it would be Willie Wells. He could hit to all fields, hit with power, bunt, and stretch singles into doubles. But it was his glove that truly dazzled..." O'Neill then went on to compare Wells favorably to the great Ozzie Smith.

Wells was also a bit of a pioneer, becoming the first player in baseball history to wear a batting helmet, in 1936, after being thrown at often by opposing pitchers. They clearly did not appreciate the fact that, from 1936 to 1939, Wells hit no lower than .346, after batting a career-high .401 in 1930.

Joe Cronin/Arky Vaughan/Luke Appling

With the exception of Honus Wagner and John Henry Lloyd, these three men were the finest shortstops of the first half of the twentieth century. As such, they are all deserving of their Hall of Fame status.

Playing for the Washington Senators and Boston Red Sox, Joe Cronin compiled a lifetime .301 batting average, .390 on-base percentage, and .468 slugging percentage (third all-time among shortstops with at least 5,000 at bats, behind only Ernie Banks and Alex Rodriguez). His 170 career home runs were the most by any shortstop during the first half of the century, and his 1,424 runs batted in and 515 doubles were second only to Honus Wagner. During his career, Cronin knocked in more than 100 runs eight times, batted over .300 eight times, had more than 40 doubles six times, and scored more than 100 runs four times. Although known more for his offense, Cronin was considered to be an above-average defensive shortstop.

Using our Hall of Fame criteria, Cronin would have to be considered one of the ten greatest shortstops in baseball history. For much of the 1930s, he was considered to be the finest shortstop in the American League, if not in all of baseball, having been named the outstanding major league shortstop by *The Sporting News* a total of seven times. That same publication selected him American League MVP in 1930, when he hit .346, knocked in 126 runs, and scored 127 others. He also finished second to Jimmie Foxx in 1933 in the official MVP voting, and placed in the top 10 another four times. Cronin was selected to the All-Star Team seven times. He also led the league in doubles twice, and in triples once, and led A.L. shortstops in fielding twice. Therefore, Cronin does fairly well in this area as well.

Arky Vaughan had the misfortune of playing the same position, for the same team, as Honus Wagner. Therefore, his offensive accomplishments for the Pittsburgh Pirates during the 1930s and early '40s were probably not appreciated as much as they should have been.

Vaughan was an above-average fielder, but it was as a hitter that he truly excelled. In fact, he is generally considered to have been one of the greatest offensive shortstops in baseball history. Among players at that position, only Wagner exceeded his .318 career batting average, and Vaughan's .406 on-base percentage is the highest ever for players at the position. His .385 batting average in 1935 won him the National League batting crown and set a 20th century league record for highest average by a shortstop. During his career, he knocked in over 90 runs four times, batted over .330 three times, had at least 10 triples eight times, and scored more than 100 runs five times.

Further analyzing his Hall of Fame credentials, Vaughan clearly ranks as one of the 10 greatest shortstops in baseball history. For much of the 1930s, he was one of the top five players in the National League, and, in one or two of those seasons, in all of baseball. He was the top shortstop in his league for virtually the entire decade, and was the best player in baseball at his position in some of those seasons. Vaughan finished in the top five in the MVP voting twice and was a perennial All-Star. He led the league in batting once, in slugging percentage once, and in on-base percentage, walks, triples, and runs scored three times each. He is clearly most deserving of his place in Cooperstown.

Although he was considered to be a below-average defensive player, having led American League shortstops in errors five times, Luke Appling's hitting justifies his place in Cooperstown. He batted .310 lifetime, and compiled an on-base percentage of .399, with 2,749 hits and 1,319 runs scored. He won two batting titles, leading the league in 1936 with a mark of .388 that remains the all-time record for shortstops. He also knocked in 128 runs, scored 111 others, and totaled 204 hits that year. Appling batted over .300 fourteen times during his career and was selected to the All-Star

Team seven times. Despite his defensive shortcomings, he was named the outstanding major league shortstop by *The Sporting News* three times, and finished in the top 10 in the MVP voting three times, finishing second twice.

George Davis/Joe Sewell/ Lou Boudreau/Robin Yount

These are the last four shortstops who clearly belong in Cooperstown.

George Davis, whose career spanned the last decade of the 19th century and the first decade of the 20th, was arguably the finest shortstop to play in the major leagues prior to Honus Wagner. Why he was not elected to the Hall of Fame by the Veterans Committee until 1998 is somewhat confusing, especially when one considers some of the lesser shortstops who were inducted long before him.

Davis finished his career with a .295 batting average, a .361 on-base percentage, 163 triples, 451 doubles, 2,660 hits, 1,437 runs batted in, 1,539 runs scored, and 616 stolen bases—all outstanding marks for a player from his era. Those figures are even more impressive when they are compared to the statistics compiled by some of the other shortstops who have been elected to Cooperstown, something we will do a bit later. Davis led the National League with 136 runs batted in 1897, one of three times he topped the 100-RBI mark. He also scored more than 100 runs five times, stole more than 40 bases five times, including a career-high 65 in 1897, and batted over .300 nine straight years, from 1893 to 1901, bettering the .340 mark four times. He was also a fine fielder, leading league shortstops in fielding no fewer than four times.

For much of the 1920s, Joe Sewell was the best shortstop playing in the major leagues. During the entire decade, he failed to hit at least .300 only one time, batting .299 in 1922. Playing for the Cleveland Indians, he was easily the best shortstop in the American League from 1921 to 1929, and he was superior to the top shortstops in the National League (Travis Jackson, Dave Bancroft, Glenn Wright, and Rabbit Maranville) in most of those seasons.

Although he was an outstanding defensive shortstop, Sewell was perhaps best known for hardly ever striking out. He is the holder of every major season and career record for fewest strikeouts by a batter, fanning only 114 times in 14 seasons and 7,132 at-bats, and setting a single-season record in 1932, when he struck out only three times in 503 at-bats. He was also a productive hitter, finishing his career with a .312 batting average, 1,055 runs batted in, 1,141 runs scored, and an on-base percentage of .391. Sewell knocked in and scored more than 100 runs in a season twice each, batted over .300 nine times, and led the A.L. in doubles once.

After leading league shortstops in fielding three times, he was moved to third base by the Yankees after they acquired him in a trade prior to the 1931 season. He spent three seasons there, solidifying New York's infield and helping them to the pennant and world championship in 1932. During his career, Sewell finished in the top 10 in the MVP voting four times.

During the 1940s, there was no finer all-around shortstop in baseball than the Cleveland Indians' Lou Boudreau. Selected to the American League All-Star Team eight times during that decade, he batted over .300 four times, drove in more than 100 runs twice, scored more than 100 once, and finished with more than 40 doubles four times. Boudreau led the American League in batting once, and in doubles three times, and was also an outstanding defensive player, leading league shortstops in fielding no fewer than eight times. He had his finest season in 1948 when, as player-manager for the Indians, he established career-highs in home runs (18), RBIs (106), and batting average (.355), en route to winning the A.L. MVP Award. Boudreau also finished in the top 10 in the voting seven other times.

Robin Yount is the only player in major league history to win an MVP Award at two of the most demanding positions on the diamond, shortstop and centerfield. Although his career numbers are not particularly overwhelming—if he were to be judged as an outfielder—they are extremely impressive when he is looked upon, primarily, as a shortstop.

That is the position Yount played for the Milwaukee Brewers in his first 11 seasons, from 1974 to 1984. Coming up to the Brewers as a skinny 18 year-old, it took Yount a few seasons to develop into the formidable player he eventually became. But, from the late 1970s to the early '80s, he was as good as any shortstop playing in the major leagues, and clearly the best in the American League.

Yount had his finest season in 1982, when he won the first of his two MVP Awards. That year, he hit 29 homers, knocked in 114 runs, batted .331, and led the league with 46 doubles, 210 hits, and a .578 slugging percentage. After being shifted to the outfield in 1985 as a result of an injury to his throwing shoulder, Yount won the award a second time in 1989. That season, he hit 21 homers, knocked in 103 runs, and batted .318.

During his career, Yount hit 251 home runs, drove in 1,406 runs, scored 1,632 others, batted .285, and compiled 3,142 hits, all outstanding numbers, especially for a shortstop. He hit more than 20 homers four times, knocked in over 100 runs three times, scored more than 100 runs five times, and batted over .300 six times.

Rabbit Maranville/Travis Jackson/ Pee Wee Reese/Luis Aparicio

These four men have been grouped together because, while they were all quite different as players, they could all be described as marginal Hall of Fame candidates. Let's examine each one's credentials separately:

Playing mostly for the Boston Braves and Brooklyn Dodgers, Rabbit Maranville spent 24 seasons in the big leagues. He was considered to be a spectacular fielder, but was a below-average hitter, even for a shortstop. Coming up to the majors in 1912, Maranville spent his first eight seasons hitting in the Deadball Era, when mediocre batting averages were the norm. However, he played until 1935, and, even after batting averages began skyrocketing during the 1920s, Maranville never hit any higher than .295, and was able to top the .280 mark only three times during his career. He never drove in more than 78 runs in any season, and scored 100 runs only once, topping 80 only four times. He finished his career with a batting average of .258, only 28 home runs, and on-base and slugging percentages of only .318 and .340, respectively.

However, Maranville, in over 10,000 career at-bats, was able to compile 2,605 hits, 1,255 runs, 380 doubles, 177 triples, and 291 stolen bases—all very respectable numbers. In addition, he led National League shortstops in fielding five times and always seemed to do well in the MVP voting, finishing in the top 10 four times, even though no award was presented in the N.L. in any of the seasons from 1915 to 1923. Another thing in his favor is that he was elected by the BBWAA, not by the Veterans Committee. In fact, prior to his election in 1954, he always did well in the balloting. Therefore, one must assume that the baseball writers of his day held him in high esteem. It is also likely that he possessed many intangible qualities that statistics simply do not reflect.

Travis Jackson, the New York Giants regular shortstop for much of the 1920s and 1930s, finished his career with a batting average of .291, 135 home runs, and a slugging percentage of .433—all very respectable numbers for a shortstop. He also drove in more than 100 runs once, finished in the top 10 in the MVP voting four times, and was selected to *The Sporting News' All-Star Team* three times.

However, in 15 big league seasons, from 1922 to 1936, Jackson appeared in more than 120 games only eight times and accumulated as many as 500 at-bats only six times. He never came close to leading the league in any offensive category, scored more than 80 runs in a season only twice, and walked as many as 40 times only twice. He finished his career with only 6,086 at-bats, 1,768 hits, and 833 runs scored. He was elected to the Hall of Fame by the Veterans Committee in 1982.

Pee Wee Reese was the captain of those great Brooklyn Dodger teams that appeared in six World Series between 1947 and 1956. He was a fine shortstop and team leader, and was one of the few

Dodger players who helped to make Jackie Robinson feel welcome when he joined the team in 1947. During his career, Reese led the National League in stolen bases, walks, and runs scored once each, and led league shortstops in fielding once.

He was selected to the All-Star Team ten times and finished in the top 10 in the MVP voting eight times. He was the top shortstop in the National League from 1946 to 1953 and, based on the support he received in the MVP voting, was obviously thought of as being an extremely valuable and important player to the Dodgers.

However, playing in a fairly decent era for hitters, and in Ebbetts Field—an excellent hitter's park—Reese finished his career with only a .269 batting average and 2,170 hits. He batted over .300 only once, and scored more than 100 runs only twice. In addition, he never had a season in which he could be classified as the best shortstop in baseball (from 1946 to 1953, that title was passed between Lou Boudreau, Phil Rizzuto, and Vern Stephens). He was selected by the Veterans Committee two years after Jackson, in 1984.

Luis Aparicio spent 18 seasons in the major leagues, playing for the Chicago White Sox, Baltimore Orioles, and Boston Red Sox. Coming up to the White Sox in 1956, Aparicio brought something to the American League that it had been lacking since the Deadball Era—daring base-running that epitomized the aggressive style of play employed by the "Go-Go Sox" of his time. Starting in 1956, he led the league in stolen bases nine straight seasons, topping the 50-mark four times. He was also an exceptional defensive player, leading the league's shortstops in fielding eight times. He was selected to the All-Star Team ten times and finished in the top 10 in the MVP voting twice.

However, aside from his base-stealing ability, Aparicio was actually a below-average offensive player. During his career, he hit over .300 only once, hitting as high as .280 only one other time. He never scored 100 runs in a season, and his career on-base percentage was only .313. If you take a look at his numbers, they actually bear a remarkable resemblance to those compiled by Rabbit

Maranville and, to a lesser degree, Bert Campaneris—someone who received very little support in the Hall of Fame balloting:

PLAYER	AB	HITS	RUNS	2B	3B	HR	RBI	AVG	SB	OBP	SLG PCT
Rabbit Maranville	10,078	2,605	1,255	380	177	28	884	.258	291	.318	.340
Luis Aparicio	10,230	2,677	1,335	394	92	83	791	.262	506	.313	.343
Bert Campaneris	8,684	2,249	1,181	313	86	79	646	.259	649	.313	.342

Maranville and Aparicio were virtually equal as run producers (that is, runs scored plus runs batted in). Aparicio hit more home runs and stole more bases, but Maranville had twice as many triples. Other than that, their numbers are practically identical.

Aparicio and Campaneris, both leadoff men, drove in runs, and scored them at virtually the same rate. Campaneris actually had a little more power and, in fewer at-bats, stole many more bases. It should be noted, though, that he was not as strong as Aparicio defensively. In addition, Aparicio was never considered to be the best shortstop in baseball. Early in his career, Ernie Banks held that distinction, and the torch was later passed to Maury Wills and, for one or two seasons, players such as Zoilo Versailles, Jim Fregosi, Rico Petrocelli, and Campaneris. Even in the American League, the only seasons in which he was rated as the top shortstop were 1959 and 1960.

The question that follows then is this: Where do Maranville, Jackson, Reese, and Aparicio stand as legitimate Hall of Famers? The feeling here is that none of the four men was truly outstanding enough to be viewed as anything more than a borderline candidate, at best. Their selections should all be viewed as extremely questionable. Of the four, due to his lack of plate appearances and relatively low career totals, Jackson's election seems to be the most fallible. Maranville, because of his repeatedly good showings in the MVP and Hall of Fame balloting, and Reese, because of the excellent support he received in the MVP voting, and for all his appearances on the All-Star team, appear to be the most legitimate. But, the selections of all four men should be viewed with a great deal of skepticism.

Dave Bancroft

In 1971, the Veterans Committee, under the influence of two of its members, Frankie Frisch and Bill Terry, both of whom played with the former shortstop, elected Dave Bancroft to the Hall of Fame. Bancroft originally came up with the Philadelphia Phillies in 1915 and, as a rookie, helped them win the National League pennant. He was an outstanding fielder who was known much more for his defense than he was for his hitting. In his five years with the Phillies, he never batted higher than .272 and, in 1916, hit only .212. However, Bancroft benefited as much as anyone from the offensive resurgence that was ushered in by the 1920s. After being traded to the New York Giants during the 1920 season, he never hit less than .299 over the next four seasons, peaking at .321 in 1922. He also scored more than 100 runs in three of those seasons. Traded to the Boston Braves after the 1923 season, Bancroft batted over .300 twice more, in 1925 and 1926, before being traded to the Dodgers and, eventually, back to the Giants for his final season.

Bancroft led National League shortstops in fielding twice. He also finished in the top 10 in the MVP voting twice, even though the award was not presented in any of the 1915-1923 seasons.

Bancroft was a good player. The problem is, he probably wasn't quite good enough, nor did he accomplish enough during his career to justify his induction into the Hall of Fame. Playing mostly in a hitter's era, Bancroft finished his career with a .279 batting average. He also compiled only 591 runs batted in and 1,048 runs scored in just over 7,000 career at-bats (roughly, the equivalent of 14 full seasons). That averages out to approximately 42 RBIs and 75 runs scored a year, hardly Hall of Fame numbers, even for a shortstop. Let's look at his numbers next to those of Rabbit Maranville and Joe Sewell, both of whom were also excellent fielders:

PLAYER	AB	HITS	RUNS	2B	3B	HR	RBI	AVG	SB	OBP	SLG PCT
Rabbit Maranville	10,078	2,605	1,255	380	177	28	884	.258	291	.318	.340
Dave Bancroft	7,182	2,004	1,048	320	77	32	591	.279	145	.355	.358
Joe Sewell	7,132	2,226	1,141	436	68	49	1,055	.312	74	.391	.413

Bancroft's numbers clearly come up far short of the figures compiled by the other two men in virtually every category. Maranville's statistical superiority is largely the result of his greater longevity. Sewell was simply a much better hitter than Bancroft. However, regardless of the reason, it becomes apparent that, in spite of his strong defense, Bancroft's statistics should not have been good enough to get him into the Hall of Fame.

Hughie Jennings

There are two things that prevent Hughie Jennings from being a legitimate Hall of Famer. The first is that he didn't play long enough, or have enough plate appearances, to be considered a valid choice. The second is that the only good offensive seasons he had were from 1894 to 1900, when batting averages throughout all of baseball were extremely high. In the previous three seasons, and in Jennings' last three years, he did virtually nothing on offense.

From 1891 to 1893, Jennings posted batting averages of .292, .224 and .181. Then, in 1894, a year in which the league average rose to over .300, Jennings batted .335. Over the next three seasons, he hit .386, .401 and .355—impressive numbers in any era. He also knocked in over 100 runs, and scored 100 more in each of those seasons. After two more good years in which he batted over .300 and scored 100 runs, the rules changes that went into effect at the turn of the century brought Jennings' numbers back down to earth, and he never again hit over .300.

Jennings ended his career after the 1903 season with less than 5,000 at-bats, not even the equivalent of ten full seasons. He was a full-time player for only seven seasons. While both his career batting average of .311 and his lifetime on-base percentage of .390 are fairly impressive, Jennings finished with only 840 RBIs, 994 runs scored, and 18 home runs. In addition, he never led his league in any offensive category and was just a mediocre fielder. Even with fielding averages being much lower at that time than they would become in later years, Jennings' career mark of .922 was below the league average of about .935 to .940.

Bobby Wallace

The Veterans Committee elected Bobby Wallace to the Hall of Fame in 1953, 45 years before George Davis was elected. Looking at their numbers, it is hard to figure out why:

PLAYER	AB	HITS	RUNS	2B	3B	HR	RBI	AVG	SB	OBP	SLG PCT
George Davis	9,031	2,660	1,539	451	163	73	1,437	.295	616	.361	.405
Bobby Wallace	8,618	2,309	1,057	391	143	34	1,121	.268	201	.326	.358

Playing in essentially the same time period, in almost the same number of at-bats, Davis finished well ahead of Wallace in every offensive category. In particular, note the discrepancy in runs scored, runs batted in, stolen bases, on-base percentage, and slugging percentage. In addition, while Davis batted over .300 nine times, scored 100 runs five times, and led the league in runs batted in once, Wallace batted over .300 just twice, never scored 100 runs in a season, and never led the league in any offensive category. While Wallace did lead the league in fielding twice, Davis finished at the top of the league rankings four times.

In short, Bobby Wallace was a good player. But, when his numbers are compared to those of a legitimate Hall of Famer like George Davis, it becomes apparent that he does not belong in Cooperstown.

Phil Rizzuto

The evaluation of the Hall of Fame credentials of this particular player is extremely difficult for me due to personal reasons. Having grown up in the Bronx as a huge Yankees fan during the 1960s and 1970s, *The Scooter* holds a special place in my heart. Although his last season as a player was 1956, the year I was born, I grew up watching him on television and listening to his voice on the radio as an announcer for the team. Rizzuto had such an endearing quality to him that it was impossible, even if you were a Yankee hater, to dislike him. He was funny, entertaining, natural, and, perhaps more than anything else, unpretentious. This ability to be himself, and to laugh at himself, was probably the quality that people most appreciated about him. When Phil passed away in 2007, millions of Yankee fans, myself included, felt as if they lost a member of their own family. Feeling as I do about *The Scooter* is what makes saying this so hard, but, looking at things completely objectively, Phil Rizzuto should not be in the Hall of Fame.

That last statement should not be misinterpreted to mean that Rizzuto was not a fine player, or that he was one of the worst players elected to Cooperstown. He was a fine player, and there are several players in the Hall of Fame who are less deserving than Phil. However, Rizzuto's resume is just not impressive enough to allow him to be classified as a legitimate Hall of Famer. Let's take a look.

In a 13-year career, Rizzuto batted .273, drove in 563 runs, scored another 877, totaled 1,588 hits, and hit 38 home runs. He batted over .300 twice, scored more than 100 runs twice, and led American League shortstops in fielding twice. He was selected to the All-Star Team five times and was named the league's Most Valuable Player in 1950. That season was Rizzuto's finest, as he established career-highs in virtually every offensive category by batting .324, scoring 125 runs, totaling 200 hits, hitting seven homers, and rapping out 36 doubles. He also finished in the top 10 in the MVP voting on two other occasions, finishing second to Ted Williams a year earlier.

However, let's take a hard look at the numbers: Aside from his two .300 seasons, Rizzuto batted as high as .270 only five other times, never hitting any higher than .284 in any other season. Not always a leadoff hitter, he never drove in more than 68 runs in any season, and, with the exception of his two 100-plus seasons, scored as many as 80 runs only two other times. Aside from his 200-hit season in 1950, Rizzuto never had more than 169 hits in any other year. Although he was said to have been the American League's most feared baserunner of his era, Rizzuto never stole more than 22 bases in a season, never led the league in that department, and stole only 149 bags in his career. While it is true that Rizzuto played during an era in which stealing bases was not heavily emphasized—especially by the Yankee teams on which he played—he was obviously not his league's version of Lou Brock, Maury Wills, or even Jackie Robinson.

It was also said that Rizzuto did the little things to help his team win; things like bunting, hitting behind the runner, and playing good defense. While this is certainly true, the little things can only do so much. A Hall of Famer needs to do much more, and Rizzuto's career totals indicate that he just did not do enough.

Others argue that he played on winning teams and was a major contributor to their success. While it is true that the Yankees won ten pennants and eight world championships during his career, and that Rizzuto was a major contributor, it is also true that they did just as well before he arrived, and just as well after he left. Rizzuto's first season was 1941, and his last was 1956. From 1936 to 1940, New York won four pennants and four world championships. From 1957 to 1964, they won seven pennants and three world championships. Therefore, how much of a factor in the team's success could Rizzuto have been? More likely, it was DiMaggio, Berra, Mantle, and Ford who had a greater impact.

In actuality, the arguments about Rizzuto doing the little things to help his team win, and being a major contributor to a winning team's success could just as easily be applied to Bert Campaneris. While Rizzuto was slightly better defensively, and was also a somewhat better all-around player, due to longevity, Campaneris posted superior career numbers in most categories. Campy was also a far better base-stealer. In addition, Campaneris, like Rizzuto, was an excellent bunter, and he played on five division-winning and three world championship teams in Oakland. Former A's owner Charlie Finley once said that Campaneris was the most valuable player on his Oakland teams during the championship years. Yet Campaneris has drawn virtually no support for induction into Cooperstown.

One other argument that has been waged on Rizzuto's behalf is that he was extremely comparable to Pee Wee Reese, who was elected to the Hall of Fame ten years earlier. While it is true that both men played shortstop in the city of New York, for winning teams at the same time, a closer look at the two men reveals that they were not truly comparable as players. Using just our Hall of Fame criteria, Rizzuto was a five-time All-Star; Reese was selected to the All-Star Team ten times. Rizzuto finished in the top 10 in the MVP voting three times, winning the award once; while Reese never won the award, he did finish in the top 10 eight times. While Reese was the best shortstop in the N.L from 1946 to 1953, Rizzuto was the best in the A.L. only in 1950 and, perhaps, in 1951 as well. A look at their career numbers, along with those of Vern Stephens, who played the same position for the St. Louis Browns and Boston Red Sox at the same time, reveals the overall disparity:

PLAYER	AB	HITS	RUNS	2B	3B	HR	RBI	AVG	SB	OBP	SLG PCT
Pee Wee Reese	8,058	2,170	1,338	330	80	126	885	.269	232	.366	.377
Phil Rizzuto	5,816	1,588	877	239	62	38	563	.273	149	.351	.355
Vern Stephens	6,497	1,859	1,001	307	42	247	1,174	.286	25	.355	.460

Reese finished well ahead of Rizzuto in virtually every offensive category, and was a comparable defensive player. Stephens, who is not in the Hall of Fame, not only finished well ahead of Rizzuto in most categories, but also had better overall numbers than Reese. While he was not as good defensively as either Reese or Rizzuto, Stephens was far from a liability in the field. He wasn't as quick as the other two men, but he had a powerful throwing arm that allowed him to accumulate more assists annually. Probably more than with his defense, however, Stephens suffers in comparison to Reese and Rizzuto in other areas. He was not as much of a team leader as either Reese or Rizzuto, and the teams he played for were not as successful as either the Dodgers or the Yankees. Furthermore, the general consensus was that Stephens did not do as many little things to help his team win.

While all of the above may be true, there are certain perceptions that were held towards Stephens that are not totally accurate. Rizzuto and Reese were viewed as being winning ballplayers who were extremely cerebral in their approach to the game. Meanwhile, Stephens was seen as being a somewhat one-dimensional player who did not know how to win. After all, he played for some Boston Red Sox teams in the late '40s and early '50s that were thought to be even more talented than the Yankee teams that repeatedly edged them out in the pennant race. The general perception was that those Red Sox teams didn't have the pitching or defense that those Yankee teams had (which was probably true), that they didn't do the little things, such as bunting and hitting behind runners, that a winning team does (which may have been true), and that Stephens was one of the primary culprits (which may or may not have been true). It was also thought that Stephens benefited greatly from playing in Fenway Park. While it is true that, as a righthanded power-hitter, he was aided somewhat playing his home games there, it is also true that Stephens put up better numbers on the road alone than many shortstops accumulated over the entire season.

Let's take a look at his numbers in 1949, which rank among the most productive ever amassed by a shortstop in a single season. That year, Stephens hit 39 home runs, led the league with 159 runs batted in, and batted .290. Of the 39 homers, 18 were hit on the road, and, of the 159 RBIs, 63 were compiled away from Fenway.

If Stephens' career is looked at in more detail, one sees that he led the American League in runs batted in three times, home runs once, and fielding once. He hit more than 30 homers twice, drove in more than 100 runs four times, and scored more than 100 runs three times. In addition, he was selected to the All-Star Team eight times, and he finished in the top 10 in the MVP voting six times, placing in the top five on three occasions. Thus, his credentials appear to be more consistent with those of a typical Hall of Famer than those of Rizzuto, and, perhaps, even Reese. Yet Stephens has never even come close to being elected.

Why?

Because, unlike the other two players, he didn't play in New York, didn't play for winning teams, and didn't have publicity campaigns run for him to get him elected. Frankly, I am not advocating that Stephens be elected; there are already too many borderline candidates who have been inducted. But, he certainly belongs in the Hall of Fame as much as Reese, and more than Rizzuto.

Joe Tinker

As was the case with his infield mates Frank Chance and Johnny Evers, Joe Tinker rode into the Hall of Fame on the heals of that famous poem written by that frustrated New York sportswriter. The fact is, though, he doesn't belong there any more than they do. One look at his career numbers tells you that:

AB	HITS	RUNS	2B	3B	HR	RBI	AVG	SB	OBP	SLG PCT
6,434	1,687	774	263	114	31	782	.262	336	.308	.353

Particularly unimpressive were Tinker's career batting average of .262, his .308 on-base percentage, and his .353 slugging percentage. He never finished any higher than fourth in the league in any major offensive category. The only time he batted over .300 was in 1913, when he hit .317 in only 382 at-bats. In addition, Tinker was never considered to be the best shortstop in the National League. During the first half of his career, he was rated far behind Honus Wagner; and George Davis was considered to be his superior as well. By the latter stages of Tinker's career, Rabbit Maranville had established himself as the league's best shortstop. Defensively, Tinker was solid but somewhat overrated since, as was mentioned earlier, the famous double-play combination of *Tinker-to-Evers-to-Chance* led the N.L. in double plays only once. It is, therefore, extremely difficult to justify Tinker's selection.

CATCHERS (16)

PLAYER	YEARS	ELECTED BY	YEAR ELECTED
Buck Ewing	1880-1897	Veterans Committee	1939
Roger Bresnahan	1900-1915	Veterans Committee	1945
Louis Santop	1910-1926	Veterans Committee	2006
Ray Schalk	1912-1929	Veterans Committee	1955
Biz Mackey	1920-1947	Veterans Committee	2006
Gabby Hartnett	1922-1941	BBWAA	1955
Mickey Cochrane	1925-1937	BBWAA	1947
Bill Dickey	1928-43,46	BBWAA	1954
Rick Ferrell	1929-1947	Veterans Committee	1984
Josh Gibson	1930-1946	Negro Leagues Committee	1972
Ernie Lombardi	1931-1947	Veterans Committee	1986
Yogi Berra	1946-1963	BBWAA	1972
Roy Campanella	1948-1957	BBWAA	1969
Johnny Bench	1967-1983	BBWAA	1989
Carlton Fisk	1969-1993	BBWAA	2000
Gary Carter	1974-1992	BBWAA	2003

Josh Gibson/Johnny Bench

Gibson, as the greatest catcher and hitter in Negro League history, and Bench, as the greatest catcher in major league history, are well deserving of their places in Cooperstown.

With the possible exception of Satchel Paige, Josh Gibson was the Negro Leagues' greatest and most famous player for 17 seasons. Along with Paige, he was the league's greatest drawing card, and he was rivaled only by Oscar Charleston as the league's greatest all-around player. Although Roy Campanella spent several seasons in the Negro Leagues prior to signing with the Brooklyn Dodgers, he was always rated behind Gibson as the leagues' top catcher. Campanella himself called Gibson, "Not only the greatest catcher, but the greatest ballplayer I ever saw."

Had Gibson's dream of playing in the major leagues been allowed to come true, he likely would have gone on to prove that he was the greatest catcher in baseball history. Although Negro League statistics are often not that reliable, Gibson is known to have averaged around 70 home runs a year. His career total is uncertain, but even the most conservative estimates place him somewhere between 800 and 950, albeit not against major league pitching. More than just a slugger, Gibson's lifetime batting average is the highest in Negro League history, at .354, or .440, depending on the source. In 16 exhibition games against major league pitching, he hit .424 with five home runs. Defensively, although he occasionally struggled with pop-ups and was not a great handler of pitchers, few runners challenged him on the basepaths because of his powerful throwing arm.

Walter Johnson said of Gibson, "He hits the ball a mile. Throws like a rifle. Bill Dickey isn't as good a catcher."

Monte Irvin, who played against Gibson in the Negro Leagues and was later a teammate of Willie Mays on the New York Giants, said: "I played with Willie Mays and against Hank Aaron. They were tremendous players, but they were no Josh Gibson. You saw him hit, and you took your hat off."

Johnny Bench is generally considered to be the greatest catcher in major league history. He was clearly the National League's best catcher from 1968 to 1977, with the exception of the 1971 and 1976 seasons, when injuries caused him to perform at less than optimum proficiency. He was the best catcher in the game for virtually all of the other seasons during that period, being rivaled only by Bill

Freehan in 1968, Thurman Munson in 1975, and Carlton Fisk in 1977. For much of that ten-year period, Bench was arguably one of the five or six best players in the game. He certainly was among the best in 1970, 1972, and 1974. In 1970, Bench won the N.L MVP Award for the first time by leading the league in both home runs (45) and runs batted in (148), while hitting a career high .293. He won the award a second time in 1972 when he once again led the league in homers (40) and RBIs (125). Two years later, in 1974, Bench led the league for the third and final time in RBIs, with 129, while hitting 33 homers and batting .280.

During his career, Bench finished in the top five in the MVP voting a total of four times, knocked in over 100 runs six times, was a perennial All-Star, and was perhaps the greatest defensive catcher the game has ever seen.

Yogi Berra/Bill Dickey/Mickey Cochrane/ Roy Campanella

These four players have been grouped together because a legitimate case could be made for any of them being among the five greatest catchers in the history of the game.

From 1948 to 1956, Yogi Berra was not only the best catcher in the American League but was arguably one of its five best players. During that period, he was selected to the All-Star Team each season, won three Most Valuable Player Awards, and was considered to be one of the best clutch hitters in the game. Over that nine-year stretch, Berra hit more than 20 home runs eight times, topping the 30-mark twice, knocked in more than 100 runs five times, and batted over .300 three times. He won the MVP Award in 1951, 1954, and 1955, and finished in the top five in the voting four other times during his career. Berra had his finest statistical season in 1950 when he finished second in the MVP balloting to teammate Phil Rizzuto. That year, Berra hit 28 home runs, knocked in 124 runs, and established career-highs in batting average (.322), doubles (30), hits (192), and runs scored (116), while striking out only 12 times in over 650 plate appearances.

During his career, Berra was selected to the A.L. All-Star Team 14 times and was named to *The Sporting News* team five times. Perhaps more than any of the individual accolades he earned, however, Berra will be remembered best for being a winner. In the 17 full seasons he spent with the Yankees, they won 14 pennants and 10 World Series, a record of success approached only by his Yankees teammate Joe DiMaggio, who played on ten pennant winners and nine world champions during his 13-year career.

Bill Dickey preceded Berra as the Yankees catcher, and as the best player in the American League at that position. From 1929 to 1935, Dickey was a very good player, rivaling Mickey Cochrane as the best catcher in the game, and hitting well over .300 in all but one of those seasons. He was selected to *The Sporting News All-Star Team*, over Cochrane, in both 1932 and 1933. However, from 1936 to 1939, Dickey was truly exceptional, establishing himself clearly as the best catcher in the game. In each of those four seasons, he hit over 20 home runs, knocked in well over 100 runs, and batted well over .300. His two finest seasons came in 1936 and 1937. In the first of those years, Dickey hit 22 homers, drove in 107 runs, and batted .362, establishing an all-time record for catchers with more than 400 at-bats (later equaled by Mike Piazza). The following season, he reached career-highs in both home runs (29) and runs batted in (133), while batting .332.

During his career, Dickey was selected to the American League All-Star Team ten times, and was named to *The Sporting News All-Star Team* six times. He finished with a .313 lifetime batting average, and was also considered to be the finest defensive catcher of his time, holding records for most putouts and highest fielding average by a catcher when he retired. In addition, he was a winner, playing for nine pennant-winners and eight world champions over his 17 big league seasons.

With the possible exception of Bill Dickey, Mickey Cochrane was the finest catcher to play in the major leagues during the first half of the 20th century. Although not as strong as Dickey defensively, Cochrane was considered to be the best hitting catcher in baseball during his career. His .320 batting average and .419 on-base percentage are both career records for catchers with more than 5,000 at-bats. He hit .300 or better nine times, scored more than 100 runs four times, and struck out only 217 times in just over 6,000 plate appearances.

Although he received stiff competition from Dickey during the second half of his 13-year career, Cochrane was clearly the American League's best receiver from 1925 to 1931, during which time he topped the .330 mark five times, hitting a career-high .357 in 1930. He was the best catcher in the majors in each season from 1927 to 1929 and then again in 1931 and 1934. In two of those seasons, 1928 and 1934, Cochrane was voted the American League's Most Valuable Player. He was also a team leader, leading the Philadelphia Athletics to pennants in 1929, 1930, and 1931, and to World Series victories in both '29 and '30. He was player/manager for the Detroit Tigers when they won the pennant in both 1934 and 1935.

By the time he arrived in Brooklyn to be the Dodgers' regular catcher for the next ten seasons, Roy Campanella was already 27 years old and had spent several seasons in the Negro Leagues (where he was a three-time All-Star). After joining the Dodgers, Campanella quickly established himself as the preeminent receiver in the National League, and, perhaps, in all of baseball, being rivaled only by the American League's Yogi Berra.

From 1948 to 1957, Campanella was the cornerstone of Dodger teams that won five pennants in ten seasons. As such, he was selected the National League's Most Valuable Player three times—in 1951, 1953, and 1955. In each of those seasons, Campanella hit more than 30 home runs, drove in over 100 runs, and batted over .300. His best season came in 1953 when hit 41 homers, led the league with 142 runs batted in, and batted .312.

In addition to being an offensive force and an outstanding team leader and handler of pitchers, Campanella was the finest defensive catcher of his time. He led National League catchers in putouts six times, and threw out two of every three runners that tried to steal against him.

Gabby Hartnett/Buck Ewing

Hartnett was the finest catcher in the National League during the first half of the 20th century, and Ewing was the game's greatest receiver during the first 50 years of major league baseball. Therefore, both men most certainly earned their places in Cooperstown.

Prior to the appearance of Johnny Bench, many people considered Gabby Hartnett to be the greatest catcher in National League history. He was certainly that league's finest receiver during the first half of the 20th century.

Although he was not a truly great player, possessing only borderline Hall of Fame numbers, Hartnett's career statistics compare quite favorably to those of the other top catchers from that 50-year period. His 1,179 RBIs and 1,912 hits were surpassed only by Bill Dickey among catchers from that period, and his 236 home runs remained a record for catchers until Yogi Berra eventually surpassed him. His .489 slugging percentage is third all-time among major league catchers, behind only Mike Piazza and Roy Campanella.

From 1924 to 1935, with the exception of the 1926 and 1929 seasons, Hartnett was clearly the best catcher in the National League. He was the top catcher in the majors in 1924, 1925, 1930, and 1935. Hartnett was selected N.L. MVP in 1935 but had his finest season in 1930 when he hit 37 home runs, knocked in 122 runs, and batted .339 for the Chicago Cubs. During his career, the Cubs won four National League pennants. In all, Hartnett was selected to six All-Star teams and finished in the top 10 in the league MVP balloting a total of four times.

When the first set of Hall of Fame elections was held in 1936, the two players who received the most support from the original Veterans Committee were Cap Anson and Buck Ewing. After subsequent tallies were taken over the next three years, both men were enshrined in Cooperstown when the Hall first opened in 1939. The results of that balloting are a clear indication of the respect that Buck Ewing garnered from baseball people of the day.

In fact, not only was Ewing considered to be unquestionably the greatest catcher to play in the major leagues prior to Mickey Cochrane and Bill Dickey, but he was thought to be one of the very best players of the 19th century. He was clearly one of the most versatile. In just under 5,400 career at-bats, Ewing batted .303, knocked in 883 runs, scored 1,129 others, amassed 178 triples, and stole 354 bases. In a career spanning parts of 18 seasons, he batted over .300 eleven times, knocked in over 100 runs once, scored more than 100 runs once, and reached double-digits in triples eleven times, once totaling as many as 20. He led the league in home runs and triples once each, and had his finest season in 1893. That year, Ewing knocked in 122 runs, batted .344, scored 117 runs, accumulated 15 triples, and stole 47 bases—one of four times during his career that he finished with at least 40 steals. While many players from that era struggled with their batting averages prior to the rules changes that went into effect in 1893, Ewing batted over .300 in every season from 1885 to 1892. He was probably, along with Dan Brouthers, Cap Anson, Billy Hamilton, Sam Thompson, and Ed Delahanty, one of the six best position players of the 19th century.

James Raleigh "Biz" Mackey

Since he was generally considered to be the second greatest catcher in Negro League history, behind only Josh Gibson, it would seem that Biz Mackey's 2006 Hall of Fame induction was long overdue. Mackey spent the better part of three decades playing for nine different teams in the Negro Leagues. Although he originally came up as a shortstop, Mackey became the regular catcher for the Philadelphia Hilldales in 1925 and subsequently developed into what most Negro League experts considered to be the greatest defensive catcher in the history of black baseball. Possessing a powerful and accurate throwing arm, Mackey typically gunned down opposing baserunners with throws made from a squatting position. A tremendous all-around receiver, Mackey was a studious observer of opposing batters and an expert handler of pitchers.

He was also extremely agile behind the plate, despite his lack of running speed.

More than just an outstanding defensive player, the switch-hitting Mackey was also a good hitter, with power from both sides of the plate. He placed among the Negro Leagues' all-time leaders in total bases, RBIs, and slugging percentage, while hitting either .322 or .335 for his career, depending on the source. Mackey won two Negro League batting titles, hitting .423 for the Hilldales in 1923, and topping the circuit once more in 1931 with a mark of .359. He also compiled a batting average of .358 against major league competition in exhibition games.

Still, it was largely Mackey's defense on which he built his reputation, and that established him, in the minds of some, as the greatest catcher in Negro League history. Indeed, Homestead Grays manager Cum Posey rated him as his number-one all-time catcher, placing him ahead of Josh Gibson. Posey is on record as having stated, "Mackey was a tremendous hitter, a fierce competitor, although slow afoot he is the standout among catchers who have shown their wares in this nation."

In 1937, while serving as player/manager for the Baltimore Elite Giants, Mackey began mentoring the 15-year-old Roy Campanella in the fine points of catching. Campanella later recalled:

"In my opinion, Biz Mackey was the master of defense of all catchers. When I was a kid in Philadelphia, I saw both Mackey and Mickey Cochrane in their primes, but, for real catching skills, I don't think Cochrane was the master of defense that Mackey was. When I went under his direction in Baltimore, I was 15 years old. I gathered quite a bit from Mackey, watching how he did things, how he blocked low pitches, how he shifted his feet for an outside pitch, how he threw with a short, quick, accurate throw without drawing back. I got all this from Mackey at a young age."

Louis Santop

Another outstanding former Negro League catcher whose long-time exclusion from the Hall of Fame seems rather dubious was Louis Santop. Referred to as "The Black Babe Ruth" long before anyone ever heard of Josh Gibson, Santop was black baseball's greatest slugger of the Deadball Era.

The six-foot four-inch, 240-pound Santop played for several teams during a 17-year career that began in 1910 with the Lincoln Giants. While with the Giants, Santop caught two of the greatest pitchers in Negro League history, Smokey Joe Williams and Cannonball Dick Redding. Considered to be an above-average defensive catcher, Santop had a powerful throwing arm that intimidated opposing baserunners.

But, it was Santop's hitting that truly frightened opposing teams. The lefthanded power hitter was known for his tape measure home runs, and for occasionally calling his shots before he hit them. Once, in 1912, he hit a ball that was said to have traveled 500 feet—particularly amazing when it is considered that the blow was struck against a Deadball Era baseball. Santop was more than just a slugger, though. While the integrity of the data surrounding his career statistics is somewhat questionable, records indicate that Santop frequently posted batting averages in excess of .400 during his 17 seasons in the Negro Leagues.

Carlton Fisk

Most people would probably say that Carlton Fisk being in the Hall of Fame should be a no-brainer. After all, prior to being surpassed in home runs by Mike Piazza, he held the record for most career home runs by a catcher (350), most stolen bases, and most games caught. He is also one of only three catchers, along with Johnny Bench and Yogi Berra, to hit 300 home runs, score 1,000 runs, and drive in 1,000 runs. The feeling here, though, is that Fisk's credentials need to be examined more closely since most of the numbers he compiled during his career were based more on longevity than on greatness.

Carlton Fisk was a regular catcher in the big leagues, first for the Boston Red Sox and, later, for the Chicago White Sox, from 1972 to 1991. One of the reasons why Fisk lasted as long as he did was that he never pushed himself to the limit, and played through injuries, the way some of his contemporaries such as Johnny Bench and Thurman Munson did. In those 20 seasons, Fisk had as many as 500 official at-bats only four times, and as many as 400 at-bats in only nine other seasons. As a basis for comparison, in his 16 seasons as a regular, Bench had at least 500 at-bats eight times, and surpassed 600 plate appearances twice; in his 10 seasons as a regular, Munson surpassed 500 at-bats seven times, and had more than 600 plate appearances on two occasions.

Nevertheless, over his 25-year major league career, Fisk was able to hit 376 home runs, drive in 1,330 runs, score 1,276 others, and steal 128 bases—all fairly impressive numbers. He hit more than 20 homers eight times, topping the 30-mark once, knocked in more than 100 runs twice, batted over .300 twice, and scored more than 100 runs once. He was also a fine defensive catcher who had a reputation for being a good handler of pitchers.

But, how does Fisk rate in terms of the Hall of Fame criteria being used here? While he was never considered to be either the best player in baseball or the best player in his league, with the possible exception of Josh Gibson and Johnny Bench, neither were any of the other catchers elected to Cooperstown. Therefore, those factors cannot be held against him. The same can be said for his not being among the five or six best players in the game at any time. However, due largely to his tremendous longevity, a valid case could be made for Fisk being one of the ten best catchers in baseball history.

Was he, for an extended period of time, considered to be the best player in the game, or in his league, at his position? Well, with the possible exception of the 1977 season, it could not be said that he was ever thought of as being the best catcher in baseball. Playing for the Red Sox that year, Fisk had his finest season by hitting 26 home runs, driving in 102 runs, and batting .315. Yet Johnny Bench's numbers were just as impressive (31, 109, .275). Throughout the rest of his career, Fisk was rated behind either Bench, Munson, Ted Simmons, or Gary Carter. In the American League, Fisk was the top catcher in 1972 (22 HR, 61 RBIs, .293 AVG), 1977 (26 HR, 102 RBIs, .315 AVG), 1978 (20 HR, 88 RBIs,

.284 AVG), 1983 (26 HR, 86 RBIs, .289 AVG), and 1985 (37 HR, 107 RBIs, .238 AVG).

In the MVP voting, Fisk finished in the top 10 four times, placing as high as third in 1983. He was also selected to the All-Star Team 11 times.

Fisk never led the league in any major offensive category, but he finished second in both home runs and runs scored once. He was also a team leader and a major contributor to his team's success.

Thus, overall, it could be said that Fisk does moderately well when using our Hall of Fame selection criteria as a benchmark. However, there were two other catchers whose careers overlapped with Fisk's who were comparable to him as players, yet who have not been elected to the Hall of Fame.

Those catchers were Joe Torre and Ted Simmons. Simmons has received virtually no support, and it has become rather apparent that, if Torre is ever going to be elected, it will have to be largely on the strength of the success he had managing the Yankees. Torre's career totals don't quite measure up to the numbers compiled by Fisk. But it was Fisk's greater longevity, not his superiority as a player, that is responsible for the statistical edge he holds over Torre. The latter hit more than 20 homers six times, knocked in more than 100 runs five times, batted over .300 four times, was selected to the All-Star Team nine times (six times as a catcher), and won a Most Valuable Player Award. And, despite Fisk's decided advantage in home runs, stolen bases, and runs scored, Simmons compares quite favorably to Fisk in most offensive categories. Indeed, Simmons may well have been a better all-around hitter than Fisk.

Let's take a look at the career statistics of all three players:

PLAYER	AB	HITS	RUNS	2B	3B	HR	RBI	AVG	SB	OBP	SLG PCT
Joe Torre	7,874	2,342	996	344	59	252	1,185	.297	23	.367	.452
Carlton Fisk	8,756	2,356	1,276	421	47	376	1,330	.269	128	.341	.457
Ted Simmons	8,680	2,472	1,074	483	47	248	1,389	.285	21	.352	.437

In addition, Simmons hit more than 20 homers six times, knocked in over 100 runs three times, batted over .300 seven times, was selected to the All-Star Team eight times, and finished in the top 10 in the MVP voting three times.

Torre was considered to be the best catcher in baseball from 1964 to 1967, in addition to his MVP season of 1971, which was as a third baseman. Simmons was ranked behind Bench for most of his career, but was actually the superior player in at least two or three seasons.

This should not be misinterpreted to suggest that Torre and Simmons should be elected to the Hall of Fame as well; there have already been too many borderline players voted in. Rather, the suggestion here is that Fisk's election should not have been viewed as having been such an obvious one. Due to the numbers he accumulated over the course of his career, he probably does deserve a place in Cooperstown. However, he should be thought of more as a borderline Hall of Famer than as a clear-cut choice. And, if he made it in so easily, both Simmons and Torre should have received far more support.

Gary Carter

While Carlton Fisk was elected to the Hall of Fame in just his second year of eligibility, it took Gary Carter six tries to make it into Cooperstown. This is somewhat surprising because, while Fisk's career numbers are slightly more impressive, Carter was actually a very similar player, and was thought of just as highly throughout most of his career.

Like Fisk, Carter had very good power, hitting more than 20 homers nine times during his career, and topping the 30-mark twice. He knocked in more than 100 runs four times, twice as many times as Fisk, and even led his league in that department once, something Fisk never did. Carter was the best catcher in baseball from 1980 to 1986, and was arguably one of the five best players in the game in at least two of those seasons. In 1984, as a member of the Montreal Expos, he hit 27 home runs, led the National League with 106 runs batted in, and batted .294. The following season, playing for the Mets, he hit 32 homers, drove in 100 runs, and batted .281.

A look at the career numbers of Fisk and Carter indicates just how similar they really were as players:

PLAYER	AB	HITS	RUNS	2B	3B	HR	RBI	AVG	SB	OBP	SLG PCT
Carlton Fisk	8,756	2,356	1,276	421	47	376	1,330	.269	128	.341	.457
Gary Carter	7,971	2,092	1,025	371	31	324	1,225	.262	39	.338	.439

Also, like Fisk, Carter finished in the top five in the league MVP voting twice, and in the top ten another two times. Like Fisk, he was selected to the All-Star Team 11 times. In addition, Carter was an excellent defensive receiver, with three Gold Gloves to his credit, as opposed to just one for Fisk. He led the league five times in assists, and six straight years in putouts.

There are three possible explanations as to why it took Carter longer to get elected to Cooperstown. The first lies in the fact that, due to his greater longevity, Fisk's career numbers are slightly superior to Carter's. Secondly, Fisk remained an effective offensive player for most of his career, becoming a liability at the plate in just his final two seasons. Meanwhile, the image that many people have of Carter towards the end of his career is probably that of someone who was hanging on to the very end. He failed to hit more than 11 home runs or drive in more than 46 runs in any of his final five seasons. Perhaps even more telling, though, is the fact that many members of the press (the people that have the final say as to who goes into the Hall) were put off somewhat by what they perceived to be Carter's constant posturing for media and fan attention during his playing days. He took every opportunity he could to talk to the press, and he enjoyed being the center of attention. This alienated some of his teammates in Montreal, and irked many outsiders as well.

Probably more than anything else, this is what also kept him out of the Hall of Fame for three or four years, because Carter should have been viewed in much the same light as Fisk. He was a very good player whose selection was a pretty good one. However, like Fisk, he should be viewed as someone who was not an obvious selection.

Ernie Lombardi

With the exception of Gabby Hartnett, Ernie Lombardi was probably the National League's best catcher during the first half of the 20th century. Playing primarily for the Cincinnati Reds and New York Giants, Lombardi succeeded Hartnett during the late 1930s as the league's top receiver. He won the batting title in 1938, with an average of .342, and was voted the league's Most Valuable Player that year. During his career, he batted over .300 ten times, surpassing the .330-mark five times. He was clearly the N.L.'s best catcher from 1936 to 1942, and was selected to the All-Star Team seven times.

However, with the possible exception of the 1938 and 1940 seasons, Lombardi was never considered to be the best catcher in baseball (Hartnett and Dickey were both rated above him for most of his career). In addition, while he was an excellent hitter, Lombardi was far from a complete player. During his career, he was well known for being the slowest player in the game and a completely immobile, below-average defensive catcher.

Because he was so slow, he never scored more than 60 runs in any season. Although he batted over .300 ten times, he never had as many as 500 at-bats in any season, and he topped 400 plate appearances only four times. Primarily because of his limited number of at-bats, Lombardi never knocked in more than 95 runs in a season, and he compiled as many as 80 RBIs only twice. If his numbers are viewed alongside those of Thurman Munson, who is not in the Hall of Fame, it appears that the two catchers were fairly comparable as offensive players:

PLAYER	AB	HITS	RUNS	2B	3B	HR	RBI	AVG	SB	OBP	SLG PCT
Ernie Lombardi	5,855	1,792	601	277	27	190	990	.306	8	.358	.460
Thurman Munson	5,344	1,558	696	229	32	113	701	.292	48	.350	.410

While, on the surface, Lombardi's statistics seem more impressive than Munson's, they really were not. To begin with, Lombardi played during the 1930s and 1940s, in much more of a hitter's era than when Munson played, during the 1970s. Lombardi also had the advantage of spending most of his career playing in good hitter's parks in Cincinnati's Crosley Field and New York's Polo Grounds. Meanwhile, Munson had to play half his games in Yankee Stadium, which has always been an extremely difficult ballpark for righthanded batters.

Furthermore, on Munson's behalf, he had more than 500 at-bats in seven of his ten seasons, something Lombardi failed to do even once. He had three straight seasons in which he knocked in over 100 runs (something else Lombardi never did) and batted over .300. Munson batted over .300 five times during his career and scored more than 80 runs three times. In addition, prior to being slowed by shoulder and knee problems that plagued him during the latter stages of his career, Munson was an excellent defensive catcher, winning three Gold Gloves. He was a superb handler of pitchers and, as captain of the Yankees, was a true team leader. He was selected to the A.L. All-Star Team seven times, was named the league's MVP in 1976, and finished in the top 10 in the voting two other times. He was the top catcher in the American League from 1973 to 1976, and the best in baseball in 1976 and, perhaps, in 1975 as well. In his prime, he was considered to be at least the equal of his Boston counterpart, Carlton Fisk, who is in the Hall of Fame.

All this is not to suggest that Thurman Munson should be elected to the Hall of Fame. Frankly, as good as he was, his career was too short, and his career numbers are not impressive enough. But, while Ernie Lombardi was a slightly better hitter, Munson was a better all-around player who deserves to be in Cooperstown as much as Lombardi. Unfortunately, when the Veterans Committee elected Lombardi in 1986, it was not a very good decision.

Rick Ferrell

The Veterans Committee's selection of Rick Ferrell in 1984 was an even worse one than it would make two years later with Lombardi. It is one of those that just leaves you scratching your head and wondering to yourself, "What were they thinking?" Ferrell, who caught for the St. Louis Browns, Boston Red Sox, and Washington Senators during his 18-year career, has, by far, the worst offensive numbers of any catcher in the Hall of Fame who played after the Deadball Era. Let's take a look at his statistics:

AB	HITS	RUNS	2B	3B	HR	RBI	AVG	SB	OBP	SLG PCT
6,028	1,692	687	324	45	28	734	.281	29	.378	.363

That's right—28 home runs, 734 RBIs and 687 runs scored in over 6,000 career at-bats! Add to that the fact that Ferrell had only six seasons in which he had as many as 400 at-bats (like Lombardi, he never had 500 in a season), never knocked in more than 77 runs in a season, and never scored more than 67, and what you have essentially is a nice player who was among the better catchers of his era. However, he was always rated far behind both Bill Dickey and Mickey Cochrane in the American League during his career, and he probably doesn't even rank among the 25 or 30 best catchers in the history of the game. Yet, Ferrell was well-liked and had friends on the Veterans Committee. Therefore, he was able to get elected to the Hall of Fame.

Roger Bresnahan/Ray Schalk

The selections of Bresnahan and Schalk, both completely unwarranted, are extreme examples of the politics involved in the Hall of Fame elections.

Roger Bresnahan played primarily with the New York Giants, St. Louis Cardinals, and Chicago Cubs at the turn of the last century. He was the Giants' regular catcher from 1903 to 1908. During that time, he established a very good relationship with Giants manager John McGraw, one of the most influential men in the game. He became one of McGraw's favorites, eventually working under him as one of the team's coaches. During his playing career, Bresnahan stole 212 bases and finished with a very respectable .386 on-base percentage. However, he also finished with just under 4,500 at-bats, 1,252 hits, 530 runs batted in, 682 runs scored, and a .279 batting average—hardly Hall of Fame numbers.

Ray Schalk spent virtually his entire 18-year career with the Chicago White Sox, and was a member of the 1919 squad that was accused of throwing the World Series. He was an excellent receiver and handler of pitchers, but was a relatively weak hitter, batting only .253, hitting only 11 home runs, driving in just 594 runs, and scoring only 579 others in just over 5,300 career at-bats. He never batted any higher than .282, knocked in more than 61 runs, or scored more than 64 runs during his 18 seasons, and he finished with a feeble .316 slugging percentage.

If you look at the numbers of both players alongside those of Wally Schang, a contemporary of Schalk who caught for the Philadelphia A's, Boston Red Sox, New York Yankees, and St. Louis Browns during a career that spanned the years 1913-1931, it becomes even more difficult to understand why Bresnahan and Schalk were elected:

PLAYER	AB	HITS	RUNS	2B	3B	HR	RBI	AVG	SB	OBP	SLG PCT
Roger Bresnahan	4,481	1,252	682	218	71	26	530	.279	212	.386	.377
Ray Schalk	5,306	1,345	579	199	49	11	594	.253	176	.340	.316
Wally Schang	5,307	1,506	769	264	90	59	710	.284	122	.393	.401

In virtually the same number of at-bats, Schang, who is not in the Hall of Fame, finished well ahead of both men in every offensive category, except stolen bases. In addition, he was considered to be a fine defensive catcher, and he played on five pennant-winning teams and three world champions in Philadelphia and New York.

Why, then, are Bresnahan and Schalk in, while Schang isn't? In Bresnahan's case, his relationship with McGraw was clearly one of the reasons. McGraw was thought of very highly in baseball circles, and his opinions drew a great deal of respect. The fact that Bresnahan was one of his favorites was certainly a contributing factor. In addition, Bresnahan passed away in December of 1944. His election in 1945 was undoubtedly aided by his passing, since many of the committee members must have voted for him out of sympathy. In the case of Schalk, his selection by the Veterans Committee in 1955 was likely his reward for not taking part in the conspiracy to throw the 1919 World Series. Whatever the reasons, the selections of both men were poor ones that did irreparable damage to the Hall of Fame by lowering the standards for future generations of players, and by lessening the integrity of the voting process.

10 CHANGE IN VOTING PHILOSOPHY, OR LOWERING OF THE STANDARDS?

This would probably be a good time to take a brief break from the player analysis and focus on the change in voting philosophy that has apparently transpired over the years. This change can be evidenced in two ways. First, there are the increasingly high voting percentages attained in recent years by players upon their election to the Hall of Fame. During the past two decades, a trend has developed that has enabled players whose credentials were less impressive than those of some of the great players from prior generations to garner a higher percentage of the total number of votes cast by the members of the BBWAA upon their election. In addition, once they become eligible for election, players are now being voted in far more rapidly than they were in the past.

A player who was not truly great, but merely very good, is now elected the first or second time his name appears on the ballot. Meanwhile, some of the greatest players in the history of the game previously had to wait several years before being elected. Let's take a closer look at these trends.

When the first elections were held in 1936, with 226 members of the BBWAA casting ballots, 170 votes were needed to satisfy the minimum 75 percent requirement for election. Only Ty Cobb (222), Babe Ruth and Honus Wagner (215 each), Christy Mathewson (205), and Walter Johnson (189) received enough support from the writers to get elected. Napoleon Lajoie (146), Tris Speaker (133), Cy Young (111), and Rogers Hornsby (105) were the others who came closest to being voted in. Lajoie, Speaker, and Young were all elected the following year, and Grover Cleveland

Alexander was the lone selection in 1938. In 1939, with 206 votes needed for election, George Sisler (235), Eddie Collins (213), and Willie Keeler (207) were all voted in. Hornsby, with 176 votes, once again fell short. Since no election was held in either 1940 or 1941, Hornsby had to wait until 1942 to finally be elected. Thus, one of the very greatest players in the history of the game, and the man considered by many to be the greatest righthanded hitter in baseball history, failed in his first four attempts to get elected to the Hall of Fame.

A primary source of the frustration Hornsby and several other outstanding players must have felt was unquestionably the backlog of qualified candidates that existed at that time. With the names of 15 or 20 former greats appearing on the ballot every year, the writers' votes tended to be more scattered, and it was more difficult for any one or two players to meet the minimum 75 percent requirement. Thus, in some years, no players were selected, and some truly great ones had to wait several years before they were eventually enshrined.

However, it also appears that the writers tended to take a different attitude with them to the elections in those years, and that they viewed a player's selection more as an *honor* than as a *right*, as they appear to do now at times. They seemed to feel that a great player eventually deserved to be voted in to the Hall of Fame, but that it would be even more of an honor if he had to wait a few years.

These days, the prevalent attitude seems to be: "Was he a very good player who probably deserves to be in Cooperstown? Yes? Okay, then let's put him in right away."

Thus, over the past two decades, some players who were clearly not among the all-time greats have been inducted into the Hall of Fame in their first year of eligibility. Following is a chart listing of all the players who have been elected to Cooperstown in the first year that their name appeared on the ballot:

HALL OF FAMERS ELECTED IN THEIR FIRST YEAR	
Jackie Robinson	(1962)
Bob Feller	(1962)
Ted Williams	(1966)
Stan Musial	(1969)
Sandy Koufax	(1972)
Roberto Clemente	(1973)*
Warren Spahn	(1973)
Mickey Mantle	(1974)
Ernie Banks	(1977)
Willie Mays	(1979)
Al Kaline	(1980)
Bob Gibson	(1981)
Frank Robinson	(1982)
Hank Aaron	(1982)
Brooks Robinson	(1983)
Lou Brock	(1985)
Willie McCovey	(1986)
Willie Stargell	(1988)
Carl Yastrzemski	(1989)
Johnny Bench	(1989)
Joe Morgan	(1990)
Jim Palmer	(1990)
Rod Carew	(1991)
Tom Seaver	(1992)
Reggie Jackson	(1993)
Steve Carlton	(1994)
Mike Schmidt	(1995)
Robin Yount	(1999)
George Brett	(1999)

*Special Election

HALL OF FAMERS ELECTED IN THEIR FIRST YEAR	
Nolan Ryan	(1999)
Kirby Puckett	(2001)
Dave Winfield	(2001)
Ozzie Smith	(2002)
Eddie Murray	(2003)
Dennis Eckersley	(2004)
Paul Molitor	(2004)
Wade Boggs	(2005)
Cal Ripken Jr.	(2007)
Tony Gwynn	(2007)

This list reveals that no player was elected in his first year of eligibility prior to 1962. A look at the names on the list also reveals that all those players who were elected the first time their name appeared on the ballot during the 1960s and 1970s were among the very greatest players of all-time. However, this trend began to change somewhat during the 1980s. While Lou Brock, Willie McCovey, and Willie Stargell were all exceptional players who clearly belong in Cooperstown, could it honestly be said that they were among the all-time greats? They were certainly not on the same level as Ted Williams, Stan Musial, Mickey Mantle, and Willie Mays.

In every year from 1988 to 1995, at least one player was elected in his first year of eligibility, and, during the 1990s, the caliber of player being elected in this manner continued to decline. From Reggie Jackson (a lifetime .262 hitter) in 1993, to Robin Yount (a very good player, but certainly not a great one) in 1999, to Kirby Puckett (a borderline Hall of Famer) in 2001, the standards for first-ballot Hall of Famers have hit an all-time low.

This should not be misinterpreted to mean that these players do not belong in the Hall of Fame; they all do, with the possible exception of Puckett. But how can their first-time elections be justified when some truly great players from previous generations had to wait several years before they were finally inducted.

As an example, one needs merely to look at the elections of 1945 and 1946, when no player satisfied the minimum 75 percent requirement despite the presence on the ballot of names such as Jimmie Foxx, Lefty Grove, Charlie Gehringer, Al Simmons, Carl Hubbell, Bill Dickey, and Mickey Cochrane. Hubbell, Cochrane, and Grove were elected in 1947, along with Frankie Frisch, but Gehringer had to wait until 1949, Foxx until 1951, Simmons until 1953, and Dickey until 1954.

Even the great Joe DiMaggio, whose name appeared on the ballot for the first time in 1953, had to wait until his third year of eligibility to be voted in. In that first year, 198 votes were needed for election, but DiMaggio was named on only 117 of the ballots, thereby falling 81 votes short. Dizzy Dean and Al Simmons were elected that year. In 1954, with 189 votes needed, DiMaggio could muster only 175, thereby finishing fourth behind Rabbit Maranville, Bill Dickey, and Bill Terry, each of whom was elected that year. Finally, in 1955, when 188 votes were needed, DiMaggio was named on 223 of the ballots, thereby gaining admittance to Cooperstown.

Other outstanding players who were not elected in their first year of eligibility include:

Frankie Frisch—elected in 1947, in his sixth time on the ballot;

Harry Heilmann—elected in 1952, in his twelfth time on the ballot;

Bill Terry—elected in 1954, in his fourteenth time on the ballot;

Joe Medwick—elected in 1968, in his eighth time on the ballot;

Roy Campanella—elected in 1969, in his fifth time on the ballot;

Yogi Berra—elected in 1972, in his second time on the ballot;

Eddie Mathews—elected in 1978, in his fifth time on the ballot

Some of the more notable injustices include:

Jimmie Foxx: When Foxx's playing career ended in 1945, it was not necessary for a player to have been retired for five seasons before he could become eligible for election. In 1946, he was named on only 26 ballots, and, in 1947, he received only 10 votes. He was finally elected in 1951, in the sixth year his name appeared on the ballot.

Lefty Grove: In 1945, his first year of eligibility, he was named on only 28 ballots. He was elected in 1947, in his third year of eligibility.

Hank Greenberg: In 1949, his first year of eligibility, he received only 67 votes. He was finally elected in 1956, in his eighth year of eligibility.

Carl Hubbell: He was elected in 1947, in his fourth year of eligibility, after receiving only 24 votes in his first year.

Al Simmons: He was elected in 1953, in his eighth year of eligibility, after receiving only one vote in his first year, and six in his second.

Charlie Gehringer: He was elected in his fifth year of eligibility, in 1949, after receiving only ten votes in his first year.

Goose Goslin: His name remained on the ballot from 1948 to 1962, when it was finally dropped after he received no more than 30 votes in any of his 15 years of eligibility. He was finally elected by the Veterans Committee in 1968.

Sam Crawford: He never received more than 11 votes during his eligibility period. He was finally elected by the Veterans Committee in 1957.

Johnny Mize: His name remained on the ballot from 1960 to 1973, until his eligibility period expired. In his first year of eligibility, he received only 45 votes. He was finally elected by the Veterans Committee in 1981.

Arky Vaughan: He was passed on by the BBWAA from 1953 to 1968. In his first year of eligibility, he received just one vote. He was elected by the Veterans Committee in 1985.

Most of these players were as good as some of those who were later elected to the Hall of Fame in their first year of eligibility. Yet they were not ushered in with the same alacrity, in part because of the circumstances surrounding the elections in the early years, and also because of a difference in voting philosophy. This difference in philosophy can also be seen in the disparity in the voting percentages garnered by certain players at the time of their election.

For example, when Nolan Ryan was elected to the Hall of Fame in 1999, he was named on 491 of the 497 ballots cast. That comes out to 98.79 percent—the second highest percentage in the history of the voting (Tom Seaver was named on 98.8 percent of the ballots when he was elected in 1992). That means that a man who lost almost as many games as he won during his career fared better in the voting than virtually every other player who has ever lived! While Ryan was an exceptional pitcher—one who, when he was at his best, was one of the most dominant hurlers the game has seen—his career was marked with inconsistency, and it would be difficult to rank him even among the 20 greatest pitchers of all time.

Then, there is George Brett, who was also elected in 1999 when he was named on 488 of the 497 ballots cast, just three fewer than Ryan. That comes out to a percentage of 98.19, or the fourth highest ever awarded to a player. While Brett was a truly great hitter, and one of the best players of his generation, was he more deserving than Willie Mays, who, when he was elected in 1979, was named on "just" 94.7 percent of the ballots?

When Reggie Jackson was elected in 1993, he was named on 93.6 percent of the ballots. Yet, Ted Williams was named on only 93.4 percent in 1966, and Stan Musial was named on just 93.2 percent in 1969. Jackson was a great slugger, but not very many people would even mention him in the same breath with either Williams or Musial.

Another example would be Carl Yastrzemski, who was elected in 1988 when he was named on 94.6 percent of the ballots cast. When Joe DiMaggio was elected in 1955, he received only 89.2

percent of the vote. When Mickey Mantle was elected in 1974, he was named on only 88.2 percent of the ballots. Yastrzemski was a superb all-around player, but would anyone in their right mind suggest that he was better than either DiMaggio or Mantle?

What all this seems to indicate is a gradual lowering of the standards deemed essential for prospective Hall of Fame candidates. While voting percentages and years of eligibility prior to actual election may seem trivial to most, they carry with them a great deal of significance if they also eventually lead to the admittance of players who do not live up to the high standards to which the players from previous generations were held.

LEFTFIELDERS (22)

PLAYER	YEARS	ELECTED BY	YEAR ELECTED
Jim O'Rourke	1873-1893	Veterans Committee	1945
Ed Delahanty	1888-1903	Veterans Committee	1945
Jesse Burkett	1890-1905	Veterans Committee	1946
Joe Kelley	1891-1908	Veterans Committee	1971
Fred Clarke	1894-1911	Veterans Committee	1945
Pete Hill	1899-1925	Veterans Committee	2006
Zack Wheat	1909-1927	Veterans Committee	1959
Goose Goslin	1921-1938	Veterans Committee	1968
Heinie Manush	1923-1939	Veterans Committee	1964
Al Simmons	1923-41,43-44	BBWAA	1953
Chick Hafey	1924-1935,37	Veterans Committee	1971
Joe Medwick	1932-1948	BBWAA	1968
Ted Williams	1939-42,46-60	BBWAA	1966
Stan Musial	1941-44,46-63	BBWAA	1969
Monte Irvin	1938-42,45-56	Negro Leagues Committee	1973
Ralph Kiner	1946-1955	BBWAA	1975
Billy Williams	1959-1976	BBWAA	1987
Carl Yastrzemski	1961-1983	BWAA	1989
Lou Brock	1961-1979	BWAA	1985
Willie Stargell	1962-1982	BBWAA	1988
Jim Rice	1974-1989	BBWAA	2009
Rickey Henderson	1979-2003	BBWAA	2009

Ted Williams/Stan Musial

No one would question the credentials of either of these two men—they were both among the very greatest players of all-time.

A very good case could be made for Ted Williams being the greatest hitter who ever lived. In addition to the obvious—his 521 career home runs, 1,839 runs batted in, 1,798 runs scored, and .344 batting average—Williams, along with Stan Musial, was the only one of the truly great hitters who played during the period that saw the game go through some of its greatest changes during the last century. During his career, night ball started to become far more prevalent than it had previously been, black players were finally allowed into the major leagues, relief pitching started to become more of a factor in games, and new pitches, such as the slider, were developed. If he was not the greatest hitter of all-time, Williams was certainly among the top two or three.

The last player to hit .400, Williams also holds the record for highest career on-base percentage (.483), and is second only to Babe Ruth in career slugging percentage, with a mark of .634. Had he not missed almost five full seasons due to two stints in the military, Williams likely would have challenged Ruth's career mark of 714 home runs.

During his career, Williams won seven batting championships and also led the American League in home runs and runs batted in four times each, runs scored six times, on-base percentage twelve times, slugging percentage nine times, and walks eight times. He won two triple crowns, leading the league in home runs, runs batted in, and batting in both 1942 and 1947. He was also a two-time winner of the league's MVP Award, winning it in both 1946 and 1949. Williams is generally considered to be among the five or ten greatest players of all-time.

Stan Musial may very well have been the finest all-around hitter in National League history. When he retired following the 1963 season, he held league records for most hits, runs scored, doubles, runs batted in, and total bases. He was clearly the league's best player from 1944 to 1953, during which time he won three Most

Valuable Player Awards. In fact, during his career, Musial finished in the top five in the MVP voting a remarkable nine times!

Musial led the league in batting seven times, runs batted in twice, runs scored five times, hits six times, triples five times, doubles eight times, and both on-base and slugging percentage six times. He also led the major leagues in total bases six times. He finished his career with 475 home runs, 1,951 runs batted in, 1,949 runs scored, 3,630 hits, and a batting average of .331. Musial is generally thought of as being one of the 10 or 15 greatest players in the history of the game.

Rickey Henderson

As the greatest leadoff hitter in baseball history and the all-time leader in both stolen bases (1,406) and runs scored (2,295), Rickey Henderson was most deserving of his 2009 election by the baseball writers in his first year of eligibility. In his 25 major league seasons, spent with nine different teams, Henderson led his league in stolen bases 12 times, runs scored five times, walks three times, hits once, and on-base percentage once. He holds the single-season mark for most stolen bases (130), set in 1982 as a member of the Oakland Athletics. He stole more than 100 bases three other times, and swiped as many as 50 bags a total of 13 times. He also scored more than 100 runs 13 times, drew more than 100 walks seven times, and batted over .300 seven times.

Henderson had one of his finest seasons for the Yankees in 1985, when he hit 24 home runs, knocked in 72 runs, batted .314, stole 80 bases, and scored 146 runs. He was voted the American League's Most Valuable Player in 1990 when, after rejoining the Athletics, he hit 28 homers, drove in 61 runs, scored 119 others, batted .325, and stole 65 bases. It was one of three times he finished in the top five in the MVP voting. He also finished in the top ten in the balloting another three times. Henderson was a 10-time All-Star and also won a Gold Glove in 1981 for his outstanding defensive work in the outfield.

Throughout much of his career, Henderson was the best leftfielder in the American League, and, in several seasons, among the five best all-around players in the game. He was clearly among the game's best players from 1980 to 1986, and, again, in 1988 and 1990 (in eight of those nine seasons, he scored more than 100 runs; in six, he stole at least 80 bases; and in five, he batted over .300). With the exception of Barry Bonds, he was the finest leftfielder of the last 25 years, and the members of the BBWAA rewarded Henderson with a resounding 94.8 percent approval rating the first time his name appeared on the ballot.

Al Simmons/Joe Medwick

Both Simmons and Medwick were among the best players in the game for extended periods of time. They are both, therefore, quite deserving of their Hall of Fame status.

For eleven straight seasons, from 1924 to 1934, Al Simmons knocked in more than 100 runs and batted over .300. During eight of those seasons, 1925 to 1932, he was among the two or three best players in the American League, and among the five or six best in all of baseball. Over that eight-year stretch, Simmons never batted below .322 and surpassed the .380 mark four times. He also hit more than 30 homers, drove in more than 150 runs, and scored more than 120 runs three times each during that period, while collecting more than 200 hits five times, including a career-best 253 safeties in 1925.

Simmons won two batting titles, leading the A.L. in batting in both 1930 and 1931, with averages of .381 and .390, respectively. In 1929, he led the league in runs batted in with 157, while being named Most Valuable Player, one of four times he finished in the top five in the voting. He also led the league in hits twice and in runs once. Simmons finished his career with 307 home runs, 1,827 runs batted in, 1,507 runs scored, 2,927 hits, and a .334 batting average. He also played on three pennant winners and two world championship teams in Philadelphia, for Connie Mack's A's.

From 1935 to 1939, Joe Medwick of the St. Louis Cardinals was the most dominant hitter in the National League and one of the five or six best players in baseball. During that five-year stretch, he never batted below .322, and he topped the .350 mark three times.

He also hit more than 20 homers three times, accumulated more than 200 hits and scored more than 100 runs four times each, and amassed more than 40 doubles and 100 runs batted in each season, including a career-high 64 doubles in 1936 and a career-best 154 RBIs in 1937. In fact, that 1937 season was Medwick's finest as he became the last National League player to win the triple crown by leading the league with 31 homers, 154 RBIs, and a .374 batting average, en route to being named the league's Most Valuable Player. He also finished in the top five in the MVP voting on two other occasions and was selected to the National League All-Star Team a total of nine times.

In all, Medwick led the league in runs batted in a total of three times, and also led the circuit in triples once, hits twice, runs once, and doubles three times. He knocked in and scored more than 100 runs six times each, had more than 40 doubles seven times, more than 10 triples seven times, and batted over .300 in ten straight seasons. In addition, he played on two pennant-winners and one world championship team during his career.

Ed Delahanty

There are some baseball historians who feel that Ed Delahanty may have been the greatest righthanded hitter in baseball history. If nothing else, he was certainly one of the greatest players of the 19th century.

Delahanty was part of the Philadelphia Phillies outfield of 1894 (along with Billy Hamilton and Sam Thompson) that batted over .400. During his career, Delahanty batted over .400 three times and became the only player ever to win a batting title in each league. During the last decade of the 19th century, he led the National League in almost every major hitting category at least once. In addition to winning two batting titles, Delahanty led the league in home runs twice, runs batted in three times, slugging percentage five times, and doubles five times. He had probably his most productive season for the Phillies in 1893 when he hit 19 home runs, knocked in 146 runs, batted .368, collected 219 hits, and scored 145 runs. In all, Delahanty drove in more than

100 runs and batted over .360 seven times each, scored more than 100 runs ten times, finished with more than 200 hits on three occasions, and totaled more than 40 doubles five times.

While it is true that Delahanty, along with the other hitters of his era, benefited greatly from the rules changes that were implemented during the 1890s, he stood out as the finest all-around hitter of the decade. In fact, even after 1900, when the size of the strike zone was increased and pitching once again began to dominate the game, Delahanty remained an exceptional hitter, posting averages of .354 in 1901 and .376 in 1902.

Carl Yastrzemski

While he was a very good player for most of his career, Carl Yastrzemski was a truly exceptional one from 1967 to 1970. For those four seasons, he was one of the two or three best players in the American League, and one of the best all-around players in baseball. In fact, it could be argued that in two of those seasons, 1967 and 1970, Yastrzemski was *the* best all-around player in the game.

After being a good player from 1961 to 1966, Yastrzemski had one of the greatest seasons a player has ever had in 1967, winning the American League triple crown and MVP Award, playing a superb leftfield, and leading the Boston Red Sox to the pennant. That year, in the middle of a pitching-dominated decade, Yaz hit 44 home runs, knocked in 121 runs, and batted .326. He also led the league with 112 runs scored, 189 hits, an on-base percentage of .421, and a slugging percentage of .622. After carrying the Sox into the World Series on his shoulders, he hit .400 with three home runs in a losing effort to Bob Gibson and the St. Louis Cardinals. The following season, Yastrzemski won the third and final batting title of his career by being the only player in the American League to bat over .300. In 1969, Yaz hit 40 homers and knocked in 111 runs, but batted a disappointing .255. However, in 1970, he was again the best all-around player in the A.L., and, perhaps, in all of baseball. That year, he hit 40 homers, knocked in 102 runs, batted .329, scored 125 runs, and walked 128 times. Although he never again put up those kinds of numbers, Yastrzemski remained an outstanding ballplayer for many more seasons.

Yastrzemski finished his career with 452 home runs, 1,844 runs batted in, 1,816 runs scored, 646 doubles, a .285 batting average, and 3,419 base hits. He is the only American League player to hit 400 home runs and compile 3,000 hits. He led the league in home runs and runs batted in once each, batting average, doubles, runs scored, and slugging percentage three times each, hits twice, and on-base percentage five times. He hit over 40 homers three times, drove in more than 100 runs five times, and batted over .300 six times. Yastrzemski was selected to the All-Star Team 18 times and finished in the top 10 in the MVP voting four times during his career.

Goose Goslin

During his 18-year career, Goose Goslin was an outstanding player who batted over .300 and knocked in more than 100 runs eleven times each. From 1924 to 1928, he was arguably one of the five or six best players in the American League. During that time, he never batted below .334, topping the .350 mark in two of those years. Over that five-year span, he also drove in more than 100 runs and finished with double-digits in triples each season, scored more than 100 runs three times, and collected more than 200 hits twice. In 1924, Goslin led the A.L. in runs batted in, with 129, and he won the batting title in 1928 with a career-high mark of .379.

Splitting time between the Washington Senators, St. Louis Browns and Detroit Tigers, Goslin topped 120 RBIs four times during his career, batted over .340 three times, scored more than 100 runs seven times, and collected at least 10 triples nine times. He finished with 248 home runs, 1,609 runs batted in, 1,483 runs scored, 2,735 base hits, 173 triples, and a .316 batting average, and did relatively well in the MVP voting, finishing in the top 10 on three different occasions. Although he played during a hitter's era, Goslin stood out as one of the very best batsmen of his time.

Lou Brock/Willie Stargell

Although their styles of play could not have been more dissimilar, Brock and Stargell have been grouped together because they were players who excelled during the same era, albeit at different aspects of the game.

Prior to Rickey Henderson, Lou Brock was the greatest leadoff hitter in major league history. Although he is remembered more as a great base-stealer, Brock was an exceptional all-around player. He finished his career with 3,023 hits, 141 triples, 1,610 runs scored, and a .293 batting average. He batted over .300 eight times, scored more than 100 runs seven times, and compiled more than 200 hits four times. Brock had probably his finest all-around season in 1967 when he established career-highs in home runs (21) and runs batted in (76), batted .299, stole 52 bases, collected 206 hits, and led the N.L. with 113 runs scored. The following season, Brock became the first National League player since Honus Wagner in 1908 to lead the league in doubles, triples, and steals.

Nevertheless, Brock's reputation was built largely on his base-stealing ability. Along with Maury Wills, he is largely responsible for changing the way the game was played. During a nine-year stretch, from 1966 to 1974, Brock led the National League in stolen bases eight times. He established a major league record by stealing 50 or more bases in 12 consecutive seasons, from 1965 to 1976. Although Rickey Henderson eventually shattered both marks, Brock once held both the career (938) and single-season (118) stolen base records.

Using our Hall of Fame criteria, although Brock was never considered to be among the five or six best players in baseball, or even the best player at his position, he does very well in all other categories. He was selected to the National League All-Star Team six times, and he finished in the top 10 in the MVP voting five times. In fact, when Brock stole 118 bases in 1974, not only did he finish second to Steve Garvey in the MVP balloting, but he was named Man of the Year by *The Sporting News*. In addition, Brock was a huge contributor to his team's success, and he clearly did the little things to help his team win. After the St. Louis Cardinals acquired him in a trade with the Chicago Cubs during the 1964 season, they went on to win three pennants and two world championships in the next five years. Brock's base running and abilities as a leadoff hitter had as much to do with that as anything. He was a selfless player who, despite possessing good power himself, sacrificed hitting home runs for getting on base and upsetting the opposing team's pitcher and defense. Brock was also a tremendous clutch performer, exhibiting his ability to perform well under pressure in every World Series in which he appeared. In the 1967 Series, he batted .414 against the Red Sox, collecting 12 hits and establishing a Series record by stealing seven bases. The following year, against Detroit, Brock batted .464, rapped out 13 hits, and equaled his own Series record by stealing another seven bases.

Although he was a mediocre outfielder and a below-average baserunner, Willie Stargell was one of the great sluggers the game has seen and was one of the most feared and dangerous hitters of the 1960s and 1970s. In fact, even though he finished his career with 475 home runs, Stargell probably would have hit many more long balls had he not spent his first seven seasons playing in Pittsburgh's cavernous Forbes Field. Although he surpassed 30 homers there once, and was able to knock in over 100 runs twice, it was not until the Pirates moved to Three Rivers Stadium prior to the 1970 season that Stargell became a truly dominant hitter. From 1971 to 1973, he was one of the five best players in the game, and, perhaps, baseball's most productive hitter. In 1971, he led the National League with 48 homers, knocked in 125 runs, batted .295, and finished runner-up to Joe Torre in the MVP voting. The following season, he hit 33 homers, drove in 112 runs, batted .293, and finished third in the MVP balloting. In 1973, he led the league with 44 homers, 119 runs batted in, 43 doubles, and a slugging percentage of .646, while batting .299 and finishing second to Pete Rose in the MVP voting.

In 1979, nearing the end of his career, Stargell was recognized for his team leadership and integral role on the Pirates' team that eventually went on to win the World Series when he was voted co-winner of the league MVP Award, along with Keith Hernandez of the Cardinals. In all, Stargell finished in the top 10 in the MVP voting seven times during his career and was selected to the N.L. All-Star Team seven times.

In addition to his other credentials, Stargell was one of the classiest men the game has known and epitomized the "integrity," "sportsmanship," and "character" traits that Hall of Famers, in theory, are supposed to possess.

Monte Irvin/Ralph Kiner/Billy Williams

Although Irvin, Kiner, and Williams would all fall just short of being ranked among the ten greatest leftfielders in baseball history, they each had some very impressive credentials that legitimized their places in Cooperstown.

Monte Irvin did not arrive in the major leagues as a member of the New York Giants until 1949, when he was already 30 years old. He spent seven seasons with the Giants and one with the Chicago Cubs before retiring at the end of the 1956 campaign. Irvin was a good major league player, having two extremely productive seasons for the Giants. In 1951, he helped lead them to the National League pennant by hitting 24 home runs, leading the league with 121 runs batted in, scoring 94 runs, and batting .312. After suffering a serious leg injury that cost him most of the following season, Irvin returned in 1953 to hit 21 homers, knock in 97 runs, and bat .329. Over the course of his eight big league seasons, Irvin hit 99 home runs and batted .293.

However, Irvin was not elected to the Hall of Fame because of his major league career. Prior to signing with the Giants, he spent ten seasons playing in the Negro Leagues and was considered by many to have been one of the finest talents ever to come out of them. Although he played mostly leftfield in the majors, Irvin made his mark in the Negro Leagues primarily as a shortstop. He had the full package: strong arm, speed and power.

"He was just a terrific talent," said Robert Ruck, a Negro League historian and a history professor at the University of Pittsburgh. "The only thing that kept him from jumping into the major leagues before Jackie Robinson was he went away to the service."

Irvin was a power hitter who hit a league-high .395 in 1941 before joining the war effort. After missing three seasons due to military service, he returned in 1946 to lead the Newark Eagles to the Negro League title, batting a league-leading .404 and being selected league MVP.

In 2000, the Negro League Baseball Museum did an unscientific survey of roughly 200 living ballplayers. The players were given a list of key players in the Negro Leagues, and they were asked to pick the "best of the best."

"Irvin was picked at outfield," said Raymond Doswell, the curator at the museum. "Again, unscientific, but they considered him a great player."

Ralph Kiner did not hit for a particularly high average (.279 lifetime), and was not a great outfielder by any stretch of the imagination. However, he was one of the greatest sluggers in the history of the game. Although he played only ten seasons, Kiner managed to hit 369 home runs and set a major league record by leading his league in home runs for seven consecutive seasons—a record that still stands.

From 1947 to 1951, only Stan Musial prevented Kiner from being the most dominant player in the National League. For those five seasons, Kiner was clearly one of the two or three best players in the N.L., and one of the five best in the majors. He hit over 40 homers and knocked in well over 100 runs in each of those seasons. He also batted over .300 three times. Kiner's two finest seasons came in 1947 and 1949. In the first of those years, he hit 51 home runs, drove in 127 runs, batted .313, and scored 118 runs. Two years later, Kiner once again topped the 50-homer mark by hitting a career-high 54 long balls, while driving in 127 runs, batting .310, and scoring 116 runs.

Over the course of his career, Kiner knocked in more than 100 runs, scored more than 100 runs, and drew more than 100 walks six times each, while batting over .300 three times. He led the league in runs batted in once, walks three times, runs scored once, on-base percentage once, and slugging percentage three times. He was selected to the N.L. All-Star Team five times and, in spite of the fact that he spent most of his career playing for weak Pittsburgh Pirates teams, finished in the top 10 in the MVP voting five times.

Billy Williams had the misfortune of coming up to the Chicago Cubs at a time when four of the greatest outfielders in the history of the game were already established on other National League teams. By the time Williams came up to stay with the Cubs in 1961, Willie Mays, Hank Aaron, Frank Robinson, and Roberto Clemente were already All-Stars on their respective teams. By the late '60s, two of Williams' contemporaries, Willie Stargell and Lou Brock had also established themselves as All-Stars. Therefore, it could not legitimately be said that, at any point during his career—with the exception of two seasons—Williams was considered to be one of the top two or three players in his league, or, for that matter, the best player at his position. He was, however, a consistently outstanding performer who, although overshadowed by others for much of his career, was one of the finest players of his era.

Billy Williams finished his career with 426 home runs, 1,475 runs batted in, 1,410 runs scored, 2,711 base hits, and a .290 batting average. During a pitcher's era, for 13 straight seasons from 1961 to 1973, he never hit fewer than 20 home runs, drove in less than 84 runs, or batted less than .276. He hit more than 30 homers five times, drove in more than 100 runs three times, scored more than 100 runs five times, collected more than 200 hits three times, and batted over .300 five times. He had three seasons that could be described as true Hall of Fame type seasons.

The first of these came in 1965, when he hit 34 home runs, drove in 108 runs, batted .315, scored 115 runs, and collected 203 hits. Then, in 1970, Williams had his finest season. That year, he hit 42 homers, knocked in 129 runs, batted .322, and led the N.L. with 205 hits and 137 runs scored, finishing second to Johnny Bench in the league MVP voting. Two years later, in 1972, Williams hit 37 homers, had 122 RBI's, and led the league with a .333 batting average and a .606 slugging percentage. Once again, he finished runner-up to Bench in the MVP voting. However, in both the 1970 and 1972 seasons, it could be argued that Williams was as good an all-around player as there was in the game. He was selected to the All-Star Team six times during his career and finished in the top 10 in the MVP voting a total of three times.

Pete Hill

It took Pete Hill more than 80 years after he played his final game to be admitted to Cooperstown. But all available evidence seems to indicate that the Veterans Committee made a wise decision when it finally elected him in 2006.

Joseph Preston "Pete" Hill spent 22 seasons playing for seven different teams in the Negro Leagues. During that time, he was considered to be the cornerstone of three of the most talented teams in the pioneer years of black baseball. From 1904 through 1907, Hill was the star leftfielder for Sol White's hard-hitting Philadelphia Giants. From 1908 to 1910, he played for Rube Foster's Leland Giants. In his years with the Giants, Foster depended heavily on Hill's leadership skills, treating him much as a second manager. In Hill's final year with the team, the Giants posted a remarkable record of 123-6 against the best talent in the Midwest. In 1911, Hill joined Foster's newly formed Chicago American Giants, and was subsequently named team captain the following year.

Hill was an excellent defensive outfielder, with outstanding speed and a strong throwing arm. At the plate, he was a lefthanded line-drive hitter who hit to all fields. With the American Giants in 1911, Hill batted safely in 115 of 116 games against all levels of competition. While it is true that the Giants faced mostly minor-league level competition that year, they also played some teams that had major-league quality pitching, including Hall of Famers Eddie Plank, Chief Bender, and Mordecai Brown.

Cum Posey, owner of the Homestead Grays, called Hill "the most consistent hitter of his time. While a lefthanded batter, he hit both lefthanders and righthanders equally well. He was the backbone, year in and year out, of great ball clubs."

Due to the extremely limited availability of statistical data surrounding the early years of the Negro Leagues, it is difficult to ascertain just how good a hitter Hill actually was. But he obviously had many of the intangible qualities desirable in a Hall of Famer. Furthermore, a poll taken in 1952 by the African-American weekly *Pittsburgh Courier* named Hill the fourth-best outfielder in Negro League history, behind only Oscar Charleston, Monte Irvin, and Cristobal Torriente.

Jim Rice

One of baseball's most dominant hitters for more than a decade was Boston Red Sox leftfielder Jim Rice. In 11 full seasons between 1975 and 1986, Rice averaged 30 home runs, 110 runs batted in, and 95 runs scored, while compiling a batting average of .305. He was particularly outstanding from 1977 to 1979, averaging 41 homers, 128 RBIs, 114 runs scored, and .320 over that three-year stretch. Rice hit at least 39 home runs four times during his career, drove in more than 100 runs eight times, batted over .300 seven times, accumulated 200 hits on four separate occasions, and scored more than 100 runs three times. He led all major league players with 1,276 runs batted in between 1975 and 1986. Rice had his greatest season in 1978 when he was named the American League's Most Valuable Player for batting .315, scoring 121 runs, and leading the league with 46 home runs, 139 runs batted in, 15 triples, 213 hits, 406 total bases, and a .600 slugging percentage. It was one of six times he finished in the top five in the MVP balloting.

Yet, there are legitimate arguments that can be waged against the legitimacy of Rice's 2009 induction into Cooperstown. Injuries caused his offensive production to fall off dramatically his last few seasons, leaving Rice with less-than overwhelming career totals of 382 home runs and 1,249 runs scored. He was not a particularly good baserunner, and he was generally considered to be a below-average fielder, with somewhat limited range and only fair instincts in the outfield.

Nevertheless, supporters of Rice can also point to his eight appearances on the All-Star team. He also was a league-leader in a major statistical category a total of 13 times, and the majority of players who competed during his era consider Rice to be one of the most dominant figures of that period. Furthermore, his credentials are actually quite comparable to those of Billy Williams, who we previously identified as a legitimate Hall of Famer:

PLAYER	AB	HITS	RUNS	2B	3B	HR	RBI	AVG	SB	OBP	SLG PCT
Billy Williams	9,350	2,711	1,410	434	88	426	1,475	.290	90	.361	.492
Jim Rice	8,225	2,452	1,249	373	79	382	1,451	.298	58	.352	.502

Williams finished slightly ahead of Rice in most offensive categories, but that was primarily because he accumulated 1,125 more at-bats during his career. Rice actually drove in runs at a faster pace and compiled a higher batting average and slugging percentage. Williams was an extremely consistent performer over the years, but Rice was the more dominant hitter. While Rice topped his league in a major statistical category a total of 13 times, Williams was a league-leader only five times. Williams placed in the top five in the MVP voting only twice, to Rice's six top-five finishes, and Williams' six appearances on the All-Star team were two fewer than Rice's eight selections. Furthermore, while Williams had only three or four truly dominant seasons that could be classified as Hall-of-Fame caliber, Rice had at least six such campaigns. Therefore, while Rice should be viewed very much as a borderline Hall of Famer, his 2009 induction certainly does not lower the Hall's standards in the least.

Jesse Burkett/Fred Clarke/Joe Kelley

These three players have been grouped together for two reasons. First, they were contemporaries of one another, each coming up to the majors during the last decade of the nineteenth century and playing through part, or all, of the first decade of the twentieth. Second, all three were very good players, although their career numbers were somewhat inflated by the rules that were in effect from 1893 to 1900. Let's take a look at the career of each man:

Jesse Burkett came up with the New York Giants in 1890, but was traded at the end of the season to the Cleveland Spiders (who eventually became the St. Louis Cardinals), where he became a full-time outfielder in 1892. That season, he had a relatively good year, batting .275, scoring 119 runs, and collecting 14 triples. The following year, though, with the pitcher's mound moved back to 60' 6" and batting averages throughout baseball soaring to record highs, Burkett's numbers took a quantum leap as well. That season, he finished with an average of .348 and scored 145 runs. Over the next several seasons, Burkett was arguably the finest leadoff hitter in the game. From 1893 to 1901, he never batted any lower than .341, and he topped the .400-mark twice. Over that nine-year stretch, he failed to score at least 100 runs only once, surpassing the 140-mark four times and tallying a career-best 160 runs scored in 1896. He also collected more than 200 hits six times and stole more than 30 bases five times.

However, after being traded to the St. Louis Browns in 1902, Burkett never again hit any higher than .306. It is hard to say if his decline was more a reflection of the times, since pitchers came to dominate the game once more shortly after the turn of the century, or if it was more an indication that he was in the twilight of his career at that juncture. Either way, Burkett remained a full-time player over his final four seasons, totaling well over 500 at-bats each year. Therefore, the Browns must have felt that he had something left. Yet, he batted over .300 in only one of those years.

Still, during his career, Burkett led the league in batting and hits three times each, and in runs scored twice. In addition, his two seasons with a batting average in excess of .400, six seasons with more than 200 hits, and nine years with more than 100 runs scored are quite impressive, regardless of the era in which he played. Burkett was elected to the Hall of Fame by the Veterans Committee in 1946.

Fred Clarke came up to the Louisville Colonels in 1894 and remained with the team long after they became the Pittsburgh Pirates prior to the start of the 1900 season. In fact, Clarke served as player/manager of the team from 1897 until he retired at the end of the 1911 season. Thus, for the first seven years of his career, Clarke was a beneficiary of the rules changes that went into effect one year prior to his arrival in the big leagues. However, he spent the last ten years of his career hitting in the Deadball Era, when pitchers dominated the sport. Therefore, his numbers can probably be viewed without a great deal of skepticism.

Although Clarke was not a big run-producer, never having driven in more than 82 runs in any season, he was a fine hitter, topping the .300 mark eleven times during his career. As might be expected, he had his finest seasons during the last decade of the 19th century, posting averages of .347 in 1895, .390 in 1897, and .342 in 1899. However, Clarke did hit .351 in 1903, clearly indicating that he was a good hitter, regardless of the rules that were in effect at any particular time. In addition, he collected 200 hits twice, scored over 100 runs five times, and finished in double-digits in triples 14 times. During his career, though, Clarke only led the league once in triples, doubles, and slugging percentage. The Veterans Committee elected him to the Hall of Fame in 1945.

Joe Kelley played for five different teams during his 18-year career that spanned virtually all of the last decade of the nineteenth century, and the first decade of the twentieth. He was similar to Burkett and Clarke in that he was a fine hitter whose career batting average was aided immeasurably by playing during the 1890s. However, he differed from the other two men in that he was far superior as a run producer. During his career, Kelley knocked in over 100 runs five times, peaking at 134 RBIs for the 1895 Baltimore Orioles. He also scored more than 100 runs six times, totaling 165 for the Orioles in 1894, and batted over .300 in eleven straight seasons, from 1893 to 1903. In 1896, he stole 87 bases for the Orioles. Still, aside from leading the league once in stolen bases, he never led the circuit in any offensive category. Kelley was elected to the Hall of Fame by the Veterans Committee in 1971.

A look at the career statistics of the three men indicates that they were all fine players:

PLAYER	AB	HITS	RUNS	2B	3B	HR	RBI	AVG	SB	OBP	SLG PCT
Jesse Burkett	8,421	2,850	1,720	320	182	75	952	.338	389	.415	.446
Fred Clarke	8,568	2,672	1,619	361	220	67	1,015	.312	506	.386	.429
Joe Kelley	7,006	2,220	1,421	358	194	65	1,194	.317	443	.401	.451

While Burkett and Clarke were basically equal as run producers, Kelley had a clear advantage there, driving in more runs in far fewer at-bats and scoring them at essentially the same rate. Burkett finished with the highest batting average and on-base percentage—both very important categories for a good leadoff hitter.

The feeling here is that all three men were decent selections by the Veterans Committee, but that none was a clear-cut Hall of Famer along the lines of an Ed Delahanty, or a few of the other outfielders from that time period whose careers we will examine shortly. Since Burkett was the only one to lead the league multiple times in any major offensive category, he should probably be viewed as the most legitimate choice of the three. But none was a dominant player, and all should be viewed as borderline Hall of Famers.

Jim O'Rourke

Nicknamed "The Orator" because he was considered to be the most eloquent player of the 19th century, Jim O'Rourke was one of the very first Hall of Famers to play in the major leagues. O'Rourke's big league career began in 1873, with the Boston Braves, and ended 21 years later, with the original Washington Senators of the National League. In between, he had stints with the Providence Grays, Buffalo Bisons, and New York Giants.

O'Rourke was known for being a good hitter, but was also considered to be a liability in the field. He led the league in home runs, triples, runs scored, and hits once each, and in on-base percentage twice. O'Rourke's finest season came in 1890, when, playing for the Giants, he hit nine home runs, drove in 115 runs, scored 112 more (one of five times during his career he scored more than 100 runs), and batted .360. He finished his career with 62 home runs, just under 1,200 runs batted in, just over 1,700 runs scored, slightly more than 2,600 hits, 150 triples, 461 doubles, and a .311 batting average. In his five best big league seasons, O'Rourke posted batting averages of .350, .362, .348, .347, and .360.

However, in only two of those years did he have as many as 400 at-bats. In fact, due to the infrequency with which games were played in the early years of professional baseball, O'Rourke never had more than 370 at-bats during his first ten seasons. In his entire career, he surpassed 500 at-bats only three times, and he had as many as 400 at-bats only seven other times. It is, therefore, extremely difficult to gauge his performance against that of other Hall of Fame players and ascertain whether or not he is truly qualified. The feeling here is that, while the Veterans Committee's 1945 selection of O'Rourke was not necessarily a bad one, it was one that was questionable, especially when taking into consideration the limited amount of playing time he experienced throughout most of his career.

Heinie Manush/Chick Hafey

Both of these men had their finest seasons from the mid-1920s to the early '30s, during one of the greatest hitting eras in the history of the game. This needs to be factored in to the equation when reviewing their Hall of Fame credentials.

Heinie Manush's 17-year major league career included stints with the Detroit Tigers, St. Louis Browns, Washington Senators, Boston Red Sox, Brooklyn Dodgers, and Pittsburgh Pirates. Manush was neither a power-hitter nor a big producer of runs. He never hit more than 14 home runs in any season, and he knocked in more than 100 runs only twice. However, he was an outstanding line-drive hitter, batting as high as .378 on two separate occasions, and surpassing the .340-mark four other times. Manush also collected more than 200 hits four times, scored more than 100 runs six times, compiled more than 40 doubles six times, and finished in double-digits in triples eight times. He led the American League in batting in 1926 when he hit .378 for the Tigers, and he matched that figure two years later while playing for the Browns. He also led the league in hits twice, doubles twice, and triples once.

However, Manush was never considered to be among the very best players in the game, and, with the possible exceptions of the 1926 and 1928 seasons, could not even be included among the five or six best players in his own league. In addition, for most of his career, he was rated well behind Al Simmons among American

League leftfielders. In other Hall of Fame criteria, he finished in the top five in the MVP voting three times, and, as was mentioned earlier, was a league-leader in various offensive categories on six different occasions. It is difficult to say whether or not Manush contributed to his team's success in other ways because he played on teams that finished in the second division for most of his career. However, he was a member of the 1933 Washington Senators team that won the American League pennant.

Chick Hafey spent his entire 13-year career in the National League, playing eight seasons with the Cardinals and five with the Reds. Rogers Hornsby, who was a teammate of his for three seasons in St. Louis, once said that Hafey was as good a righthanded hitter as he ever saw. Hafey is said to have hit the ball as hard as any righthanded batter of that era, with the exception of Jimmie Foxx. During his career, he hit more than 20 home runs, drove in more than 100 runs, and scored more than 100 runs three times each. He also batted over .330 in five straight seasons, from 1928 to 1932, winning the N.L. batting title in 1931 with a mark of .349.

The thing about Hafey, though, is that he was a full-time regular for only six seasons, totaling more than 500 at-bats only four times, and topping 400 plate appearances only two other times. As a result, his career numbers pale by comparison to those of most legitimate Hall of Famers. In addition, like Manush, he was never considered to be among the very best players in the game, or even, for that matter, in his own league. He was also ranked well behind Al Simmons among leftfielders throughout his career.

Let's take a look at the career numbers of both Manush and Hafey, alongside those of Bob Johnson, the man who succeeded Simmons in leftfield for the Philadelphia Athletics, and who is not in the Hall of Fame:

PLAYER	AB	HITS	RUNS	2B	3B	HR	RBI	AVG	SB	OBP	SLG PCT
Heinie Manush	7,654	2,524	1,287	491	160	110	1,183	.330	114	.377	.479
Bob Johnson	6,920	2,051	1,239	396	95	288	1,283	.296	96	.393	.506
Chick Hafey	4,625	1,466	777	341	67	164	833	.317	70	.372	.526

Looking at this graphic, several things become quite apparent. First, while Hafey was a very good hitter, he just didn't do enough to be considered a legitimate Hall of Famer. Other than his .317 batting average and .526 slugging percentage—both of which were somewhat inflated by the era in which he played—none of his numbers are even close to being Hall of Fame worthy. It is also apparent that Johnson was easily the most productive and powerful hitter of the three. Playing from 1933 to 1945, in somewhat less of a hitter's era, he put up the most impressive numbers. In approximately 700 fewer at-bats, Johnson hit more than twice as many homers as Manush, knocked in 40 more runs, scored almost as many runs, and finished with a higher slugging percentage. His batting average was considerably lower, but much of that discrepancy is due to the fact that Manush's average was padded somewhat during the 1920s. In addition, due to his greater ability to draw bases on balls, Johnson finished with a higher on-base percentage despite his lower batting average. Manush had more doubles and triples, but Johnson was a far more dangerous hitter. He hit more than 30 homers three times, knocked in more than 100 runs eight times, scored more than 100 runs six times, and batted over .300 four times.

Johnson also does rather well using our Hall of Fame criteria. Although it could not be said that he was among the very best players in the game for most of his career, he was arguably the best leftfielder in the American League from 1935 to 1938. He was also selected to the All-Star Team eight times, and he finished in the top 10 in the MVP voting three times.

Once again, this is not to suggest that someone who is not in the Hall of Fame should be. Johnson probably does not deserve to be in. However, he belongs just as much as Manush, and more than Hafey. Of course, Frankie Frisch, when he was on the Veterans Committee, had a lot to do with his former Cardinals teammate being elected in 1971. As for Manush, he was not a bad choice, but his selection should also be looked upon with a great deal of skepticism.

Zack Wheat

Before ending his career with the Philadelphia Athletics in 1927, Zack Wheat spent his first 18 seasons playing for the Brooklyn Dodgers. For much of the second decade of the 20th century, Wheat was considered to be one of the top sluggers in the National League, even though he never hit more than nine home runs or drove in more than 89 runs during that period. He was also one of the league's top three outfielders for much of the decade, batting over .300 six times and finishing in double-digits in triples seven times. When a livelier ball was put into play for the first time in 1920, Wheat's productivity, along with that of virtually every other major league hitter, increased dramatically. During the 1920s, he failed to bat over .300 only once, twice reaching the .375 mark. He also reached double-digits in home runs four times, knocked in over 100 runs twice, scored more than 100 runs once, collected more than 200 hits three times, and reached double-digits in triples four more times.

However, while Wheat was thought of as being one of the top players in the National League for much of his first ten years with the Dodgers, he was never looked upon as being one of the five or six best players in the game. He wasn't even considered to be one of the four or five best outfielders (he was ranked well behind Ty Cobb, Tris Speaker, Shoeless Joe Jackson, and Sam Crawford). Even though Wheat became a more productive hitter during the first half of the 1920s, there were many outfielders who were far more productive—Babe Ruth, Harry Heilmann, Bobby Veach, Ken Williams, Cy Williams, Cobb, and Speaker, just to name a few. While Wheat did hit .375 twice during the decade, he failed to win the batting title either year (Rogers Hornsby won it both times). In fact, Wheat was a league-leader only twice during his career, winning the batting title once and leading the league in slugging percentage once. Here are his career numbers:

AB	HITS	RUNS	2B	3B	HR	RBI	AVG	SB	OBP
9,106	2,884	1,289	476	172	132	1,248	.317	205	.361

Those are good numbers, probably strong enough to earn him serious consideration for induction into the Hall of Fame.

Consider, though, that this is what they look like if they are split between the figures he accumulated prior to 1920 and those he compiled during the 1920s:

	AB	HITS	RUNS	2B	3B	HR	RBI	AVG	SB	OBP
Pre-1920	5,166	1,547	635	251	107	51	640	.300	162	.345
Post-1920	3,940	1,337	654	225	65	81	608	.339	43	.385

This is an indication of how much greater Wheat's productivity was during the 1920s, and what kind of impact hitting with a livelier ball had on him. While his power numbers could be expected to jump drastically during this period, note the discrepancy in his batting averages. From this, it would seem that Wheat was a good, solid player, but that he benefited greatly from playing in one of the greatest hitting decades in baseball history. As a result, Wheat would probably fall just short of being Hall of Fame worthy.

CENTERFIELDERS (22)

PLAYER	YEARS	ELECTED BY	YEAR ELECTED
Hugh Duffy	1888-1901, 04-05	Veterans Committee	1945
Billy Hamilton	1888-1901	Veterans Committee	1961
Ty Cobb	1905-1928	BBWAA	1936
Tris Speaker	1907-1928	BBWAA	1937
Max Carey	1910-1929	Veterans Committee	1961
Cristobal Torriente	1913-1928	Veterans Committee	2006
Edd Roush	1913-1929,31	Veterans Committee	1962
Oscar Charleston	1915-1942	Negro Leagues Committee	1976
Cool Papa Bell	1922-1946	Negro Leagues Committee	1974
Turkey Stearnes	1923-1940	Veterans Committee	2000
Hack Wilson	1923-1934	Veterans Committee	1979
Earle Combs	1924-1935	Veterans Committee	1970
Lloyd Waner	1927-42,44-45	Veterans Committee	1967
Earl Averill	1929-1941	Veterans Committee	1975
Joe DiMaggio	1936-42,46-51	BBWAA	1955
Willard Brown	1936-44,47-50	Veterans Committee	2006
Larry Doby	1947-1959	Veterans Committee	1998

PLAYER	YEARS	ELECTED BY	YEAR ELECTED
Duke Snider	1947-1964	BBWAA	1980
Richie Ashburn	1948-1962	Veterans Committee	1995
Mickey Mantle	1951-1968	BWAA	1974
Willie Mays	1951-52,54-73	BBWAA	1979
Kirby Puckett	1984-1995	BBWAA	2001

Willie Mays/Ty Cobb

Mays and Cobb are at the top of the list of great centerfielders whose Hall of Fame credentials would not be questioned by anyone.

Many people consider Willie Mays to be the greatest all-around player in baseball history. There is nothing on a ball field he could not do. He had great power, was a lifetime .300 hitter, was a superb baserunner, and was one of the finest defensive centerfielders in the history of the game. As if his 660 career home runs, 1,903 runs batted in, 3,283 hits, and 11 Gold Gloves weren't enough, he was also the first man to hit 300 home runs and steal 300 bases. He led the National League in home runs four times, batting average once, triples three times, slugging percentage five times, runs scored and on-base percentage two times each, and stolen bases four times.

From 1954 to 1966, Mays was one of the five best players in baseball and, in most of those years, the best centerfielder in the game. In several of those seasons, he was viewed as being the sport's greatest player. He certainly was just that in 1954, 1955, 1962, 1964, and 1965. In the first of those seasons, Mays hit 41 homers, knocked in 110 runs, scored 119 more, and led the N.L. with a .345 batting average, .667 slugging percentage and 13 triples, en route to leading the Giants to the world championship and winning the first of his two Most Valuable Player Awards. The following season, he hit 51 homers, knocked in 127 runs, and batted .319. In 1962, he led the league with 49 homers, drove in 141 runs, batted .304, and scored 130 runs to finish second to

Maury Wills in the MVP voting. Two years later, he hit 47 home runs, knocked in 111 runs, scored 121 others, and finished with a batting average of .296. Mays won the MVP Award for the second time in 1965, when he hit 52 homers and finished with 112 runs batted in, 118 runs scored, and a .317 batting average.

In all, Mays finished in the top five in the MVP voting an astonishing nine times during his career and was selected to the All-Star Team twenty times.

From 1907 to 1919, Ty Cobb was considered to be the most dominant player in baseball. During that 13-year period, he won ten batting titles and hit .383, .368, and .371 in the three seasons he failed to do so. He batted over .350 in all but one of those seasons, topping the .400-mark twice. Over that stretch he also collected more than 200 hits seven times, knocked in over 100 runs five times, scored more than 100 runs seven times, stole over 50 bases eight times, finished in double-digits in triples every season, won the American League's triple crown once, and was also named its MVP once.

In addition to his ten batting titles, during his career Cobb led the league in stolen bases six times, runs batted in four times, triples four times, doubles three times, hits eight times, runs scored five times, on-base percentage six times, and slugging percentage eight times. He finished his career with 1,937 runs batted in, 2,246 runs scored, 295 triples, 724 doubles, 4,189 hits, 891 stolen bases, and the highest batting average (.367) of any player in baseball history. Although many of his records have since been broken, when Cobb retired in 1928 he held almost every major career and single season batting and base-running record.

Yet, despite his incredible list of achievements, if the Hall of Fame voters truly considered "character," "sportsmanship," and "integrity" when evaluating potential candidates during the selection process, they would have thought twice before admitting Cobb, instead of making him one of the five original members in 1936. Cobb was a bitter, contentious, antagonistic, and violent man, who felt stronger than most about keeping black players out of the major leagues. We will take a closer look at this side of

Cobb in a later chapter, but, suffice to say, the Hall of Fame clearly is more stringent at some times than at others in its admissions policy.

Joe DiMaggio/Mickey Mantle

The two greatest centerfielders in New York Yankees history were also among the five greatest of all-time.

For virtually his entire career, Joe DiMaggio was the best centerfielder in baseball, and among its five best players. In fact, from 1936 to 1942, prior to his three-year stint in the military, the young DiMaggio may very well have been the finest all-around player in baseball history. Certainly, from 1937 to 1941, and again in 1948, a valid case could be made for him being the best player in the game.

In 1937, DiMaggio led the American League with 46 home runs, knocked in 167 runs, scored 151 others, and batted .346, while compiling 418 total bases and 215 base hits. Only his teammate Lou Gehrig, Detroit's Hank Greenberg, and the National League's Joe Medwick had comparable seasons. The following year, DiMaggio hit 32 homers, knocked in 140 runs, and batted .324. However, he would probably have to be rated just behind Jimmie Foxx and Greenberg that year, since both men reached the 50-homer plateau. In 1939, DiMaggio won the first of his three Most Valuable Player Awards by leading the league with a .381 batting average, while hitting 30 homers and driving in 126 runs, despite missing more than 30 games due to injuries. He was clearly the best player in baseball that season and quite possibly the next year as well. In 1940, he won his second consecutive batting title, hitting .352 while collecting 31 homers and 133 runs batted in, to finish just behind Greenberg in the MVP voting. The following year, DiMaggio hit in 56 straight games, batted .357, hit 30 homers, drove in 125 runs, won his second Most Valuable Player Award, and vied with Ted Williams (who batted .406) for the title of greatest player in the game. After coming out of the service two years earlier, DiMaggio had another great season in

1948 when he led the league in homers (39) and runs batted in (155), while batting .320.

During his career, DiMaggio won three MVP Awards, two home run titles, three RBI crowns, and two batting championships. He was selected to the All-Star Team in each of his 13 big-league seasons, and was selected to *The Sporting News All-Star Team* eight times. In addition to his three MVP seasons, he finished in the top five in the voting three other times. One particularly amazing statistic about DiMaggio is that he hit 361 home runs and struck out only 369 times during his career.

Had Mickey Mantle taken better care of himself and been able to play most of his career injury-free, he may have gone on to become the greatest baseball player in history. As it is, he is generally considered to be one of the 15 greatest players of all-time. He was clearly the greatest switch-hitter in the history of the game, and he probably possessed the greatest combination of speed and power that the game has ever seen.

Although he never quite lived up to his full potential, Mantle's 536 career home runs, 1,509 runs batted in, 1,677 runs scored, and .423 on-base percentage are all quite impressive figures. In spite of the constant pain and injuries he had to play through much of the time, Mantle was still one of the two or three best players in the American League for a good portion of his career, and among the five or six best in the game. From 1955 to 1958, then again, from 1960 to 1962, Mickey was one of the very best players in baseball. In fact, in at least three of those seasons, he may very well have been *the* best player in the game. Mickey's greatest season came in 1956 when he won the first of his three Most Valuable Player Awards by leading the major leagues in home runs (52), runs batted in (130), batting average (.353), runs scored (132), and slugging percentage (.705). He became just the second player (Jimmie Foxx was the first) to hit 50 homers and win a batting title in the same season. He followed that up with another great year in 1957 by hitting 34 homers, knocking in 94 runs, batting .365, walking 146 times, and winning his second consecutive MVP Award. Mantle was again arguably the best player in the game in 1961, even though he was beaten out for MVP honors by his teammate Roger Maris. That year, Mantle hit 54 home runs, knocked in 128 runs, and batted .317.

In all, Mantle led the American League in home runs four times, runs batted in once, batting average once, runs scored six times, on-base percentage three times, slugging percentage four times, and walks five times. He won three Most Valuable Player Awards and finished in the top five in the voting five other times. Mantle was also selected to the American League All-Star Team a total of 16 times, and to *The Sporting News All-Star Team* six times.

Tris Speaker

During the second decade of the 20th century, only Ty Cobb prevented Tris Speaker from being widely acknowledged as the greatest player in the game. From 1910 to 1919, Speaker batted well over .300 in all but one season, topping the .340-mark five times. During that 10-year period, he finished in double-digits in triples nine times, collected more than 40 doubles four times, scored more than 100 runs four times, and led the American League in home runs and batting average once each. He was named the league's Most Valuable Player in 1912 when, playing for the Boston Red Sox, he batted .383 and amassed 53 doubles. Speaker was also regarded as the finest defensive centerfielder in the game. In fact, to this day, many baseball experts consider him to be the greatest defensive centerfielder in baseball history.

In the 1920s, playing for the Cleveland Indians, Speaker continued to stand out as one of the finest all-around players in the game. With a livelier ball being used that decade, he batted over .360 five times, drove in over 100 runs twice, and became the only man to ever lead his league in doubles four straight years, from 1920 to 1923. His .345 career batting average, 222 triples, 1,882 runs scored, and 3,514 hits all place him in the top 10 all-time, and he is the career leader in doubles, with 792.

Oscar Charleston/Cool Papa Bell

Charleston and Bell were the two greatest outfielders in Negro League history and were generally regarded to be among the league's five greatest players.

Oscar Charleston's career in the Negro Leagues spanned 28 years, from 1915 to 1942. For much of that time, he was considered to be the league's finest all-around player, rivaling Josh Gibson as its top slugger and Cool Papa Bell as its best centerfielder. In fact, during his career, Charleston was compared favorably to Tris Speaker as a fielder, Ty Cobb as a baserunner, and Babe Ruth as a hitter. Many who saw him play insisted there was never anyone better.

Charleston played for 12 different teams during his 28-year Negro League career. Among his numerous stops were two seasons with the Homestead Grays, for whom he performed in 1930 and 1931. The Grays' 1931 squad is considered to be among the greatest baseball teams ever assembled. Joining Charleston on the roster were future Hall of Famers Josh Gibson, Smokey Joe Williams, and Jud Wilson. Charleston batted .380 for the Grays that year.

A tremendously gifted athlete, there was nothing Charleston could not do on the ball field. He had great running speed, was an instinctive and aggressive baserunner, had superb range, good hands, and a powerful arm in the outfield, and could hit for both power and average. The 1921 season was perhaps the greatest example of Charleston's all-around brilliance. Playing for the St. Louis Giants that year, the lefthanded hitting Charleston compiled a .434 batting average, and led the league with 35 stolen bases, 14 doubles, 11 triples, and 15 home runs in only 60 league games.

Charleston was equally proficient as an outfielder. Rightfielder Dave Malarcher, who played alongside Charleston, said, "He could play all the outfield. I just caught foul balls. I stayed on the lines." Buck O'Neill, who played against him in the Negro Leagues, said, "Willie Mays was the best major league player I ever saw, but Oscar Charleston was the best baseball player I ever saw."

Cool Papa Bell might have been the fastest man ever to play organized baseball. The 5'11", 150-pound Bell was once clocked circling the bases in an amazing 12 seconds. He used his speed and daring to become the foremost base-stealer in baseball, once being credited with stealing over 170 bases in a 200-game season. Bell was so fast that he frequently beat out infield hits on two-hoppers hit directly to infielders, scored from second base on sacrifice flies, and advanced from first to third on bunts. Legend has it that he even scored all the way from first base on a bunt against Bob Lemon and a team of major league all-stars. Bell also utilized his speed to become an outstanding defensive outfielder, playing a shallow centerfield and often outrunning pitcher's mistakes by turning his back on home plate and tracking down long fly balls.

An outstanding switch-hitter who consistently batted well over .300, Bell compensated for his lack of power at the plate by hitting down on the ball to use his great running speed, and by smacking line drives to all fields. Various sources have his lifetime batting average in Negro League play approaching the .340-mark, and he batted .395 in exhibition games against major league players. During his career, Bell played on 11 championship teams and was an annual selection for the East-West All-Star Game.

Bill Veeck, owner of several major league teams, said, "Defensively, he was the equal of Tris Speaker, Joe DiMaggio or Willie Mays."

Pro basketball pioneer and baseball scout Eddie Gottlieb said, "If he had played in the major leagues, he would have reminded people of Willie Keeler as a hitter and Ty Cobb as a baserunner—and he might have exceeded both."

Billy Hamilton/Hugh Duffy

These two men were the greatest centerfielders of the 19th century.

Billy Hamilton was not only the finest centerfielder of the 19th century, but was one of the five or six greatest players of that period. Although many people are not aware of it, it was Hamilton's stolen base record that Lou Brock broke—and not Ty Cobb's—when he stole 938 bases during the 1960s and 1970s. Although Cobb had been credited with the "modern" record for stolen bases all those years, his 891 steals actually fell 21 short of the 912 Hamilton stole for the Philadelphia Phillies from 1888 to 1901.

However, Hamilton was far more than just a great base-stealer. He finished his career with a .344 batting average, a .455 on-base percentage, 1,690 runs scored, and 2,158 hits in only 6,268 at-bats. By scoring 1,690 runs in just 1,593 games, Hamilton became one of only two players in major league history to average more than a run a game. As part of the Philadelphia outfield that batted over .400 in 1894, he had his greatest season that year. Not only did Hamilton hit a career-high .404, but he stole 98 bases and scored an all-time record 192 runs. He also batted over .380 two other times and led the league in on-base percentage five times, walks five times, batting average twice, hits once, and runs scored four times. Hamilton's election to the Hall of Fame by the Veterans Committee in 1961 was long overdue.

Hugh Duffy was the other outstanding centerfielder of the 19th century. Although he was not the prolific base-stealer that Hamilton was, he still managed to swipe 574 bags during his 16-year career. In addition, he finished with a .324 batting average, 1,302 runs batted in, 1,552 runs scored, 2,282 hits, and 119 triples. He won the National League triple crown in 1894 by hitting 18 home runs, driving in 145 runs, and compiling the highest batting average in baseball history—.438. While it is true that averages throughout baseball that year were extremely high (Philadelphia's team batting average was .349), Duffy's mark of .438 was still 30 points higher than that of the runner-up in the batting race. He was also a league-leader in various other offensive categories during the course of his career. He led the league in home runs, runs batted in, and hits twice each, and in doubles and runs scored once each. He knocked in over 100 runs eight times, and scored more than 100 runs nine times, including 161 in 1890 and 160 in 1894. In fact, in that triple crown season of 1894, Duffy also collected 51 doubles and 237 hits, and compiled a .694 slugging percentage. During the 1890s, he batted over .300 in eight straight seasons.

As good as Duffy was, it is still somewhat curious that the Veterans Committee elected him in 1945, 16 years before Billy Hamilton gained admittance. Perhaps the reason lies in the limited availability of historical statistics during the early years of the elections.

Turkey Stearnes

Norman "Turkey" Stearnes may well have been the most underrated, underappreciated, and unheralded player in Negro League history. Possessing both exceptional power at the plate and outstanding running speed in the field and on the basepaths, Stearnes was one of the finest all-around players in the history of black baseball.

Satchel Paige said of Stearnes, "He was one of the greatest hitters we ever had. He was as good as Josh (Gibson)." Cool Papa Bell expressed his admiration for his centerfield rival by saying, "That man could hit the ball as far as anybody. But they don't say too much about him. And he was one of our best all-around players. He could field, he could hit, he could run. He had plenty of power."

Indeed, Stearnes provided the stiffest competition to Bell as the greatest leadoff hitter in Negro League history. Possessing superior power to Bell, Stearnes won six home run crowns during his 18-year career, spent predominantly with the Detroit Stars. He also captured three batting titles. In 1932, as a member of the Chicago American Giants, Stearnes became one of only two players in the history of organized baseball (Oscar Charleston being the other) to lead his league in home runs, doubles, triples, and stolen bases. Unofficial records show that Stearnes, a perennial .300 hitter, posted batting averages of .342, .374, and .430, from 1933 to 1935 for the Giants.

Prior to Stearnes' induction into Cooperstown, Cool Papa Bell said, "If they don't put Turkey in the Hall of Fame, they should take me out." Fortunately, the Veterans Committee rectified its earlier oversight when it selected Stearnes in 2000.

Duke Snider/Earl Averill

Both Snider and Averill were excellent players whose prime years were relatively few in number. Yet, at their peaks, they were both among the very best players in the game.

Duke Snider first came up to the Brooklyn Dodgers during the 1947 season. At that time, the great Joe DiMaggio still reigned supreme among New York outfielders. By 1951, although Snider was already beginning to establish himself as a true star, Willie Mays had come up to the Giants, and Mickey Mantle had been called up by the Yankees. Therefore, Snider never really had the New York spotlight all to himself, and was overshadowed somewhat by his New York counterparts for much of his career. However, in virtually every season from 1949 to 1957, Snider would have to be ranked among the five or six best players in the Major Leagues. In fact, he hit more home runs (326) than any other player in baseball during the 1950s.

From 1949 to 1953, Snider was the best centerfielder in the National League, and arguably in all of baseball. Over that five-year stretch, he averaged 29 home runs, 104 RBIs, and 103 runs scored, while hitting over .300 three times. Although Mays established himself as the best player in the game in 1954, he received stiff competition from Snider over the next few seasons. From 1954 to 1957, Snider hit more than 40 homers each year, knocked in and scored over 100 runs three times, and batted over .300 twice. He had his three finest seasons from 1953 to 1955. In 1953, he hit 42 homers, knocked in 126 runs, batted .336, and led the league with 132 runs scored. The following year, he hit 40 homers, drove in 130 runs, batted .341, and led the league with 120 runs scored. In 1955, he hit 42 homers, knocked in 136 runs, batted .309, and again led the league in runs scored, with 126. Snider was named *The Sporting News* Player of the Year for that 1955 season.

During his career, Snider led the National League in homers, RBIs, and on-base percentage once each, in runs scored three times, and in slugging percentage twice. He was selected to the N.L. All-Star Team eight times, and he finished in the top 10 in the

MVP voting six times, making it into the top five on three separate occasions.

Earl Averill played only 13 seasons in the major leagues and was a full-time regular in only 10 of those. However, from 1929 to 1936, he was the best centerfielder in the American League, and from 1931 to 1936, the best in all of baseball. Averill had his two finest seasons for the Cleveland Indians in 1931 and 1936. In the first of those years, he established career-highs in home runs (32), runs batted in (143), and runs scored (140), while batting .333. In 1936, Averill hit 28 homers, knocked in 126 runs, batted a career-best .378, and scored 136 runs while collecting 232 hits. Although it could not honestly be said that he was among the five or six best players in the game for most of his career, he certainly was in those two seasons. And he was clearly among the ten best players in the game from 1929 to 1936.

During his career, Averill only led the league in triples and hits once each, but he finished with more than 100 runs batted in five times, and with more than 100 runs scored in nine of his ten full seasons. Even though the All-Star game was not played in any of Averill's first four big league seasons, he was still selected to the All-Star Team six times. He also fared very well in the MVP voting, finishing in the top 10 four times, and in the top five on three of those occasions.

Larry Doby

Jackie Robinson is widely remembered, among other things, for being the first black player to play in the major leagues. For some reason, however, Larry Doby never received the credit he deserved for being the first black man to play in the American League. In fact, while Robinson spent one season in the Brooklyn Dodgers farm system prior to joining the big league club in 1947, Doby was the first player to go directly from the Negro Leagues to the majors, joining the Cleveland Indians just 11 weeks after Robinson began playing for the Dodgers.

Doby played second base for the Newark Eagles for four seasons and teamed with shortstop Monte Irvin to form one of the most talented double-play combinations in Negro League history. In his final season with Newark, in 1946, Doby batted .341 and led the Eagles to the league championship. However, when he joined the Cleveland Indians the following season he was quickly converted into a centerfielder. With Cleveland, he went on to lead the league in home runs twice and in runs batted in, runs scored, on-base percentage and slugging percentage once each. He knocked in more than 100 runs five times, and scored more than 100 runs three times. Over the course of his 13 major league seasons, Doby hit 253 home runs, drove in 970 runs, scored 960 others, and batted .283. He was selected to the American League All-Star Team seven times and finished in the top 10 in the MVP voting twice.

On the surface, it would seem that Doby's Hall of Fame credentials are modest ones and that he should be thought of as a borderline Hall of Famer, at best. However, consider the following:

- He was the first black man to play in the American League.
- He was the first player to go from the Negro Leagues straight to the majors.
- He was the first black player to hit a home run in the World Series.
- He was the first player to win championships in the Negro Leagues and the major leagues.
- He was the first black player to win a home run title in the majors.
- He was the first black player to win an RBI title in the American League.

Todd Bolton, an authority on the Negro Leagues and a researcher for the Society for American Baseball Research, said of Doby, "I don't think Lary ever got the credit he deserved for going through what he did. He's been on the backburner."

All things considered, while Lary Doby was not a truly great player, his selection by the Veterans Committee in 1998 was a pretty good one.

Cristobal Torriente/Willard Brown

Many observers felt that both Torriente and Brown wasted a good deal of their tremendous natural ability. But both men were among the most talented players in Negro League history, with some extremely impressive Hall of Fame credentials.

Cristobal Torriente is generally considered to be the greatest Cuban position player of the first half of the 20th century, and is arguably the greatest Cuban player ever. A five-tool player, Torriente also pitched on occasion during his 16-year Negro League career, spent predominantly with the Cuban Stars. Possessing fine speed, good hands, and a strong throwing arm, Torriente is said to have been an excellent defensive player. In addition to playing the outfield and pitching, he also played second base and third base during his career, an extremely unusual feat considering Torriente was a lefthanded thrower.

But it was Torriente's hitting on which he built his reputation. Known as a "bad-ball" hitter and nicknamed the "Cuban Strongman" for his broad shoulders, the lefthanded Torriente drove the ball with power to all fields. He holds the record for the highest lifetime batting average in Cuban League play, with a mark of .350, and led that league in every batting category in both 1919 and 1920. He batted over .400 once for the Cuban Stars of the Negro Leagues, and surpassed the .300-mark at least seven other times. Various sources have him hitting somewhere between .333 and .339 over the course of his Negro League career. He won three Negro National League championships as a member of the Chicago American Giants.

Torriente had two things working against him in the analysis of his Hall of Fame credentials. First, his fondness for alcohol and high living in general caused his physical skills to deteriorate rapidly. As a result, Torriente was an exceptional player for a relatively brief amount of time. In addition, the statistics for the first half of his career are extremely limited due to the lack of an organized Negro League at that point. Nevertheless, Torriente's reputation as arguably the greatest Cuban player in history is difficult to ignore. We will, therefore, assume that his 2006 induction into Cooperstown was a valid one.

Willard Brown was one of the most talented athletes ever to play in the Negro Leagues. He was exceptionally fast in the field, a good baserunner, and an excellent outfielder with a good throwing arm. Brown was most famous, though, for being black baseball's premier home-run hitter of the 1940s. The free-swinging Brown was a notorious bad-ball hitter who, using a 40-ounce bat, hit with power to all fields. Playing in the western-based Negro American League, Brown won seven home-run crowns during his 13-year career, which was interrupted for two seasons by World War II. More than just a slugger, Brown also captured three batting titles, leading the league with averages of .371 in 1937, .356 in 1938, and .333 in 1941. He played on the great Kansas City Monarch teams that won five NAL pennants between 1937 and 1942, and ended his career with a .355 lifetime batting average and six Negro League All-Star Game appearances.

Unfortunately, Brown failed in his one brief trial period in the major leagues. Signed by St. Louis Browns owner Bill Veeck during the 1947 campaign, the 36-year-old Brown batted only .179 in 21 games, before being released by St. Louis. Yet, he managed to hit one home run for the Browns, the first ever by a black player in the American League. Many attributed Brown's lack of success in St. Louis to the fact that he jumped directly from the Negro Leagues to the majors, without the same sort of minor-league adjustment period earlier accorded Jackie Robinson with the Dodgers.

Regardless of Brown's failure at the major-league level, there can be no questioning his ability. Tommy Lasorda said, "Willard Brown was one of the greatest hitters I ever saw." The one thing that others often questioned about Brown, though, was his desire. Many observers felt he never fully lived up to his potential since he lacked drive. They viewed him as someone who loved to play in front of large crowds, but who was also lazy, stubborn, and lackadaisical at times.

Speaking of Brown, one former Negro League player, Quincy Trouppe, said, "He could have been a great ball player. He could hit the long ball, but he was so doggone triflin'! He would walk to the outfield...sometimes causing the pitcher to wait to throw the first pitch. He could hit the ball to rightfield, centerfield, leftfield. He was a great hitter."

But Buck O'Neil, who played with Brown and later managed him, said, "Willard was so talented, he didn't look as if he was hustling. Willard Brown stole bases standing up; he didn't slide because he didn't have to. He could do all the things in baseball—hit, run, field, throw, and hit for power...But Willard was like Hank Aaron—you always thought he could do a little more. Both Brown and Aaron were so talented, they didn't look as if they were hustling. Everything looked so easy for them."

Whether or not Willard Brown ever played up to his great ability is subject to conjecture. However, he clearly accomplished enough during his playing career to earn his place in Cooperstown.

Max Carey

The National League's top centerfielder, leadoff hitter, and base-stealer for much of the second decade of the 20th century, and for part of the third, was the Pittsburgh Pirates Max Carey. From 1911 to 1925, Carey was the Pirates' regular centerfielder, and in many of those seasons, the best player in the league at that position. He certainly was in 1912, 1913, and from 1922 to 1925. In 1912, he batted .302, scored 114 runs, and stole 45 bases. The following year, Carey batted .277, scored 99 runs, and led the league with 61 stolen bases. From 1922 to 1925, he batted well over .300 three times, scored well over 100 runs each season, and stole no fewer than 46 bases. His finest season came in 1922 when he batted .329, scored a career-high 140 runs, collected 207 hits, stole 51 bases, and established career bests in home runs (10) and runs batted in (70).

During his career, Carey led the league in stolen bases 10 times en route to finishing with 738 steals, a figure good enough to place him in the top 10 all-time. He was also a league-leader in triples twice, and in runs scored once. Carey batted over .300 six times, scored more than 100 runs five times, stole more than 50 bases six times, and was one of the finest defensive centerfielders the game has seen. In fact, during his career, only Tris Speaker was thought to be his superior as a defensive centerfielder.

However, Carey was never considered to be one of the very best players in the game, or even one of the five or six best outfielders. Among centerfielders alone, he was always rated well behind both Speaker and Ty Cobb as an all-around player, and was thought to be more on a level with the Cincinnati Reds' Edd Roush, a borderline Hall of Famer, at best. Although he did spend a large portion of his career playing in the Deadball era, Carey's lifetime batting average of .285 is not particularly impressive.

Nevertheless, if Carey's greatest strengths are emphasized, he becomes a viable Hall of Fame candidate. He was the National League's top base-stealer of his time, only slightly less prolific in that area than Ty Cobb. He was an outstanding leadoff hitter, tallying 1,545 runs and collecting 2,665 hits during his career, as well as finishing with a solid .361 on-base percentage. In addition, Carey is considered by most baseball historians to be among the finest defensive centerfielders in baseball history. All things considered, Carey was a borderline Hall of Famer. Though not a truly great player, he excelled in enough areas of the game to have his 1961 election by the Veterans Committee viewed with only minor skepticism.

Kirby Puckett

Kirby Puckett's election to the Hall of Fame by the BBWAA in 2001, in his first year of eligibility, symbolized the degree to which the Hall's standards have dropped over the years. It isn't that Puckett wasn't a fine player whose career numbers did not merit a great deal of consideration by the voters. His selection was not a particularly bad one. However, Puckett's election in his very first year of eligibility can be looked upon as a slight to the earlier greats who failed to gain admittance to Cooperstown the first time their names appeared on the ballot. There is little doubt that Puckett's tremendous popularity with both the media and the fans facilitated his speedy induction. But the fact remains that he had only three truly "dominant" seasons during a career that was ended prematurely by an eye injury. Let's take a closer look at his qualifications.

Puckett played 12 seasons for the Minnesota Twins, from 1984 to 1995. He finished with an outstanding .318 batting average and 2,304 hits. He batted over .300 eight times, topping the .330-mark on three occasions. Puckett hit more than 20 homers six times, drove in over 100 runs three times, scored more than 100 runs three times, and collected more than 200 hits five times. He won a batting title, and also led the league in hits four times. He was selected to the American League All-Star Team nine times, and he finished in the top 10 in the MVP voting six times, making it into the top five on three occasions.

However, it should be noted that Puckett played during a relatively good era for hitters, in one of the best-hitting ballparks in the major leagues—Minnesota's Metrodome. It's artificial surface and relatively shallow outfield fences greatly inflated Puckett's numbers, padding his batting average, home run, and RBI totals considerably. To illustrate the degree to which the Metrodome affected Puckett's offensive statistics, here are the numbers he compiled during his career playing at home and on the road:

	AB	HITS	RUNS	2B	3B	HR	RBI	AVG	OBP	SLG PCT
HOME	3,689	1,269	626	239	38	113	600	.344	.388	.521
AWAY	3,555	1,035	445	175	19	94	485	.291	.331	.430

Clearly, Puckett was a much better player in Minnesota than he was everywhere else. In virtually the same number of at-bats, he finished well ahead in every offensive category playing at home. In particular, note the huge discrepancies in batting average, on-base percentage, slugging percentage, hits, and runs scored. It would, therefore, not be totally unreasonable to conclude that Puckett was a somewhat overrated player.

Using our Hall of Fame criteria, Puckett was never considered to be either the best player in baseball or the best player in his league. He was, however, considered to be among the five or six best players in the game, and the best centerfielder in baseball, in at least a few seasons. In 1988, 1992, and 1994 he was clearly among the game's best players, and arguably the best centerfielder in the majors. In the first of those seasons, he hit 24 home runs, knocked in 121 runs, batted .356, scored 109 runs, and collected 234 hits. In 1992, he hit 19 homers, drove in 110 runs, batted .329, scored 104 runs, and totaled 210 hits. In 1994, he finished with 20 homers and 112 RBIs, and batted .317. Puckett also had outstanding seasons in 1986, 1987, 1989, and 1991 that made him the best centerfielder in the American League. We saw earlier that he fared well in the MVP voting, and that he was selected to nine All-Star teams. He was also a league-leader in a major offensive category five times, and he was a major contributor to his team's success, helping Minnesota to two world championships. So, overall, Puckett does rather well in these areas.

Consider, however, that his career statistics are actually quite comparable to those compiled by two other players who were even more dominant in their primes, yet who are not in the Hall of Fame. Those two players were Tony Oliva and Don Mattingly.

Let's take a look at the numbers of all three players:

PLAYER	AB	HITS	RUNS	2B	3B	HR	RBI	AVG	SB	OBP	SLG PCT
Tony Oliva	6,301	1,917	870	329	48	220	947	.304	86	.353	.476
Kirby Puckett	7,244	2,304	1,071	414	57	207	1,085	.318	134	.360	.477
Don Mattingly	7,003	2,153	1,007	440	20	222	1,099	.307	14	.358	.471

Mattingly's numbers are amazingly similar, and he was a contemporary of Puckett. In addition, he won an MVP Award (something Puckett never did), he was considered to be the best player in baseball at his position for at least four years (1984-1987), and he was considered by many to be the best player in the game from 1985 to 1987.

Oliva, in almost 1,000 fewer at-bats, put up numbers that were quite comparable to those of Puckett. Furthermore, he played during the 1960s and 1970s, a period during which it was far more difficult to compile outstanding offensive numbers. Oliva also played for the same team as Puckett, but in a different ballpark that was far less advantageous to hitters. He was considered to be one of the very best players in the American League, and he was arguably its finest hitter for much of his career. Indeed, a look at the batting statistics compiled by Oliva during his career while playing at home, and on the road, indicate just how good a hitter he was:

	AB	HITS	RUNS	2B	3B	HR	RBI	AVG	OBP	SLG PCT
HOME	3,075	935	443	161	28	95	433	.304	.357	.467
AWAY	3,226	982	428	168	20	125	514	.304	.350	.485

These numbers not only illustrate that Oliva was an extremely consistent hitter, but they also indicate that he didn't have the "home-field advantage" that Puckett had throughout his career. Thus, it could be argued that Oliva, who was also a good outfielder and a fine baserunner, was actually a better player than Puckett. Yet, for some reason, Puckett was elected to the Hall of Fame in his first year of eligibility while both Oliva and Mattingly have received only minimal support. Perhaps the reason for this lies in the fact that Puckett played on two world championship teams while neither Oliva nor Mattingly was fortunate enough to have done so. Furthermore, Puckett was an outstanding player right to the end, while Oliva and Mattingly both experienced a considerable drop-off in performance after their early years of dominance. Whatever the reason, though, it is something of an injustice that Puckett was ushered into the Hall with such alacrity while the other two men remain on the outside looking in. Once again, this is not to suggest that Oliva and Mattingly should be elected, although, in truth, neither man would be a particularly bad choice. However, the thing I am suggesting is that perhaps Puckett's qualifications should have been considered a little more carefully before he was voted in. In any case, he should be viewed more as a borderline Hall of Famer than as an automatic, first-time selection.

Hack Wilson

During his 12-year major league career, Hack Wilson played for the Giants, Cubs, Dodgers, and Phillies. It was with the Cubs that he had his finest seasons, leading the National League in home runs four times, and in runs batted in and slugging percentage twice each between 1926 and 1930. His 1929 and 1930 seasons were both superb, as he hit 39 home runs, drove in 159 runs, scored another 135, and batted .345 in the first of those years, and hit 56 homers, knocked in an all-time record 191 runs, scored 146 others, and batted .356 in the second. Over the course of his career, Wilson hit more than 30 homers four times, drove in more than 100 runs six times, batted over .300 five times, and scored more than 100 runs three times.

However, Wilson was a full-time player for only six seasons, compiling as many as 400 at-bats only those six times. He had those tremendous 1929 and 1930 campaigns, along with another four very good ones. But he failed to hit more than 13 home runs, knock in more than 61 runs, score more than 66 runs, or bat any higher than .295 in any other year. In addition, Wilson, with his squatty frame and beer-barrel chest (he stood only 5'6" and weighed over 200 pounds), was not particularly fleet afoot, and was generally considered to be a below-average outfielder.

Using our Hall of Fame criteria, Wilson was never considered to be the best player in baseball, but it could be said that, in his two finest seasons, he was ranked among the top two or three players in the National League (along with Chuck Klein and Mel Ott in 1929, and Klein and Bill Terry in 1930). He also would have been ranked among the game's elite players those two seasons. It could also be argued that he was the best centerfielder in the National League from 1926 to 1930. However, Wilson certainly was not one of the ten best centerfielders in the history of the game, nor was he the best player in the game at his position for more than two seasons.

Wilson finished in the top 10 in the MVP voting four times, even though the award was not presented in 1930, his greatest season. However, he never finished any higher than fifth in the balloting. We have already seen that he led his league in some major offensive category eight times during his career. He did help the Cubs to the National League pennant in 1929, but, if anything, he was probably not as good as his statistics indicate. He was not a good defensive player or baserunner, and he had a drinking problem and a surly disposition that made him unpopular with most of his teammates, and that eventually shortened his career.

Thus, overall, it would seem that Wilson does no better than average on the Hall of Fame criteria board. Let's look at his career numbers next to those of Earl Averill, a legitimate Hall of Famer whose career overlapped with Wilson's:

PLAYER	AB	HITS	RUNS	2B	3B	HR	RBI	AVG	SB	OBP	SLG PCT
Earl Averill	6,353	2,019	1,224	401	128	238	1,164	.318	70	.395	.534
Hack Wilson	4,760	1,461	884	266	67	244	1,062	.307	52	.395	.545

Due to the relative brevity of both players' careers, the numbers they posted are not particularly overwhelming. In most categories, they are actually fairly similar, although Averill does have a sizeable lead in runs scored, doubles, and triples. However, Averill was a better outfielder and a more complete player. If he is viewed as being a legitimate Hall of Famer, but not an obvious choice, how should Wilson be viewed? That really all depends on how liberal approach one wishes to take in considering potential Hall of Fame candidates. While Wilson was an outstanding player for a few seasons, he truly did not have a Hall of Fame type career. Nor, with the exception of two years, was he ever a *great* player. The feeling here is that the Veterans Committee's 1979 selection of Wilson was not a particularly bad one, but was one that probably should not have been made.

Richie Ashburn

It was Richie Ashburn's fate to play in the major leagues during an era in which some of the greatest centerfielders in baseball history were performing for other teams. His first year with the Philadelphia Phillies was 1948, when a man named DiMaggio was still playing centerfield for the Yankees. One year earlier, Duke Snider was called up by the Dodgers, and three years later, both Willie Mays and Mickey Mantle arrived in the big leagues. As a result, Ashburn was relegated to second-tier status among major league centerfielders throughout most of his career, playing in the shadow of these all-time greats. However, he was a fine player whose career was certainly deserving of Hall of Fame consideration. Let's take a look at his qualifications.

Ashburn was perhaps the finest leadoff hitter of his time, collecting 2,574 hits and scoring 1,322 runs during a career that saw him finish with a .308 batting average and an outstanding .397 on-base percentage. He won two batting titles and also led the National League in on-base percentage and bases on balls four times each, hits three times, triples twice, and stolen bases once. Although he scored more than 100 runs only twice, he topped the 90-mark seven other times. Ashburn batted over .300 in nine of his 15 seasons, topping .330 five times. He collected more than 200 hits three times, stole more than 30 bases twice, and finished in double-digits in triples three times. Ashburn was selected to the All-Star Team five times and was considered to be one of the finest defensive outfielders of his time.

However, due to the presence of Snider and Mays, he was never considered to be the best centerfielder in the National League. Ashburn also finished in the top 10 in the MVP voting only twice during his career. In addition, his overall statistics are actually less impressive than those of Vada Pinson, whose career spanned the entire 1960s and much of the 1970s—less of a hitter's era than when Ashburn played. Here are the numbers of both players:

PLAYER	AB	HITS	RUNS	2B	3B	HR	RBI	AVG	SB	OBP	SLG PCT
Richie Ashburn	8,365	2,574	1,322	317	109	29	586	.308	234	.397	.382
Vada Pinson	9,645	2,757	1,366	485	127	256	1,170	.286	305	.327	.442

While Ashburn finished with a higher batting average and a much higher on-base percentage, Pinson was well ahead in virtually every other offensive category. He hit almost ten times as many home runs as Ashburn and knocked in twice as many runs. Pinson hit more than 20 homers seven times, drove in more than 100 runs twice, scored more than 100 runs four times, batted over .300 four times, and stole more than 20 bases nine times. In addition, he was an excellent outfielder with a much stronger throwing arm than Ashburn. Yet he received only minimal support during his eligibility period.

Why, then, was Ashburn elected instead of Pinson? Ashburn was very popular and stayed around the game much longer than Pinson. After his career ended, Ashburn became a broadcaster for the Phillies and, as such, became even more popular than he was as a player. While he was a good player, he probably never quite reached the level at which a true Hall of Famer needs to perform. As a result, while his 1995 selection by the Veterans Committee was certainly not the worst one it has ever made, it is one that should be looked upon with a great deal of skepticism.

Edd Roush

During his 18-year major league career, Edd Roush played for five different teams, but it was with the Cincinnati Reds that he had his finest seasons. Playing for the Reds from 1916 to 1926, Roush failed to hit over .300 only once. In fact, over that 11-year stretch, he batted at least .321 ten times, surpassing the .340 mark on five different occasions. He won the National League batting title two times, in both 1917 and 1919, with averages of .341 and .321, respectively. He also led the league in triples and doubles once each. Roush batted over .300 thirteen times during his career, stole more than 20 bases six times, and finished in double-digits in triples eleven times. He was the best centerfielder in the National League from 1917 to 1921.

However, at no point during his career was Roush considered to be the best centerfielder in the game, or even among the five best players in his league. The American League's Ty Cobb and Tris Speaker were always rated well above him and, for much of his career, he was also ranked behind the Pittsburgh Pirates' Max Carey, who, as we saw earlier, was a borderline Hall of Famer himself. A look at the career numbers of Carey and Roush indicates how tenuous the latter's status as a legitimate Hall of Famer really is:

PLAYER	AB	HITS	RUNS	2B	3B	HR	RBI	AVG	SB	OBP	SLG PCT
Max Carey	9,363	2,665	1,545	419	159	70	800	.285	738	.361	.386
Edd Roush	7,363	2,376	1,099	339	182	68	981	.323	268	.369	.446

Roush compiled a much higher batting average and slugging percentage than Carey. He also drove in more runs, collected more triples, and hit virtually the same number of home runs in 2,000 fewer at-bats. However, Carey's overall numbers were more impressive. He finished with almost 300 more hits and almost 450 more runs scored than Roush, and he also stole almost three times as many bases. In addition, Carey walked much more frequently than Roush, thereby finishing with an on-base percentage that was nearly as good. As a leadoff hitter, Carey's primary job was to get on base and score a lot of runs, two things he did very well. Since he was batting at the top of the order, he could not be expected to drive in as many runs as Roush, who usually batted in the middle of his team's lineup. Therefore, the discrepancy in their RBI totals is really insignificant. Carey was also the better outfielder of the two.

In addition, Roush knocked in as many as 90 runs only once during his career, reaching the 80-mark only two other times. He never scored more than 95 runs in a season, and he scored as many as 80 runs only six times. Having many of his best years during the 1920s at a time when runs were being scored at a record pace, Roush was simply not a big run-producer. While he did hit for some high batting averages during the decade, the figures he posted did not exceed the league norm by enough to compensate for his lack of productivity. When compared to the numbers accumulated by other players of his era who were legitimate Hall of Famers, Roush's totals pale by comparison. In short, Roush was a good player, but he just did not accomplish enough during his career to merit his 1962 selection by the Veterans Committee.

Earle Combs

The centerfielder and leadoff hitter for the team many people still consider to be the greatest in baseball history—the 1927 New York Yankees—was Earle Combs. He played 12 seasons for the Yankees, from 1924 to 1935, but that 1927 season was his finest. Combs established career-highs in batting average (.356), hits (231), and triples (23) that magical year, while also scoring

137 runs and fulfilling his role as leadoff hitter better than perhaps anyone else in the game. He also had outstanding seasons in 1925, 1929, 1930, and 1932, never batting any lower than .321 or scoring less than 117 runs in any of those seasons, and scoring a career-high 143 runs in 1932.

During his career, Combs led the American League in triples three times and in hits once. He finished with more than 20 triples three times, batted over .300 ten times, topping the .340-mark on four separate occasions, collected more than 200 hits three times, and scored more than 100 runs eight times. In each of his nine full seasons, he finished in double-digits in triples.

The problem with Combs, though, was that he was a full-time player for only those nine seasons. His career was relatively short, and in three of his 12 seasons, he failed to accumulate as many as 300 at-bats, totaling only 417 plate appearances in a fourth campaign. A player with such a short career must be truly dominant in order to be thought of as a legitimate Hall of Fame candidate. While Combs was a fine player, he was not a dominant one. He was never considered to be among the very best players in the game, or even in his own league. He was the best centerfielder in the American League in only 1925 and 1927, being ranked behind Earl Averill for most of his career, and he was never thought to be the best player in the game at his position. Combs finished in the top 10 in the MVP voting only once, and he was a league-leader in a major offensive category only four times. In addition, playing in an era during which big offensive numbers were rather commonplace, he had only five seasons that even remotely resembled those of a legitimate Hall of Famer. His offensive numbers were somewhat inflated by the era in which he played, and by the team for which he played. Combs' status as New York's leadoff hitter enabled him to precede Babe Ruth and Lou Gehrig in the Yankee lineup for virtually his entire career. Batting in front of two of the greatest run-producers in the history of the game unquestionably enabled Combs to score many more runs than he otherwise would have.

There is also little doubt that the aura of the 1927 Yankees contributed significantly to Combs' selection by the Veterans

Committee in 1970. There is no question that Combs had an integral role on that team, and that he was a very good player. But his career was too short, and he was not dominant enough to allow us to overlook that last fact. Therefore, his selection by the Committee was one that probably should never have been made.

Lloyd Waner

Prior to both players being dealt to other clubs at the end of the 1940 season, Lloyd Waner spent 14 years playing alongside his older brother Paul in the Pittsburgh Pirates' outfield. While Paul usually batted either third or fourth in the Pirates' lineup, Lloyd was the leadoff hitter for much of his career, and was one of the better ones in the game.

The younger of the Waner brothers batted over .300 ten times, finishing his career with a .316 batting average. He collected more than 200 hits four times and scored more than 100 runs three times. He led the National League in hits, runs scored, and triples once each. Waner's first three seasons were his best. In 1927, he batted .355, scored 133 runs, and collected 223 hits. The following year, he finished with a batting average of .335, 121 runs scored, and 221 base hits. Waner had probably his finest season in 1929, though. That year, he batted .353 and established career-highs in runs scored (134), hits (234), triples (20), and runs batted in (74).

Those first three seasons, however, turned out to be the only truly exceptional ones Waner had during his career. Playing mostly during a hitter's era, he never again batted any higher than .333, scored more than 90 runs, or knocked in more than 57 runs, and he had only one other season with more than 200 hits. Waner had absolutely no power, never hitting more than five home runs in a season, and he stole only 67 bases during his career. In addition, due to the fact that he hardly ever walked (his single-season high was only 40), his career on-base percentage was a modest .349—not particularly high for a leadoff hitter. As a result, he was not an exceptionally good run-producer.

Waner was never considered to be one of the very best players in his league, and he was never thought to be among the top two or three centerfielders in the game. He finished in the top 10 in the MVP voting only one time, and he was generally considered to be only the third or fourth best player on his own team (behind his brother, Paul, Pie Traynor, and, later, Arky Vaughan).

If the selection of Earle Combs to the Hall of Fame was not a particularly good one, Waner's selection was downright puzzling. Take a look at the career numbers of both players:

PLAYER	AB	HITS	RUNS	2B	3B	HR	RBI	AVG	SB	OBP	SLG PCT
Earle Combs	5,746	1,866	1,186	309	154	58	632	.325	96	.397	.462
Lloyd Waner	7,772	2,459	1,201	281	118	27	598	.316	67	.353	.393

The two men played at essentially the same time, albeit in different leagues. While it is true that Combs had a better supporting cast in New York, the Pirate teams that Waner played for usually had a potent lineup as well. In approximately 2,000 fewer at-bats, Combs finished well ahead of Waner in virtually every offensive category. He was clearly the better player of the two. Therefore, if Combs' selection is looked upon as being a bad one, what does that say for the selection of Waner? He clearly does not belong in the Hall of Fame.

RIGHTFIELDERS (24)

PLAYER	YEARS	ELECTED BY	YEAR ELECTED
Mike "King" Kelly	1878-1893	Veterans Committee	1945
Tommy McCarthy	1884-1896	Veterans Committee	1946
Sam Thompson	1885-1898	Veterans Committee	1974
Willie Keeler	1892-1910	BBWAA	1939
Elmer Flick	1898-1910	Veterans Committee	1963
Sam Crawford	1899-1917	Veterans Committee	1957
Harry Hooper	1909-1925	Veterans Committee	1971
Harry Heilmann	1914-1930,32	BBWAA	1952
Babe Ruth	1914-1935	BBWAA	1936
Sam Rice	1915-1934	Veterans Committee	1963
Ross Youngs	1917-1926	Veterans Committee	1972
Kiki Cuyler	1921-1938	Veterans Committee	1968
Martin Dihigo	1923-1945	Negro Leagues Committee	1977
Paul Waner	1926-1945	BBWAA	1952
Mel Ott	1926-1947	BBWAA	1951
Chuck Klein	1928-1944	Veterans Committee	1980
Enos Slaughter	1938-42,46-59	Veterans Committee	1985
Al Kaline	1953-1974	BWAA	1980
Hank Aaron	1954-1976	BBWAA	1982
Roberto Clemente	1955-1972	BBWAA	1973

PLAYER	YEARS	ELECTED BY	YEAR ELECTED
Frank Robinson	1956-1976	BBWAA	1982
Reggie Jackson	1967-1987	BBWAA	1993
Dave Winfield	1973-1995	BBWAA	2001
Tony Gwynn	1982-2001	BBWAA	2007

Babe Ruth/Hank Aaron

Ruth and Aaron were not only the two greatest rightfielders in the history of the game, but were among the very greatest players in baseball history.

Babe Ruth was the greatest, most dominant player of all time. He dominated his era as no other player ever has, and he was undoubtedly the most famous player who ever lived. Perhaps the most amazing thing about Ruth, though, is that if he hadn't been converted from a starting pitcher into an outfielder early in his career to take greater advantage of his hitting skills, he likely would have eventually made it into the Hall of Fame as a *pitcher*. After all, starting for the Boston Red Sox from 1916 to 1918, Ruth was acknowledged to be the best lefthanded pitcher in the game. However, it was as a hitter that he gained his greatest fame.

Ruth was the greatest offensive performer the game has ever seen, setting numerous records, most of which have since been broken. No other player has, by himself, hit more home runs in a season than *entire teams*, a feat that Ruth accomplished on more than one occasion. From 1918 to 1931, he led the American League in home runs and slugging percentage 12 times each, in runs batted in six times, in batting average once, in runs scored eight times, in walks 11 times, and in on-base percentage 10 times. He ranks among the all-time leaders in home runs, runs batted in, runs scored, batting average, walks, and on-base percentage, and his career slugging percentage of .690 is 56 points higher than that of Ted Williams, who, at .634, is second on the all-time list.

Ruth missed extensive playing time in 1922 due to a suspension, and again in 1925, due to an illness. However, in every other season from 1920 to 1931, he was either the very best player in the game, or among the top two or three. He won an MVP Award and was selected to *The Sporting News All-Star Team* each season from 1926 to 1931, the first six years that publication announced its selections. No other player deserves to be in the Hall of Fame more than Ruth.

For quite some time, Hank Aaron was one of the most overlooked superstars ever to play in the major leagues. His low-key personality certainly contributed to his virtual anonymity, as did the fact that he spent the first half of his career playing in Milwaukee, while contemporaries Willie Mays and Mickey Mantle performed in much larger media markets. Only towards the end of his career as he drew inexorably closer to Babe Ruth's cherished home run record did Aaron begin to garner the attention he so richly deserved. It was also only then that people began to realize that he was one of the five greatest players who ever lived.

Aaron's name is all over the record books: first all-time in runs batted in and total bases; second in home runs, third in runs scored and base hits; ninth in doubles. While he never had one particular year that could be identified as his signature season, Aaron was a study in long-term excellence, putting up outstanding numbers year after year. Aaron led the National League in home runs, runs batted in, doubles, and slugging percentage four times each, in runs scored three times, and in batting average and base hits twice each. He was named the National League's Most Valuable Player in 1957, when he led the Braves to the world championship by leading the league in homers (44), runs batted in (132), and runs scored (118), while batting .322. He finished in the top five in the MVP voting seven other times.

Aaron was a superb player for virtually his entire career, and he was one of the five best players in baseball from 1957 to 1971. In several of those seasons, he was the best player in the game. He was particularly outstanding in 1957, 1959, 1960, 1962, 1963, 1966, 1967, and 1971. In each of those years, Aaron knocked in well over 100 runs, compiled a batting average that either approached or exceeded .300, hit no fewer than 39 homers, and scored over

100 runs (except for 1971, when he crossed the plate 95 times). Unfortunately, it seems that only over the past two decades have people come to realize how great a player Hank Aaron was.

Frank Robinson/Roberto Clemente

Robinson and Clemente were also superb players whose Hall of Fame credentials would not be questioned by anyone.

While Hank Aaron's excellence was overlooked for much of his career, Frank Robinson is someone who still does not get the credit he deserves for being one of the greatest players in baseball history. Robinson is sixth on the all-time home run list, with 586, and he also ranks in the top 10 in total bases. He finished his career with 1,812 runs batted in, 1,829 runs scored, and 2,943 hits. Even in this age of free agency when players change teams and leagues so frequently, Robinson remains the only player in baseball history to win the Most Valuable Player Award in each league. During his career, Robinson finished in the top five in the MVP voting a total of six times. He was also a 12-time All-Star.

Robinson was one of the best players in the game in virtually every season from his rookie year of 1956 to 1969. His most outstanding years were 1959, 1961, 1962, 1965, and 1966—all seasons in which he was among the two or three best players in baseball. In each of those campaigns, he hit no fewer than 33 home runs, knocked in well over 100 runs, batted well over .300 (except for 1965, when he batted .296), and scored well over 100 runs. In his first MVP season of 1961, he was the league's best player as he led the Cincinnati Reds to the National League pennant by hitting 37 homers, knocking in 124 runs, and batting .323. The following year, his numbers were even better as he hit 39 homers, drove in 136 runs, batted .342, and led the league with 51 doubles, 134 runs scored, an on-base percentage of .424, and a slugging percentage of .624. Robinson was baseball's greatest player in 1966, after switching leagues prior to the start of the season. He captured the American League triple crown and his second Most Valuable Player Award en route to leading the Baltimore Orioles to the world championship. That year, Robinson led the league with

49 homers, 122 RBIs, a .316 batting average, 122 runs scored, an on-base percentage of .415, and a slugging percentage of .637.

In addition to being a great player, Robinson was also an exceptional team leader and a fierce competitor. Although he is not always viewed as such, Robinson was one of the 15 greatest position players in the history of the game.

For virtually all of the 1960s, and even into the early '70s, Roberto Clemente was one of the five best players in baseball. He finished the decade of the sixties with the highest batting average of any player during that ten-year period, with a mark of .328. During his career, Clemente won four batting titles, hitting over .350 three times, and topping the .340 mark two other times. He batted over .300 in 14 of his 18 big league seasons, finishing his career with a .317 batting average. He also collected 3,000 hits, compiling as many as 200 safeties in a season four times, and leading the league in that department twice.

Though somewhat overshadowed earlier in his career by Hank Aaron, Al Kaline, Roger Maris, and Frank Robinson, by the mid-sixties Clemente established himself as a truly great player who only Aaron and Robinson could challenge for supremacy among major league rightfielders. Although Robinson was the best player in the game in 1966, Clemente was a close second. Establishing career highs in home runs (29), runs batted in (119), and runs scored (105), while also batting .317 that year, Clemente was named the National League's Most Valuable Player. The following year, he finished in the top five in the MVP voting once more, and only Carl Yastrzemski's triple crown season for the Red Sox prevented him from being the best player in baseball. That season, Clemente finished with 23 home runs, 110 runs batted in, 103 runs scored, 209 hits, and a major league leading batting average of .357. In all, he finished in the top five in the MVP voting four times during his career.

Of course, Clemente was more than just a great hitter. He was perhaps the finest defensive rightfielder in baseball history. He had great range and a powerful and accurate throwing arm. During his career, Clemente was the winner of 12 straight Gold Gloves; only

Al Kaline rivaled him defensively among players at the position. In addition, Clemente was a tremendous postseason performer. He hit safely in each of the 14 World Series games in which he played, leading the Pirates to Series victories in 1960, over the Yankees, and in 1971, over the Orioles. In that 1971 Series, Clemente hit two homers, batted .414, had 12 hits, and gave a memorable performance in rightfield to earn Series MVP honors.

Harry Heilmann

Many players posted impressive offensive numbers during the hitting-dominated 1920s. However, one player whose numbers surpassed those of almost every other major leaguer during that period was the Detroit Tigers' Harry Heilmann. From 1921 to 1927, Heilmann was one of the four or five best players in the American League, and one of the very best players in baseball. With the exception of Babe Ruth, he was the best rightfielder in the game over that stretch. In fact, with Ruth missing good portions of both the 1922 and 1925 seasons, Heilmann was the best player at that position in each of those years. During that seven-year period, he won four batting titles, never hit less than .346, topped the .390 mark four times, and batted over .400 once. He also led the league in doubles and hits one time each.

During his career, Heilmann knocked in over 100 runs eight times, and he also scored more than 100 runs four times. He finished in double-digits in triple nine times, collected more than 40 doubles eight times, and amassed more than 200 hits four times. He finished his career with 183 home runs, 1,539 runs batted in, 1,291 runs scored, 151 triples, 542 doubles, and a superb .342 batting average. He also fared well in the MVP voting, finishing in the top 10 five times and placing in the top five on four separate occasions.

While it is true that Heilmann's numbers were somewhat inflated by playing predominantly during a hitter's era, it is also true that he was one of the most outstanding hitters of that era, and one of the best players of his day. His election to Cooperstown, therefore, is one that cannot be questioned.

Tony Gwynn

In his 20 seasons with the San Diego Padres, Tony Gwynn established himself as the finest scientific hitter of his era, and as one of the best ever. He finished his career with 3,141 base hits and a batting average of .338, the highest of any player whose career began after 1940, and the highest since Ted Williams retired with a mark of .344. During his career, Gwynn won seven batting titles and also led the National League in hits six times, and in runs scored twice. Gwynn batted over .350 seven times and collected more than 200 hits five times. He was not a tremendous run-producer, having surpassed the 100-RBI mark only once, and topping 100 runs scored only twice in his 20 big-league seasons. However, the fact that the Padres were a mediocre team for most of Gwynn's career is largely responsible for his inability to compile huge numbers in either of those offensive categories.

Although Gwynn batted .394 in the strike-shortened 1994 campaign, and also batted .370 while scoring a career-high 119 runs in 1987, his most productive season was 1997. That year, Gwynn established career highs in home runs (17), runs batted in (119), hits (220), and doubles (49), while batting .372. In each of those three seasons, Gwynn was arguably the best rightfielder in the game, and among its top five players. He was also clearly among the game's elite in 1989, 1993, and 1995, never hitting any lower than .336 in any of those years. In all, Gwynn was selected to 15 All-Star teams and finished in the top 10 in the league MVP voting a total of seven times, placing as high as third in 1984.

In addition to being a superb hitter, Gwynn was a solid outfielder and a good baserunner, winning five Gold Gloves and stealing more than 30 bases four times in the early stages of his career. His 2007 induction into Cooperstown, in his first year of eligibility, was well-deserved.

Mel Ott/Paul Waner/Chuck Klein

Ott, Waner, and Klein have been grouped together because they all starred in the National League at the same time, and were all clearly deserving of their elections to the Hall of Fame.

The New York Giants Mel Ott was the National League's top slugger for much of the 1930s. Although not on the same level with the American League's Lou Gehrig, Jimmie Foxx, Hank Greenberg, and Joe DiMaggio, Ott was rivaled only by Chuck Klein and Joe Medwick during that decade as the N.L.'s top home run threat. Though diminutive in stature, Ott became one of the game's top home run hitters by learning to pull the ball in order to take full advantage of the Polo Grounds' short rightfield porch. As a result, he led the N.L. in home runs six times, and he also led the league in runs batted in once, walks six times, on-base percentage four times, and runs scored twice.

Though never considered to be one of the four or five best players in baseball, Ott was consistently ranked among the top five players in the National League for much of the 1930s. He was selected to 12 All-Star teams and finished in the top 10 in the MVP voting six times during his career. With Babe Ruth retiring in 1935, and with both Chuck Klein and Paul Waner on the decline, Ott was the best rightfielder in baseball from 1934 to 1939. Over that stretch, he averaged 32 homers, 113 runs batted in, and 109 runs scored, while batting well over .300 in all but one season. During his career, Ott hit more than 30 homers eight times, knocked in and scored more than 100 runs nine times each, and batted over .300 ten times, topping the .320 mark on six different occasions. His most productive season came in 1929, when he established career-highs in home runs (42), runs batted in (151), and runs scored (138), while batting .328. He also had particularly outstanding years in 1930 (25 HR, 119 RBIs, .349 AVG, 122 RUNS), 1932 (38 HR, 123 RBIs, .318 AVG, 119 RUNS), 1934 (35 HR, 135 RBIs, .326 AVG, 119 RUNS), and 1936 (33 HR, 135 RBIs, .328 AVG, 120 RUNS).

On the negative side, Ott's home run totals were greatly inflated by the ballpark in which he played. The friendly rightfield porch at New York's Polo Grounds enabled him to hit 324 of his 511 career homers at home, while hitting only 187 on the road. Therefore, Ott's reputation as a great slugger is somewhat exaggerated. However, he was regarded as being the National League's greatest slugger of the first half of the twentieth century, and as one of the most dominant players of his era.

During his 20-year career, Paul Waner was, in many ways, the Tony Gwynn of his era. Like Gwynn, he did not have a great deal of power, never hitting more than 15 home runs in a season, and knocking in more than 100 runs only twice. However, also like Gwynn, he was a superb line drive hitter who was perhaps the finest scientific hitter of his era.

During his career, Waner won four batting titles and also led the league in runs batted in once, and in triples, doubles, hits, and runs scored twice each. Although not a home run hitter, Waner had some power, as can be evidenced by his ten seasons with at least ten triples, and five seasons with more than 40 doubles. In fact, Waner's career-high in triples was 22 (1926), and he once finished with as many as 62 doubles (1932). He also scored more than 100 runs nine times, collected more than 200 hits eight times, and batted well over .300 in each season, from 1926 to 1937.

Playing for the Pittsburgh Pirates during that 12-year period, Waner was considered to be one of the five best players in the National League in almost every season. He was certainly the league's best rightfielder from 1926 to 1928, compiling averages of .336, .380, and .370, and scoring more than 100 runs in each of those years. He was voted the league's top player in 1927, when he won the Most Valuable Player Award by leading the Pirates to the pennant. That year was Waner's best, as he led the league with 131 runs batted in, 237 hits, and a .380 batting average, while scoring 114 runs and collecting 18 triples. He finished in the top five in the MVP voting three other times.

Waner also fared well in the All-Star voting, being selected to the team four times, even though the game was not played until 1933, his eighth year in the league. Waner finished his career with a .333 batting average, 3,152 hits, 1,309 runs batted in, 1,627 runs scored, 191 triples, and 605 doubles.

There are those who consider Chuck Klein a marginal Hall of Famer due to the fact that he was a dominant player for only five seasons. But, from 1929 to 1933, there was no better all-around player in the game. Over that stretch, he was clearly the best player in the National League, leading the senior circuit in home runs four times, runs batted in twice, batting average once, on-base percentage once, slugging percentage three times, doubles twice, hits twice, and runs scored three times. In fact, for those five years, Klein was so dominant that he rivaled Babe Ruth as the best rightfielder in baseball. Though Ruth was a slightly better player in 1929, 1930, and 1931, by 1932 Klein supplanted the Babe as the game's top player at the position.

The National League did not present a Most Valuable Player Award at the end of either the 1929 or 1930 season, but, had a vote been taken, the Philadelphia Phillies' Klein certainly would have received a great deal of support. In 1929, he hit 43 homers, knocked in 145 runs, batted .356, scored 126 runs, and finished with 219 hits and 45 doubles. The following year, he hit 40 homers, drove in 170 runs, batted .386, scored 158 runs, and collected 250 hits and 59 doubles, while setting a 20th century record for outfielders by accumulating 44 assists. Klein finished in the top five in the MVP voting in each of the next three seasons, winning the award in 1932. That year, he led the league with 38 home runs, 152 runs scored, and 226 base hits, while knocking in 137 runs and batting .348. Although he finished second in the balloting to Giants pitcher Carl Hubbell the following year, Klein won the National League's triple crown by leading the league with 28 homers, 120 runs batted in, and a batting average of .368.

Over the course of his career, Klein topped the 30-homer mark four times, knocked in and scored more than 100 runs six times each, batted over .330 six times, collected more than 200 hits five times, and finished with more than 40 doubles four times. He also accomplished the outstanding feat of collecting more than 400 total bases in a season three times. Unfortunately, after 1933, Klein's productivity was hampered by a series of hamstring pulls and a growing drinking problem that prevented him from accumulating as many as 500 at-bats in a season more than one other time, or being the dominant force he was during his peak seasons. However, while he faltered during the latter stages of his career, he remained a solid player through the 1937 season. Thus, by the time he retired at the end of the 1944 campaign, Klein accumulated 300 home runs, 1,201 runs batted in, and 1,168 runs scored, while compiling a lifetime batting average of .320. Many far less-deserving players were elected to the Hall of Fame prior to the Veterans Committee's selection of Klein in 1980.

Sam Thompson

The greatest slugger and run-producer, and one of the very greatest players of the 19th century, was Sam Thompson. In fact, Thompson was the most prolific player ever at driving in runs, finishing his career with a ratio of .921 runs batted in per game.

With the Detroit Wolverines in 1887, Thompson established a 19th century record by knocking in 166 runs, while scoring another 118, collecting 203 hits, and batting .372. Two years later, with the Philadelphia Phillies, Thompson set another 19th century record by hitting 20 home runs. From 1893 to 1895, he posted batting averages of .370, .407, and .392, respectively, while scoring well over 100 runs each season. In the last of those seasons, he hit 18 home runs and knocked in 165 runs, to come within two homers and one RBI of equaling his own records.

Over the course of his career, Thompson led the league in home runs, runs batted in, doubles, and slugging percentage twice each, hits three times, and batting average and triples once each. He knocked in more than 100 runs eight times, scored more than 100 runs ten times, batted over .370 four times, finished with more than 20 triples three times, and collected more than 200 hits three times. He ended his career with 126 home runs (second among 19th century players to Roger Connor's 138), a .331 batting average, 160 triples, 1,299 runs batted in, and 1,256 runs scored, in just over 1,400 games and slightly less than 6,000 at-bats.

With the possible exceptions of Dan Brouthers and Ed Delahanty, Thompson was the finest all-around hitter of the 19th century and, undoubtedly, one of its five or six greatest players. His selection by the Veterans Committee in 1974 was long overdue.

Willie Keeler

Nobody benefited more from the rules changes that were implemented in the early 1890s than "Wee" Willie Keeler. From his first full season in 1894 up until the 1900 campaign, Keeler never batted any lower than .362. Nor did he collect fewer than 200 hits or score less than 100 runs over that seven-year stretch. Included during that period were seasons in which he compiled batting averages of .424, .386, and .385, hit totals of 239, 219, and 216 (twice), runs scored totals of 165, 162, and 153, and stolen base totals of 67 and 64. Although he had little power, hitting only 33 home runs during his career, Keeler's knack for getting base hits by being able to place the ball where he wanted to, seemingly at will, earned him the nickname of "Hit 'em Where They Ain't."

A superb leadoff hitter, he was surpassed only by the Phillies' Billy Hamilton as a run-scorer and table-setter during the 1890s. Keeler led the league in batting twice, hits three times, and runs scored once. During his career, he batted over .370 six times, scored more than 100 runs eight times, collected more than 200 hits eight times, and stole more than 40 bases five times.

Although the larger strike zone that was implemented at the turn of the century adversely affected "Wee Willie's" offensive output, he remained a solid performer for the next several seasons, never batting below .300 through 1906. Playing primarily for the National League's Baltimore Orioles and Brooklyn Dodgers, and the American League's New York Highlanders (who eventually became the Yankees), Keeler finished his career with a .341 batting average, a .387 on-base percentage, 2,932 base hits, and 1,719 runs scored. He was selected by the BBWAA in the last set of elections that were held prior to the original opening of the Hall in 1939.

Reggie Jackson

Reggie Jackson's inability to finish his career with a batting average any higher than .262, along with his reputation for being a below-average outfielder, kept him from being a truly great player. Both factors could have also very easily prevented him from being elected to the Hall of Fame, as he was, in his first year of eligibility.

Nevertheless, Jackson was one of the best and most dynamic players of his era. As such, he clearly earned his place in Cooperstown.

Reginald Martinez Jackson's 563 career home runs, 1,702 runs batted in, and 1,551 runs scored were probably enough to justify his selection to the Hall of Fame. However, Jackson had many other things going for him. He was one of the most colorful and controversial players of his time, and he was also a tremendous clutch performer. During his career, Jackson played on six pennant-winners and five world-championship teams, and he was one of the best players in postseason history. He is the only player to have been named MVP in two World Series, having led the Oakland A's to the championship in 1973 and the New York Yankees to the title in 1977. In that 1977 Series against the Dodgers, Jackson set World Series records for home runs (5), slugging percentage (.755), runs scored (10), and total bases (25), and became only the second player to hit three home runs in one Series game (Babe Ruth did it twice).

Jackson was also among the five best players in the American League for a good portion of his career, and one of the very best players in the game in several seasons. Jackson's first truly outstanding year was 1969, when, playing for Oakland, he hit 47 home runs, drove in 118 runs, batted .275, and led the league with 123 runs scored. After three less-productive seasons from 1970 to 1972, Jackson reached his apex in 1973. That year, he hit 32 homers, knocked in a league-leading 117 runs, batted .293, and led the league in runs scored and slugging percentage, en route to being named the American League's Most Valuable Player. In virtually every season from 1973 to 1980, Jackson was one of the top five players in the A.L., and also the league's top rightfielder. His outstanding performances in 1973, 1974, 1976, and 1980 were probably good enough to also have him ranked among the five best players in the game.

Jackson finished in the top 10 in the MVP voting seven times, making it into the top five on five separate occasions. He was selected to 14 All-Star teams and led his league in home runs four times, runs batted in once, runs scored twice, and slugging percentage three times. In addition, he was a winner who helped his teams reach their ultimate goal of winning the championship.

Al Kaline/Dave Winfield

Neither Kaline nor Winfield was a truly dominant player. However, both excelled in many different aspects of the game, were exceptional all-around players, and would have to be viewed as being among the very best players of their respective eras.

Al Kaline never hit 30 home runs in a season, knocked in 100 runs only three times, and scored 100 runs only twice. But he was one of the best and most complete players of his time. He could hit for both average and power, and he was an outstanding baserunner. The winner of 10 Gold Gloves, he was also a superb outfielder with a powerful throwing arm.

Playing for the Detroit Tigers, from 1955 to 1963 Kaline was the second best player in the American League, behind only Mickey Mantle. While others such as Ted Williams, who was in the twilight of his career by then, Roger Maris, Rocky Colavito, and Harmon Killebrew had two or three outstanding seasons during that period, Kaline was consistently excellent over that nine-year stretch, being surpassed only by Mantle. With the exception of Maris' two MVP seasons of 1960 and 1961, Kaline was also the league's top rightfielder. Although he faced stiff competition from the National League's Hank Aaron, Frank Robinson, and Roberto Clemente, only Aaron was consistently ranked ahead of Kaline among major league players at the position during that period.

Kaline was the best rightfielder, and one of the five best players in baseball, in both 1955 and 1956. In 1955, he hit 27 home runs, knocked in 102 runs, scored 121 others, and led the league with a .340 batting average and 200 base hits. Although he finished second behind Yogi Berra in the MVP voting that year, he was named the A.L. Player of the Year by *The Sporting News*. The following year, he finished in the top five in the MVP voting once more by hitting 27 homers, knocking in a career-high 128 runs, and batting .314. Over the course of his career, Kaline finished in the top five in the MVP voting two other times, and placed in the top ten of the balloting a total of nine times. He also batted over .300 and hit more than 20 homers nine times each, and he was selected to 15 All-Star teams. Kaline finished his career with 399 home runs, 1,583 runs batted in, 1,622 runs scored, 3,007 hits, and a .297 batting average.

Although he had a little more power than Kaline, hitting 465 home runs during his career and topping the 30-homer mark three times, Dave Winfield was similar to the Tiger outfielder in many ways. He never dominated his league, but he did everything extremely well and put up outstanding numbers year-after-year. He was an outstanding run-producer, an excellent baserunner, and a great outfielder.

After spending eight seasons with the National League's San Diego Padres, Winfield joined the Yankees in 1981 where he subsequently became the American League's best rightfielder, and one of its best players, for the next eight seasons. Before leaving San Diego, however, Winfield had perhaps his finest season in 1979. That year, playing in a pitcher's park, he hit 34 home runs, led the league with 118 RBIs, batted .308, and was the best rightfielder in baseball, and arguably the finest all-around player in the game. With the Yankees, Winfield hit more than 30 homers twice, knocked in over 100 runs six times, batted over .300 twice, and established himself as one of the league's top players. His most outstanding seasons in New York were 1982 (37 HR, 106 RBIs, .280 AVG), 1983 (32 HR, 116 RBIs, .283 AVG), 1984 (19 HR, 100 RBIs, .340 AVG), and 1988 (25 HR, 107 RBIs, .322 AVG). In each of those years, Winfield was one of the five or six best players in baseball, and the best rightfielder in the game.

Although Winfield was a league-leader only one time during his career, he put up some very impressive numbers. In addition to his 465 home runs, he finished with 1,833 runs batted in, 1,669 runs scored, and 3,110 base hits. He hit more than 20 homers 15 times, knocked in more than 100 runs eight times, scored more than 100 runs three times, batted over .300 four times, and stole more than 20 bases four times. Winfield was selected to the All-

Star team 12 times and finished in the top 10 in the MVP voting seven times, making it into the top five on three occasions.

Sam Crawford

Though overshadowed by his Detroit Tigers' teammate Ty Cobb for much of his career, Sam Crawford was one of the finest players of the Deadball Era. In virtually every season from 1901 to 1915, he was among the five best players in baseball.

For most of the first decade of the 20th century, only Honus Wagner and Napoleon Lajoie were better, and Crawford was clearly the American League's best rightfielder. With both Wagner and Lajoie in the twilight of their careers by the start of the century's second decade, players such as Cobb, Tris Speaker, Shoeless Joe Jackson, and Eddie Collins established themselves as the best players in the game. However, right behind them, still ranked among the game's elite players, was Crawford. Only Jackson was rated above him as a rightfielder, and Crawford was still considered to be perhaps the top slugger and run-producer in baseball.

During the Deadball Era, the measure of a player's slugging ability was not so much in the number of home runs he hit, but, rather, in the number of triples he compiled. During his career, Crawford slugged more triples (309) than any other player in history. From 1900 to 1916, he never failed to hit at least 10 three-baggers in a season, and he finished with at least 20 on five separate occasions. Crawford led the league in that department six times, and he also finished first in runs batted in three times, home runs twice, and runs scored once. He is one of just a handful of players to lead both major leagues in home runs (he hit 16 for the Cincinnati Reds in 1901). Crawford knocked in over 100 runs six times, scored more than 100 runs three times, and batted over .300 eleven times. He finished runner-up to Eddie Collins in the 1914 MVP voting and ended his career with 1,525 runs batted in, 1,391 runs scored, 2,961 base hits, 366 stolen bases, and a .309 batting average. His 1957 election by the Veterans Committee was well-deserved.

Mike "King" Kelly

It is difficult to gauge just how good a player Mike "King" Kelly truly was because of the era in which he played. As we saw earlier, in the very early days of major league ball, games were scheduled far more sporadically than they were in later years and, as a result, players' statistics from those days need to be interpreted differently. Although Kelly spent 16 seasons in the big leagues, he appeared in more than 100 games, and had as many as 400 at-bats, only seven times. In only one season did he come to the plate more than 500 times. As a result, even though he had a rather lengthy career, Kelly finished with slightly less than 6,000 at-bats.

Needless to say, it would have been difficult for him to have many seasons in which he accumulated huge totals of runs batted in and runs scored. In fact, if you look at his career numbers, they are rather modest, even when compared to those of some of the other 19th century players who were elected to the Hall of Fame: only 950 RBIs and a .308 batting average. However, Kelly did manage to score more than 100 runs and steal more than 50 bases five times each, hit over .300 eight times, and lead his league in batting average twice, runs scored three times, on-base percentage twice, and doubles three times. In fact, although his productivity was curtailed even further by a bout with alcoholism and a general disinclination to take care of himself, for a few years some considered Kelly to be the finest player in the game. From 1884 to 1888, playing first for the Chicago Cubs and then for the Boston Braves, he averaged 121 runs scored and batted well over .300 four times. His three best seasons were 1884, 1886, and 1887. In the first of those years, he hit 13 home runs, knocked in 95 runs, batted .354, and scored 120 runs. In 1886, he established career-highs by hitting .388 and scoring 155 runs. The following year, he batted .322, scored 120 runs, and stole 84 bases.

Kelly was one of the most versatile players in the game, at one time or another playing every position on the field. He was also somewhat of an innovator, and he has a certain amount of historical significance. In addition to playing the outfield, he frequently caught, and he has been credited with being the first catcher to use signals to alert his infielders as to the type of pitch being thrown.

All things considered, it would seem that Kelly's 1945 election by the Veterans Committee was not a bad choice.

Sam Rice/Kiki Cuyler

Both Rice and Cuyler benefited greatly from having their prime seasons during the hitting-dominated 1920s. As a result, their statistics were somewhat inflated. However, both men were outstanding all-around players who could hit, run, and field, and whose claim to Hall of Fame legitimacy is a valid one.

The career of Sam Rice spanned 20 years and was spent almost entirely with the Washington Senators. In his first several seasons with the team, the Senators were an also-ran, finishing in the second division in the standings virtually every year. However, with the development of Rice into an outstanding player, the emergence of a young Goose Goslin, and the presence of an aging, but still effective Walter Johnson, Washington spent a good portion of Rice's career contending for the American League pennant.

While it could not legitimately be said that Rice was the best rightfielder in the American League at any point during his career, or even among the circuit's five or six best players, he starred throughout the entire decade of the 1920s. Over that ten-year period, he was among the top 15 players in the game. From 1919 to 1932, Rice failed to hit over .300 only twice, and he batted .295 and .297 in the other two seasons. He batted over .320 ten times, topping the .340 mark twice. Rice's two finest seasons came in 1925 and 1930. In the first of those years, he helped Washington to the pennant by establishing career-highs in batting (.350), hits (227), and runs batted in (87), while scoring 111 runs. In 1930, he batted .349, scored 121 runs, and collected 207 hits.

Although Rice hit only 34 home runs during his career, he had good extra-base power. He finished his career with 184 triples and 498 doubles, finishing in double-digits in triples and with more than 30 doubles ten times each. He also scored more than 100 runs five times, collected more than 200 hits six times, and stole more than 20 bases nine times, swiping a career-high 63 bags in 1920. Rice led the American League in hits twice, and in triples and stolen bases once each. He also finished in the top five in the league MVP voting twice.

The fact that his offensive numbers were somewhat inflated by the era in which he played should make Rice something less than an obvious choice for the Hall of Fame. However, his .322 career batting average, 1,514 runs scored, and 2,987 base hits are probably enough to validate his 1963 selection by the Veterans Committee.

The 18-year career of Kiki Cuyler included stints with the Pittsburgh Pirates, Chicago Cubs, Cincinnati Reds, and Brooklyn Dodgers. Cuyler's prime years were spent with the Pirates and Cubs, between 1924 and 1934. Over that 11-year stretch, he failed to hit over .300 only twice, topping the .350-mark four times. He batted .354 for the Pirates in 1924, then followed that up the next season by batting .357, hitting 18 home runs, knocking in 102 runs, scoring 144 others, and collecting 220 hits, 26 triples, 43 doubles, and 41 stolen bases. For those two seasons, Cuyler was the National League's best rightfielder, and one of its top five players. However, at no other point during his career could either of those statements legitimately be made.

Over the next several years, Cuyler was supplanted as the league's best player at that position by the likes of Paul Waner, Chuck Klein, and Mel Ott. Nevertheless, he continued to perform at a very high level, having superb seasons for the Cubs in both 1929 and 1930. In the first of those years, he hit 15 home runs, knocked in 102 runs, batted .360, and scored 111 runs. The following year, he knocked in a career-best 134 runs, while batting .355, scoring 155 runs, and collecting 228 hits, 50 doubles, and 17 triples.

Over the course of his career, Cuyler led the National League in runs scored, triples, and doubles once each, and in stolen bases four times. He knocked in over 100 runs three times, scored more than 100 runs five times, collected more than 200 hits three times, batted over .300 ten times, and finished in double-digits in triples six times. In addition, although he played during an era in which the stolen base became almost obsolete, Cuyler stole more than 30 bases six times. He placed in the top 10 in the MVP voting twice and finished his career with a .321 batting average, 1,065 runs batted in, 1,305 runs scored, and 2,299 hits. Considering that his peak seasons were from 1924 to 1934, during a great hitter's era, Cuyler's numbers were not particularly overwhelming. However, when one also factors into the equation his integral role on five pennant-winning teams (two in Pittsburgh, and three in Chicago), his selection by the Veterans Committee in 1968 was not a bad one.

Martin Dihigo

Cuban-born Martin Dihigo may very well have been the most versatile man to ever play the game. It is one thing to play all nine positions on the field, but it is something else to *excel* at all of them. That is something Dihigo did during his 23-year Negro League career.

While he was quite capable of playing every position on the diamond, Dihigo's greatest success came as a rightfielder, and, later in his career, as a pitcher. Renowned for his powerful throwing arm, which was compared favorably to that of Roberto Clemente by those who saw both men play, Dihigo was also an excellent hitter. Although statistics from the Negro Leagues are not totally reliable, he is reported to have batted over .300 in at least eleven seasons, and surpassed the .400-mark in at least three others. With the Cuban Stars of the Eastern Colored League, he led the league in home runs in 1926, while hitting .421. The following year, he tied for the league lead in home runs and batted .370. With the Hilldale Daisies of the American Negro League in 1936, Dihigo hit .358 to win the batting title, while simultaneously occupying a regular spot in the pitching rotation. In fact, during his career, Dihigo often lead his team in most hitting and pitching categories.

Hall-of-Famer Johnny Mize once said that Dihigo was the best player he ever saw and recalled that when the two men were teammates in the Dominican Republic, opponents sometimes intentionally walked Dihigo to pitch to him.

All evidence seems to indicate that the Negro Leagues Committee did a good job when it elected Dihigo to the Hall of Fame in 1977.

Enos Slaughter

Enos Slaughter is a prime example of the type of player who has caused disagreement over the years between those who feel that only the great players should be elected to the Hall of Fame, and those who are less stringent in their approach to the elections.

Slaughter played 19 years for the St. Louis Cardinals, Kansas City Athletics, New York Yankees, and Milwaukee Braves. His peak years were spent with the Cardinals, from 1938 to 1953, with three years of playing time lost due to his stint in the military. During his years in St. Louis, Slaughter never hit less than .276, and he topped the .300-mark eight times. Although he never hit more than 18 home runs in any season, Slaughter knocked in and scored more than 100 runs three times each, finished in double-digits in triples seven times, and compiled as many as 52 doubles one year. His most productive season was 1946, when he helped lead the Cardinals to the world championship by hitting 18 home runs, knocking in a league-leading 130 runs, batting .300, and scoring 100 runs. He also had outstanding seasons in both 1942 and 1949. In his last year of play prior to joining the war effort, Slaughter hit 13 home runs, drove in 98 runs, scored 100 others, and batted .318. In 1949, he hit 13 homers, knocked in 96 runs, and batted .336.

In his years with St. Louis, Slaughter led the league in batting once, runs batted in once, triples twice, and doubles and hits once each. He was selected to the All-Star Team ten times, and finished in the top 10 in the league MVP voting five times, making it into the top five on three separate occasions.

However, while Slaughter was an extremely consistent player who had many good years, he was never able to put together that one *great*, truly dominant Hall-of-Fame-type season. In his prime, he was not as good as several other outfielders who are not in the Hall of Fame. Players such as Bob Johnson, Bob Elliott, and Tony

Oliva were all, at their peaks, superior players to Slaughter. They just didn't hang around as long as he did. Elliott, in particular, is a good example because he was a National League contemporary of Slaughter, playing for the Pirates and Braves, among others, from 1939 to 1953. A look at the career numbers of both players indicates that they were actually quite comparable:

PLAYER	AB	HITS	RUNS	2B	3B	HR	RBI	AVG	SB	OBP	SLG PCT
Enos Slaughter	7,946	2,383	1,247	413	148	169	1,304	.300	71	.382	.453
Bob Elliott	7,141	2,061	1,064	382	94	170	1,195	.289	60	.372	.440

Elliott, who played both third base and the outfield during his career, hit as many home runs as Slaughter and knocked in only 100 fewer runs in 800 fewer at-bats. He was also quite comparable in most other offensive categories. Elliott hit more than 20 homers three times (something Slaughter never did), knocked in over 100 runs six times, and was named the National League's MVP in 1947 when, playing for the Braves, he hit 22 homers, knocked in 113 runs, and batted .317. Yet, Elliott received only minimal support during his eligibility period.

Using our other Hall of Fame criteria, Slaughter was never considered to be even among the 10 best players in the game, much less the top five, and, with the possible exception of 1946, was never even among the five best players in his own league. He was, however, the best rightfielder in baseball in at least a few seasons. He certainly was in 1941, 1942, 1946, 1948, and 1949, all seasons in which he batted over .300 and, with the exception of 1941, knocked in over 90 runs. In addition, Slaughter's offensive productivity and hustling style of play—epitomized by his "mad-dash" around the bases to score the winning run in the 1946 World Series against the Boston Red Sox—contributed greatly to his teams' success. He played on five pennant-winners and four world champions in St. Louis and New York.

The inevitable question that follows: was the Veterans Committee's 1985 selection of Slaughter justified? Once again, the answer lies in the manner in which one chooses to evaluate the credentials of potential Hall of Fame candidates. Slaughter was clearly not a great player. In fact, he was a very good one in only about six or seven seasons. He was, however, a good player for a very long time. The feeling here is that Slaughter should be viewed as a borderline Hall of Famer, at best. While he was far from the worst selection ever made by the Veterans Committee, he is someone who, in all probability, should never have been elected.

Elmer Flick

The man who replaced Sam Thompson in the Philadelphia Phillies' outfield in 1898 was Elmer Flick. Flick's 13-year major league career included four seasons with the Phillies and nine with the American League's Cleveland Indians. Over his 13 seasons, Flick batted over .300 eight times, scored more than 100 runs twice, collected more than 200 hits and knocked in more than 100 runs once each, stole more than 30 bases seven times, and finished in double-digits in triples ten times. He led his league in runs batted in, batting average, and runs scored once each, and triples three times. Flick finished his career with a .313 batting average, a .389 on-base percentage, 164 triples, and 330 stolen bases.

However, Flick was never considered to be the best rightfielder in his league, being ranked behind both Willie Keeler and Sam Crawford in virtually every season. In addition, his career was a relatively short one, his 5,600 at-bats permitting him to accumulate only 756 runs batted in, 948 runs scored, and 1,752 hits—paltry numbers by Hall of Fame standards. Flick was a good player, but he just didn't do enough to merit his 1963 selection by the Veterans Committee, which is one that never should have been made.

Ross Youngs

The career of New York Giants outfielder Ross Youngs was an abbreviated one that was halted by a fatal illness he incurred during the 1926 season. Prior to that, Youngs was one of the better players in the National League, hitting over .300 in nine of his ten big-league seasons. His finest years came from 1920 to 1924. In those five seasons, he never batted below .327, surpassing the .350-mark twice. He also scored more than 100 runs three times, collected more than 200 hits twice, and finished in double-digits in triples in each of those years. From 1920 to 1923, Youngs was the National League's best rightfielder.

However, hitting mostly during the 1920s, Youngs' batting statistics were somewhat inflated by the offensive explosion that took place at the time. He never came close to leading the league in hitting, finishing well behind Rogers Hornsby in the batting race in each season, from 1920 to 1925. He led the National League in runs scored and doubles once each, but had little power, hitting as many as 10 home runs only once, and knocking in 100 runs only one time. In fact, in no other season did Youngs drive in as many as 90 runs. He was never considered to be among the best players in the game, or even in his own league. A look at his career numbers, next to those of Sam Rice, is quite revealing:

PLAYER	AB	HITS	RUNS	2B	3B	HR	RBI	AVG	SB	OBP	SLG PCT
Ross Youngs	4,627	1,491	812	236	93	42	592	.322	153	.399	.441
Sam Rice	9,269	2,987	1,514	498	184	34	1,078	.322	351	.374	.427

The two players were virtually equal in productivity throughout their careers. In twice the number of at-bats, Rice finished with twice as many runs batted in, runs scored, hits, triples, doubles, and stolen bases. While Youngs hit more home runs and finished with slightly higher on-base and slugging percentages, the two men finished with the exact same batting average. Yet, in spite of their comparable level of offensive productivity, Rice played twice as long as Youngs and, therefore, compiled far more impressive numbers during his career. Youngs' career numbers suffer greatly when compared to those posted by Rice and are clearly not Hall of Fame caliber. In short, Youngs was a good player, but his selection by the Veterans Committee in 1972, due largely to the influence of his former teammate, Committee member Frankie Frisch, was a big mistake.

Tommy McCarthy

The 13-year career of Tommy McCarthy included stints with the Boston Braves, Philadelphia Phillies, St. Louis Cardinals, and Brooklyn Dodgers. After struggling in his first few seasons, McCarthy came into his own in 1888, when he stole 93 bases and scored 100 runs for the first of seven consecutive seasons. Over that seven-year period, he also knocked in over 100 runs twice, batted over .300 four times, and stole more than 40 bases six times.

McCarthy's finest years came in 1890, 1893, and 1894. Playing for the Cardinals in 1890, he batted .350, stole 83 bases, and scored 137 runs. With the Braves in 1893, he hit .346, knocked in 111 runs, and scored 107 others. The following season, he established career highs in home runs (13) and runs batted in (126), while batting .349 and scoring 118 runs.

However, McCarthy led his league only once in any major offensive category (stolen bases), and was never considered to be an exceptional player, or even the best at his own position. Playing rightfield at the same time as Sam Thompson, McCarthy was rated well behind the 19th century slugger throughout his career. A look at the numbers of both players illustrates the disparity in their skill levels:

PLAYER	AB	HITS	RUNS	2B	3B	HR	RBI	AVG	SB	OBP	SLG PCT
Sam Thompson	5,984	1,979	1,256	340	160	127	1,299	.331	229	.384	.505
Tommy McCarthy	5,128	1,496	1,069	192	53	44	735	.292	468	.364	.376

In approximately 800 fewer at-bats, the only edge that McCarthy had was in stolen bases. In all other categories, there really is no comparison. Thompson was a far-superior player to McCarthy, who was a good player for seven years, and a very good one for only two or three. Those few good years should not have been enough to get McCarthy elected to the Hall of Fame. His selection by the Veterans Committee in 1946, 28 years before Thompson's induction in 1974, is indefensible and another indication of how uninformed the Committee members were in the early years of the balloting.

Harry Hooper

Another selection by the Veterans Committee that is difficult to fathom is that of Harry Hooper, who was elected in 1971. Hooper's major league career lasted 17 seasons, 12 with the Boston Red Sox and five with the Chicago White Sox. With Boston from 1909 to 1920, Hooper was fortunate enough to play alongside the great

Tris Speaker in the Red Sox outfield for seven seasons, and, also, with Babe Ruth for six. As a result, he played on several pennant-winning teams and three world champions.

However, just how much Hooper contributed to the success of those teams is somewhat debatable. In his 12 seasons in Boston, he stole more than 20 bases nine times, scored more than 90 runs four times, and finished in double-digits in triples nine times. However, he batted .300 only twice, hitting less than .270 six times, scored 100 runs only once, never knocked in more than 53 runs, and never finished with more than 169 hits. During his entire career, Hooper batted over .300 only five times, scored more than 100 runs only three times, never knocked in more than 80 runs, and never finished with more than 183 hits. He never led the American League in any offensive category and was never considered to be among even the ten best players in the league. In fact, he was never rated any higher than third among rightfielders alone. Throughout his career, he was ranked well behind the likes of Shoeless Joe Jackson and Sam Crawford, and, later, Babe Ruth, Harry Heilmann, and Sam Rice. A look at his career numbers, along with those of Bobby Veach, causes one to wonder what the Veterans Committee was thinking when it selected him:

PLAYER	AB	HITS	RUNS	2B	3B	HR	RBI	AVG	SB	OBP	SLG PCT
Harry Hooper	8,785	2,466	1,429	389	160	75	817	.281	375	.359	.387
Bobby Veach	6,656	2,063	953	393	147	64	1,166	.310	195	.356	.442

Veach, who played simultaneously with Hooper from 1912 to 1925, had his finest seasons playing alongside Ty Cobb and Sam Crawford, and, later, Harry Heilmann, in the Detroit Tiger outfield. In approximately 2,000 fewer at-bats than Hooper, he hit almost as many home runs, knocked in 350 more runs, hit 30 points higher, and finished with almost the same number of doubles and triples. The only real edge that Hooper had was in runs scored and stolen bases. In addition, Veach knocked in more than 100 runs six times (something Hooper never even came close to doing even once), batted over .300 nine times, reaching a career-best of .355 for the Tigers in 1919, collected more than 200 hits twice, stole more than 20 bases five times, and finished in double-digits in triples ten times. He was a more productive and dangerous hitter than Hooper, and a better ballplayer. Yet he received practically no support in the Hall of Fame voting. Should Veach have been elected? The answer is no. His numbers just were not outstanding enough. But he was certainly more deserving than Hooper, who never should have been voted in.

14 SHOELESS JOE JACKSON AND PETE ROSE

There is no doubt, based strictly on their playing ability, that both Shoeless Joe Jackson and Pete Rose belong in the Hall of Fame. Among non-pitchers, Jackson was one of the greatest players of the Deadball Era, surpassed only by Ty Cobb, Honus Wagner, and, perhaps, Tris Speaker. His lifetime batting average of .356 is the third highest ever (behind only Cobb and Rogers Hornsby), he is the only player in baseball history to hit .400 in his first full season in the major leagues, and he was a terrific outfielder and baserunner.

Pete Rose, while not as talented as Jackson, got the most out of his ability and parlayed a 24-year career in the majors into becoming the all-time leader in base hits, games played, and at-bats. He is also second in doubles, fifth in runs scored, and sixth in total bases. He was an All-Star at five different positions, and he won a Most Valuable Player Award.

The thing that is keeping both men out of the Hall of Fame is the issue of morality, since both were found guilty of breaking the rules of baseball by being involved with gambling on the sport, albeit on totally different levels. Rose was banned from baseball, for life, on August 23, 1989, at the conclusion of a six-month investigation into allegations that he bet on baseball. Jackson and eight other players were banned, for life, by then-Commissioner Kenesaw Mountain Landis in June of 1921 for doing the unthinkable—throwing the 1919 World Series. Perhaps a review of the circumstances surrounding the Black Sox scandal of 1919 is in order.

In September of 1920, a Chicago grand jury convened to investigate charges about the 1919 World Series between the

Chicago White Sox and Cincinnati Reds. Meanwhile, an article appeared on September 27, 1920, in the *Philadelphia North American* in which local gambler Bill Maharg described how White Sox pitcher Ed Cicotte volunteered to fix the Series; how Maharg and his partner, former major leaguer Billy Burns, promised to pay $100,000 to eight White Sox players; how the gamblers double-crossed the players by paying them only $10,000 at first; how the players double-crossed the gamblers by winning a game they were supposed to lose; and how Burns and Maharg got double-crossed by a rival fixer, New York gambler Abe Attell, who *also* was bribing the players. The following day, Cicotte agreed to testify to the grand jury and named the players who, from that point on, became known as the *Black Sox*. The eight players named were Cicotte, fellow-pitcher Claude "Lefty" Williams, outfielders "Shoeless" Joe Jackson and Oscar "Happy" Felsch, infielders Buck Weaver (who had "guilty knowledge" of the fix, but refused to take part in it), Swede Risberg, Chick Gandil, and utility player Fred McMullin.

In grand jury testimony, Gandil emerged as the ringleader, pocketing $35,000. Cicotte received $10,000, and Jackson was paid $5,000 (he was earning about $6,000 a year from tight-fisted White Sox owner Charles Comiskey). Arnold Rothstein, the notorious gangster, reputedly masterminded the fix, although his role was never legally proven and he was never charged with a crime. However, following the mysterious disappearance of their confessions, and other legal machinations, the eight Black Sox won acquittal during their June, 1921 conspiracy trial. But the newly appointed baseball commissioner, Kenesaw Mountain Landis, in an extraordinarily bold move aimed at restoring public confidence in the game, suspended all eight players for life.

From all this, it becomes quite clear that Joe Jackson was no saint. For that matter, neither was Pete Rose. Throughout his career, and subsequent to his playing days as well, Rose often displayed his egocentricity, arrogance, and self-absorption. Away from the field, he cheated on his wife openly, causing her great public embarrassment and humiliation. Neither man was a role model for youngsters, or the type of person anyone should try to emulate.

However, being a nice guy has never been a prerequisite for entering the Hall of Fame, since it already has several members who were of rather questionable character. The most obvious example would be Ty Cobb, who was the most hated man in baseball during his playing days. He was ruthless, argumentative, vindictive, and violent. During his career, Cobb engaged in drawn-out, knockdown fights with umpires, teammates, opposing players, and fans alike.

Perhaps the most famous of these incidents occurred on May 15, 1912, at Hilltop Park in Manhattan, during a game between Cobb's Tigers and the New York Highlanders. A heckling fan had been shouting insults at Cobb from the stands all game. However, when he yelled at Cobb that he was a "half-nigger" (considered, in those days, to be the ultimate insult given to a white man), Cobb vaulted the fence and began stomping and kicking the fan with his spikes. When fans began yelling that the man was helpless because he had no hands, Cobb replied, "I don't care if he doesn't have any feet," and kept kicking him until park police eventually pulled him away. When he was informed of the incident, American League President Ban Johnson suspended Cobb indefinitely from organized ball. However, the suspension was lifted when Cobb's Tiger teammates went on strike to show their support for him, since, at that time, being called a "half-nigger" was considered to be more than any white man could reasonably be expected to take. In the end, Cobb was reinstated after paying just a $50 fine.

As a result of his involvement in incidences such as this, in spite of the fact that he was one of the greatest players who ever lived, Cobb was an embarrassment to the game in many ways. Yet, he was one of the original five members elected to the Hall of Fame in 1936, receiving more votes than any other player. It is, therefore, safe to assume that the writers who voted for him did not place too much importance on "character," "integrity," and "sportsmanship" when making their selections.

While Cobb is the most flagrant example, there are many other people in the Hall of Fame who were not chosen based on the quality of their character. In an earlier chapter, it was mentioned that Cap Anson threatened to organize a players' strike to bar black players from competing in the major leagues prior to a game in 1885. His protest was upheld and it eventually led to the gentlemen's agreement among owners that prevented blacks from playing in the majors, no matter how good they were, until 1947.

Babe Ruth, as a member of the Boston Red Sox in 1917, attacked umpire Brick Owens. He also went into the stands one time with a bat to chase a heckler. In 1922 alone, he was suspended five times, usually for swearing at umpires. Of course, this was nothing compared to his actions off the field. A legendary philanderer, Ruth once bragged that he had slept with every girl in a St. Louis whorehouse, and, even when his first wife Helen accompanied him on road trips, teammates facilitated his romantic trysts by making their rooms available to him for his liaisons. Ruth also had huge appetites for food and beverage, and was a known drunkard. Mickey Mantle was another who was anything but a model citizen, and drinking problems also came to be associated with players such as Hack Wilson, Chuck Klein, Grover Cleveland Alexander, and Paul Waner.

Another player who was elected to the Hall of Fame despite his off-the-field transgressions was pitcher Ferguson Jenkins. The former Chicago Cub, then pitching for the Texas Rangers, was arrested at the Toronto airport on August 25, 1980 for possession of two ounces of marijuana, two grams of hashish, and four grams of cocaine. He was later found guilty of cocaine possession.

But neither Shoeless Joe Jackson nor Pete Rose has been banned from the game because they were bad people, or because of anything they did in their personal lives. They were banned from baseball because they broke the rules of the game and threatened its integrity. Rose broke the rule against gambling, and Jackson took a bribe to throw the World Series. A look back into baseball history reveals, however, that certain Hall of Fame players were, at one time or another, involved in some rather suspicious activities that threatened the integrity of the game.

There was a reported attempt to bribe players in the first two World Series, in 1903 and 1905. In the 1905 Series, Philadelphia A's pitcher Rube Waddell did not play due to an injury, while he had allegedly received a $17,000 offer not to play. Yet any reports regarding the offer were never fully investigated and Waddell was eventually voted into Cooperstown.

Although there were many reports of attempted fixes during the first two decades of the 20th century, under Judge Landis' stern tutelage, baseball became far less tolerant of gamblers than it had been in the past. Still, stories of corruption continued to surface. In 1926, player-managers Ty Cobb of the Tigers and Tris Speaker of the Indians both resigned under a cloud of suspicion. The public later learned that ex-pitcher Dutch Leonard alleged that they had conspired to fix the last game of the 1919 season so that Detroit could win third-place money, and that Smoky Joe Wood allegedly placed bets for Cobb and Speaker. In 1927, "Black Sox" Swede Risberg publicly charged that some 50 players had known of a four-game series in 1917 that the Tigers threw to the White Sox. Yet, both Cobb and Speaker went unscathed because Landis felt that they were too big to be prosecuted. So much for the integrity of Judge Landis.

While we are on the subject of Landis, who was elected to the Hall of Fame by his former cronies in 1944, it might be worthwhile to take a closer look at his character and integrity, or lack thereof.

Throughout his term of office, Kenesaw Mountain Landis presided over the game of baseball in much the same manner that a despot rules a nation, often coming across as pompous, arrogant, and self-righteous. He always enjoyed accepting credit for "saving" the game of baseball with his banishment of the eight "Black Sox" players who threw the World Series. Meanwhile, he did more to hurt the game than anything else. He showed preferential treatment to those men who helped him get elected to office. Prime examples of this were his handling of the 1919 "Black Sox" scandal, and his subsequent dealings with White Sox owner Charles Comiskey.

Comiskey was notoriously cheap and, as a result, was universally disliked by everyone on the White Sox. In fact, even prior to the 1919 World Series, the White Sox players were nicknamed the "Black Sox." The story goes that, one year, Comiskey refused to pay for the laundering of his players' uniforms, so they played with dirty uniforms. Finally, Comiskey relented and agreed to foot the bill. Then, at the end of the season, he took it out of their World Series paychecks. Such parsimoniousness, and the resentment it caused among his players, as much as anything, is what resulted in the throwing of the 1919 Series.

It later surfaced that, shortly after the Series ended, Joe Jackson wrote a letter to Comiskey stating that the Series outcome was questionable and he volunteered to meet with the owner to provide details. This was actually almost a year before the scandal broke. But Comiskey—said to be concerned about the effect of such revelations on attendance and profits, not to mention his equity in the franchise—never followed up on Jackson's offer. Yet, when Judge Landis announced his edict, banishing the eight players for life, Comiskey went unscathed. In fact, he was eventually elected to the Hall of Fame by the Old-Timers Committee, of which Landis was a member.

Of even greater significance, though, is the fact that it was Landis, more than anyone else, who fostered the notion that black players should not be allowed in the major leagues. While this was never officially announced by anyone, or written anywhere into the rules, it was an understanding amongst the owners, enforced by Landis. Not until he passed away in 1944, and "Happy" Chandler took over as Commissioner, were the gates opened for everyone to participate in major league baseball.

The point here is that baseball has always been an hypocrisy, and, for years, Landis was a symbol of that hypocrisy. Anything that happened during his term of office, any decisions he handed down, and any rules he made should be taken lightly. How could the rulings of a man who excluded such a large segment of the population from the national pastime be taken seriously? How could the rules created even after his term ended be taken seriously when the powers that be have never fully enforced them? Just look at former pitcher Steve Howe. After six violations of baseball's anti-drug policy, which included a year-long suspension in 1984, Howe was suspended "for life" in June of 1992 by then-commissioner Fay Vincent. However, he was eventually reinstated, only to suffer a seventh suspension.

Therefore, those who say that Shoeless Joe Jackson and Pete Rose should not be allowed to enter the Hall of Fame because they were banished for life for "breaking the rules" of the game should take a long look back into baseball history. Doing so might cause them to reevaluate their position. Jackson and Rose should be no more excluded than men such as Cobb, Speaker, Waddell, Comiskey, and Landis. Their names should be included on the eligible list, and the current members of the Hall of Fame should be the ones to determine their fate. Some of them have already gone on record as saying that they do not wish to have the names of Jackson and Rose intermingled with theirs. They certainly have a right to feel that way, but that should be *their* decision to make. It should not be made for them by other individuals who, over the years, have contributed to the hypocrisy that has come to symbolize major league baseball. Jackson, who was banished from the game "for life," has been dead for almost 50 years. Rose should never be permitted to either manage or coach again, but his name should appear on the eligible list as well.

As far as an assessment of the relative evils committed by both men, there are two possible interpretations. The first views Jackson's act as the more heinous of the two. After all, he took a bribe to throw the World Series and actually performed at less than 100 percent of his full capabilities, something Rose never did. Jackson's actions directly affected the outcomes of his team's games and were, in essence, the same as betting against his own team. Rose was never found guilty of betting against his own team. What he did seems almost harmless, by comparison.

However, things could also be viewed from a different perspective. Shoeless Joe Jackson was a poor South Carolina farm boy who could neither read nor write. He was naïve about the ways of the world, easily influenced by others, and probably didn't even fully comprehend the overall impact his actions would have on the game. He was also grossly underpaid by his team's tight-fisted owner. More importantly, he was contrite—something Rose never was. He offered to provide details of his wrongdoing to his team's owner, but was ignored. Rose, on the other hand, was fully aware of what he was doing, and what the possible consequences might be. His actions were not prompted so much by greed, but, rather, by an insatiable desire to compete, as well as a serious addiction to gambling. He also remained defiant and lied openly for 14 years, denying that he ever bet on baseball. Finally, desperate for reinstatement, Rose admitted his guilt in 2004. However, even his confession was an insincere one since it conveniently coincided with the publication of his book, in which he finally accepted culpability for his actions.

So, take your pick. Which one was worse?

PITCHERS (68)

PLAYER	YEARS	ELECTED BY	YEAR ELECTED
Pud Galvin	1875-1892	Veterans Committee	1965
Mickey Welch	1880-1892	Veterans Committee	1973
Tim Keefe	1880-1893	Veterans Committee	1964
Charley Radbourn	1881-1891	Veterans Committee	1939
John Clarkson	1882-1894	Veterans Committee	1963
Amos Rusie	1889-1895, 97-98	Veterans Committee	1977
Kid Nichols	1890-1901,04-06	Veterans Committee	1949
Cy Young	1890-1911	BBWAA	1937
Vic Willis	1898-1910	Veterans Committee	1995
Joe McGinnity	1899-1908	Veterans Committee	1946
Jack Chesbro	1899-1909	Veterans Committee	1946
Rube Waddell	1899-1910	Veterans Committee	1946
Christy Mathewson	1900-1916	BBWAA	1936
Eddie Plank	1901-1917	Veterans Committee	1946
Addie Joss	1902-1910	Veterans Committee	1978
Chief Bender	1903-1917	Veterans Committee	1953
Mordecai Brown	1903-1916	Veterans Committee	1949
Ed Walsh	1904-1917	Veterans Committee	1946
Walter Johnson	1907-1927	BBWAA	1936

PLAYER	YEARS	ELECTED BY	YEAR ELECTED
Rube Marquard	1908-1925	Veterans Committee	1971
Jose Mendez	1908-1926	Veterans Committee	2006
Joe Williams	1910-1932	Veterans Committee	1999
Grover C. Alexander	1911-1930	BBWAA	1938
Eppa Rixey	1912-1933	Veterans Committee	1963
Herb Pennock	1912-1934	BBWAA	1948
Red Faber	1914-1933	Veterans Committee	1964
Dazzy Vance	1915,1922-35	BBWAA	1955
Stan Coveleski	1916-1928	Veterans Committee	1969
Burleigh Grimes	1916-1934	Veterans Committee	1964
Waite Hoyt	1918-1938	Veterans Committee	1969
Jesse Haines	1920-1937	Veterans Committee	1970
Bullet Rogan	1920-1938	Veterans Committee	1998
Andy Cooper	1920-1941	Veterans Committee	2006
Bill Foster	1923-1938	Veterans Committee	1996
Ted Lyons	1923-1942,46	BBWAA	1955
Red Ruffing	1924-1942, 45-47	BBWAA	1967
Lefty Grove	1925-1941	BBWAA	1947
Satchel Paige	1926-1953	Negro Leagues Committee	1971
Carl Hubbell	1928-1943	BBWAA	1947
Lefty Gomez	1930-1943	Veterans Committee	1972
Ray Brown	1930-1948	Veterans Committee	2006
Dizzy Dean	1932-1941	BBWAA	1953
Hilton Smith	1933-1948	Veterans Committee	2001
Leon Day	1935-1949	Veterans Committee	1995
Bob Feller	1936-1941, 45-56	BBWAA	1962
Hal Newhouser	1939-1955	Veterans Committee	1992

PLAYER	YEARS	ELECTED BY	YEAR ELECTED
Early Wynn	1941-1944, 46-63	BBWAA	1972
Bob Lemon	1946-1958	BBWAA	1976
Warren Spahn	1946-1965	BBWAA	1973
Robin Roberts	1948-1966	BBWAA	1976
Whitey Ford	1950,1953-67	BBWAA	1974
Hoyt Wilhelm	1952-1972	BBWAA	1985
Jim Bunning	1955-1971	Veterans Committee	1996
Sandy Koufax	1955-1966	BBWAA	1972
Don Drysdale	1956-1969	BBWAA	1984
Bob Gibson	1959-1975	BBWAA	1981
Juan Marichal	1960-1975	BBWAA	1983
Gaylord Perry	1962-1983	BBWAA	1991
Phil Niekro	1964-1987	BBWAA	1997
Ferguson Jenkins	1965-1983	BBWAA	1991
Catfish Hunter	1965-1979	BBWAA	1987
Jim Palmer	1965-1984	BBWAA	1990
Steve Carlton	1965-1988	BBWAA	1994
Don Sutton	1966-1988	BBWAA	1998
Nolan Ryan	1966-1993	BBWAA	1999
Tom Seaver	1967-1986	BBWAA	1992
Rollie Fingers	1968-1985	BBWAA	1992
Goose Gossage	1972-1994	BBWAA	2008
Dennis Eckersley	1975-1998	BBWAA	2004
Bruce Sutter	1976-1988	BBWAA	2006

Walter Johnson/Lefty Grove

As the greatest righthanded and lefthanded pitchers of all time, Johnson and Grove head the list of exceptional pitchers whose Hall of Fame credentials would not be questioned by anyone.

During the Deadball Era, there were many outstanding pitchers, some of whom totally dominated the hitters of the day. However, the most dominant hurler of all, and quite possibly the greatest pitcher in the history of the game was the Washington Senators Walter Johnson. Although the Senators were a second-division team for much of Johnson's career, the big righthander still managed to win 416 games (against 279 losses) and compile a .599 career winning percentage. During his career, Johnson won 38 games by a score of 1-0, and lost 27 others by the same score. He holds the major league record for lifetime shutouts (110), his career ERA of 2.16 is the lowest of any American League pitcher with more than 2,000 innings, and his 416 wins are the most by any pitcher during the 20th century.

Johnson led the American League in wins six times, ERA five times, strikeouts twelve times, innings pitched five times, and shutouts seven times. He captured the pitcher's version of the triple crown—by leading the league in wins, ERA, and strikeouts in the same season—three times. Johnson won more than 20 games twelve times during his career, surpassing 30 victories on two separate occasions. He won at least 20 games in every season from 1910 to 1919. Over that 10-year stretch, Johnson was clearly the best pitcher in the American League, and he was the finest pitcher in the game in many of those seasons. In nine of those years, his ERA was less than 2.00, and his mark of 1.14 in 1913 is the best in A.L. history for pitchers with more than 200 innings. In that remarkable 1913 season, Johnson also finished with a won-lost record of 36-7, 243 strikeouts, and 12 shutouts. That year, Johnson won the first of his two Most Valuable Player Awards, a feat accomplished by only two other pitchers in baseball history.

If anyone could rival Johnson as the greatest pitcher in baseball history, that man would be Lefty Grove. Pitching for the Philadelphia Athletics and Boston Red Sox from 1925 to 1941, during much more of a hitter's era, Grove was the dominant pitcher of his time. He finished with 300 wins and only 141 losses, thereby compiling a lifetime winning percentage of .680, one of the best in baseball history. He led the American League in wins four times, ERA a record nine times, strikeouts seven times, and winning percentage five times. While Grove's career earned run average of 3.06 runs per game may not seem particularly impressive on the surface, it was a truly exceptional mark considering the era during which it was compiled. In both 1930 and 1931, Grove's ERA was more than two runs a game below the league average. The 1931 season was the best of Grove's career. Not only did he capture the pitcher's version of the triple crown for the second of three times that year by finishing 31-4, with a 2.06 ERA and 175 strikeouts, but Grove was also named the American League's Most Valuable Player.

During his career, Grove won more than 20 games eight times, including seven consecutive years from 1927 to 1933. For those seven seasons he was clearly the best pitcher in the game, and his won-lost record of 152-41 from 1928 to 1933 has to go down as one of the greatest accomplishments ever.

Christy Mathewson/Grover Cleveland Alexander

With the exception of Walter Johnson, Mathewson and Alexander were the most dominant pitchers of the Deadball Era. They were clearly the best pitchers in the National League during that period, and they were arguably the greatest hurlers in the history of the league.

Many baseball historians consider Christy Mathewson to be the greatest pitcher in National League history. Pitching almost exclusively for the New York Giants from 1900 to 1916, Mathewson won more than 20 games 13 times, compiling as many as 30 victories on four different occasions. From 1903 to 1914 he won no fewer than 22 games in any season, leading the National League in wins four times, ERA and strikeouts five times each, and shutouts four times. He finished with an earned run average under 2.00 five times, with his personal best coming in 1909 with a mark of 1.14. However, his finest season was the previous year, when he finished 37-11, with a 1.43 ERA, 259 strikeouts, 11 shutouts, 390 innings pitched, and 34 complete games to win the pitcher's triple crown for the second time. He also won at least 30 games in each year from 1903 to 1905.

Mathewson was one of the two or three best pitchers in baseball, and the best pitcher in the National League, in virtually every season from 1903 to 1914. Until Walter Johnson came along, and later, Grover Cleveland Alexander during the second decade of the 20th century, he was clearly the best pitcher in the game. Mathewson finished his career with a record of 373 wins against only 188 losses, and an earned run average of 2.13—one of the best ever.

As dominant as Mathewson was during the first decade of the 20th century, Grover Cleveland Alexander was just as dominant over the next ten seasons. From 1911 to 1920, pitching first for the Phillies and then the Cubs, Alexander won at least 22 games seven times, including six seasons with at least 27 victories. He won the pitcher's triple crown in each season from 1915 to 1917, finishing with records of 31-10, 33-12, and 30-13, and ERA's of 1.22, 1.55, and 1.83 in those years. Over his career, Alexander won at least 20 games nine times, and he finished with an earned run average under 2.00 six times. He led the league in wins five times, ERA four times, strikeouts six times, and shutouts seven times. His 16 shutouts in 1916 remain the major league record, and his 90 career shutouts are second only to Walter Johnson's 110. Alexander was clearly the National League's best pitcher from 1913 to 1917, and he was rivaled only by Johnson as the best pitcher in the game over that stretch.

Cy Young

Cy Young was the most durable pitcher the game has ever seen, and also one of the greatest. He holds several records that will never be broken. Among them are his records for most career wins (511), most innings pitched (7,354), most games started (815), and most complete games (749). Pitching for five different teams during his 22-year career, Young had 15 seasons with at least 20 wins, including five seasons with more than 30 victories. He won at least 20 games in all but one season from 1891 to 1904. Young led his league in wins four times, ERA, strikeouts, and innings pitched two times each, and shutouts seven times. Although he had many great seasons, Young was at his very best in 1901, when, pitching for the Boston Red Sox, he finished 33-10 with an ERA of 1.62, 38 complete games, and five shutouts. Young was among the two or three best pitchers in baseball in virtually every season from 1892 to 1904, and was among the five or ten greatest pitchers in the history of the game.

Satchel Paige

The most legendary figure, and the greatest pitcher in the history of the Negro Leagues, was Satchel Paige. The first Negro League player to be inducted into the Hall of Fame, Paige was the league's greatest drawing card and was rivaled only by Josh Gibson as its most famous player.

On barnstorming tours against major league players Paige regularly got the best of the likes of Dizzy Dean and Bob Feller, and he was known to walk hitters intentionally to get to Joe DiMaggio. DiMaggio once said that Paige "was the best I ever faced."

Although he didn't get to pitch in the major leagues until he was already in his forties, Paige was still extremely effective when he joined the Cleveland Indians in 1948, helping them win the American League pennant that year.

Cool Papa Bell was quoted in *Baseball When the Grass Was Real* as saying, "Satchel Paige was the fastest…I've seen Walter Johnson, Dizzy Dean, Bob Feller, Lefty Grove, all of them. All he threw for years was that fastball."

Sandy Koufax/Warren Spahn

Although Spahn was a study in consistency and durability, while Koufax was brilliant for only a few seasons, these two men have been grouped together because they were the two greatest lefthanded pitchers of the second half of the 20th century.

While some baseball historians object to Sandy Koufax being included among the very greatest pitchers of all time due to the relative brevity of his career, few of them would argue that he may well have been the greatest pitcher the game has ever seen for four seasons.

Koufax pitched in the major leagues for the Dodgers for only 12 seasons, and he was a good pitcher for only half his career. After struggling with his control his first six seasons, Koufax finally became a "pitcher" instead of a "thrower" in 1961. Over the next two seasons he was very good, winning 18 and 14 games, respectively, and leading the league with 269 strikeouts in 1961, and with a 2.54 ERA in 1962.

However, from 1963 to 1966, Koufax dominated baseball as no other pitcher ever has. In those four seasons, he won the Cy Young Award three times, even though only one trophy was presented for both leagues combined, won the pitcher's triple crown three times, won the N.L. MVP Award once, and finished second in the balloting two other times. For those four years, he was not only the best pitcher in baseball, but he was arguably the best player in the game. Here is his record for those four seasons:

1963: 25 wins, 5 losses; 1.88 ERA; 306 strikeouts; 311 innings pitched; 11 shutouts; 20 complete games.
1964: 19 wins, 5 losses; 1.74 ERA; 223 strikeouts; 7 shutouts.
1965: 26 wins, 8 losses; 2.04 ERA; 382 strikeouts; 335 innings pitched; 8 shutouts; 27 complete games.
1966: 27 wins, 9 losses; 1.73 ERA; 317 strikeouts; 323 innings pitched; 5 shutouts; 27 complete games.

From 1962 to 1966, Koufax's won-lost record was an amazing 111-34. That mark is rivaled only by Lefty Grove's six-season record of 152-41 from 1928 to 1933. Although the 1960s featured many outstanding pitchers, none of them came close to Koufax. In spite of the fact that he won only 165 games during his career (against only 87 losses), he was the greatest pitcher of his time, and one of the greatest ever.

In his 22-year major league career, spent mostly with the Braves, Warren Spahn won more games (363) than any other lefthander in baseball history. His thirteen seasons with 20 or more victories tied Christy Mathewson for the most by any pitcher during the 20th century. He led the National League in wins eight times, including five consecutive seasons from 1957 to 1961. He also led the league in ERA three times, strikeouts, innings pitched, and shutouts four times each, and complete games nine times, including seven in a row from 1957 to 1963.

Spahn won only one Cy Young Award during his career, but that was primarily because the award wasn't presented prior to 1956, Spahn's eleventh full season in the majors. Even after that, only one award was presented annually throughout the remainder of his career. However, Spahn was one of the five best pitchers in baseball in virtually every season from 1953 to 1961, failing to win at least 20 games only once during that period, and averaging 21 wins a season. He was the best pitcher in the game in at least three or four of those years, with probably his finest season coming in 1953. That year, Spahn finished 23-7, with a 2.10 ERA, 24 complete games, and five shutouts. He was selected to the National League All-Star Team 14 times and finished in the top five in the MVP voting four times.

Bob Feller

In his 18 seasons with the Cleveland Indians, Bob Feller won 266 games, while losing 162. However, if he hadn't lost almost four full seasons during the peak of his career due to time spent in the military, he would have won well over 300 games. In the three seasons immediately preceding his enlistment in the service, Feller won 24, 27, and 25 games, respectively, and he was the best pitcher in baseball. In 1946, his first full season back, Feller picked up right where he left off, having perhaps his finest season. That year, he finished 26-15, with an ERA of 2.18, and a league-leading 348 strikeouts, 371 innings pitched, 36 complete games, and 10 shutouts.

During his career, Feller led the league in wins six times, strikeouts seven times, and ERA once. He was a 20-game winner six times, threw three no-hitters, twelve one-hitters, and once struck out 18 batters in a game. He was the best pitcher in baseball from 1939 to 1941, and arguably in both 1946 and 1947 as well. He also played on two pennant-winners and one world championship team in Cleveland.

Bob Gibson/Juan Marichal

Gibson and Marichal were the dominant righthanders of the 1960s and, with the exception of Sandy Koufax, they were the decade's finest pitchers.

Bob Gibson was probably the most intimidating pitcher of his era, and one of the very, very best. Although he struggled with his control early in his career, as well as with the racial stereotypes that were prevalent at that time about black pitchers—that they were not intelligent and that they had no heart—by 1962, under new St. Louis manager Johnny Keane, Gibson started to turn things around. That year, he won 15 games while losing 13, compiled an ERA of 2.85, and struck out 208 batters—the first of nine times during his career he surpassed the 200-strikeout mark. The next two years he won 18 and 19 games, respectively, and he beat the Yankees twice in the 1964 World Series to begin to build his legacy as one of the greatest big-game pitchers in baseball history. Over the next six seasons, from 1965 to 1970, Gibson won more than 20 games and struck out more than 200 batters five times each, compiled an ERA under 3.00 four times, led the National League in shutouts four times, and in wins, ERA, strikeouts, and complete games once each.

After missing the final two months of the 1967 regular season with a broken leg suffered after being hit by a line drive off the bat of Roberto Clemente, Gibson led the Cardinals to the world championship by defeating the Boston Red Sox three times in the World Series. The following season, he won the first of his two Cy Young Awards and was also voted the National League's Most Valuable Player—one of two times he finished in the top five of the voting. Gibson was practically unhittable that year, finishing 22-9, with 28 complete games and a league-leading 1.12 ERA, 268 strikeouts, and 13 shutouts. Although Gibson lost the decisive seventh game of the World Series to Mickey Lolich to break his string of seven consecutive Series victories, he struck out a Series record 17 Detroit Tiger batters in winning Game One. Gibson won his second Cy Young Award in 1970 by finishing 23-7 with a 3.12 ERA and 274 strikeouts.

For his career, Gibson finished with a won-lost record of 251-174, an ERA of 2.91, and 3,117 strikeouts. From 1963 to 1972, he was one of the five best pitchers in baseball, being selected to the All-Star Team eight times during that period, and he was the best pitcher in the game in both 1968 and 1970.

Nobody won more games (191) during the 1960s than San Francisco Giants righthander Juan Marichal. From 1963 to 1969, he won more than 20 games six times, and he won at least 18 games eight times during his career. Marichal led the National League in wins, complete games, shutouts, and innings pitched twice each, and in ERA once. He won at least 25 games three times, and he finished with an ERA under 3.00 nine times, compiling a mark below 2.50 on six separate occasions. He also struck out more than 200 batters six times, and threw more than 300 innings three times.

Although Marichal never won the Cy Young Award, he was a consistently great pitcher. It was simply Marichal's misfortune that he had to compete against the brilliant Sandy Koufax. Nevertheless, he was one of the five best pitchers in baseball from 1962 to 1969, and he was among the top two or three hurlers in the sport in most of those years. In 1963, he finished 25-8 with a 2.41 ERA, 248 strikeouts, and 321 innings pitched. The following year, he finished 21-8 with a 2.48 ERA. In 1965 and 1966, Marichal won 22 and 25 games, respectively, while finishing with ERAs of 2.13 and 2.23. Marichal was also among the two or three best pitchers in the game in both 1968 and 1969, when he won 26 and 21 games, respectively.

A look at the record shows that Marichal won 243 games, while losing only 142 during his career. He also finished with a 2.89 ERA and struck out more than three times as many men as he walked. He was a nine-time All-Star and finished in the top ten in the league MVP voting three times, making it into the top five once. He was one of the finest pitchers of his era, and one of the best ever.

Tom Seaver/Steve Carlton/Jim Palmer

These three men all began their major league careers during the mid-1960s and went on to become the three best pitchers in the game for much of the 1970s.

After coming to the New York Mets in 1967, Tom Seaver almost instantly brought respectability to an organization that previously had very little to be proud of. That year, he was the National League's Rookie of the Year and he helped lead the team to its first world championship just two years later. In 1969, Seaver finished 25-7 with a 2.21 ERA, 208 strikeouts, and 273 innings pitched, won the first of his three Cy Young Awards, and finished second to Willie McCovey in the league MVP voting. Seaver also won the Cy Young Award in 1973 and 1975. In the first of those seasons, he compiled a record of 19-10 with a league-leading 2.08 ERA and 251 strikeouts, while throwing 290 innings. In 1975, he won 22 games, against only 9 losses, and finished with an ERA of 2.38 and a league-leading 243 strikeouts. Seaver finished in the top five in the Cy Young voting two other times.

During his career, Seaver led the National League in wins and earned run average three times each, and in strikeouts five times. He was a 20-game winner five times and won at least 16 games in 11 of the 13 seasons between 1967 and 1979. He also struck out more than 200 batters ten times and finished with an ERA under 3.00 twelve times, allowing fewer than 2.50 runs per contest on five separate occasions. He finished his career with 311 wins against 205 losses, an ERA of 2.86, and 3,640 strikeouts. Seaver was among the five best pitchers in baseball in virtually every season from 1969 to 1977 and, then again, in 1981. He was arguably the best pitcher in the game in 1969, 1971, 1973, 1975, 1977, and 1981, winning at least 20 games in all but two of those seasons, and finishing with an ERA of no higher than 2.58 in any of them. With the possible exception of Steve Carlton, Seaver was the best pitcher in the National League during the 1970s.

The winner of 329 games and four Cy Young Awards during a 24-year major league career spent primarily with the Philadelphia Phillies and St. Louis Cardinals, Steve Carlton was one of the greatest pitchers of his time, and one of the finest of the last half of the 20th century. Carlton was a 20-game winner six times, and he won at least 16 games four other times. From 1967, when he first joined the Cardinals' starting rotation, to 1984, his last productive season with the Philadelphia Phillies, Carlton failed to win at least 13 games only once. Over that 18-year stretch, he also finished with an earned run average under three runs a game eight times, struck out more than 200 batters eight times, and failed to throw at least 250 innings only five times.

Carlton led the National League in wins four times, ERA once, strikeouts and innings pitched five times each, and complete games three times. He had his finest season, and one of the most dominant years ever recorded by a pitcher, in 1972. Carlton won a record 45 percent of the last-place Phillies' 59 wins that year, en route to capturing the Cy Young Award for the first time. He led all N.L. pitchers in wins (27), ERA (1.97), strikeouts (310), innings pitched (346), and complete games (30), and was clearly the best pitcher in baseball. It could also be argued that he was the best pitcher in the game in his three other Cy Young Award years of 1977, 1980, and 1982. In the first of those years, he finished 23-10 with an ERA of 2.64, 198 strikeouts, and 283 innings pitched. In 1980, he helped lead the Phillies to the world championship by compiling a 24-9 record with an ERA of 2.34, and a league-leading 286 strikeouts and 304 innings pitched. Two years later, Carlton won the award for the final time by finishing 23-11 with a 3.10 ERA, and a league-leading 286 strikeouts, 295 innings pitched, six shutouts, and 19 complete games. At his peak, he was so dominant that he finished in the top five in the league MVP voting three times. Carlton is fourth on the all-time strikeout list, and is tenth in career victories.

The best pitcher in the American League, and one of the very best in baseball for most of the 1970s, was the Baltimore Orioles Jim Palmer. In eight of the nine seasons between 1970 and 1978,

Palmer won at least 20 games and allowed fewer than 3 earned runs per contest. During that nine-year period, he won three Cy Young Awards, led the league in ERA twice, in innings pitched four times, and in wins three consecutive seasons, beginning in 1975.

After winning 15 games during the 1966 regular season, and another in the World Series, Palmer missed virtually all of the next two seasons with arm trouble. However, he returned in 1969 to finish 16-4 with a 2.34 ERA. Palmer won at least 20 games and finished with an ERA well under 3.00 in each of the next four seasons, establishing himself as one of the game's finest pitchers. He won his first Cy Young Award in 1973, when he finished 22-9, led the league with a 2.40 ERA, and threw 296 innings. He also won the award in both 1975 and 1976, leading the league in wins both times, with totals of 23 and 22, respectively, and finishing with ERA's of 2.09 and 2.51.

During his career, Palmer finished with an ERA under 3.00 nine times, under 2.50 five times, and threw more than 300 innings four times. He ended his career with a won-lost record of 268-152 and an outstanding ERA of 2.86.

Carl Hubbell/Dizzy Dean

Hubbell and Dean were the National League's top two pitchers for much of the 1930s. Between them, they dominated most N.L. pitching categories from 1932 to 1937. With the exception of the American League's Lefty Grove, they were clearly the best pitchers in the game at that time.

Carl Hubbell's career won-lost record of 253-154 and earned run average of 2.98 are both outstanding figures. However, neither mark is a true indication of just how dominant he actually was at the peak of his career. During the mid-1930s, not only was Hubbell, along with Dizzy Dean, the National League's best pitcher, he was its most dominant player. The greatest evidence of this dominance can be seen by the fact that he is one of only three pitchers in baseball history to win his league's Most Valuable Player Award twice.

From 1929 to 1937, Hubbell was an outstanding pitcher, winning more than 20 games five times, and failing to win at least 17 games only once. From 1933 to 1937, though, he was rivaled only by the St. Louis Cardinals Dizzy Dean as the National League's best pitcher. During that five-year period, Hubbell won more than 20 games each season, finished with an ERA well under 3.00 three times, threw more than 300 innings four times, and completed more than 20 games four times. He had perhaps his finest season in 1933, when he won the MVP Award for the first time. That year, he won 23 games while losing 12, compiled a superb 1.66 ERA, and also led the league with 308 innings pitched and 10 shutouts. Hubbell was named the league's Most Valuable Player a second time in 1936, when he finished with a record of 26-6, an ERA of 2.31, 304 innings pitched, and 25 complete games. He was unquestionably the best pitcher in baseball in both those seasons, and one of the two or three best in the game in each season from 1933 to 1937. During his career, Hubbell led the league in wins and ERA three times each, and in complete games, shutouts, and innings pitched once each.

The career of Dizzy Dean was not as long as that of Hubbell, but Dean was just as dominant at his peak. Although he won only 150 games (against just 83 losses) during his 12-year major league career, Dean was outstanding from 1932 to 1937, and was the best pitcher in the game in both 1934 and 1935. From 1932 to 1936, he won at least 20 games four times, notching 18 victories in the other season. He was well on his way to another 20-win season in 1937 when a line-drive off the bat of A.L. outfielder Earl Averill at the All-Star Game broke his toe. The injury prompted Dean to alter his pitching motion and eventually caused him to damage his right arm. As a result, Dean was never the same pitcher again.

However, prior to his injury, Dean was named the National League's MVP in 1934, when he led the St. Louis Cardinals to the World Championship by becoming the last N.L. pitcher to win 30 games in a season. That year, Dean finished 30-7 with an ERA of 2.66, and led the league with 195 strikeouts and seven shutouts. He also finished runner-up in the MVP voting in each of the next two seasons. In 1935, he won 28 games while losing only 12, and, in 1936, he finished just behind Hubbell in the MVP voting after winning another 24 games during the regular season. In all, Dean led the league in wins twice, strikeouts four times, shutouts twice, complete games three times, and innings pitched three times.

Eddie Plank/Mordecai Brown

Both Plank and Brown were outstanding pitchers who began their careers at the turn of the last century. Neither man was considered to be the best pitcher in the game at any point during his career, but they were both among the five best pitchers in baseball for extended periods of time.

During his 17-year major league career, spent mostly with Connie Mack's Philadelphia Athletics, Eddie Plank was often overshadowed by some of the other top pitchers in the game, some of whom pitched for the same team as him. Plank never led the American League in any major pitching category, and, for quite a few seasons, he had to compete with fellow A's pitchers Rube Waddell, Chief Bender, and Jack Coombs for preeminence on his own team's staff. However, Plank won at least 20 games eight different times, twice compiling as many as 26 victories. He was a 20-game winner five times between 1902 and 1907, winning 19 games the other season.

Plank performed at a particularly high level in 1904, 1905, 1907, 1909, 1911, and 1912, winning at least 23 games in five of those six seasons, and finishing with an ERA no higher than 2.26 in any of them. In 1909, the one year he failed to win 20 games, he may have been the most effective, compiling an ERA of 1.76 while winning 19 games. In each of those six seasons, as well as one or two others, he was among the five best pitchers in the game.

Plank ended his career with 326 victories, the third highest win total of any lefthanded pitcher in baseball history, behind only Warren Spahn and Steve Carlton. He also compiled an outstanding earned run average of 2.35. In addition to winning at least 20 games eight times, Plank finished with at least 16 victories six other times. He also finished with an ERA under 2.50 thirteen times.

"Three Fingered" Mordecai Brown's 14-year major league career included stints with seven different teams. However, Brown's peak seasons were spent with the Chicago Cubs, on some of the greatest teams of the first decade of the 20th century.

Although overshadowed by the great Christy Mathewson, from 1906 to 1910 Brown was a truly great pitcher, second only to the New York Giants righthander among National League hurlers. In each of those five seasons Brown was a 20-game winner, and, in four of the five, he surpassed 25 victories. He also finished with an ERA of less than 2.00 in each of those seasons. Brown's ERA of 1.04 in 1906 was the lowest of the 20th century, and he followed that up the next four seasons with marks of 1.39, 1.47, 1.31, and 1.86. In fact, his career ERA of 2.06 is the third lowest ever. Brown led the N.L. with 27 wins in 1909, after winning 29 games the previous year, and he also led the league in shutouts and complete games twice each. He was a 20-game winner a total of six times, won as many as 17 games two other times, and finished with an ERA under 2.00 six times. Brown ended his career with 239 victories, against only 130 defeats.

Nolan Ryan

When the baseball writers elected Nolan Ryan to the Hall of Fame in 1999, naming him on 491 of the 497 total ballots cast (a percentage of 98.79, the second highest ever attained by any player), few people disagreed. After all, in his 28 major league seasons, Ryan struck out more batters (5,714) and threw more no-hitters (7) than any other pitcher in baseball history. He finished with an ERA under 3.00 eight times, twice surrendering less than 2.50 runs per contest, struck out over 300 batters six times, fanned more than 200 another nine times, and threw more than 300 innings twice. Ryan was an eight-time All-Star who led his league in ERA twice, shutouts three times, and strikeouts eleven times. His six seasons with more than 300 strikeouts, and 15 years with at least 200 Ks, are both major league records.

At his best, Ryan was one of the most dominating pitchers ever. There is no disputing that he belongs in the Hall of Fame.

What is debatable, however, is whether or not he truly deserved to be ushered in with such alacrity, and in such overwhelming fashion. For Ryan's career was marked with inconsistency since he often failed to pitch at the dominating level his strikeout totals and no-hit performances would seem to indicate.

While it is true that Ryan won 324 games during his career, he also lost 292, finishing with a winning percentage of only .526, the second lowest of any starting pitcher ever elected to the Hall of Fame. Some might argue that he had the misfortune of playing on bad teams throughout his career, but that was not entirely true. While many of his peak seasons were spent with a below average California Angels team from 1972 to 1979, the Angels became a contender during the latter portion of his tenure there. Following the free agent signings of players such as Don Baylor, Joe Rudi, and Bobby Grich, they were a solid team his last few years with the team, and even won their division in 1979. That year, Ryan's record was 16-14, and he finished just 10-13 the previous year.

Ryan signed as a free agent with the Houston Astros in 1980 and spent the next nine seasons with that franchise. With Ryan, Houston won the division in both 1980 and 1986. In those two seasons, he compiled records of 11-10 and 12-8, respectively. Thus, Ryan's rather mediocre winning percentage cannot be attributed solely to the fact that he spent a good portion of his career pitching for average teams. He was erratic and, especially early in his career, prone to issuing an inordinate number of bases on balls.

Ryan's career earned run average of 3.19 was good, but hardly spectacular, especially when one considers that he spent most of his career pitching in good pitchers' parks. New York's Shea Stadium and Houston's Astrodome were both very favorable for pitchers, and the ballparks in California and Texas were quite fair, to say the least.

In spite of his 324 victories, Ryan was a 20-game winner only twice, and he won as many as 16 games only six other times. He never led his league in wins, and he never won the Cy Young Award. In fact, in only three seasons could a legitimate case be made for him being among the five best pitchers in the game. In

1973, pitching for the Angels, he finished 21-16, with a 2.87 ERA, 383 strikeouts, and 26 complete games. That year, he finished second in the American League Cy Young voting to Jim Palmer. The following year, he finished 22-16, with an ERA of 2.89, 367 strikeouts, and another 26 complete games. That year, he finished third in the Cy Young voting, with the award going to Catfish Hunter. With the Astros, during the strike-shortened 1981 season, Ryan won 11 games, against only 5 losses, and led the league with a 1.69 ERA in finishing fourth in the N.L. Cy Young balloting. Although he did finish in the top five in the voting two other times, in no other season would he have been ranked among the five best pitchers in baseball. During the first half of the 1970s, pitchers such as Tom Seaver, Steve Carlton, Jim Palmer, Catfish Hunter, and Ferguson Jenkins were all better. Later that decade, Seaver, Carlton, and Palmer were joined by Ron Guidry. At different times during the 1980s, Guidry, Jack Morris, Dwight Gooden, Fernando Valenzuela, and Roger Clemens were more consistent winners.

In short, Nolan Ryan is one of the most overrated players in baseball history. Strikeouts and no-hitters are quite glamorous, and they tend to leave a lasting impression on those who witness them. But the game is all about *winning*, and there were many pitchers who were superior to Ryan in that regard. Throughout most of his career, Walter Johnson pitched for teams that were inferior to those Ryan played on. Yet he was able to compile a lifetime winning percentage of .599—73 points higher than Ryan's mark. Other outstanding Hall of Fame pitchers such as Dazzy Vance, Burleigh Grimes, and Robin Roberts also spent large portions of their careers pitching for mediocre teams. Yet, they too compiled winning percentages that were much better than Ryan's (Vance's was .585; Grimes' was .560; Roberts' was .539). A truly great pitcher should be able to win the vast majority of his games, even if the team he plays for is not particularly strong. That is something Ryan was unable to do during his career. Thus, he should not even be ranked among the 20 greatest pitchers of all-time. Ryan was a very good pitcher. He just wasn't as good as the BBWAA made him out to be when it made him the second most popular choice in the history of the Hall of Fame voting.

Ed Walsh

Chicago White Sox righthanded spitball artist Ed Walsh spent 14 seasons in the major leagues, and was a top-flight pitcher in only seven of those. In the other seven seasons, he failed to win more than eight games. However, in virtually all of the other years, he was among the top two or three pitchers in the American League, and one of the five best in baseball. As a result, he would have to be considered a legitimate Hall of Famer.

Walsh won more than 20 games four times, compiling win totals of 24 in 1907, and 27 in both 1911 and 1912. In each of those seasons, he was among the five best pitchers in the game. However, Walsh was clearly the best pitcher in baseball in 1908. That year, he finished 40-15 with an ERA of 1.42, 269 strikeouts, 464 innings pitched, 11 shutouts, and 42 complete games. He finished with an ERA under 2.00 five straight seasons from 1906 to 1910, and his career mark of 1.82 is the lowest of any pitcher from the 20th century. In an era when hitters struck out far less than they would in future generations, Walsh also struck out more than 200 batters five times. In all, he led the American League in ERA twice, wins once, strikeouts twice, innings pitched four times, and shutouts three times. He ended his career with 195 wins, against 126 losses.

Joe McGinnity

In the first few years of the 20th century, no pitcher was more durable than "Iron Man" Joe McGinnity. Although his major league career lasted only ten seasons, McGinnity managed to win 246 games, while losing only 142, and he completed 314 of his 381 starts. It was not at all unusual for him to pitch both ends of a doubleheader, and he won a record three twin-bills in one month for the New York Giants in 1903.

In his first four seasons, spent with the original Baltimore Orioles and Brooklyn Dodgers, McGinnity won 28 games twice, 26 games once, and 21 once. He had his finest seasons with the

Giants, though, from 1903 to 1906, winning no fewer than 21 games, and topping the 30-mark twice. In fact, in 1904, McGinnity even surpassed teammate Christy Mathewson as the best pitcher in the National League. That year, he finished 35-8, to lead the league in victories, while also topping the circuit with a 1.61 ERA, 408 innings pitched, and 9 shutouts. Although McGinnity pitched in Mathewson's shadow for much of his career, he was probably the league's second best pitcher for much of the first decade of the 20th century. He led the N.L. in wins five times, ERA once, innings pitched four times, and complete games twice. Despite the relative brevity of McGinnity's career, it would be difficult to questions his 1946 election to Cooperstown by the Veteran's Committee.

Bob Lemon

In his 13 seasons with the Cleveland Indians, from 1946 to 1958, Bob Lemon pitched alongside some very fine pitchers. At different times during his tenure there, the Indians staff included the likes of fellow Hall of Famers Bob Feller and Early Wynn, tough righthander Mike Garcia, and the ill-fated Herb Score. Nevertheless, for most of his career, Lemon stood out as the ace of the Indians staff.

From 1948 to 1956, Lemon was one of the two or three best pitchers in the American League, and one of the five best in baseball. During that nine-year period, he won at least 20 games seven times, never failing to post at least 17 victories. Over that same stretch, he also completed more than 20 games seven times, and, during a pretty good era for hitters, finished with an ERA under 3.00 four times. He led the American League in wins three times, innings pitched four times, complete games five times, and shutouts and strikeouts once each.

Lemon's first outstanding season was 1948, when he won 20 games for the first time, compiled a 2.82 ERA, and led the league with 10 shutouts. He was the A.L.'s best pitcher that year and again the following year, when he finished 22-10, with an ERA of 2.99 and 22 complete games. After winning 23 games in 1950, and another 17 the following year, Lemon had another outstanding year in 1952. That year, he finished 22-11 with a 2.50 ERA and 28 complete games. Only Bobby Shantz's MVP season for the Philadelphia A's prevented Lemon from being the best pitcher in the league that year. However, in 1954, Lemon had perhaps his finest season, winning 23 games, while losing only 7, compiling a 2.72 ERA, and leading the Indians to the pennant. He was clearly the best pitcher in the league that year.

During his career, Lemon was selected to the All-Star Team seven times and finished in the top 10 in the league MVP voting six times, making it into the top five on three separate occasions. He was one of the top pitchers of his day and a worthy Hall of Famer.

Robin Roberts

Righthander Robin Roberts was a dominant pitcher in only six of his 19 major league seasons. However, for those six seasons, Roberts rivaled Warren Spahn as the National League's best pitcher, and was one of the five best hurlers in baseball.

Although he later pitched for the Orioles, Astros, and Cubs as well, Roberts' best years were with the Philadelphia Phillies, for whom he won at least 15 games ten times in 14 seasons. He was a 20-game winner each year from 1950 to 1955, winning as many as 28 games in 1952, and posting 23 victories three other times. In that 1952 season, Roberts was arguably the best pitcher in baseball. His won-lost record was 28-7, and he finished with an ERA of 2.59, 30 complete games, and 330 innings pitched. He was also among the two or three best hurlers in the game in each of the next three seasons, winning 23 games each year, finishing with an ERA under 3.00 twice, and throwing more than 300 innings and completing close to 30 games each year. Though his productivity declined considerably after 1955 due to the strain put on his arm by throwing more than 300 innings in six consecutive seasons, Roberts managed to win 286 games over his career (against 245 losses). Had the Phillies teams he pitched for in many of those seasons been stronger, his record would have been even better.

While Roberts' career ERA of 3.41 is less than spectacular, the 1950s were a pretty good hitter's era and Philadelphia's Shibe Park was a good hitter's ballpark. Still, he managed to finish with an ERA under 3.00 six times and complete more than 20 games eight times. Roberts was selected to the All-Star Team seven times and finished in the top 10 in the league MVP voting five times, making it into the top five twice. Roberts' status as one of baseball's dominant pitchers from 1950 to 1955, along with the fact that he won 286 games playing for weak teams throughout most of his career, clearly legitimize his place in Cooperstown.

Whitey Ford

The career statistics of Whitey Ford were aided immeasurably by the fact that he was a lefthander pitching in Yankee Stadium, with its distant outfield fences for righthanded batters, and that he played for the dominant team of his era. Yet, he was still an excellent pitcher and a worthy Hall of Famer.

In fact, for much of his career, Ford was one of the two or three best pitchers in the American League, and one of the five best in baseball. His 236 victories, against only 106 defeats, give him the highest winning percentage (.690) of any pitcher with more than 200 wins since 1900. He also finished with an outstanding earned run average of 2.75. Although Ford won 20 games only twice during his career, that was mostly because Casey Stengel, who managed Ford for nine seasons, preferred to manipulate his pitching rotation so that he could save his ace for the better teams in the league. After Ralph Houk replaced Stengel as Yankee manager in 1961, Ford had his two biggest seasons, winning 25 games (against only 4 losses) that year, and winning another 24 (against only 7 defeats) in 1963. In 1961, Ford won the Cy Young Award. He would have won it again two years later had one been presented to the best pitcher in each league. However, that year's award went to the National League's Sandy Koufax, who was also named N.L. MVP.

Ford was also the best pitcher in the American League in both 1955 and 1956, winning 18 and 19 games, respectively, and finishing with ERA's of 2.63 and 2.47. Although he won 20 games only twice, Ford won at least 16 games eight other times. During his career, he led the American League in wins three times and in ERA, innings pitched, and shutouts twice each. He finished with an ERA under 3.00 ten times, and with one under 2.50 five times. Ford was an eight-time All-Star, and he finished in the top five in the league MVP voting twice.

Dazzy Vance

At first glance, one is hardly overwhelmed by Dazzy Vance's career record of 197-140 and ERA of 3.24. However, when it is considered that he compiled those numbers during one of the greatest hitting eras in baseball history, pitching mostly for the second-division Brooklyn Dodgers, Vance's numbers become far more impressive.

For much of the 1920s, Vance was the National League's top pitcher, winning more than 20 games three times, and compiling at least 16 victories three other times. He led the league in strikeouts each season from 1922 to 1928, and he also finished first in wins twice, ERA three times, shutouts four times, and complete games twice. His greatest season was 1924, when he finished 28-6 with a league-leading 2.16 ERA, 262 strikeouts, 308 innings pitched, and 30 complete games in winning league MVP honors. Vance was also the league's best pitcher in both 1925 and 1928, finishing fifth in the MVP voting in 1925. In each of those seasons, he won 22 games and struck out over 200 batters, and he led the league with a 2.09 ERA in 1928.

Four times during his career, Vance finished with an ERA under 3.00, with one of his greatest achievements coming in 1930. That was the year the National League experienced one of the greatest offensive explosions in history, with Hack Wilson knocking in a record 191 runs, Bill Terry batting .401, and runs being scored at a record pace throughout the league. In the midst of all that, Vance finished with a rather remarkable 2.61 ERA, making him the best pitcher in baseball, with the exception of the American League's Lefty Grove. Therefore, in spite of the fact that he had only seven truly outstanding seasons, Vance was a dominant pitcher at his peak, and would have to be considered a worthy Hall of Famer.

Early Wynn

Early Wynn was not a great pitcher, and a case could be made for him being among the five best hurlers in baseball in only five of his 23 major league seasons. However, he was a very good pitcher for a long time, and he had enough outstanding years to be considered a legitimate Hall of Famer.

Wynn was one of the few players in baseball history to spend parts of four different decades in the majors, having lengthy stints with the Washington Senators, Cleveland Indians, and Chicago White Sox. He had his breakout season for the Senators in 1943, finishing 18-12 with a 2.91 ERA. After being dealt to the Indians prior to the start of the 1949 campaign, Wynn won at least 17 games in seven of his nine years in Cleveland, topping the 20-victory mark four times. He was among the five best pitchers in baseball in 1951, 1952, 1954, and 1956, winning 23 games in two of those seasons, and compiling 20 victories in the other two years. He also finished with an ERA under 3.00 in three of those seasons. Wynn's greatest season, though, was 1959, when, pitching for the pennant-winning White Sox, he finished 22-10 with a 3.17 ERA to earn the Cy Young Award as baseball's best pitcher.

In all, Wynn was a 20-game winner five times during his career, winning at least 17 games five other times. He led the league in wins twice, ERA once, strikeouts twice, and innings pitched three times. Wynn finished in the top 10 in the MVP voting three times, making it into the top five twice.

Hoyt Wilhelm/Rollie Fingers/Dennis Eckersley/ Bruce Sutter/Goose Gossage

These five men have been grouped together because they were the first five relief pitchers to be elected to the Hall of Fame.

Hoyt Wilhelm was a pioneer of sorts, being the first pitcher to have a lengthy major league career being used almost exclusively in relief. Prior to World War II, most pitchers who entered a game in relief were either starters who were past their prime, or those who simply were not good enough to become members of their team's starting rotation. While others, such as Johnny Murphy and Joe Page of the Yankees, and Jim Konstanty of the Phillies previously experienced fleeting success as relief specialists, Wilhelm was the first man to make a career out of coming out of the bullpen. In acknowledgement, the BBWAA elected him to the Hall of Fame in 1985.

Yet, Wilhelm was not voted in simply because he was a baseball pioneer. He was an excellent pitcher. After a brilliant rookie season with the New York Giants in 1952 in which he saved 11 games and won 15 others, all in relief, Wilhelm won 12 more games for the Giants in 1954. He was converted briefly into a starter by Baltimore in 1959, but, despite winning 15 games that year, returned to the bullpen shortly thereafter. After being traded to the Chicago White Sox prior to the start of the 1963 season, Wilhelm became a full-time reliever once more, and gradually developed into the best the game had seen up to that point. Over the next three seasons, he saved a total of 68 games while winning another 24. From 1964 to 1968, his ERA never got as high as 2.00 as he used his knuckleball to baffle American League hitters. During his career, Wilhelm won more than 10 games five times, four times strictly as a reliever. He finished with a record of 143 wins and 122 losses, an ERA of 2.52, and 227 saves.

If Hoyt Wilhelm was the first true relief specialist the game ever saw, Rollie Fingers, along with Sparky Lyle, was the first to bring relief pitching to the next level. In 18 big league seasons, Fingers filled the closer role better than any other man had, up to then. Pitching for the Oakland Athletics, San Diego Padres, and Milwaukee Brewers, Fingers was among the best relief pitchers in the game for much of his career. Four times he finished in double-digits in victories, twice he saved more than 30 games, three times he finished with an ERA of less than 2.00, and eight times he struck out more than three times as many men as he walked. He also led his league in both saves and appearances three times.

After helping the Oakland Athletics to three world championships from 1972 to 1974, and then spending four seasons with the Padres, Fingers had his greatest season with the Milwaukee Brewers in 1981. That year, he became one of only three relief pitchers to win both the Cy Young and MVP Award in the same season. That strike-shortened season, Fingers compiled a record of 6-3, a 1.04 ERA, and a league-leading 28 saves, while surrendering only 55 hits in 78 innings of work, walking only 13 batters, while striking out 61.

As one of the two or three greatest relief pitchers in the history of the game, Dennis Eckersley is most deserving of his place in Cooperstown. He was the premier closer of his time, and is rivaled only by Rollie Fingers and Mariano Rivera as the top relief pitcher ever. Eckersley is one of just a handful of relief pitchers to win both the Cy Young and MVP Award in the same season. He accomplished the feat in 1992 when he compiled a 7-1 record and a 1.91 ERA for the Oakland Athletics, while leading the American League with 51 saves. Eckersley also led the league in saves in 1988, when he closed out 45 contests for Oakland, while compiling a 2.35 ERA and allowing just 52 hits in 73 innings of work. Eckersley was even better in 1990, when he finished second in the A.L. with 48 saves, while pitching to a brilliant 0.61 earned run average and permitting only 41 safeties in 73 innings pitched. Eckersley was so dominant as a closer that he finished in the top five in the league MVP voting three times during his career. He also placed in the top five in the Cy Young balloting on four separate occasions. In all, Eckersley saved more than 30 games eight times, compiling as many as 40 saves four different times. He led the A.L. in that department twice. He finished his career with a won-lost record of 197-171, 390 saves, and an ERA of 3.50.

Of course, many of those decisions came during the first half of Eckersley's career when he was a solid starting pitcher for three different teams. He originally broke into the big leagues with the Cleveland Indians in 1975 as a starter. Eckersley also pitched for the Boston Red Sox and Chicago Cubs before being converted into a relief pitcher by Oakland A's manager Tony LaRussa prior to the start of the 1987 season. As a starter, Eckersley compiled a won-lost record of 151-128 over his first 12 seasons. He had his finest season in that role for the Red Sox in 1978 when he finished 20-8 with a 2.99 ERA. However, Eckersley truly made his mark as a relief specialist, and that is what he went into the Hall of Fame as.

The BBWAA's 2006 selection of Bruce Sutter to Cooperstown, in the former closer's 13th year of eligibility, was long overdue. Not only was Sutter the preeminent relief pitcher of his era, but he was the originator of the split-finger fastball that has become so popular in baseball over the last two decades.

Sutter had his finest seasons for the Chicago Cubs and the St. Louis Cardinals. He first became Chicago's closer in 1977 when he finished second in the National League with 31 saves while compiling a 1.34 ERA. Two years later, he began a string of four consecutive seasons in which he led the league in saves. In 1979, Sutter saved 37 games for the Cubs, pitched to a brilliant 2.22 ERA, and allowed only 67 hits in 101 innings of work, while striking out 110 batters. His split-finger fastball made him virtually unhittable, enabling him to become only the third relief pitcher in either league to capture the Cy Young Award. Sutter had another phenomenal season for the Cardinals in 1984 when he saved a league-leading 45 games, while compiling an ERA of 1.54.

In all, Sutter led the National League in saves a total of five times, and also finished in the top five on three other occasions. In addition to his 1979 Cy Young, he placed in the top five in the voting three other times, and also finished in the top ten in the league MVP balloting a total of five times. One can only wonder why it took the members of the BBWAA so long to admit him to Cooperstown.

Another dominant reliever who probably waited longer than he should have to be selected by the baseball writers was Rich "Goose" Gossage, who was elected to the Hall of Fame in his ninth year of eligibility. Gossage was the most intimidating relief pitcher of his time, and may well have been the most imposing one ever.

Gossage spent 23 seasons terrorizing opposing batters with his blazing fastball that often approached 100 miles per-hour on the radar gun. Five times during his career, Gossage compiled more strikeouts than innings pitched, and he allowed fewer hits than innings pitched in 18 of his 23 seasons.

Gossage had his first big year with the Chicago White Sox in 1975, winning nine games coming out of the bullpen, compiling a 1.84 ERA, and leading the American League with 26 saves. Goose had another brilliant season as a member of the Pittsburgh Pirates in 1977, winning 11 games, saving 26 others, pitching to a 1.62 ERA, and allowing only 78 hits in 133 innings of work while striking out 151 batters. After joining the Yankees the following year, Gossage established himself as the American League's dominant closer, leading the circuit with 27 saves, compiling a 2.01 earned run average, and allowing only 87 hits in 134 innings pitched. He was even more dominant during the strike-shortened 1981 campaign, finishing second in the league with 20 saves, compiling a magnificent 0.77 ERA, and allowing just 22 hits in 47 innings of work.

During his career, Gossage led the American League in saves three times, compiling more than 30 in a season twice, and finishing with more than 20 eight other times. He posted an ERA under 2.00 four times. Gossage placed in the top five in the Cy Young balloting four times, and finished in the top ten in the league MVP balloting twice, placing as high as third in 1980. He was also a nine-time All-Star.

Ferguson Jenkins/Gaylord Perry

Perry and Jenkins had a few things in common. For one thing, they pitched during the same era, for several different teams. They also pitched for a very long time. Furthermore, while both men were very good pitchers, neither ever had a season in which they were considered to be the best pitcher in baseball.

During his 19-year major league career, Ferguson Jenkins pitched for four different teams. However, most of his finest seasons were spent with the Chicago Cubs. As a member of the Cubs, Jenkins was somewhat overlooked, even though he surpassed 20 victories six consecutive seasons from 1967 to 1972. Jenkins always seemed to be the forgotten man because, during his prime, the National League also featured several other outstanding hurlers such as Bob Gibson, Juan Marichal, Tom Seaver, and Steve Carlton. As a result, Jenkins never got the credit he deserved for being among the very best pitchers in the game. Nevertheless, in each of those six seasons, he was among the three or four best pitchers in the National League, and one of the five best in baseball.

Jenkins finally received the recognition he so richly deserved in 1971 when he was voted the league's Cy Young Award winner. That year, he finished 24-13, with a 2.77 ERA, 263 strikeouts, 325 innings pitched, and 30 complete games to beat out Seaver for the award. Even that year, though, he was somewhat overshadowed by Oakland's Vida Blue, who won both the Cy Young and MVP Awards in the American League.

After being traded to Texas following the 1973 campaign in the deal that brought Bill Madlock to the Cubs, Jenkins had another great season for the Rangers in 1974. That year, he finished 25-12, with a 2.82 ERA, 225 strikeouts, 328 innings pitched, and 29 complete games. However, he finished second to Catfish Hunter in the A.L. Cy Young voting. Jenkins had only one more big year, winning 18 games for Texas in 1978, but, at his peak, he was a dominant pitcher and a well-qualified Hall of Famer.

During his career, Jenkins won 20 games seven times, compiled at least 16 victories three other times, finished with an ERA under 3.00 four times, struck out more than 200 batters six times, surpassing the 250-mark on four separate occasions, threw more than 300 innings five times, and completed more than 20 games eight times. He finished with 284 wins, against 226 losses.

In his 22 big league seasons, Gaylord Perry pitched for eight different clubs. He spent his peak years with the San Francisco Giants and Cleveland Indians. In ten seasons with the Giants, from 1962 to 1971, Perry was a 20-game winner twice, and he won at least 15 games four other times. While he was a good pitcher from 1966 to 1971, he was a very good one in only two of those seasons—1966 and 1970. In 1966, Perry finished 21-8 with a 2.99 ERA and 201 strikeouts. In 1970, he finished 23-13 with a 3.20 ERA, 214 strikeouts, 328 innings pitched, and 23 complete games.

In each of the other four seasons during that stretch, Perry's ERA was well below 3.00, but his wins barely outnumbered his losses. In 1967, he finished 15-17; 1968, 16-15; 1969, 19-14; and 1971, 16-12. Perry's rather mediocre won-lost record those years cannot be blamed on the fact that the Giants were a bad team because they were a perennial contender. Thus, in his years with San Francisco, Perry was a good pitcher; but he was not a Hall of Fame caliber hurler.

However, after being traded to the Cleveland Indians for Sam McDowell prior to the start of the 1972 season, Perry had his greatest season. That year, pitching for a mediocre team, he led the league with 24 wins (against 16 losses), and compiled a 1.92 ERA, 234 strikeouts, 342 innings pitched, and 29 complete games in winning the A.L. Cy Young Award. After an unspectacular 1973 season, Perry returned to top form in 1974, winning 21 games and finishing with a 2.51 ERA, 216 strikeouts, 322 innings pitched, and 28 complete games.

After three more mediocre seasons for the Indians and Texas Rangers, Perry won his second Cy Young Award in 1978 as a member of the San Diego Padres. That year, he won 21 games while losing only 6 and compiling a 2.73 ERA. The rest of his career, Perry was merely a .500 pitcher, never again winning more than 12 games. In all, he was a 20-game winner five times and finished with an ERA under 3.00 nine times. He finished his career with 314 victories, against 265 losses.

Perry was a very good pitcher. But was he good enough to be considered a legitimate Hall of Famer? If one ascribes to the theory that 300 wins should automatically guarantee a pitcher election to Cooperstown the answer is yes. The feeling here, though, is that other things must be factored into the equation as well. A win total in excess of 300 certainly goes a long way towards justifying a pitcher's place in Cooperstown since it is indicative of a certain amount of sustained excellence over a lengthy period of time. However, a pitcher's overall performance must be evaluated, and the level of dominance he displayed throughout his career needs to be examined before his name can be linked to the all-time greats.

In Perry's case, while he won two Cy Young Awards, he was never considered to be the best pitcher in baseball. In 1972, that honor went to the Phillies Steve Carlton, and in 1978, New York's Ron Guidry was clearly the best pitcher in the game. In fact, in only a few seasons could it even be said that Perry was the best pitcher on his own team's staff, since, in his years with San Francisco, Juan Marichal was generally considered to be the staff ace. However, Perry was among the five best pitchers in baseball in at least four seasons—1970, 1972, 1974, and 1978. He led his league in wins three times, innings pitched twice, complete games twice, and shutouts once. As was noted earlier, he won two Cy Young Awards, and he also finished in the top five in the Cy Young voting two other times. In addition, Perry placed in the top 10 in the MVP voting twice and was selected to the All-Star Team five times.

Overall, it would seem that Perry fared moderately well when using our Hall of Fame criteria to examine his credentials. That, in conjunction with his 314 victories, is probably enough to justify his 1991 election by the BBWAA. However, he should be viewed as a somewhat borderline selection, and as a prime example of how a simple standard such as 300 wins or 500 home runs should not be used as the sole criteria for judging whether or not a player belongs in Cooperstown.

Pud Galvin/Charley Radbourn/Mickey Welch/ Tim Keefe/John Clarkson/Kid Nichols

While on the subject of pitchers who won 300 games, there were six 19th century hurlers who were elected to the Hall of Fame by the Veterans Committee prior to 1973. Just looking at their win totals, one would assume they earned their places in Cooperstown. However, when these men pitched, the sport of baseball differed drastically from the game it eventually became—even the one that was played during the early years of the 20th century.

In the very early days of baseball, prior to the turn of the last century, it was not at all unusual for a team's best pitcher to start as much as 40, or even, 50 percent of his team's games. Top pitchers typically made between 55 and 75 starts, and came away with anywhere from 50 to 70 decisions. Therefore, it was not that unusual for a good pitcher to win as many as 40 games, and lose as many as 25. That being the case, 300 victories, while still an impressive figure, was not nearly as difficult a mark to reach as it would become in later years. As a result, there really is a need to look more closely at the careers of these six men to determine if they truly belong in the Hall of Fame.

The first of these 19th century pitchers was Jim "Pud" Galvin, who pitched for four different teams during a career that started in 1875 and ended in 1892. Twice Galvin started more than 70 games in a season, once 66, and five other times more than 50. Needless to say, he had an inordinate number of decisions, winning and losing more than 20 games ten times each. Galvin won 46 games twice, and 37 once. However, he also lost 35 games once, and 29 another time. His best season came in 1884, when, pitching for the Buffalo Bisons, he finished 46-22 with a 1.99 ERA, 369 strikeouts, 12 shutouts, and an incredible 71 complete games and 636 innings pitched. Amazingly enough, though, Galvin didn't lead the league that year in any major pitching category. In fact, he never led the league in wins, ERA, or strikeouts. However, in 1883, he was the league-leader in games (76), complete games (72), shutouts (5), and innings pitched (656). Galvin ended his career with a record of 365-310 and a 2.85 ERA.

While he was not the best pitcher of his era, and probably should not be thought of as having been anything more than a very good pitcher, Galvin was able to distinguish himself in two distinct ways. First, he won more games than any other hurler who pitched exclusively during the 19th century. He is also the only pitcher in history to win at least 20 games ten times without ever playing on a pennant winner. On the other hand, Galvin had only two truly great years, and just three other very good ones. He also finished with a losing record in five of his 15 big league seasons. The Veterans Committee elected him to the Hall of Fame in 1965.

The career of Charley "Old Hoss" Radbourn did not last as long as that of Galvin, but he still managed to win over 300 games. Pitching for three different teams during his 11-year major league career, Radbourn had his greatest seasons with the Providence Grays. Pitching for Providence from 1881 to 1885, he won at least 25 games every season, never finishing with an ERA any higher than 2.43. He was baseball's greatest pitcher in both 1883 and 1884. In the first of those years, he finished 48-25, with a 2.05 ERA, 315 strikeouts, 66 complete games, and 632 innings pitched. The following season, he was even better, leading the league's pitchers in every major statistical category by compiling a record of 59-12, with an ERA of 1.38, 441 strikeouts, 11 shutouts, 73 complete games, and 678 innings pitched. Unfortunately, after throwing so many innings those two seasons, Radbourn was never quite the same pitcher after 1884. Yet he still managed to win more than 20 games nine times (while losing over 20 games five times) and compile a career record of 309 wins against only 195 losses, and an ERA of 2.67. He led the league in wins, winning percentage, strikeouts, and games pitched twice each, and in complete games, innings pitched, shutouts, and ERA once each. Radbourn was elected by the Veterans Committee in 1939.

Mickey Welch broke in with the Troy Trojans in 1880 and spent three seasons there, never truly distinguishing himself. His record over those three seasons was a very mediocre 69-64. However, after one more less-than-spectacular season with the New York Giants in 1883, Welch developed into one of the finest pitchers in baseball. Over the next three seasons, he compiled records of 39-21, 44-11, and 33-22, and finished with an ERA under 3.00 each year. He was at his best in 1885, when, in addition to winning 44 games, he finished with an ERA of 1.66, 258 strikeouts, 492 innings pitched, 55 complete games, and seven shutouts. He also won more than 20 games in each season from 1887 to 1889, compiling a 1.93 ERA in 1888, and finishing 27-12 the following year. He ended his career with a won-lost record of 307-210 and a 2.71 ERA.

The problem with Welch, though, is that he was an exceptional pitcher for only three seasons, and a very good one for only two others. In addition, he was not the dominant pitcher of his era, never having led the league in any major pitching category. He was selected by the Veterans Committee in 1973.

A teammate of Welch's for a good portion of his career was Tim Keefe. Like Welch, Keefe broke in with the Troy Trojans in 1880 and spent three seasons there. After losing more games than he won with the Trojans, Keefe moved on to the New York Metropolitans in 1883 with whom he accumulated win totals of 41 and 37 over the next two seasons. Keefe rejoined his former teammate Welch with the Giants in 1885, where he won more than 30 games in each of the next four seasons and twice finished with an ERA of less than 2.00. Over the course of his career, Keefe won more than 40 games twice, topped the 30-mark four other times, and once won 28 games. He struck out more than 300 batters three times and finished with an ERA under 3.00 eight times. Unlike Welch, he led the league in every major pitching category at least once during his career, topping the N.L. in wins, ERA, strikeouts, innings pitched, and complete games twice each. Keefe finished with a record of 342-225, and an ERA of 2.62. The Veterans Committee elected him to the Hall of Fame in 1964.

Perhaps the best of the 19th century pitchers was John Clarkson, who, in his 13 big-league seasons, managed to win 328 games, while losing only 178, for an outstanding winning percentage of .648. During his career, Clarkson led the league in wins, strikeouts, and complete games three times each, ERA once, innings pitched four times, and shutouts twice. He had his finest season in 1885, when he led the league in virtually every statistical category. That year, he finished 53-16, with an ERA of 1.85, 308 strikeouts, 623 innings pitched, 68 complete games, and 10 shutouts. Four years later, he had another brilliant season, compiling a record of 49-19, with a 2.73 ERA, 284 strikeouts, 620 innings pitched, 68 complete games, and 8 shutouts. He won more than 30 games three other times and finished his career with a 2.81 ERA. He was elected by the Veterans Committee in 1963.

Kid Nichols is the only one of these six men whose career extended into the first few years of the 20th century. Pitching mostly for the Boston Beaneaters (who eventually became the Braves) during his 15-year major league career, Nichols was, along with Cy Young, the finest pitcher in the game during the last decade of the 19th century. He was a 20-game winner in every season from 1890 to 1899, and he won at least 30 games seven times during that period. Unlike most top pitchers of his era, Nichols never lost as many as 20 games in a season, and he finished his career with an outstanding .634 winning percentage. He led the league in wins and shutouts three times each, and in innings pitched once.

Nichols had perhaps his finest season for the Braves in 1892, when he finished 35-16 with a 2.84 ERA, 453 innings pitched, and 49 complete games. He had another great year for Boston in 1898, when he compiled a record of 31-12 with an ERA of 2.13. Nichols was a 20-game winner eleven times and compiled an ERA of less than 3.00 nine times. He finished his career with a record of 361-208 and an ERA of 2.95, pitching mostly during an era (1892-1900) in which the rules governing the game favored the batter. Nichols was elected by the Veterans Committee in 1949.

Now, back to the issue at hand. Should these men be thought of as legitimate Hall of Famers? When one considers the extent to which the game differed when these six baseball pioneers pitched, the answer to this question is not a simple one. It would seem that Clarkson, Radbourn, and Nichols had the most impressive credentials, followed closely by Keefe. Each of those four men clearly earned their places in Cooperstown. Welch and Galvin were obviously fine pitchers, but they would have to be considered a notch below the other four hurlers. Thus, one must view them as somewhat borderline Hall of Famers, although it is awfully difficult to argue against the admission of pitchers who compiled such prodigious win totals. We will not do that here.

However, the Veterans Committee may have been somewhat remiss by excluding another outstanding pitcher from that era named Bob Caruthers, who was also a part-time outfielder. Although he spent only nine seasons in the majors, from 1884 to 1892, Caruthers compiled some outstanding numbers. Splitting his time between Brooklyn and St. Louis, he won 40 games twice, 30 once, 29 twice, and 23 another time. Here are his numbers from 1885 to 1890:

1885: 40 wins, 13 losses; 2.07 ERA; 482 innings pitched; 53 complete games
1886: 30 wins, 14 losses; 2.32 ERA; 387 innings pitched; 42 complete games
1887: 29 wins, 9 losses; 3.30 ERA; 341 innings pitched; 39 complete games
1888: 29 wins, 15 losses; 2.39 ERA; 391 innings pitched; 42 complete games
1889: 40 wins, 11 losses; 3.13 ERA; 445 innings pitched; 46 complete games
1890: 23 wins, 11 losses; 3.09 ERA; 300 innings pitched; 30 complete games

Caruthers led the league in wins twice and ERA once. In spite of the fact that he was a regular starter in his team's pitching rotation only seven seasons, he managed to compile a career won-lost record of 218-99, for a brilliant .688 winning percentage, finish with an ERA of 2.83, and complete 298 of his 310 starts. While he wasn't able to accumulate the career totals of his six contemporaries, he was as effective as any of them, and probably better than Keefe, Welch, and Galvin.

Joe Williams/Leon Day/Bullet Rogan/ Bill Foster/Hilton Smith

Though not nearly as famous as Satchel Paige, these five men were all outstanding Negro League pitchers who were elected by the Veterans Committee near the turn of the century.

Even though Satchel Paige is generally considered to have been the greatest pitcher in Negro League history, there are those who feel differently. In fact, a 1952 *Pittsburgh Courier* poll of black sportswriters and baseball players voted "Smokey" Joe Williams the greatest pitcher in Negro League history, ahead of Paige.

Williams pitched in the Negro Leagues from 1910 to 1932 and had his greatest years with the New York Lincoln Giants from 1912 to 1923. There he teamed with Cannonball Dick Redding to give the New York team a devastating one-two punch in their rotation. His signature season was 1914, when, pitching against all levels of competition, he won 41 games while losing only 3 (in league play, he was 12-2 with 100 strikeouts in 17 games). In exhibition games against major league competition, Williams went 20-7, defeating Hall of Famers Grover Cleveland Alexander, Walter Johnson, Waite Hoyt, Chief Bender, and Rube Marquard in the process. In fact, in a 1917 game against the National League champion New York Giants, Williams struck out 20 batters and pitched a no-hitter, although he lost the game, 1-0, on an error.

After being released in a Lincoln Giants' youth movement in 1924, Williams joined the Brooklyn Royal Giants for one season, then moved on to the Homestead Grays. There, he joined Josh Gibson, Oscar Charleston, and others to form what some consider to have been the greatest team in Negro League history.

Ty Cobb, noted for his racial intolerance and general surliness, once said that Williams would have been a sure 30-game winner had he been a major leaguer. He was elected by the Veterans Committee in 1999.

Leon Day was one of the most versatile of all Negro League players, playing second base and the outfield on the days he wasn't pitching. Although he was a fine hitter as well, Day was best known for being one of the best Negro League pitchers of all-time. His 95-mph fastball and nasty curveball made him the top strikeout artist of the late 1930s and '40s. Day's best overall season came in 1937, when he went 13-0 in league play, in addition to batting .320. He set many strikeout records over the course of his career, setting the Puerto Rican mark with 19 in an 18-inning marathon in 1940. He also set a Negro League record with 18 strikeouts against the Baltimore Elite Giants in 1942, fanning Roy Campanella three times. That same season, with Day's team out of the playoffs, he was recruited by the Homestead Grays to pitch in the World Series against Satchel Paige. Day bested Paige with a five-hitter in the classic match-up. He also played in a record seven East-West All-Star games between 1935 and 1946, fanning five of the seven batters he faced in the 1942 contest.

In the introduction of *"Dandy, Day and the Devil,"* a book by James A. Reilly about Ray Dandridge, Day and Willie Wells, Hall of Famer Monte Irvin wrote, "In a must-win situation, the manager always gave the ball to Leon, and he failed very few times. In those important games, he would ask his teammates for one run and if they couldn't do it, he would step up to the plate and do it himself. I compare him to Bob Gibson."

The Veterans Committee elected Day to the Hall of Fame in 1995.

Another versatile Negro League player was the Kansas City Monarchs Joe "Bullet" Rogan, who played every position except catcher at some point during his professional career. In his 19 seasons, Rogan compiled a .339 batting average, tenth among all Negro Leaguers, and led the league in homers and stolen bases three times each. However, it was as a pitcher that Rogan gained his greatest fame. Possessing a great fastball and curve, and superb control as well, he led the league in wins twice and compiled a record of 111-43, for a .721 winning percentage. Monarchs pitcher Chet Brewer held him in particularly high regard, believing that Rogan should have been inducted into the Baseball Hall of Fame before Satchel Paige.

Hall of Fame manager Casey Stengel referred to Rogan as "one of the best—if not the best—pitcher that ever pitched." Rogan was elected by the Veterans Committee in 1998.

Half-brother of Negro League pitcher and pioneer Rube Foster, Bill Foster was the greatest lefthanded pitcher in Negro League history. Over his 16 seasons, he compiled a winning percentage close to .700. Foster won pennants with the Chicago American Giants in 1926, 1927, 1932, and 1933, excelling in the postseason. After compiling a regular season record of 11-4 in 1926, Foster faced the Kansas City Monarchs, down two games to one, for the

Negro National League title. Needing wins in both games of a doubleheader for the pennant, Foster won both games, beating Bullet Joe Rogan twice.

During that season's Negro World Series against the Bacharach Giants, Foster pitched three complete games, relieved in a fourth, won two games including a shutout, and compiled a 1.27 ERA. The following year, he finished 21-3, and once again won two World Series games. After the 1929 season, Foster participated in a two-game series against an American League All-Star team. He pitched poorly in the first contest, but shut out the major leaguers in the rematch, striking out nine and yielding no hits over eight innings. After the series, Detroit Tigers Hall of Fame second baseman Charlie Gehringer told Foster, "If I could paint you white, I could get $150,000 for you right now."

Foster was elected to the Hall of Fame by the Veterans Committee in 1996.

Righthander Hilton Smith was best known for being Satchel Paige's "relief" with the Kansas City Monarchs. After Paige pitched three innings, Smith typically threw the final six frames and was just as effective. However, due to his quiet manner, he was overshadowed by the more flamboyant Paige.

Still, many Negro League players felt that the man who possessed the best curve in black baseball was the game's best all-around pitcher. With the Monarchs, from 1937 to 1948, Smith was certainly among the very best, frequently winning more than 20 games. His best years were from 1939 to 1942, when he finished with records of 25-2, 21-3, 25-1, and 22-5. He retired from the Negro Leagues with a career record of 161-32. The Veterans Committee elected Smith to the Hall of Fame in 2001.

In spite of the limited availability of statistical data surrounding the careers of Williams, Day, Rogan, Foster, and Smith, it is quite clear that all five men were exceptional pitchers who were most deserving of their places in Cooperstown.

Ray Brown/Andy Cooper/Jose Mendez

Each member of this second tier of outstanding Negro League pitchers was elected to the Hall of Fame by the Veterans Committee in 2006.

Ray Brown spent 19 years in the Negro Leagues, beginning his career with the Dayton Marcos in 1930. It was with the Homestead Grays, though, that Brown gained general recognition as one of black baseball's finest hurlers. Pitching for the Grays from 1932 to 1945, Brown appeared in four World Series, posting a record of 3-2 in his seven Series starts. Among his victories was a one-hit shutout of the Birmingham Black Barons in the 1944 World Series. Over the course of his career, Brown played in four All-Star games and was a member of eight pennant-winning teams.

Brown had a wide assortment of pitches but depended heavily on his curveball to baffle opposing hitters. Brown had such fine control of his curve that he wasn't afraid to throw it at any point in the count. His wide array of pitches enabled him to throw a seven-inning perfect game against the Chicago American Giants in 1945. Ranking high in career winning percentage among Negro League pitchers, Brown posted marks of 12-3, 18-3, 15-8, and 13-6 in different seasons, and, at one point, won 28 straight games between 1936 and 1937. In 1938, Brown was one of five players designated as certain major-league stars in a wire sent to the Pittsburgh Pirates by *The Pittsburgh Courier*. The other four players identified were Josh Gibson, Satchel Paige, Buck Leonard, and Cool Papa Bell.

Andy Cooper pitched for four teams during a 22-year Negro League career that lasted until he was age 45. Cooper spent most of his time with the Detroit Stars and Kansas City Monarchs, although he also pitched briefly for the Chicago American Giants and St. Louis Stars. The 6'2" 220-pound lefthander was a master at mixing pitches and changing speeds, and kept opposing batters off-balance with his wide array of breaking pitches.

After struggling somewhat in his first two years with Detroit, Cooper came into his own in 1922. Over his next six seasons with the Stars he posted a combined record of 72-30 in league play.

Cooper joined the Monarchs in 1928 and, after several successful seasons with them, had his best year for the team in 1936. With the Monarchs playing as an independent team against all levels of competition, Cooper compiled a record of 27-8. Over the course of his career, Cooper posted an overall record of 116-57 in league play, and established the Negro League career record for saves, with 29. He played for five pennant-winning clubs in his 22 seasons.

Jose Mendez was one of the first Latino baseball legends. In his homeland of Cuba, he was called *El Diamante Negro*—The Black Diamond. Mendez threw a hard, rising fastball and a sharp-breaking curve with a deceptively easy motion that made him extremely difficult for opposing hitters to properly time.

Mendez compiled a record of 9-0 in his first Cuban League season, which lasted from January through March of 1908. In the fall of that year, he pitched the games that made him a legend. Pitching against the Cincinnati Reds in a series of exhibition games played in Havana, Mendez threw 25 consecutive scoreless innings in his three appearances, two of which were starts. He finished the series with a record of 2-0, an ERA of 0.00, and allowed just 8 hits while striking out 24 batters. Over the next six Cuban League seasons, Mendez continued to dominate, topping the circuit's pitchers in wins three times, and leading his team to three pennants. Mendez was also extremely effective when he performed in the Negro Leagues during the summer. Some sources indicate that Mendez posted a 44-2 record with the Cuban Stars in 1909, although another source lists him with a more modest mark of 14-2 that year.

During his peak seasons of 1908-1913, Mendez frequently pitched against America's best teams and best pitchers of all colors. In his native country he outpitched Hall of Famers Christy Mathewson and Eddie Plank in exhibition games, although his combined record against major league teams was a mediocre 9-11.

After facing John McGraw's New York Giants, Mendez was proclaimed by the legendary manager as being "sort of Walter Johnson and Grover Alexander rolled into one."

Ira Thomas, a catcher for Connie Mack's Philadelphia Athletics, discussed Mendez in a 1913 article in *Baseball Magazine*: "Mendez is a remarkable man...It is not alone my opinion, but the opinion of many others who have seen Mendez pitch, that he ranks with the best in the game. I do not think he is Walter Johnson's equal, but he is not far behind. He has terrific speed, great control and uses excellent judgment. He is a natural ballplayer if there ever was one and, with his pitching, it is no wonder that the Cubans win games."

And, John Henry Lloyd, who faced most of baseball's finest pitchers, both black and white, during the first quarter of the 20th century, said that he had never seen a pitcher superior to Mendez.

Unfortunately, Mendez developed arm trouble at the end of the 1913 season and was never again a dominant pitcher. He was removed from his team's regular pitching rotation and spent the remainder of his career primarily at shortstop, although he also played the outfield and took an occasional turn on the mound.

Evaluating the Hall of Fame credentials of Brown, Cooper, and Mendez, all three men were obviously outstanding pitchers. They received a great deal of acclaim during their careers, and those who saw them pitch respected them highly. But, while the statistics surrounding the careers of the three pitchers are quite incomplete, all available evidence suggests that they were a notch below the five other former Negro League hurlers inducted into Cooperstown at the turn of the century. Williams, Day, Rogan, Foster, and Smith all had more impressive resumes and were generally more highly-regarded by most Negro League experts.

Of the three men, Brown appears to be the most qualified. Certainly, his endorsement by *The Pittsburgh Courier* is a point in his favor. Being included with the likes of Josh Gibson, Satchel Paige, Buck Leonard, and Cool Papa Bell is most impressive. Mendez also had an outstanding reputation, and he received very high praise from those fortunate enough to have seen him play. But he was an exceptional pitcher for only six seasons. Furthermore, he achieved much of his glory playing in the Cuban Leagues. As a result, one can only guess as to the level of competition he typically faced. Therefore, Mendez's selection would have to be considered the most questionable of the three. Yet, as is the case with all the former Negro League stars, the limited availability of statistical data surrounding the careers of Brown, Cooper, and Mendez makes it extremely difficult to find fault with their 2006 selections by the Veterans Committee.

Ted Lyons

Ted Lyons' career won-lost record of 260-230 left him with the third lowest winning percentage (.531) of any starting pitcher in the Hall of Fame. However, when one considers that, in Lyons' 21 seasons with the Chicago White Sox, the team finished out of the second division only five times, his record becomes far more impressive.

Lyons had the misfortune of joining the White Sox in 1923, just three years after several of the team's best players were banned for life by Commissioner Landis for throwing the 1919 World Series. The commissioner's edict relegated the Sox to second-division status for the next several seasons, and, unfortunately for Lyons, they remained a weak team throughout much of his career.

Yet Lyons still managed to win 260 games, and was a 20-game winner three times. His first 20-win season was in 1925, when he finished 21-11 with a 3.26 ERA and a league-leading 5 shutouts. Two years later, he had arguably his finest season, leading the league with 22 wins, against 14 losses, compiling a 2.84 ERA, and also leading the league with 30 complete games and 307 innings pitched. He finished third in the league MVP voting that year. Lyons won 20 games for the last time in 1930, going 22-15 with a 3.78 ERA, and leading the league with 29 complete games and 297 innings pitched. He also had two more outstanding seasons later in his career, finishing 14-6 with a 2.76 ERA in 1939, and going 14-6 with a 2.10 ERA in 1942. In addition to his three 20-win seasons, Lyons won at least 15 games three other times, and won 14 games three times as well. During his career, he led the league in wins, shutouts, complete games, and innings pitched twice each, and in ERA once.

However, in six seasons when he was a regular member of the starting rotation, Lyons lost more games than he won, twice losing as many as 20 games. In several other seasons, he was barely over .500, and in six seasons when he was a regular member of the rotation, his ERA was more than 4.00. He finished his career with an ERA of 3.67. On a superficial level, this figure hardly seems overwhelming. However, when one takes into account that most of his prime years were between 1925 and 1935, during a hitter's era, 3.67 becomes much more impressive. Also, when one factors into the equation the poor teams he played for during his career, his sub-par won-lost records become much more tolerable.

Looking beyond just the sheer numbers, Lyons was an outstanding pitcher for nine seasons, and a good one in another two. Though he was not a dominant pitcher, he was arguably the best pitcher in the game in both 1925 and 1927, and among the top five in both 1926 and 1930. That might not be enough to make him a clear-cut choice for the Hall of Fame, but it should be sufficient to justify his 1955 selection by the BBWAA.

Hal Newhouser

Lefthander Hal Newhouser had a winning record in only seven of his 17 major league seasons, finishing at exactly .500 five other times. However, at his peak, he was the most dominant pitcher of his era, and he was clearly the best pitcher in baseball over a six-year stretch.

Although Newhouser struggled in his first five seasons with the Detroit Tigers, never finishing above the .500-mark, he came into his own in 1944. With most of the game's top players serving in the military, Newhouser went on a three-year run comparable to any that the game has seen. In that first year, he finished 29-9 with a 2.22 ERA, 6 shutouts, 312 innings pitched, and 25 complete games. He was voted the American League's Most Valuable Player that year and then again the following season, when he led A.L. pitchers in every major statistical category by compiling a record of 25-9, with an ERA of 1.81, 212 strikeouts, 313 innings pitched, 8 shutouts, and 29 complete games. In 1946, Newhouser fell just short of winning his third MVP Award, something that no pitcher in baseball history has done. That season, with most of the game's greatest players back from the war, he finished runner-up in the voting to Ted Williams by finishing 26-9 with a league-leading 1.94 ERA, and totaling 275 strikeouts, 292 innings pitched, and 29 complete games.

Although Newhouser's record fell to 17-17 in 1947, he was still a fine pitcher, compiling an ERA of 2.87, with 24 complete games and 285 innings pitched. He was the best pitcher in baseball once more in 1948, when he finished with a record of 21-12, an ERA of 3.01, and 19 complete games. Newhouser had two more good seasons in 1949 and 1950, winning 18 and 15 games, respectively, before arm problems prevented him from ever again being a dominant pitcher. However, prior to that, in the six seasons from 1944 to 1949, he compiled a record of 136- 67, won more than 20 games four times, led the league in wins four times, and won two MVP Awards. He ended his career with a won-lost record of 207-150 and an ERA of 3.06.

The sole argument against Newhouser would be that two of his greatest seasons occurred while most of the best players in baseball were away from the game. However, his great season of 1946 and his fine performances from 1947 to 1949 serve as proof that, at his peak, he was truly an outstanding pitcher. Therefore, his 1992 selection by the Veterans Committee should not be questioned.

Burleigh Grimes

During his 19-year major league career, spent almost entirely in the National League, Burleigh Grimes pitched for seven different teams. Most of his finest seasons were spent with the Brooklyn Dodgers and Pittsburgh Pirates during the 1920s, seasons in which he rivaled Dazzy Vance as the league's best pitcher.

After two uneventful seasons with the Pirates in 1916 and 1917, Grimes was traded to the Dodgers, with whom he spent the next nine years. In his nine years in Brooklyn, Grimes won at least 17 games six times, surpassing the 20-victory mark on four separate occasions. He was particularly outstanding in 1920 and

1921, when he finished with won-lost records of 23-11 and 22-13, respectively, and ERAs of 2.22 and 2.83.

After compiling a record of 19-8 with the Giants in 1927, Grimes was traded back to the Pirates, with whom he had his finest season in 1928. That year, he finished 25-14 with an ERA of 2.99, and led the league with 28 complete games and 330 innings pitched. He finished third in the league MVP voting and was the best pitcher in the game for that one season. He followed that up with 17 wins in 1929, which was good enough to place him fourth in the MVP balloting.

In all, Grimes was a 20-game winner five times, won at least 16 games six other times, and finished with an ERA less than 3.00 four times. He led the league in wins twice, strikeouts once, innings pitched three times, and complete games four times. Grimes ended his career with a won-lost record of 270-212 and an ERA of 3.53—very respectable, considering the era in which he pitched. His selection by the Veterans Committee in 1964 would have to be considered a good one.

Red Ruffing/Lefty Gomez

Both Ruffing and Gomez were fine pitchers who were fortunate enough to play on Joe McCarthy's great New York Yankees teams of the 1930s.

Red Ruffing is a perfect example of how playing on a good team can make a pitcher better. In six-plus seasons with the struggling Boston Red Sox from 1924 to 1930, he failed to win more than 10 games in any season, and was a two-time 20-game loser. His overall record with Boston and with the Chicago White Sox, with whom he ended his career in 1947, was a poor 42-101. In addition, only once in all those years did he finish with an ERA under 4.00 (3.89 in 1928). However, in his 15 seasons with the Yankees, Ruffing compiled an outstanding won-lost record of 231-124 and finished with an ERA under 4.00 thirteen times, three times compiling a mark under 3.00.

The thing that makes Ruffing so unusual is that, in his years with Boston and Chicago, his .293 winning percentage was below that of the rest of the team. Meanwhile, in his years with New York, Ruffing's winning percentage of .650 was better than the overall mark posted by his team. From this, one could surmise that, when Ruffing was bad, he was really bad, and, when he was good, he was really good. One would also have to conclude that his success with the Yankees was not based solely on the fact that he pitched for a good team. Ruffing must have become a better pitcher once he came to New York because his winning percentage would not otherwise suddenly have become better than the rest of the team's.

From 1930 to 1942, Ruffing failed to win at least 15 games only twice. He was a 20-game winner four times, won 19 games another season, and finished with 18 victories in yet another. His four best years were 1936-1939, during which time he was a 20-game winner each season, while compiling an overall record of 82-33. He also finished with an ERA under 3.00 in two of those seasons. He was among the five best pitchers in baseball during that period, and was arguably the top American League hurler in both 1937 and 1938.

During his career, Ruffing led the league in wins, strikeouts, shutouts, and complete games once each. He was selected to the American League All-Star team six times and finished in the top 10 in the MVP voting three times, making it into the top five twice. Ruffing ended his career with a won-lost record of 273-225 and an ERA of 3.80.

Ruffing's teammate on the Yankees for 13 seasons was Lefty Gomez. Like Ruffing, Gomez benefited greatly from playing on some truly outstanding teams. However, unlike Ruffing, he spent virtually his entire career pitching for New York, making only one start for the Washington Senators in 1943. Therefore, his career winning percentage of .649 was considerably higher than Ruffing's mark of .548, and ranks among the best ever.

In ten full seasons with the Yankees, Gomez was a 20-game winner four times, won at least 15 games three other times, and had only one losing season. Although he won 21 games in 1931, and another 24 the following year, his two best seasons were in

1934 and 1937, when he won the pitcher's triple crown. In 1934, he finished 26-5, with a 2.33 ERA, 158 strikeouts, and 25 complete games. In 1937, he compiled a record of 21-11, with an ERA of 2.33, 194 strikeouts, and 25 complete games. Gomez was the American League's best pitcher in each of those years, and among the top two or three in all of baseball (the N.L.'s Dizzy Dean and Carl Hubbell were the number one hurlers in 1934 and 1937, respectively). He was also among the top five pitchers in the game in 1931, 1934, and 1938.

Gomez led American League pitchers in wins and ERA twice each, strikeouts and shutouts three times each, and complete games and innings pitched once each. He was selected to the All-Star Team seven times, and he finished in the top 10 in the MVP voting three times, making it into the top five twice. He was a very good pitcher. But was he any more deserving of Hall of Fame honors than two of his contemporaries, Wes Ferrell and Lon Warneke?

Let's take a look at the career numbers of all three pitchers:

PITCHER	W	L	PCT	ERA	GS	CG	IP	HITS	BB	SO
Lefty Gomez	189	102	.649	3.34	320	173	2,503	2,290	1,095	1,468
Wes Ferrell	193	128	.601	4.04	323	227	2,623	2,845	1,040	985
Lon Warneke	192	121	.613	3.18	343	192	2,782	2,726	739	1,140

Both Ferrell and Warneke were actually quite comparable to Gomez. Although both men pitched for lesser teams throughout most of their careers—Ferrell for the Indians and Red Sox, and Warneke for the Cubs and Cardinals—they finished with outstanding winning percentages, and compared favorably to Gomez in most other categories. Gomez was more of a strikeout pitcher, but both Ferrell and Warneke had better control. Gomez's earned run average was considerably lower than Ferrell's, but the discrepancy could be attributed largely to the fact that the former was a lefthander pitching all his home games in spacious Yankee Stadium, while Ferrell pitched in smaller ballparks. Also, Ferrell's last five seasons were poor ones in which his ERA never fell below 4.66.

From 1929 to 1932, then again in 1935 and 1936, Ferrell was one of the two or three best pitchers in the American League, winning at least 20 games in each of those seasons, and surpassing 25 victories on two separate occasions. With the Indians in 1930, he finished 25-13 with an ERA of 3.31 and 25 complete games. With Boston in 1935, he compiled a record of 25-14 with a 3.52 ERA and 31 complete games. Ferrell led the league in wins once, complete games four times, and innings pitched three times, and was one of the greatest hitting pitchers in baseball history. He finished in the top 10 in the MVP voting twice, making it into the top five once.

With the Chicago Cubs and St. Louis Cardinals from 1932 to 1941, Lon Warneke won at least 20 games three times, and finished with at least 16 victories five other times. His four best years were with the Cubs, from 1932 to 1935. In 1932, Warneke won 22 games while losing only 6, and he also finished with an ERA of 2.37 and 25 complete games. The following season, he won 18 games and compiled a brilliant 2.00 ERA. He won 22 and 20 games the next two seasons, and only Carl Hubbell and Dizzy Dean were rated above him in the National League over that four-year period. He also had some fine seasons for the Cardinals from 1937 to 1941, and played on two pennant-winning teams in Chicago.

It would appear that Ferrell and Warneke may well have been just as good as Gomez. However, due to the ballpark he played in, and the team he pitched for, Gomez's numbers—at least on a superficial level—are slightly more impressive. The same could be said for Ruffing. However, the bottom line is this: both Ruffing and Gomez were very good pitchers who, for the most part, were made better by the team they played on. Had they pitched for most other teams, there is a strong possibility that neither man would have been a legitimate Hall of Famer. But that was not the case, and they were both fortunate enough to pitch for the best team in baseball. Therefore, while neither Ruffing nor Gomez should be viewed as a clear-cut choice, it is difficult to find fault with their selections.

Stan Coveleski

Righthander Stan Coveleski had a winning record in eleven of his thirteen major league seasons and won at least 15 games nine times. Pitching for the Cleveland Indians from 1916 to 1924, Coveleski was one of the best pitchers in baseball for five consecutive seasons, beginning in 1917.

In that first season, Coveleski won 19 games while losing 14, compiled an ERA of 1.81, and threw 9 shutouts and 24 complete games. Only Walter Johnson and Chicago's Ed Cicotte had better years in the American League. In 1918, Coveleski finished 22-13 with a 1.82 ERA. Only Johnson was better that year. The following season, he compiled a record of 24-12 and a 2.61 ERA. Again, only Johnson and Cicotte had better seasons. In 1920, Coveleski helped lead Cleveland to the American League pennant by finishing 24-14 with a 2.49 ERA. He also won three games against the Dodgers in the World Series. Only teammate Jim Bagby, who won 31 games, was better that year. The following season, Coveleski finished 23-13 and rivaled New York's Carl Mays as the league's best pitcher. He was once again among the league's best pitchers in 1925 when, pitching for the Senators, he compiled a record of 20-5 and led the league with an ERA of 2.84.

In all, Coveleski was a 20-game winner five times, finished with an ERA under 3.00 six times, threw more than 300 innings three times, and completed more than 20 games six times. He led the league in ERA and shutouts twice each, and in strikeouts once. He ended his career with a won-lost record of 215-142 and an ERA of 2.89.

The arguments against Coveleski would be that he pitched on mostly good teams during his career, and that he had only six truly outstanding seasons. In his nine years with Cleveland, the team contended for the A.L. pennant four times and finished well above .500 six times. The Washington Senators team he pitched for in 1925 and 1926 won the A.L. pennant in '25 and was strong once again the following year. It is also true that he had only six dominant-type seasons. However, he was a good pitcher in four of his five other seasons as a full-time starter. Overall, it would seem that, while Coveleski's Hall of Fame credentials were not overwhelming, his 1969 selection by the Veterans Committee was a valid one.

Amos Rusie

Although his career was abbreviated by two bitter holdouts against the New York Giants that limited him to less than ten full seasons in the majors, Amos Rusie was still able to win 246 games and establish himself as the greatest strikeout pitcher of the 1890s. Even though both Cy Young and Kid Nichols would have been ranked ahead of him during the last decade of the 19th century, Rusie won more than 30 games four consecutive seasons, and finished with more than 20 victories four other times. Pitching during a hitter's decade, he finished with an ERA less than 3.00 five times and struck out more than 300 batters three times. Rusie led the league in wins once, ERA twice, and strikeouts five times. His best season was 1894, when he led the National League with 36 wins (against only 13 losses), an ERA of 2.78, and 195 strikeouts. He finished his career with a won-lost record of 246-174 and an ERA of 3.07.

There are two valid arguments against Rusie being in the Hall of Fame. The first is that he actually spent only nine full seasons in the major leagues (he was 0-1 with the Cincinnati Reds in his final season of 1901). The second is that he had only five truly outstanding seasons. In 1891, he finished 33-20 with a 2.55 ERA and 337 strikeouts. Two years later, his record was 33-21, and he compiled an ERA of 3.23. His 1894 season was touched on earlier, and, in 1897, he finished 28-10 with a 2.54 ERA. He also had a fine season in 1898, when he compiled a 20-11 record with an ERA of 3.03. Although he won 32 games in 1892, he also lost 31 that year. In 1890, he won 29 games, but also lost 34, and, in 1895, he finished 23-23.

Should five outstanding seasons be enough to validate Rusie's 1977 election by the Veterans Committee? That is a debatable issue. However, it would seem that, while his selection should probably be viewed as being somewhat questionable, he was not a bad choice. The Committee has made worse.

Rube Waddell

Due to a poor work ethic that exasperated Philadelphia Athletics manager and owner Connie Mack, flame-throwing lefthander Rube Waddell's major league career lasted only 12 seasons, and he was a full-time starter in only nine of those. However, at his peak, Waddell was one of the very best pitchers in baseball.

The first great strikeout pitcher of the 20th century, Waddell led the American League in strikeouts for six consecutive seasons, beginning in 1902. He was the league's best pitcher in both 1902 and 1905. In the first of those seasons, he finished with a won-lost record of 24-7, an ERA of 2.05, 210 strikeouts, and 26 complete games in 27 starts. Waddell surpassed those figures in 1905 by compiling a record of 27-10, a 1.48 ERA, and 287 strikeouts. He also won 21 games in 1903, while striking out 302 batters, and 25 games in 1904, while allowing just 1.62 earned runs a game and compiling 349 strikeouts, a 20th century record for lefthanders that stood until it was eventually eclipsed by Sandy Koufax. Waddell was among the five best pitchers in baseball in each of those seasons as well, and also in 1908, when, pitching for the Browns, he won 19 games, compiled an ERA of 1.89, and struck out 232 batters. In addition to leading the league in strikeouts six times, Waddell topped the circuit in wins once and in ERA twice. He won more than 20 games four times, finished with an ERA of less than 2.00 three times, and struck out more than 200 batters six times. He ended his career with a won-lost record of 193-143 and an ERA of 2.16.

The arguments against Waddell would be that his four 20-win seasons were his only true Hall of Fame type seasons and that, due to the relative brevity of his career, he only won 193 games. While there is a certain amount of validity to each of those arguments, it is also true that, in addition to his four 20-win seasons, Waddell won 19 games two other times. He was also considered to be one of the most dominant pitchers of his era, albeit for just a few seasons. As a result, while he should be viewed as a somewhat borderline Hall of Famer, Waddell's 1946 selection by the Veterans Committee should be looked upon with only minor skepticism.

Addie Joss

The career of Addie Joss was the shortest of any player ever elected to the Hall of Fame, lasting only eight full seasons, and part of a ninth. Pitching exclusively for the Cleveland Indians from 1902 to 1909, Joss was stricken with tubercular meningitis during the 1910 campaign, and he later passed away on April 14, 1911. However, prior to that, he was able to compile the second lowest career earned run average (1.89) of any starting pitcher in history, and the highest career winning percentage (.623) of any pitcher with more than 200 decisions who was never on a pennant winner.

Joss had four truly great seasons with Cleveland, from 1905 to 1908, winning no fewer than 20 games, and finishing with an ERA no higher than 2.01. His two finest seasons were 1907 and 1908, when he finished with records of 27-11 and 24-11, respectively, and compiled ERAs of 1.83 and 1.16. He also had an outstanding year in 1906, when he won 21 games, while losing only 9, and finished with an ERA of 1.72. Joss led the league in wins once and ERA twice, and finished with an ERA under 2.00 five times. In all, he was a 20-game winner four times, won 18 games once, 17 once, and 14 twice, and he never finished with an ERA any higher than 2.77. His final won-lost record was 160-97.

Of course, the criticism of Joss would be that his career was too short. This is certainly a valid argument and prevents him from being considered anything more than a borderline Hall of Famer. However, he was arguably the best pitcher in the American League in both 1906 and 1907, he had an outstanding winning percentage, and he had a superb ERA, even for the era in which he pitched. These factors would seem to legitimize his place in Cooperstown.

Catfish Hunter

Jim "Catfish" Hunter accomplished something very few pitchers have over the last 50 years by winning more than 20 games for five consecutive seasons. Pitching for the Athletics and Yankees, Hunter was a 20-game winner each year, from 1971 to 1975. Over that five-year period, he was also among the top two or three pitchers in the American League, and among the five best in baseball.

Hunter won 21 games for the Athletics in 1971, and again in both 1972 and 1973, compiling an overall record during that three-year stretch of 63-23. He also finished with ERAs those three years of 2.96, 2.04, and 3.34. Each time, though, the Cy Young Award went to someone else—teammate Vida Blue in 1971, Cleveland's Gaylord Perry in 1972, and Baltimore's Jim Palmer in 1973. However, Hunter beat out Ferguson Jenkins for the award in 1974 by finishing 25-12 for the A's, thereby leading the league in wins, and also topping the circuit with a 2.49 ERA. He also completed 23 games and threw 318 innings that year. After signing with the Yankees as a free agent, Hunter had another outstanding season in 1975, leading the league with 23 victories (against 14 defeats), 328 innings pitched and 30 complete games, while compiling a 2.58 ERA. That year, Hunter was again beaten out for the Cy Young Award by Palmer.

During his career, Hunter led American League pitchers in wins twice and in ERA, innings pitched and complete games once each. He was an eight-time All-Star and, in addition to his one Cy Young Award, he finished in the top five in the voting three other times. He also finished in the top 10 in the league MVP voting once. He ended his career with a record of 224-166 and an ERA of 3.26.

The problem with Hunter, though, is that those five 20-win seasons were the only truly outstanding ones he ever had. He had some other *good* years, but nothing that could be classified as Hall of Fame caliber. With Oakland in 1970, he finished 18-14, but his 3.81 ERA was hardly spectacular. With New York in 1976, he won 17 games but also lost 15, and his 3.53 ERA was only slightly better than the league average. In no other season did Hunter win more than 13 games. Part of the explanation for that last fact lay in the arm problems he experienced during his last three seasons in New York. Another factor was that the A's teams he pitched for early in his career were quite poor, and winning 13 games for them—something he accomplished twice—was actually fairly impressive. On the other hand, from 1971 to 1978, Hunter was fortunate enough to pitch on some pretty good teams in Oakland and New York. Those teams won seven division titles, six pennants, and five world championships. The fact that Hunter was an outstanding big-game pitcher and an integral part of the success that those teams experienced is definitely a point in his favor. Nevertheless, the extent to which his won-lost record was improved playing on those squads should not be overlooked.

Hunter was elected to the Hall of Fame by the BBWAA in 1987, in just his third year of eligibility. But another American League pitcher from the same era who was actually quite comparable to Hunter has yet to be voted in. That pitcher is Luis Tiant. A look at the numbers of both players indicates a remarkable similarity:

PITCHER	W	L	PCT	ERA	GS	CG	IP	HITS	BB	SO
Catfish Hunter	224	166	.574	3.26	476	181	3,449	2,958	954	2,012
Luis Tiant	229	172	.571	3.30	484	187	3,486	3,075	1,104	2,416

During a 19-season career, spent with six different teams, Tiant was a 20-game winner four times, and he also won 18 games once, and 15 once. Twice he finished with an ERA under 2.00—something Hunter never did—and three times he struck out more than 200 batters, something else Hunter never did. Unlike Hunter, Tiant never led the league in wins and never won the Cy Young Award. However, he had a truly remarkable season in 1968 that went largely unnoticed because of the great years turned in by both Bob Gibson and Denny McLain. Even though McLain won 31 games for the world champion Tigers that year, was named the recipient of the A.L. Cy Young and MVP Awards, and received far more notoriety, Tiant was arguably the better pitcher. Pitching for the light-hitting fourth-place Cleveland Indians (fellow Indians hurler Sam McDowell compiled a 1.81 ERA and struck out 283 batters that year, yet won only 15 of 29 decisions), Tiant finished 21-9, with 264 strikeouts and a league-leading 1.60 ERA and 9 shutouts. He was also among the league's best pitchers in 1972, when, pitching for Boston, he won 15 games and compiled an ERA of 1.91, and in 1973, 1974, and 1976, winning at least 20 games in each of those seasons. Tiant was also named to three All-Star teams, finished in the top five in the Cy Young voting twice, and finished in the top 10 in the MVP balloting twice, making it into the top five once.

It would seem that the greater amount of exposure Hunter received from his many postseason appearances (Tiant's teams made it into the playoffs only twice), his reputation as a big-game pitcher, and his colorful nickname all worked in his favor. But, was he really a better pitcher than Tiant, and should he be in the Hall of Fame if Tiant is not? Both questions are debatable. However, Hunter was a very good pitcher, albeit for only about six or seven years, and he probably does belong in Cooperstown. It just seems that the writers may have moved just a little too quickly in enshrining him in just his third year of eligibility.

Red Faber

Red Faber's entire 20-year major league career was spent with the Chicago White Sox, and, for much of it, he wasn't the best pitcher on his own team. During his first six seasons, from 1914 to 1919, Ed Cicotte was the staff ace. Then, during his last nine seasons, from 1925 to 1933, Ted Lyons was the Sox best pitcher. Thus, Faber was the best starter on the White Sox staff for only five seasons, from 1920 to 1924. However, over an eight-year stretch, from 1915 to 1922, he was among the five best pitchers in baseball in virtually every season.

Faber had his first big year in 1915, when he finished 24-14 with a 2.55 ERA. The following year, he won 17 games while losing only 9 and compiling a 2.02 ERA. After winning another 16 games and compiling a 1.92 ERA in 1917, Faber missed portions of the 1918 and 1919 seasons due to World War I. However, he had his three finest seasons from 1920-1922, winning 23, 25, and 21 games, respectively, and finishing with an ERA under 3.00 in each season. Over the course of his career, Faber led American League pitchers in ERA twice, complete games twice, and innings pitched once. He finished with a won-lost record of 254-213 and an ERA of 3.15.

Faber does not possess overwhelming Hall of Fame credentials. He was never considered to be the best pitcher in his own league, and he was among the top two or three hurlers in only three seasons. His career winning percentage of .544 was good, but hardly spectacular. In addition, he had only five or six truly outstanding seasons. However, Faber had several very good years, winning more than 20 games four times and posting at least 15 victories three other times. Also, when one considers that the White Sox were a losing team in virtually all of Faber's last 12 seasons, his .544 winning percentage becomes far more impressive. All things considered, while Faber wasn't a clear-cut Hall-of-Famer, his 1964 election by the Veterans Committee was not a particularly bad one.

Vic Willis

During his 13-year major league career, Vic Willis pitched for three different teams. He spent his first eight seasons with the Boston Beaneaters, his next four with the Pittsburgh Pirates, and ended his career with the St. Louis Cardinals. In 1898 and 1899, Willis' first two seasons for Boston, he was outstanding, compiling records of 25-13 and 27-8, and ERA's of 2.84 and 2.50. However, despite allowing less than 3 earned runs a game in four of the next six seasons, his remaining years in Boston were marked with inconsistency. Although he won 20 games one year and 27 another, he finished with losing records the other four years, losing as many as 29 games one year, and 25 another.

After being traded to Pittsburgh following the 1905 season, though, Willis returned to top form. With an outstanding team led by Honus Wagner, Willis won more than 20 games in each of the next four seasons and posted outstanding earned run averages that repeatedly hovered around the 2.00 mark. His two finest seasons were 1906 and 1908, as he won 23 games both years and compiled ERAs of 1.73 and 2.07. Over the course of his career, Willis was a 20-game winner eight times, and he led the league in ERA and strikeouts one time each. His won-lost record was 249-205, and he finished with an ERA of 2.63.

However, while Willis had some outstanding seasons, he had only three in which he could legitimately be referred to as one of the five best pitchers in baseball—1898, 1899, and 1906. At different times during his career he was ranked behind the likes of Christy Mathewson, Joe McGinnity, Cy Young, and Mordecai Brown in the National League, and Eddie Plank and Ed Walsh in the American League. Although Boston was not a strong team in his last few seasons there, Willis' won-lost records from 1903 to 1905 of 12-18, 18-25, and 12-29 are difficult to overlook. Few Hall of Fame pitchers have ever posted three-season records even approaching that. It would seem that, while the Veterans Committee's 1995 election of Willis was not a particularly bad one, it may have been a bit of a stretch.

Jim Bunning

Although it may no longer seem like a major accomplishment in this day of free agency, Jim Bunning was the first major league pitcher to win at least 100 games in each league. While he also pitched for the Pirates and, very briefly, for the Dodgers during his 17-year career, Bunning's finest seasons were spent with the Detroit Tigers and Philadelphia Phillies.

With Detroit from 1955 to 1963, Bunning compiled a record of 118-87 and established himself as one of the American League's better pitchers. He had his best season with the Tigers in 1957 when he compiled a record of 20-8 and a 2.69 ERA and finished ninth in the A.L. MVP voting. In his six other seasons as a regular member of the Tigers pitching rotation, he won 19 games once, and 17 twice.

It was with the Phillies, though, that Bunning truly established himself as one of the game's best pitchers. He won 19 games for three consecutive seasons, from 1964 to 1966, won another 17 in

1967, finished with an ERA well below 3.00, struck out well over 200 batters in each of those seasons, and even pitched a perfect game. In 1967, he finished runner-up to San Francisco's Mike McCormick in the N.L. Cy Young Award voting. In all, Bunning led his league in wins once, strikeouts three times, shutouts twice, and innings pitched twice. He finished with an ERA under 3.00 and struck out more than 200 batters six times each, and, although he was a 20-game winner only once, he won 19 games four times and posted 17 victories three other times. Bunning was a seven-time All-Star and ended his career with a won-lost record of 224-184 and an ERA of 3.27.

While, with the exception of 1957 and 1967, Bunning was never considered to be among the top two or three pitchers in his league, he was one of the five best pitchers in baseball in 1957, and from 1964 to 1967 as well. His career winning percentage of .549 was not particularly impressive, but it should be noted that, except for two years in Detroit and two in Philadelphia, he always pitched on mediocre teams. Bunning was not a great pitcher, but he was a very good one for about 10 years. He should be viewed as a borderline Hall of Famer who was not among the best choices the Veterans Committee has made over the years. However, he was far from the worst.

Jack Chesbro/Chief Bender

Both Chesbro and Bender were very good pitchers who played at the turn of the last century. They both had some good seasons, but a couple of great ones propelled them into the Hall of Fame.

Righthander Jack Chesbro's major league career lasted only 11 seasons, and he had a winning record in only seven of those. Pitching for the Pittsburgh Pirates from 1899 to 1902, he had outstanding seasons in both 1901 and 1902. In the first of those years, Chesbro finished 21-10 with an ERA of 2.38. In 1902, he compiled a record of 28-6 and an ERA of 2.17, while tossing a league-leading 8 shutouts. In each of those years, he was among the top five pitchers in baseball. After finishing 21-15 for the New York Highlanders in 1903, Chesbro had an absolutely phenomenal season for New York in 1904. That year, he finished 41-12 with a 1.82 ERA, 239 strikeouts, 454 innings pitched, and 48 complete games. He was clearly the best pitcher in the game that season. He also won 19 and 23 games for New York over the next two seasons. In all, Chesbro led his league in wins twice, and in innings pitched, complete games, and shutouts once each. He won more than 20 games five times, and he finished with an ERA of less than 3.00 eight times.

The thing about Chesbro, though, is that he only had those two great seasons of 1902 and 1904. While he was also very good in 1901, and quite effective in both 1903 and 1906 as well, he was nothing more than an average pitcher the rest of his career. In his six other seasons, he finished with won-lost records of 6-9, 15-13, 19-15, 10-10, 14-20, and 0-5. Chesbro was among the game's elite pitchers for only three seasons, and he was dominant in only two of those. He ended his career with a fine winning percentage of .600, but won only 198 games—a relatively low number for a Hall of Famer.

Like Chesbro, righthander Chief Bender had some very solid seasons, and two or three exceptional ones. Pitching primarily for the Philadelphia Athletics during his 15-year career, Bender was one of the better pitchers in the American League from 1905 to 1914. He was among the top five pitchers in the league in seven of those seasons, winning more than 20 games twice, at least 16 five other times, and finishing with an ERA well below 3.00 every year. His best years were 1909, 1910, 1913, and 1914. Here are his records in those seasons:

1909: 18 wins, 8 losses; 1.66 ERA; 250 innings pitched; 24 complete games
1910: 23 wins, 5 losses; 1.58 ERA; 250 innings pitched; 25 complete games
1913: 21 wins, 10 losses; 2.21 ERA
1914: 17 wins, 3 losses; 2.26 ERA

In those four seasons, Bender was among the top five pitchers in the game. During his career, he was a 20-game winner only twice, but he won at least 15 games seven other times. He also finished with an ERA under 3.00 in 12 of his 15 seasons, coming in at less than 2.00 four times. He ended his career with 212 wins, against only 127 losses, for an excellent .625 winning percentage, and with an ERA of 2.46—outstanding, even for the Deadball Era.

However, Bender never led the league in any major statistical category and only won 20 games twice, despite pitching for several pennant-winning teams in Philadelphia. While he was one of the better pitchers in the American League for a good portion of his career, he was an outstanding one for only four or five seasons. He was a very good pitcher, but was he any better than Deacon Phillippe, another pitcher from that era who never received much support in the Hall of Fame voting? Let's take a look at their numbers, along with those of Chesbro:

PITCHER	W	L	PCT	ERA	GS	CG	IP	HITS	BB	SO
Chief Bender	212	127	.625	2.46	334	255	3,017	2,645	712	1,711
Deacon Phillippe	189	109	.634	2.59	289	242	2,607	2,518	363	929
Jack Chesbro	198	132	.600	2.68	332	260	2,896	2,642	690	1,265

Phillippe spent his entire career with the Pittsburgh Pirates, from 1899 to 1911. Playing with some outstanding Pirate teams that featured Hall of Famers Honus Wagner and Fred Clarke, among others, he was a 20-game winner six times. He also won at least 14 games on three other occasions. His two most outstanding seasons were 1902 and 1903, when he finished 20-9 and 25-9, respectively, with ERAs of 2.05 and 2.43. Phillippe was arguably one of the five best pitchers in baseball from 1900 to 1903, then again, in 1905. Even though his career was shorter than that of Bender, he won almost as many games and finished with a higher winning percentage. In fact, he compares quite favorably to both Bender and Chesbro in most statistical categories. Yet, for some reason, they were both elected, and he wasn't.

Once again, this is not an attempt to get another borderline candidate elected to the Hall of Fame. However, it should bring to light the fact that both Bender and Chesbro should be viewed as just that—borderline Hall of Famers. It is more difficult to find fault with the Veterans Committee's 1953 election of Bender than it is with their 1946 selection of Chesbro due to Bender's greater number of quality seasons. However, both choices should be looked upon with a certain amount of skepticism.

Don Sutton/Phil Niekro

These two men, probably more than any others, test the theory that 300 wins should automatically qualify a pitcher for the Hall of Fame. Neither pitcher was dominant. Neither had more than three or four truly outstanding years. But both had several good years, hung around the majors for a very long time, and put together enough quality seasons to eventually reach the 300-win plateau. The question is, though, was that enough to legitimize their places in Cooperstown?

In his 23-year major league career Don Sutton pitched for five different teams. His best years were spent with the Los Angeles Dodgers, with whom he pitched from 1966 to 1980, before ending his career with them in 1988. After struggling in his first five seasons with the Dodgers, compiling an overall record of 66-63, Sutton began to establish himself as one of the better pitchers in baseball in 1971, compiling a 17-12 record and a 2.54 ERA. Over the next seven seasons, from 1972 to 1978, Sutton won no fewer than 14 games, winning 21 once and 19 twice, and finishing with an ERA less than 3.00 three times. He had his only 20-win season in 1976, when he finished 21-10 with a 3.06 ERA. He had perhaps his finest season in 1972, when he finished 19-9 with an ERA of 2.08, 9 shutouts, and 18 complete games.

In all, Sutton won at least 17 games seven times, and at least 14 on six other occasions. That's 13 seasons with at least 14 victories—a rather impressive number. He also finished with an ERA under 3.00 eight times. He ended his career with a won-lost record of 324-256 and an ERA of 3.26. However, at no point during his career was Sutton considered to be the best pitcher in baseball, or in the National League. In his peak years, he was consistently ranked well behind Tom Seaver and Steve Carlton, and in only a few seasons ('71, '72, '73, '74 and '76) could a legitimate case be made for him even being among the five best pitchers in the N.L. Sutton was among the top five pitchers in baseball in only 1972 and 1976, and, even in his best years with the Dodgers, he struggled to be recognized as the ace of his own team's pitching staff, vying for that title with the likes of Tommy John and Burt Hooten.

Using our other Hall of Fame criteria, Sutton led the league in a major statistical category only twice; once in ERA and once in shutouts. He was selected to the All-Star Team four times, a relatively low number for a Hall of Famer. He finished in the top five in the Cy Young voting three times, and he never finished in the top ten in the league MVP balloting. However, Sutton did play on a total of six pennant-winning teams in Los Angeles and Milwaukee, and he was a major contributor on four of those teams. Overall, it would seem that Sutton has not fared too well using these criteria. Yet, there still are those 13 seasons with at least 14 victories and the fact that, if you look at his overall numbers for each season, he had four outstanding seasons and another nine good ones. Certainly that last fact, combined with his 324 victories, says something of his ability to sustain a quality level of play for an extended period of time.

Knuckleballer Phil Niekro played for four different teams during a 24-year career that began with the Braves in 1964, before they left Milwaukee. After spending most of his first four seasons working out of the Braves' bullpen, Niekro was converted to a full-time starter in 1968, a role he held for the next 20 years, 16 of which were spent with the Braves.

From 1968 to 1985, Niekro was a 20-game winner three times, won at least 16 games seven other times, and won at least 14 games four other times. He finished with an ERA less than 3.00 six times, completed more than 20 games four times, and threw more than 300 innings four times. He had perhaps his finest season in 1969, when he won a career-high 23 games, while losing 13 and compiling a 2.56 ERA. He had another outstanding year for the Braves in 1974, when he finished 20-13 with a 2.38 ERA.

However, those were Niekro's only two truly outstanding seasons, and the only two in which he could legitimately be ranked among the top five pitchers in the National League. He was certainly never the league's best pitcher, nor was he ever among the five best pitchers in baseball. Although there were several other years in which he won a significant number of games, Niekro also lost too many contests to be considered among the game's best pitchers in any of those seasons. For example, in his years with the Braves he posted records of 12-18, 15-14, 16-12, 13-10, 15-15, 16-20, 19-18, 21-20, and 15-18. That is just too much mediocrity for a Hall of Famer to demonstrate, even when one considers that the Braves teams he played on in many of those years were not very good. Aside from his two outstanding seasons, Niekro had only three other very good years. In 1976, he finished 17-11 with a 3.29 ERA, in 1982, he compiled a record of 17-4 and an ERA of 3.61, and, with the Yankees in 1984, he finished 16-8 with a 3.09 ERA. Other than that, Niekro was essentially a .500 pitcher for most of his career. Therefore, his 14 seasons with at least 14 victories do not carry as much weight as they would have otherwise. The same could be said for his 318 career victories (against 274 losses).

Using our other Hall of Fame criteria, Niekro did lead the National League in wins twice, in ERA once, in strikeouts once, and in innings pitched and complete games four times each. Thus, in that regard, he fares relatively well. He was selected to the All-Star Team five times, a moderate number for a Hall of Famer. He also finished in the top five in the Cy Young voting three times, and he made it into the top ten in the MVP voting once. He played on two division-winners, but none of his teams ever won a pennant. So, overall, when evaluating Niekro using our Hall of Fame criteria, you would have to say that the reviews are mixed.

Now, where does that leave us? Were Sutton and Niekro legitimate Hall of Famers? While the general school of thought seems to be that 300 victories should guarantee a pitcher a place in Cooperstown, the feeling here is that, in these two instances, that is not the case. While Sutton was the more viable candidate of the two, he should be viewed as a borderline Hall of Famer, at best. Niekro, due to the mediocrity he displayed throughout much of his career, probably should never have been elected.

Don Drysdale

One of the most intimidating pitchers of the 1960s was Dodger righthander Don Drysdale. He was big and nasty, and he had a reputation for knocking down hitters that was second to none. The prevalent feeling about Drysdale that seems to have been carried down through the years is that he was not only one of the most intimidating pitchers of his era, but also one of the very best. However, there were many external factors that came into play with Drysdale that may have created an image of him that was not totally accurate.

Don Drysdale was tall, blond, and good-looking. He was from California, played in Los Angeles, and pursued a career in broadcasting after his baseball playing days were over. He also pitched for one of the most colorful and successful teams of his time. In his years as a full-time starter with the Dodgers, they won four pennants and three world championships. He combined with teammate Sandy Koufax to form the most imposing pitching duo of that era, and was widely acknowledged to be one of the game's top pitchers. However, an in-depth look at Drysdale's career indicates that his pitching prowess may have been somewhat exaggerated.

Drysdale spent his entire 14-year major league career with the Dodgers. He was a regular member of the starting rotation in 12 of those years. He had two exceptional seasons, and four other good ones. He won the Cy Young Award in 1962 by finishing with a record of 25-9 to lead the majors in wins, while compiling an ERA of 2.83 and a league-leading 232 strikeouts and 314 innings pitched. He was baseball's best pitcher that year, and he was also among the sport's top five hurlers in 1965 when he finished 23-12, with a 2.77 ERA, 7 shutouts, and 20 complete games. Drysdale was also very good in 1957 when he compiled a record of 17-9 and an ERA of 2.69. However, those were the only three years in which he could legitimately be referred to as one of the five best pitchers in baseball. He had several other seasons in which he pitched effectively, but in none of those was he able to post an exceptional won-lost record.

In 1959, pitching for a Dodger team that went on to win the world championship, Drysdale finished just 17-13 with a 3.46 ERA. In other seasons, he finished with records of 12-13, 15-14, 13-10, 19-17, 18-16, 13-16, and 13-16. Even in 1968, the year of the pitcher, when he compiled an ERA of 2.15 and established a record for consecutive scoreless innings pitched (later broken by Orel Hershiser), Drysdale's record was only 14-12. There are those who would attempt to trivialize his rather mediocre won-lost records by stating that his 2.95 career ERA is an indication that he was a fine pitcher who was victimized by his team's inability to score a lot of runs. However, that is not entirely true. Drysdale's 2.95 earned run average was certainly good, but it must be remembered that he spent most of his career pitching during the 1960s, when ERAs were typically lower than they were in most other periods. There were some other good pitchers from that era who posted comparable ERAs who have received virtually no support for election to the Hall of Fame (Mel Stottlemyre's career ERA was 2.97 and Bob Veale's was 3.07, just to name two).

More importantly, there is a general misconception that most people seem to have about the Dodger teams that Drysdale played for. Those Dodger teams are usually thought to have been weak-hitting, low-scoring teams that had little power. It is true that their lineup was not usually loaded with power hitters, and that they relied largely on speed to score their runs. It is also true that they depended heavily on their pitching to hold down the opposing team's offense. But those Dodger teams also had some pretty good offensive players, and they were quite capable of scoring their fair share of runs.

At the top of the lineup was Maury Wills, who regularly led the league in stolen bases and finished among the leaders in runs scored. In fact, he scored as many as 105 runs in 1961, and 130 in 1962. Then, there were the Davis brothers, Tommy and Willie, who were both solid hitters and run-producers. Indeed, prior to breaking his ankle during the 1965 season, Tommy was actually one of the top hitters and run-producers in the game, winning two batting titles and leading the league with 153 runs batted in

1962. Other solid offensive performers on some of those teams included Frank Howard, Wes Parker, and Ron Fairly. Thus, the Dodgers actually could score runs: Drysdale just was not the dominant pitcher he was portrayed to be.

Nevertheless, he did have some fairly impressive credentials. He led the league in wins once, strikeouts three times, shutouts once, and innings pitched twice. He struck out more than 200 batters in a season six times, threw more than 300 innings four times, and compiled an ERA less than 3.00 nine times. Drysdale was selected to the All-Star Team eight times and finished in the top five in the league MVP voting twice. Although he was a 20-game winner only twice, he won at least 17 games four other times. However, he also lost at least 16 games four times.

At his best, Don Drysdale was very good. As his career won-lost record of 209-166 indicates, however, he wasn't at his best nearly enough. While it is certainly understandable how the baseball writers allowed themselves to be taken in by the glitz and glamour that surrounded Drysdale throughout much of his career, it is difficult to embrace his 1984 election.

Herb Pennock/Waite Hoyt

The top two pitchers on the fabled "Murderers Row" Yankee teams of the 1920s were Pennock and Hoyt. Both men were good pitchers who were aided immeasurably by having one of the greatest lineups in baseball history supporting them.

Lefthander Herb Pennock pitched for three different teams during his 22-year major league career. With the Philadelphia Athletics from 1912 to 1915, he worked mostly in relief. After two more seasons as a reliever for the Red Sox, and one year in the military, Pennock became a full-time starter for Boston in 1919. He was quite effective in his new role that first season, winning 16 games while losing only 8, and finishing with a 2.71 ERA. Pennock, though, was nothing more than mediocre over the next three years for a Boston team that had been depleted by the sale of most of its best players to other teams, including Babe Ruth to the Yankees. From 1920 to 1922, his won-lost records were 16-13,

13-14, and 10-17, and his ERA was less than 4.00 only once (3.68 in 1920).

However, after being dealt to New York prior to the 1923 season, Pennock became one of the best pitchers in the American League. In fact, with the exception of 1925, he was one of the top five pitchers in baseball in every season, from 1923 to 1928. Here are his records from his five most outstanding seasons:

1923: 19 wins, 6 losses; 3.13 ERA; 21 complete games
1924: 21 wins, 9 losses; 2.83 ERA; 25 complete games
1926: 23 wins, 11 losses; 3.62 ERA; 19 complete games
1927: 19 wins, 8 losses; 3.00 ERA; 18 complete games
1928: 17 wins, 6 losses; 2.56 ERA; 18 complete games

That 1928 season, though, was Pennock's last good one, since he never again won more than 11 games. Yet, even though he was a 20-game winner only twice, he compiled as many as 16 victories six other times. Also, pitching primarily during a hitter's era, he finished with an ERA under 3.00 five times, and completed more than 20 games three times. He finished in the top five in the league MVP voting twice and was selected to *The Sporting News* All-Star Team once. He ended his career with a won-lost record of 241-162, and an ERA of 3.60.

However, Pennock never led the league in any major statistical category and, with the possible exception of the 1926 season, was never considered to be the best pitcher in the American League. He definitely contributed to his team's success, but, no doubt, the Yankee teams he played for contributed more to *his* success. After all, in each of his five best seasons, with the exception of 1924, they won the pennant and were considered to be the best team in baseball. Pennock really had only seven good seasons, and five very good ones, but he never had any truly great years.

Pennock's teammate for eight seasons in New York was righthander Waite Hoyt, who actually joined the Yankees two years earlier, after three rather uneventful years with the Giants and Red Sox. Hoyt was a mainstay of the Yankee staff from 1921 to 1928, winning more than 20 games twice, and posting at least

17 victories four other times. He was one of the top five pitchers in the American League from 1921 to 1924, winning 19 games twice, 18 once, and 17 once. After a sub-par season in 1925, Hoyt won 16 games in 1926, then had his two best years in 1927 and 1928. In the first of those years, he led the league with 22 victories, against only 7 defeats, finished with a 2.63 ERA, and completed 23 games. In 1928, he compiled a record of 23-7 with a 3.36 ERA and finished tenth in the league MVP voting. He was among the two or three best pitchers in the American League, and one of the five best in baseball, in each of those years.

However, those were Hoyt's last big seasons, and the only two Hall of Fame type years he ever had. Even though he was also a fine pitcher from 1921 to 1924, it could not honestly be said that he was among the top five pitchers in the game in any of those seasons. He only had those two 20-win seasons and, with the exception of his 22 victories in 1927, never led the league in any other statistical category. He was a good pitcher, but, like Pennock, was aided tremendously by the Yankee teams he played for. As proof of this, his career record with New York was 157-98; with all other teams he played for, it was 80-84.

Both Pennock and Hoyt were fine pitchers who were among the better ones of their era. However, if either man had spent the majority of his career pitching for a team other than the Yankees, it is unlikely he would even have been considered for the Hall of Fame. While neither pitcher was a particularly bad choice, Pennock's 1948 election by the BBWAA and Hoyt's 1969 selection by the Veterans Committee were both ones that probably should never have been made.

Jesse Haines

Jesse Haines spent his entire 18-year career with the St. Louis Cardinals and was a member of four pennant-winning teams and three world champions. Haines, a regular member of the St. Louis pitching rotation from 1920 to 1931, was a key contributor to much of the success the Cardinals had during that time.

He had his first big season in 1921 when he finished 18-12 with a 3.50 ERA. Two years later, Haines won 20 games for the first time when he compiled a record of 20-13 and an ERA of 3.11. His best seasons, though, were 1927 and 1928 when he finished 24-10 and 20-8, respectively, with ERAs of 2.72 and 3.18. He led the National League with 25 complete games and 6 shutouts in 1927, and finished eighth in the MVP voting. Haines also had two other fine years. In the Cardinals' world championship season of 1926, he compiled a 13-4 record with a 3.25 ERA. When St. Louis won the championship again in 1931, he finished 12-3 with a 3.02 ERA.

However, those were the only six good years Haines ever had. In no other year did he win more than 13 games, and he failed to finish above .500 six times. In 1920, his won-lost record was 13-20, and he finished 8-19 in 1924. He was the National League's best pitcher in 1927, but was rated behind Dazzy Vance and Burleigh Grimes in his other top seasons. In fact, he would have been ranked among the league's top five pitchers in only his three 20-win seasons. Haines led the N.L. in complete games once, and in shutouts twice, but he never led in wins or ERA. He was a good pitcher, but there were many others who were just as good who have not been elected to the Hall of Fame. One of those pitchers was Bob Shawkey. Let's take a look at the career numbers of both men:

PITCHER	W	L	PCT	ERA	GS	CG	IP	HITS	BB	SO
Jesse Haines	210	158	.571	3.64	386	208	3,208	3,460	871	981
Bob Shawkey	195	150	.565	3.09	333	197	2,937	2,722	1,018	1,360

Shawkey spent parts of three seasons with the Philadelphia Athletics before joining the Yankees for good in 1915. During his 15-year major league career, Shawkey won at least 20 games four times, and at least 15 four other times, even though many of his best years came before the Yankees became a powerhouse ballclub. He had his finest season in 1916 when he finished 24-14 with a 2.21 ERA. Shawkey also won 20 games and finished with an ERA less than 3.00 in 1919, 1920, and 1922. He was arguably among the five best pitchers in baseball in each of those years. Yet, he was never given serious consideration for the Hall of Fame. Shawkey was a good pitcher, but his credentials were not quite good enough for election to Cooperstown. Neither were those of Haines. His 1970 selection by the Veterans Committee was a mistake.

Eppa Rixey

Of his 21 major league seasons, lefthander Eppa Rixey spent eight with the Philadelphia Phillies and 13 with the Cincinnati Reds. Rixey's best season for the Phillies was 1916 when he finished 22-10 with a 1.85 ERA. After being traded to Cincinnati prior to the 1921 season, he had three more 20-win seasons for the Reds. In 1922, he won 25 games while losing 13 and finishing with a 3.53 ERA and 26 complete games. The following year, he finished 20-15 with a 2.80 ERA and 23 complete games. Then, in 1925, he compiled a 21-11 record with a 2.88 ERA and 22 complete games. However, those were the only outstanding seasons Rixey ever had, and the only ones in which he would have been ranked among the top five National League pitchers.

In his eight seasons in Philadelphia, Rixey topped the .500-mark only twice, and he was a 20-game loser on two different occasions, finishing 16-21 in 1917 and 11-22 in 1920. While it is true that, in his years in Cincinnati, he was a 20-game winner three times and a 19-game winner two other times, he also lost 18 games twice, finished with a losing record three times, and finished no better than one game above .500 on four other occasions. Rixey did win 266 games during his career, but he also lost 251. He managed to lead National League pitchers in wins and shutouts one time each, but he never led in any other statistical category. Rixey had only five or six good seasons, and only two or three in which he could have been included among the best pitchers in baseball. His 1963 selection by the Veterans Committee was one of the most questionable ones ever made, and one of the most mystifying.

Rube Marquard

Just as mystifying as the selection of Rixey was that of lefthander Rube Marquard, who pitched for four different National League teams during his 18-year major league career.

With John McGraw's New York Giants from 1908 to 1915, Marquard had several mediocre seasons, losing as many as 22 games in 1914. However, he was one of the best pitchers in baseball from 1911 to 1913, winning well over 20 games in each of those years. In 1911, he finished 24-7 with a 2.50 ERA and a league-leading 237 strikeouts. The following season, he led the league with 26 victories, against only 11 defeats, while compiling a 2.57 ERA. In 1913, he finished 23-10 with a 2.50 ERA. Marquard had two more good years with Brooklyn, finishing 13-6 with a 1.58 ERA in 1916, and going 19-12, while compiling a 2.55 ERA the following season. In all, he led N.L. pitchers in wins once, and in strikeouts once.

However, those three 20-win seasons with the Giants were the only Hall of Fame type seasons he ever had. Furthermore, those other two years with Brooklyn were the only other good ones he ever had. Five times during his career, as a regular member of his team's pitching rotation, Marquard finished with a record below .500. He won as many as 14 games only five times, and he lost at least 14 games five times as well. Marquard's career won-lost record of 201-177 and ERA of 3.08, pitching mostly in the Deadball Era, were far from spectacular, and he was a good pitcher for only five years. Even at his best, he was not the ace of his own team's pitching staff, being ranked well behind teammate Christy Mathewson. In fact, he would have been hard-pressed to be ranked among the five best pitchers in baseball in any single season, since he would also have taken a backseat to the likes of Grover Cleveland Alexander, Walter Johnson, Eddie Plank, Ed Walsh, and Smokey Joe Wood at different times.

In short, Marquard was a very good pitcher for three years, and a good one for a few others. But at no time was he a great one, and his 1971 selection by the Veterans Committee was one of the poorest ones it has ever made.

FUTURE HALL OF FAMERS

Having reviewed the qualifications of all the current members of the Hall of Fame, let's take a look ahead and see which players are looming as future inductees into baseball's greatest shrine. As we have seen, there have been many players elected to Cooperstown in the past who were not truly deserving. No doubt, that trend will continue, and there will be others voted in who don't really belong, thereby lowering the standards even further. The approach taken here, though, will be to acknowledge only those players who have established themselves as legitimate Hall of Famers by attaining a level of excellence during their careers not even approached by most of their contemporaries. Outstanding players who might perhaps qualify as borderline candidates will also be mentioned. However, too many such players have already been voted in, so it will not be possible, with a clear conscience, to endorse their elections. The criteria used for selecting these Future Hall of Famers will be the same ones used throughout this book. Therefore, the standards will be fairly high, and several players who many might consider to be legitimate candidates will probably be missing from the list.

These Future Hall of Famers can be divided into four groups. The first is comprised of those players who are either not yet eligible to be voted in since their playing careers ended within the last five years, or who recently became eligible for induction. The second consists of players who are still active, but who have already accomplished enough during their careers to merit induction, even if they were never to play another game. The third consists of players who have performed exceptionally well at the major-league level for an extended period of time, but who must accomplish more before they can be deemed worthy of induction into Cooperstown. The final group is comprised of players whose career accomplishments clearly make them legitimate Hall of Fame candidates, but whose names have been linked to the use of performance-enhancing drugs. Thus, their status as Future Hall of Famers is somewhat tenuous, since, if guilty, the extent to which their career numbers may have been affected by the use of steroids must be factored into the equation.

Let's take a look at these four groups of Future Hall of Famers.

RECENTLY RETIRED FUTURE HALL OF FAMERS

Roberto Alomar
Jeff Kent
Edgar Martinez
Jeff Bagwell
Mike Piazza
Greg Maddux

Roberto Alomar

For more than a decade, the finest all-around second baseman in baseball was Roberto Alomar. While playing for seven different teams, Alomar was also one of the best all-around players in the game in several of those seasons.

Alomar first established himself as the game's premier second baseman with the San Diego Padres in the late 1980s. After being dealt to the Toronto Blue Jays, he quickly became one of the very best players in the American League. With Toronto in 1993, with Baltimore in 1996, and with Cleveland in 1999 and 2001, a case could be made for Alomar having been not only the best second baseman in baseball, but one of the top five all-around players in the game. Here are his numbers from those four seasons:

1993: 17 HR, 93 RBIs, .336 average, 109 runs scored
1996: 22 HR, 94 RBIs, .328 average, 132 runs scored
1999: 24 HR, 120 RBIs, .323 average, 138 runs scored
2001: 20 HR, 100 RBIs, .336 average, 113 runs scored

Those figures are quite impressive. However, the thing that truly set Alomar apart from other second basemen was his fielding ability. The winner of 10 Gold Gloves, Alomar's career fielding percentage of .984 is the highest of any American League second baseman in history.

Alomar finished in the top five in the league MVP voting twice, and placed in the top ten another three times. He was selected to the All-Star team a total of 12 times. Alomar hit more than 20 homers three times, drove in more than 100 runs twice, scored more than 100 runs six times, batted over .300 nine times, and stole more than 30 bases eight times. Although the majority of baseball historians probably would not consider him as such, a valid case could be made for Alomar being one of the five or six greatest second basemen in baseball history. If not, he was certainly among the top ten. That, in itself, should be sufficient to earn him a place in Cooperstown, quite possibly in his first year of eligibility.

Jeff Kent

Jeff Kent was always just an average defensive second baseman, with limited range. He also was never particularly popular with most of his teammates. Of course, the same things could be said about Rogers Hornsby, the man considered by many to be the greatest second sacker in baseball history. However, another thing that Kent shared with Hornsby was a propensity for compiling huge offensive numbers. Indeed, not since Joe Gordon slugged home runs and drove in large numbers of runs for the Yankees from 1938 to 1942, did any second baseman put together a string of offensively productive seasons comparable to the one that Kent compiled for the San Francisco Giants from 1997 to 2002.

After five seasons with the Mets, Blue Jays, and Indians, Kent arrived in San Francisco in 1997 and immediately provided the Giants with the kind of offensive firepower rarely supplied by a second baseman. Over the next six seasons, he averaged 29 home runs, 115 runs batted in, and 95 runs scored, while batting over .300 twice. He was voted the National League's MVP in 2000, one of three times he finished in the top ten in the balloting. That year,

Kent hit 33 home runs, knocked in 125 runs, scored 114 others, and batted .334. Kent also had outstanding seasons for the Astros in 2003 and 2004, and for the Dodgers in 2005, averaging 26 home runs and 102 runs batted in those three seasons.

In all, Kent topped the 20-homer mark twelve times, surpassing 30 on three separate occasions. He also drove in more than 100 runs eight times and batted over .300 three times. Kent was selected to the All-Star Team five times, and he was the best second baseman in the National League in virtually every season from 1997 to 2002. Although Roberto Alomar was a better all-around player for most of their careers, Kent was arguably the better player, and the top second baseman in the game, in 1997, 1998, and 2000. With 377 career home runs, most of which came as a second baseman, Kent hit more homers than any other second sacker in baseball history. He also had 1,518 runs batted in and 1,320 runs scored, along with a lifetime batting average of .290—all extremely impressive numbers for a second baseman. Factoring into the equation Kent's reputation for being just a mediocre fielder, those figures may not be good enough to get him elected to the Hall of Fame the first time his name appears on the ballot. But they should earn him admittance at some point during his period of eligibility.

Edgar Martinez

It is difficult to endorse the election of a player who was essentially one-dimensional, so much so that he was strictly a designated hitter for the better part of his career. However, the Seattle Mariners' Edgar Martinez was just that good a hitter.

Originally a third baseman when he first came up to the majors in 1987, Martinez served almost exclusively as a DH, beginning in 1993. From that point on, though, he filled that role better than any other player ever has. During his career, Martinez batted over .300 ten times, topping .330 on four separate occasions. He hit more than 20 home runs eight times, drove in more than 100 runs six times, scored more than 100 runs five times, collected more than 40 doubles five times, and drew more than 100 walks four times.

Martinez won his first batting title in 1992, when he batted .343 for Seattle. He led the league again in 1995, when he batted .356 and hit 29 home runs, knocked in 113 runs, scored 121 others, and collected 52 doubles. His .356 average that year was the highest by a righthanded hitter in more than 40 years. Martinez's most productive season, however, was the 2000 campaign. That year, he established career highs in home runs (37) and runs batted in (145), while batting .324.

Martinez led the American League in runs batted in once, batting average twice, doubles twice, runs scored once, and on-base percentage three times. He finished in the top ten in the league MVP voting twice, and was selected to the All-Star Team six times. He was one of the five best hitters in baseball in 1992, and from 1995 to 2000. In those seven seasons, he never batted below .322, while hitting more than 20 home runs six times and knocking in over 100 runs five times.

Martinez ended his career with 309 home runs, 1,261 runs batted in, 1,219 runs scored, 2,247 base hits, 514 doubles, a .312 lifetime batting average, and a career on-base percentage of .418. Those are, for the most part, borderline Hall of Fame type numbers. That fact, coupled with the one-dimensional nature of Martinez's game, may cause many of the baseball writers to withhold their vote when he eventually becomes eligible for induction. Therefore, it will probably take Martinez several tries before he is finally admitted. But, in the end, his stature as one of the finest hitters of his generation should elevate him to his rightful place in Cooperstown.

Jeff Bagwell

One of the best-kept secrets in major league baseball for the longest time was the Houston Astros' Jeff Bagwell. For 12 consecutive seasons, from 1993 to 2004, he hit at least 20 home runs, surpassing 30 homers in nine of those years, and topping the 40-mark three times. Bagwell also drove in more than 100 runs eight times, scored over 100 runs nine different times, batted over .300 six times, and drew more than 100 bases on balls seven times. In addition, he is the only first baseman in history to hit more than 30 home runs and steal more than 30 bases in the same season, accomplishing the feat in both 1997 and 1999.

Bagwell had his first truly dominant season during the strike-shortened 1994 campaign. In only 400 official at-bats that year, he hit 39 home runs, knocked in 116 runs, batted .368, and scored 104 runs, to earn N.L. MVP honors. With the possible exception of Frank Thomas, he was the best first baseman in baseball and the game's most dominant hitter that year. Bagwell was also the league's top first baseman, and one of the five or six best players in baseball, in both 1997 and 2000. In 1997, he finished with 43 home runs, 135 runs batted in, 109 runs scored, 127 bases on balls, 31 stolen bases, and a .286 batting average. In 2000, he hit 47 homers, knocked in 132 runs, scored 152 others, and batted .310. Although frequently overlooked, Bagwell was among the ten best players in baseball in seven of the eight seasons between 1994 and 2001, averaging 37 home runs, 120 RBIs, and 120 runs scored over that stretch. He led the National League in runs batted in once, runs scored three times, and bases on balls, doubles, and slugging percentage one time each.

Further evaluating the legitimacy of Bagwell's Hall of Fame credentials, he was selected to the All-Star Team only four times—a relatively low number for a potential Hall of Famer. But, in addition to winning the MVP Award once, he finished in the top ten in the balloting five other times, placing in the top five a total of four times.

Bagwell ended his career with 449 home runs, 1,529 runs batted in, 1,517 runs scored, and a .297 batting average. While those are all outstanding numbers, considering the era during which he compiled them, some might feel they make Bagwell somewhat of a borderline Hall of Fame candidate. Furthermore, Bagwell had only seven or eight true Hall of Fame type seasons. Consider, though, that he posted exceptional on-base (.408) and slugging (.540) percentages over the course of his 15 big league seasons, was a consistently productive player for 12 consecutive years, and was both a good baserunner and a solid fielder, even winning a

Gold Glove in 1994 for his outstanding defensive work at first base. Indeed, it could be argued that Bagwell was the finest all-around first baseman of his era, and one of the two or three best of the last 50 years. The members of the BBWAA should strongly consider those arguments when Bagwell's name is added to the eligible list. Although it may take him a few tries to gain admittance, Bagwell should eventually be voted into Cooperstown.

Mike Piazza

Although Mike Piazza's reputation as an all-around catcher suffered through the years because of his inability to throw out opposing baserunners, he more than compensated for that particular shortcoming by establishing himself as arguably the greatest hitting catcher in major league history.

A look at Piazza's career numbers elicits the inevitable question: has there ever been a better hitting catcher to play in the major leagues? (We will exclude Josh Gibson from this debate). Piazza compiled 427 home runs during his career, and the 397 he hit as a catcher are the most by any receiver in history. He also places high on the all-time list of catchers in both runs batted in (1,335) and runs scored (1,048). Furthermore, his .308 career batting average places him third among receivers, behind only Mickey Cochrane (.320) and Bill Dickey (.313), neither of whom had nearly as much power as Piazza. Piazza's career .377 on-base percentage also places him third on the all-time list, behind only Cochrane (.419), and Dickey (.382), and his .545 slugging percentage is 45 points higher than that of runner-up Roy Campanella. Thus, although it would be difficult to compare Piazza favorably to the likes of Johnny Bench, Yogi Berra, Bill Dickey, and Roy Campanella as an all-around receiver, a strong argument could be made that he is indeed the greatest hitting catcher of all-time.

Piazza first began to establish himself as one of the game's most dominant hitters in 1993, with the Los Angeles Dodgers. In winning N.L. Rookie of the Year honors, he hit 35 home runs, knocked in 112 runs, and batted .318. Piazza continued his assault on National League pitching the next nine years, before injuries and age began to take their toll on him during the 2003 season. Prior to that, though, he hit more than 30 home runs in nine of his first ten seasons, twice hitting as many as 40 long balls. During that period, he also drove in more than 100 runs six times and batted over .300 nine times, topping the .320 mark on five separate occasions.

Piazza had perhaps his finest season for the Dodgers in 1997. That year, he hit 40 home runs, knocked in 124 runs, and batted .362. He had another great season for the Mets in 1999, when he hit 40 homers and knocked in 124 runs, while batting .303.

During the first 10 years of his career, Piazza was the National League's top catcher, and, in many of those seasons, the very best in baseball. He was clearly the game's top receiver from 1993 to 1998, and, once again, in 2001. Rivaled only by Ivan Rodriguez for much of his career, it would be difficult to classify Piazza as the complete player that Rodriguez was at his peak. But the latter never swung as potent a bat as Piazza, who would have to be regarded as this generation's top receiver as a result. Piazza was selected to the N.L. All-Star Team in each of his first ten seasons, and also finished in the top ten in the league MVP voting seven times, making it into the top five on four separate occasions.

Piazza's defensive shortcomings may dissuade some of the members of the BBWAA from electing him to the Hall of Fame in his first year of eligibility. However, there is little doubt that his hitting prowess will earn him a spot in Cooperstown shortly thereafter.

Greg Maddux

As one of the top two or three pitchers of his generation, Greg Maddux is certain to gain admittance to Cooperstown in his first year of eligibility. Although he was never as overpowering as either Roger Clemens or Randy Johnson, Maddux was arguably the most effective, and, certainly, the most consistent pitcher of his era.

In 2008, Maddux completed his 23rd season in the big leagues, and his 22nd as a regular member of his team's starting rotation. For 17 consecutive seasons, between 1988 and 2004, he won at least 15 games, establishing a new major league record. In so doing, he also surpassed 300 victories, becoming one of the last of a vanishing breed.

Relying primarily on outstanding ball movement and exceptional control, Maddux was the National League's top pitcher, and one of the two or three best in baseball, for much of the 1990s. In the nine seasons from 1992 to 2000, he won at least 18 games seven times, finished with an ERA under 2.50 six times, compiled an overall won-lost record of 165-71, and won four Cy Young Awards. He is one of only two pitchers in baseball history to win as many as four consecutive Cy Young Awards (Randy Johnson is the other). Maddux won the award each season, from 1992 to 1995. Here are his numbers from those four years:

1992: 20 wins, 11 losses; 2.18 ERA
1993: 20 wins, 10 losses; 2.36 ERA
1994: 16 wins, 6 losses; 1.56 ERA
1995: 19 wins, 2 losses; 1.63 ERA

In each of those years, Maddux was not only the best pitcher in the National League, but the best in baseball. Furthermore, Maddux would have to be included with Roger Clemens, Randy Johnson, and Pedro Martinez in any discussions involving the greatest pitcher of the last 25 years. He led the National League in wins three times, ERA four times, shutouts five times, complete games three times, and innings pitched five times. He won at least 17 games ten times and finished with an ERA below 3.00 nine times, twice allowing less than two earned runs per contest. Maddux finished in the top five in the league MVP voting twice, and placed in the top five in the Cy Young voting a total of nine times. He was selected to the All-Star team eight times and was awarded 18 Gold Gloves for his fielding excellence. Upon his retirement at the conclusion of the 2008 season, Maddux's career won-lost record stood at 355-227, and his ERA was 3.16. Those 355 victories are the most by any pitcher whose career began after 1950, and place him second to only Warren Spahn among hurlers who began pitching after 1920.

Recently Retired Borderline Candidates

There are eight other players with some extremely impressive credentials whose careers ended within the last six or seven years. It will be interesting to see how these men fare in the balloting in the upcoming elections. The feeling here is that four of the eight players should be considered stronger candidates than the other four, and that only those four men should be seriously considered for enshrinement at Cooperstown.

Following is a list of these borderline candidates:

Fred McGriff
Craig Biggio
Barry Larkin
Tim Raines
Albert Belle
Juan Gonzalez
Larry Walker
Mike Mussina

Fred McGriff

Fred McGriff came within seven home runs of testing the theory that 500 home runs are no longer enough to guarantee election into Cooperstown. With 493 career homers, McGriff was a dangerous hitter and a very solid player for most of his career. But he was never a truly dominant one.

Playing in an era when lofty home run totals became rather commonplace, McGriff never hit 40 homers, and scored more than 100 runs only twice. He led his league in home runs twice, but never finished first in any other offensive category. In addition, he was selected to the All-Star Team only five times—not a particularly high number for a potential Hall of Famer—and he was never regarded as the best first baseman in baseball. In fact, in only the 1993 season could it legitimately be said that McGriff was even the best first baseman in his own league. That year, splitting time between the San Diego Padres and Atlanta Braves, he hit 37 home runs, knocked in 111 runs, scored another 111, and batted .290.

Nevertheless, McGriff's supporters will point to some rather impressive figures when he becomes eligible for induction in 2010. He hit more than 30 homers ten times, drove in more than 100 runs eight times, batted over .300 four times, and finished in the top ten in his league's MVP voting six times. In addition to his 493 home runs, he finished with 1,550 runs batted in, 1,349 runs scored, 2,490 hits, a .284 batting average, and a .377 on-base percentage.

With the fairly liberal approach many members of the BBWAA seem to take towards the elections, there is a strong possibility that McGriff will eventually be voted into Cooperstown. However, the feeling here is that he probably falls just a bit short of being a worthy Hall of Famer.

Craig Biggio

In this era of free agency, Craig Biggio was an oddity in that he spent his entire career with one team. Originally a catcher when he first came up to the Astros in 1988, Biggio spent the majority of his 20-year career with Houston as a second baseman, becoming one of the game's best players at that position for virtually all of the 1990s. After making the National League All-Star Team as a catcher in 1991, Biggio was shifted to second base prior to the start of the 1992 season. Between 1992 and 2002, Biggio made six appearances on the All-Star Team, and won four Gold Gloves and four Silver Sluggers.

Biggio had his five most productive seasons from 1995 to 1999, hitting more than 20 homers in three of those years, knocking in at least 73 runs and scoring at least 113 times every year, and batting over .300 three times. His two finest seasons were 1997 and 1998. In 1997, he hit 22 homers, drove in 81 runs, scored 146 others, stole 47 bases, and batted .309. Biggio followed that up the next year by hitting 20 homers, knocking in 88 runs, scoring another 123, stealing 50 bases, collecting 210 hits, 51 of which were doubles, and batting a career-high .325. Even though Jeff Kent knocked in more runs both seasons, Biggio was arguably the best all-around second baseman in baseball in each of those years.

He may well have been the best second sacker in the game in 1995 as well. That year, he hit 22 home runs, drove in 77 runs, scored 123 others, and batted .302, while committing only 10 errors in the field.

In all, Biggio hit more than 20 homers eight times, knocked in more than 75 runs four times, scored more than 100 runs eight times, batted over .300 four times, collected more than 50 doubles twice, and stole more than 30 bases five times. He led the National League in runs scored twice, doubles three times, and stolen bases once. Biggio finished in the top ten in the league MVP voting three times, making it into the top five twice.

Upon his retirement at the conclusion of the 2007 campaign, Biggio's stat-line read thusly:

AB	HITS	RUNS	2B	3B	HR	RBI	AVG	SB	OBP	SLG PCT
10,876	3,060	1,844	668	55	291	1,175	.281	414	.363	.433

Biggio's numbers are better than the statistics compiled by more than half of the 19 second basemen currently in the Hall of Fame. They are comparable to the overall figures posted by legitimate members such as Frankie Frisch and Ryne Sandberg, and are somewhat better than those compiled by borderline inductees such as Billy Herman, Bobby Doerr, Red Schoendist, and Nellie Fox. And they are vastly superior to the numbers posted by unworthy members such as Johnny Evers and Bill Mazeroski. Thus, a strong case could certainly be made on Biggio's behalf. He had six or seven truly exceptional years, and was one of the top two or three second baseman of his generation.

Yet, Biggio was not generally considered to be among the very best players of his era. It must also be considered that his figures were compiled during a hitter's era, and that, during the last several seasons of his career, after the Astros moved out of the Astrodome, Biggio played in a ballpark that was a hitter's paradise. As a result, in spite of the outstanding offensive numbers he posted for a second baseman, Biggio should be viewed as a somewhat borderline candidate. Nevertheless, his 3,000 hits are likely to gain him admittance to Cooperstown in his first few years of eligibility.

Barry Larkin

Though overshadowed for much of his career by the great Ozzie Smith, Barry Larkin was the National League's finest all-around shortstop for the better part of his 19-year major league career. While Smith received more publicity in many of those seasons, Larkin was the league's best shortstop for the entire decade of the 1990s. Over that ten-year period, he batted over .300 seven times, hit more than 20 homers twice, scored more than 100 runs twice, stole more than 30 bases four times, and developed into one of the finest defensive shortstops in baseball.

The greatest shortstop in Cincinnati Reds history, Larkin was named the National League's Most Valuable Player in 1995, even though he posted relatively modest numbers that season, hitting only 15 home runs, knocking in just 66 runs, and scoring only 98 others, while batting .319 and stealing 51 bases. The following year was actually Larkin's best, with him establishing career highs in home runs (33), runs batted in (89), and runs scored (117), while batting .298. In all, Larkin finished in double-digits in home runs nine times, batted over .300 nine times, and stole more than 30 bases five times. He also won three Gold Glove Awards, finished in the top ten in the league MVP voting twice, and was selected to 12 All-Star teams. He ended his career with 198 home runs, 960 runs batted in, 1,329 runs scored, 2,340 base hits, 379 stolen bases, and a batting average of .295. That .295 average is the third highest of any shortstop with more than 5,000 at-bats in the last 50 years.

However, Larkin was never thought of as being a *great* player. He never led his league in any offensive category, was never considered to be one of the very best players in the game, and was never even rated as the best shortstop in baseball. Furthermore, in only seven of his 19 seasons with the Reds did Larkin appear in as many as 140 games and compile as many as 500 official at-bats.

Nevertheless, Larkin was a fine player for a very long time, and his statistics compare quite favorably to several shortstops already in the Hall of Fame. Of the 22 shortstops who have been inducted thus far, 20 of whom played in the major leagues, only three (Ernie Banks, Cal Ripken Jr., and Robin Yount) hit more home runs, only six scored more runs, only four stole more bases, and only six finished with a higher lifetime batting average. Although it must be remembered that the two men competed during different eras, Larkin's offensive statistics are slightly better than those of Pee Wee Reese.

PLAYER	AB	HITS	RUNS	2B	3B	HR	RBI	AVG	SB	OBP	SLG PCT
Pee Wee Reese	8,058	2,170	1,338	330	80	126	885	.269	232	.366	.377
Barry Larkin	7,937	2,340	1,329	441	76	198	960	.295	379	.371	.444

Furthermore, Larkin's numbers are vastly superior to those compiled by Dave Bancroft, Hughie Jennings, Phil Rizzuto, and Joe Tinker. In addition, Larkin was an excellent defensive player, an outstanding baserunner, and the leader of a Cincinnati team that won the world championship in 1990. Thus, it could be said, without too much hesitation, that Larkin was clearly better than at least one-third of the shortstops currently in the Hall of Fame, including Dave Bancroft, Travis Jackson, Luis Aparicio, Hughie Jennings, Phil Rizzuto, Bobby Wallace, and Joe Tinker. Therefore, while Larkin should be viewed very much as a borderline candidate when his name is added to the eligible list, his induction would certainly not lower the Hall's standards.

Tim Raines

For many years, Tim Raines was the National League's version of Rickey Henderson. In 12 seasons with the Montreal Expos, 10 of which were as a full-time player, he led the league in stolen bases four times, runs scored twice, and doubles, batting average, and on-base percentage once each. He stole more than 70 bases six times, swiping as many as 90 bags in 1983, and stealing 71 in only 88 games during the strike-shortened 1981 season. Raines was actually a better hitter than Henderson, topping the .320 mark three times, and leading the N.L. with a .334 batting average in 1986. Raines was selected to the All-Star Team each year, from 1981 to 1987, and finished in the top ten in the league MVP voting three times during that period. In fact, from 1983 to 1987, it could be argued that he was one of the four or five best players in the National League, and one of the ten best in baseball. Over that five-year period, he batted well over .300, scored well over 100 runs, and stole more than 70 bases four times each.

Raines first established himself as one of the best players in the game in 1983. That year, he hit 11 homers, knocked in 71 runs, scored a league-leading 133 runs, stole 90 bases, and batted .298. In 1987, he hit 18 homers, knocked in 68 runs, scored 123 others, stole 50 bases, and batted .330. In all, Raines batted over .300 seven times, scored more than 100 runs six times, and stole more than 40 bases eleven times. He ended his career with 170 home runs, 980 runs batted in, 1,571 runs scored, 2,605 base hits, 808 stolen bases, a .294 lifetime average, and an excellent .385 on-base percentage. His 808 stolen bases place him fifth on the all-time list.

Raines was a fine player in his day, but was he a Hall of Famer? From 1981 to 1987 he certainly was. However, while he remained a productive player for several more seasons, those were the only dominant years he ever had. He scored 102 runs for the White Sox in both 1991 and 1992, while stealing 51 and 45 bases, respectively, but he failed to bat over .300 in either season. He was a part-time player in eight of his last ten seasons, finishing with as many as 400 at-bats only twice during that period. His career numbers would seem to make him a borderline candidate, but they are clearly superior to those of many other outfielders currently in the Hall of Fame. In fact, they are actually quite comparable to those compiled by Lou Brock, certainly a legitimate Hall of Famer:

PLAYER	AB	HITS	RUNS	2B	3B	HR	RBI	AVG	SB	OBP	SLG PCT
Lou Brock	10,332	3,023	1,610	486	141	149	900	.293	938	.344	.410
Tim Raines	8,872	2,605	1,571	430	113	170	980	.294	808	.385	.425

Brock reached the magic number of 3,000 hits, something Raines failed to do, but the former also had almost 1,500 more at-bats. Raines drove in more runs, scored almost as many times, hit more home runs, and finished well ahead of Brock in both on-base and slugging percentage. Considering that, like Brock, he was a tremendous offensive catalyst for much of his career, Raines' contributions to his teams cannot be judged merely by looking at his numbers. Viewing Raines in that light gives him a great deal of credibility as a potential Hall of Famer.

However, the fact that Raines had only seven truly exceptional years apparently weighed quite heavily on the minds of the baseball writers, who named him on only 24.3 percent of their ballots the first time his name appeared on the list of eligible candidates in 2008. They followed that up by entering his name on only 22.6 percent of their ballots in 2009. Perhaps support for Raines will grow in the upcoming years because he is certainly more worthy of induction than several players currently in the Hall of Fame. He also is more deserving than men such as Bert Blyleven, Lee Smith, and Jack Morris, each of whom has historically received far more support from the members of the BBWAA in the balloting.

Albert Belle

Considering that his major league career lasted only 12 seasons, and that he was a full-time player in only 10 of those, Albert Belle put up some pretty impressive numbers. He finished his career with 381 home runs, 1,239 runs batted in, 974 runs scored, 389 doubles, and a .295 batting average. He hit more than 30 home runs in eight straight seasons, from 1992 to 1999, hitting as many as 50 four-baggers once, and also totaling 49 and 48 in other seasons. Belle also knocked in more than 100 runs in nine straight years, batted over .300 four times, scored more than 100 runs four times, and collected more than 30 doubles nine times. He led the American League in home runs once, runs batted in three times, runs scored once, doubles once, and slugging percentage twice. Even in a day when big offensive numbers were the norm, Belle was one of the most prolific hitters in the game, and one of its most potent offensive weapons.

While Belle had several productive seasons, he had five true Hall of Fame type years. Here are his numbers from those five seasons:

1993: 38 HR, 129 RBIs, .290 average, 93 runs scored, 36 doubles
1994: 36 HR, 101 RBIs, .357 average, 90 runs scored, 35 doubles
1995: 50 HR, 126 RBIs, .317 average, 121 runs scored, 52 doubles
1996: 48 HR, 148 RBIs, .311 average, 124 runs scored, 48 doubles
1998: 49 HR, 152 RBIs, .328 average, 113 runs scored, 48 doubles, 200 hits

Those numbers are certainly very impressive, and it could be argued that Belle was among the top five players in the game in each of those five seasons. In each of those years he finished in the top ten in the league MVP voting, making it into the top five on three separate occasions. He was also selected to the American League All-Star team five times.

On the surface, it would seem that Belle may have done enough to merit election to Cooperstown. However, numbers can be somewhat deceiving since they don't give one a complete picture of the player. To begin with, Belle's numbers at season's end were usually outstanding, but he had a tendency to pad his statistics during the second half of the season, after his team was already eliminated from playoff contention. For the most part, his first-half statistics were rather mediocre. It was usually during the last two or three months of the season that Belle's productivity tended to increase dramatically, thereby giving one the impression that his year was a successful one. This might help to explain why only one team he ever played for, the 1995 Cleveland Indians, made it to the postseason. In addition, Belle's surly disposition made him a disruptive force in the clubhouse, and a cancer to every team he played on. This might provide an explanation as to why a player of his caliber ended up playing for three different teams in four years. It might also explain why Cleveland made it into the 1997 World Series, after ridding itself of Belle during the offseason.

In short, Albert Belle was an extremely talented player, far more talented than many players currently in the Hall of Fame.

In fact, he probably deserves to be in the Hall as much as several players who are already in. However, the overall negative impact he had on the teams he played for prevented him from being the kind of player who truly deserves to be enshrined in Cooperstown. As a result, it is impossible to endorse his election. The baseball writers, to whom he refused to speak throughout his career, apparently felt the same. When Belle's name appeared on the ballot for the first time in 2006, they failed to give him the necessary five percent vote he needed to remain on the eligible list.

Juan Gonzalez

Juan Gonzalez was one of baseball's top run-producers for more than a decade. After becoming a regular with the Texas Rangers in 1991, he drove in more than 100 runs eight times, topping 140 RBIs on three separate occasions. He also hit more than 40 homers five times, scored more than 100 runs three times, and batted over .300 five times. He led the American League in home runs twice, runs batted in once, doubles once, and slugging percentage once.

Gonzalez was named the league's Most Valuable Player twice, winning the award at the conclusion of both the 1996 and 1998 seasons. In 1996, he hit 47 homers, knocked in 144 runs, and batted .314. He had an even better year in 1998, when he hit 45 home runs, drove in 157 runs, scored 110 others, batted .318, and collected 50 doubles. He was not only the best player in the American League in each of those years, but was also among the two or three best in all of baseball. He was also among the game's top players in 1993, 1997, 1999, and 2001. In those four years, he averaged 41 homers and 129 RBIs, and batted over .300 three times. In addition to his two MVP trophies, Gonzalez finished in the top five in the voting two other times, and made it into the top ten a total of five times. He was also selected to the All-Star team three times.

It would seem that Gonzalez's resume is quite an impressive one. At the top of his game, he was a dominant hitter—a veritable RBI machine. However, his career was ended prematurely at the end of the 2004 campaign by a bad back that greatly limited his offensive productivity over his final few seasons. With Detroit in 2000, Gonzalez hit only 22 home runs and knocked in only 67 runs in 461 at-bats. After making a comeback with the Indians in 2001 (35 HR, 140 RBIs, .325 AVG), he hit a combined 37 home runs, while driving in only 122 runs, playing sparingly in his final three years with Texas and Kansas City.

Gonzalez ended his career with 434 home runs, 1,404 runs batted in, 1,061 runs scored, 1,936 hits, and a .295 batting average. At his peak, he was a tremendous offensive player. But, considering that Gonzalez had only seven truly exceptional seasons, his numbers are probably not quite good enough to earn him admittance to Cooperstown. Gonzalez's chances are further diminished by persistent rumors that he used steroids to help build his extremely muscular physique, and by his reputation for being a selfish player. He once refused to participate in the All-Star Game unless he was voted in as a starter; on another occasion, he demanded that the Detroit Tigers bring in the outfield fences of spacious Comerica Park if the team wished to re-sign him as a free agent at the end of the season.

Larry Walker

Larry Walker began his major league career with the Montreal Expos in 1989, becoming a regular with the team the following season. Walker was a very solid player in his five full years in Montreal, twice hitting more than 20 home runs and batting over .300. He appeared to be just coming into his own in his final year with the Expos before that 1994 season ended prematurely with the players' strike. In only 395 at-bats over 103 games that year, Walker hit 19 home runs, drove in 86 runs, and batted .322.

After Walker joined the Colorado Rockies the following season, his career really took off. Over the next eight seasons, between 1995 and 2002, he developed into one of the best all-around players in baseball. During that eight-year period, Walker batted over .300 seven times, surpassing the .350 mark on four separate occasions. He also hit more than 35 homers four times, drove in more than 100 runs five times, scored more than 100 runs four times, and won seven Gold Glove Awards.

Walker had his finest season in 1997, when he led the National League with 49 home runs, 44 doubles, an on-base percentage of .452, and a slugging percentage of .720, while knocking in 130 runs, scoring 143 others, batting .366, and winning the league MVP Award. He also had magnificent seasons in both 1999 and 2001. In the first of those years, Walker hit 37 home runs, drove in 115 runs, and led the league with a .379 batting average. Two years later, he hit 38 homers, knocked in 123 runs, and, once again, won the batting title, this time with a mark of .350. In all, Walker led the league in batting three times, in home runs and doubles once each, and in on-base and slugging percentage two times each. He finished in the top ten in the league MVP voting a total of four times, and was named to the All-Star Team five times.

Larry Walker had some truly exceptional seasons. In at least four of those, it could be said that he was among the five best all-around players in baseball. When he retired at the conclusion of the 2005 season, his stat-line read thusly:

AB	HITS	RUNS	2B	3B	HR	RBI	AVG	SB	OBP	SLG PCT
6,907	2,160	1,355	471	62	383	1,311	.313	230	.400	.565

Those are very good stats, but borderline Hall of Fame numbers. However, Walker's statistics will always be viewed with a great deal of skepticism since he compiled the majority of them playing in Colorado's Coors Field, a notoriously good hitter's ballpark. Colorado's thin air enables balls to travel much further than they do in other ballparks, resulting in significantly higher home run totals and batting averages for hitters fortunate enough to call Colorado their home. The members of the BBWAA are certain to take that into consideration when they evaluate Walker's qualifications once his name is added to the eligible list. Thus, in all likelihood, Walker will rightly be denied admission to Cooperstown.

Mike Mussina

One of baseball's winningest pitchers for much of the past two decades was Mike Mussina. In 2008, the righthander finished with double-digit victories for the 17th consecutive season, winning his 270th game in the process.

Mussina spent the first 10 years of his career with the Baltimore Orioles, becoming a regular member of the team's starting rotation in 1992, his second year with the club. Mussina was one of the American League's best pitchers that year, compiling a record of 18-5, along with an outstanding 2.54 earned run average. He finished fourth in the Cy Young voting at the end of the season. Mussina also pitched extremely well for the Orioles in 1994, 1995, and 1999, posting won-lost records of 16-5, 19-9, and 18-7, respectively, along with earned run averages of 3.06, 3.29, and 3.50. Mussina continued his excellent pitching after signing on with the Yankees as a free agent prior to the start of the 2001 season. In his first year in pinstripes, he finished 17-11 with a 3.15 ERA. Mussina also posted records of 18-10, 17-8, and 20-9 in his eight years in New York, becoming, in 2008, the oldest pitcher in baseball history to win 20 games for the first time in his career.

In all, Mussina won at least 18 games six times, posting at least 15 victories five other times. He also pitched to an ERA below 3.30 six times. Mussina ended his career in 2008 with a record of 270-153. His earned run average over 18 major league seasons was 3.68. Considering the hitter's era during which Mussina compiled those numbers, they might be good enough to earn him admittance to Cooperstown some time during his period of eligibility. Furthermore, it must be remembered that the Orioles were not a very good ballclub his first few years with the team and, also, that he spent many of those years pitching in Camden Yards, a veritable hitter's paradise.

Nevertheless, Mussina's detractors will point to the fact that he was never considered to be the best pitcher in the American League. In fact, he finished higher than fourth in the Cy Young balloting only once. He also led league pitchers in a major statistical category only three times, and he never particularly distinguished himself during the postseason. In nine playoff and World Series appearances, covering 16 postseason series, Mussina compiled a won-lost record of only 7-8, while pitching to a 3.42 earned run average. In addition, Mussina's earned run average exceeded 4.40 in five different seasons, and, in his years in New York, he was rarely considered to be the best pitcher on his own team's staff.

Still, Mussina's total body of work is quite impressive. Few pitchers of his generation won as many as 15 games 11 different times, and few posted as many as 270 victories over the course of their careers. Although he finished as high as second in the Cy Young voting only once, Mussina placed in the top five in the balloting a total of six times. And, although he was a league-leader in a major statistical category only three times, Mussina finished second in wins three times, and placed in the top five in earned run average a total of nine times. He also was named to five All-Star teams and collected seven Gold Gloves during his career.

After winning 20 games for the first time in 2008, Mussina surprisingly elected to retire at the conclusion of the season, just 30 victories short of the magical 300-mark. Had Mussina hung around long enough to reach that plateau, it would have been extremely difficult to deny him a place in Cooperstown when he eventually decided to call it quits. But, as things stand now, the feeling here is that Mussina probably falls just a bit short, and should be viewed very much as a borderline candidate. Nevertheless, he deserves to be elected at least as much as about a dozen other pitchers currently in Cooperstown, including 300-game winners Don Sutton and Phil Niekro.

STILL ACTIVE FUTURE HALL OF FAMERS

This next group of Future Hall of Famers is comprised of those players who are currently active, but who have already accomplished enough during their careers to merit induction. In most cases, these are players who are in the twilight of their careers. However, in some instances, the players still appear to have several fine seasons ahead of them, but have performed at such a dominant level during their time in the major leagues that it would be impossible to find fault with their elections even if they were never to play another game. Following is a list of these men:

Ken Griffey Jr.
Frank Thomas
Manny Ramirez
Randy Johnson
Pedro Martinez
Tom Glavine
Mariano Rivera

Ken Griffey Jr.

Once considered the leading candidate to break Hank Aaron's career home run record, Ken Griffey Jr. was victimized by a series of devastating injuries that ended his 2001–2004 seasons prematurely, and all but ended his pursuit of that cherished mark. But, prior to that, Griffey already established himself as one of the most dominant players of his era, as one of the finest all-around centerfielders ever to play the game, and as a certain Hall of Famer when his playing days are over.

After arriving in the big leagues four years earlier, Griffey had his first great season for the Seattle Mariners in 1993, hitting 45 home runs, knocking in 109 runs, scoring another 113, and batting .309. After hitting 40 homers, driving in 90 runs, scoring 94 others, and batting a career-high .323 during the strike-shortened 1994 campaign, Junior missed much of the 1995 season with an injury. However, he returned the following year, and, over the next four seasons, was arguably the best all-around player in baseball. Here are his numbers from those years:

1996: 49 HR, 140 RBIs, .303 average, 125 runs scored
1997: 56 HR, 147 RBIs, .304 average, 125 runs scored
1998: 56 HR, 146 RBIs, .284 average, 120 runs scored
1999: 48 HR, 134 RBIs, .285 average, 123 runs scored

Griffey was selected as the American League's Most Valuable Player in 1997, one of seven times he has finished in the top 10 in the balloting. He has also been chosen for the All-Star Team 13 times. Griffey has hit more than 40 homers seven times, driven in more than 100 runs eight times, scored more than 100 runs six times, and batted over .300 eight times. In all, he has led his league in home runs four times, runs batted in once, runs scored once, and slugging percentage once. At the conclusion of the 2008 campaign, he had 611 home runs, 1,772 RBIs, 1,611 runs scored, and a batting average of .288.

After appearing in a total of only 337 games for the Cincinnati Reds between 2001 and 2004, Griffey made a stirring comeback in 2005, hitting 35 home runs, driving in 92 runs, scoring 85 others, and batting .301. Despite missing 92 games over the next three seasons, Griffey combined for 75 home runs and 236 runs batted in. Griffey will be 39 at the start of the 2009 campaign and has lost any chance he once had of establishing a new home run record. But the time he missed due to injury did not prevent him from claiming the fifth spot on the all-time home run list. Nor will it prevent him from being elected to Cooperstown the first time his name appears on the ballot.

Frank Thomas

Four injury-marred, mostly unproductive seasons during the second half of his career appeared to greatly diminish Frank Thomas' chances of eventually being inducted into Cooperstown. His claim to baseball immortality was made even more tenuous by the somewhat one-dimensional nature of his game, which forced him to spend the second half of his career almost exclusively as a designated hitter. But, in the end, the tremendous offensive productivity displayed by Thomas throughout much of his long and illustrious career should earn him a spot in the Hall of Fame.

After joining the White Sox in 1990, Thomas became the team's regular first baseman the following year. In each of the next eight seasons, he hit more than 20 homers, knocked in more than 100 runs, drew more than 100 bases on balls, and scored more than 100 runs. In seven of those eight years, he batted well over .300. In fact, Thomas is the only player in baseball history to hit .300 with at least 20 homers, 100 RBIs, 100 runs scored, and 100 walks in seven consecutive seasons. He is also one of only four players to drive in at least 100 runs in his first seven years in the big leagues.

In his first seven seasons, Thomas won a batting title, led the American League in walks and on-base percentage four times each, and in slugging percentage, runs scored, and doubles once each. He won two Most Valuable Player Awards, finished in the top ten in the voting every year, and was named to five All-Star teams. He was arguably the most feared hitter in the game, and was one of its ten best players and top two first basemen in every season.

Thomas was the best first baseman in baseball in both 1993 and 1994, being named the American League's MVP at the end of each of those seasons. In 1993, he hit 41 home runs, knocked in 128 runs, batted .317, scored 106 runs, and walked 112 times. In the strike-shortened 1994 campaign, Thomas hit 38 homers and drove in 101 runs in only 399 official at-bats, while batting .353, scoring 106 runs, and walking 109 times. He was, once again, the best first baseman in the game in 1996, when he finished with 40 home runs, 134 runs batted in, a .349 batting average, and 110 runs scored. Thomas was also among the game's elite players in both 1997 and 2000. In the first of those years, he hit 35 home runs, drove in 125 runs, scored 110 others, and led the league with a .347 batting average. Three years later, he established new career highs with 43 homers, 143 runs batted in, and 115 runs scored, while batting .328 and finishing second in the league MVP voting.

Nevertheless, Thomas' status as an eventual Hall of Famer appeared to take a major hit over the next five seasons. Due to injuries, and to what some perceived to be a somewhat apathetic attitude, Thomas had only one quality season between 2001 and 2005. In three of those years, he failed to appear in more than 75 games for the White Sox. He missed almost all of the 2001 and 2005 seasons, and played in only 74 games in 2004. He did put up good numbers in 2003, though, hitting 42 home runs and driving in 105 runs. But Thomas' ineffectiveness throughout much of that period seemed to make him a borderline Hall of Fame candidate. So, too, did his reputation for being a total liability in the field, which has caused him to spend the better portion of his career serving primarily as a designated hitter.

Yet, after leaving Chicago at the end of the 2005 season, Thomas had extremely productive years for Oakland in 2006 and Toronto in 2007. Over those two seasons, he combined for 65 home runs and 209 runs batted in, helping to restore his somewhat damaged reputation. More importantly, Thomas surpassed the 500-homer mark, practically guaranteeing him a place in Cooperstown when his career is over. If the baseball writers need any more convincing, they need only look at his other outstanding credentials.

Thomas has put together eight true Hall-of-Fame type seasons during his career. Aside from winning the MVP Award twice, Thomas has finished in the top ten in the balloting seven other times. He has been selected to the All-Star Team five times, a decent number for a potential Hall of Famer. He has won a batting title, and has led his league in on-base percentage four times. In fact, his career on-base percentage of .419 is the fourth highest among active players, and places him 21st on the all-time list. His .555 career slugging percentage also places him among the top 25 all-time. In addition to his 521 career home runs, Thomas has driven in 1,704 runs, scored 1,494 others, and compiled a .301 lifetime batting average. Those numbers should be good enough to get him into the Hall of Fame when his playing days are over.

Manny Ramirez

Manny Ramirez is far from a complete player. He is a below-average outfielder, a poor baserunner, and he possesses horrible baseball instincts. Furthermore, his attitude and mental approach to the game have often been questioned by management, the fans, the media, and, in some instances, even his own teammates. Ramirez has been known to sit out pivotal games with minor injuries, he frequently doesn't hustle, and he generally seems to place his own personal interests ahead of those of his team. Perhaps that explains why, in spite of the prodigious offensive numbers he posts annually, Boston Red Sox management finally decided to rid itself of his exorbitant contract this past season, after beginning to explore opportunities to do so as early as 2002.

However, Ramirez is also a tremendous offensive player—one of the finest of his era. He has outstanding power, hits for an extremely high batting average, and is one of the best clutch hitters and greatest run producers of the modern era.

Ramirez first came up with the Cleveland Indians in 1993. In six full seasons with the Indians, he topped 30 homers and 100 runs batted in five times each, scored more than 100 runs twice, and batted over .300 five times. His two most productive seasons in Cleveland came in 1998 and 1999, both years in which he led the league in slugging percentage. In 1998, he hit 45 home runs, knocked in 145 runs, scored 108 others, and batted .294. The following year, he hit 44 homers, drove in a league-leading 165 runs, scored another 131, and batted .333. In 2000, his final year in Cleveland, Ramirez batted a career-high .351.

After signing on with the Boston Red Sox as a free agent prior to the start of the 2001 season, Ramirez continued his tremendous offensive productivity. He has hit more than 30 home runs and driven in more than 100 runs in seven of the last eight years, surpassing 40 homers and 125 runs batted in three times each. He has also scored more than 100 runs four times and batted over .300 six times during that period. In 2002, Ramriez led the American League with a .349 batting average. He had his two most productive seasons in Boston in 2004 and 2005. In the first of those years, Ramirez hit 43 home runs, knocked in 130 runs, scored another 108, batted .308, and finished third in the league MVP voting. The following season, he hit 45 homers, drove in 144 runs, scored 112 others, batted .292, and placed fourth in the MVP voting.

Over 14 full major league seasons, Ramirez has averaged 36 home runs and 118 runs batted in. He has topped the 30-homer mark 12 times, surpassing 40 on five separate occasions. He has also batted over .300 eleven times, topping the .320-mark seven times. A veritable RBI-machine, Ramirez has driven in more than

100 runs 12 times, knocking in at least 120 runs on seven separate occasions. He has also scored more than 100 runs six times. In addition to his batting title, Ramirez has led the league in home runs and runs batted in once each, and in on-base percentage and slugging percentage three times each. He has been selected to 11 All-Star teams, and has finished in the top ten in the league MVP voting a total of nine times, placing as high as third twice. Going into the 2009 season, here are his career statistics:

AB	HITS	RUNS	2B	3B	HR	RBI	AVG	SB	OBP	SLG PCT
7,610	2,392	1,444	507	18	527	1,725	.314	37	.411	.593

In spite of the amount of baggage Ramirez has always brought along with him throughout his career, those numbers should be good enough to get him into the Hall of Fame. But, at age 36, he figures to add to them significantly before his career is over. Ramirez would have to be considered a virtual lock for the Hall once his playing days are over.

Randy Johnson

As the dominant lefthander of the past 25 years, and as one of the very best pitchers of that same period, Randy Johnson is another who most certainly has a plaque waiting for him at Cooperstown when his playing days are over. With the possible exception of Steve Carlton, no lefthanded pitcher dominated opposing hitters the way Johnson did for much of his career since Sandy Koufax mesmerized National League batters during the 1960s. And, without question, not since Koufax did any lefthander intimidate opposing hitters the way Johnson did throughout much of his brilliant 21-year career.

Yet, it took Johnson time to develop into the great pitcher he eventually became. In his first five big league seasons, he struggled with his control, walking well over 100 batters three times. But, after gaining a greater command of the strike zone in 1993, Johnson became one of the best pitchers in baseball. In the 16 seasons since, he has been a 20-game winner three times, has won at least 16 games eight other times, and has garnered five Cy Young Awards.

Johnson had some truly outstanding seasons for the Seattle Mariners, finishing with records of 19-8, 18-2, and 20-4, in 1993, 1995, and 1997, respectively. However, he became the most dominant pitcher in baseball after moving to the National League during the 1998 campaign. Pitching for the Arizona Diamondbacks from 1999 to 2002, Johnson put together a string of seasons reminiscent of the ones Koufax compiled for the Dodgers during the 1960s. Here are his numbers from those four seasons:

1999: 17 wins, 9 losses; 2.48 ERA; 364 strikeouts
2000: 19 wins, 7 losses; 2.64 ERA; 347 strikeouts
2001: 21 wins, 6 losses; 2.49 ERA; 372 strikeouts
2002: 24 wins, 5 losses; 2.32 ERA; 334 strikeouts

Johnson led National League pitchers in strikeouts in each of those years, and also finished first in ERA three times, and in wins once. In being named winner of the Cy Young Award at the end of each of those seasons, Johnson joined Greg Maddux as the only pitchers ever to be so honored four consecutive years.

During his career, Johnson has led his league in wins once, ERA four times, strikeouts nine times, shutouts twice, and complete games four times. He has finished with an ERA under 3.00 seven times during his career, and has struck out more than 300 batters six times, surpassing the 200-mark on seven other occasions. Johnson has finished in the top ten in the league MVP voting twice, in the top five in the Cy Young balloting eight times, and has been selected to the All-Star team ten times. As of this writing, Johnson's career record is 295-160, his ERA is 3.26, and, with 4,789 strikeouts, he trails only Nolan Ryan on the all-time list.

Pedro Martinez

While he has not been as durable as the other great pitchers of his era—Roger Clemens, Greg Maddux, and Randy Johnson—when healthy, Pedro Martinez has been as dominant as any of them. With a career record of 214-99 as of this writing, he has the best won-lost percentage, and his ERA of 2.91 is significantly lower than that of the other three men. Martinez has led his league in wins once, in ERA five times, and in strikeouts three times. He has been an eight-time All-Star, has placed in the top five in the league MVP voting twice, and has won the Cy Young Award three times, finishing in the top five in the voting another four times.

With the exception of his injury-plagued 2001 season, Martinez was at his very best from 1997 to 2002, rivaling Randy Johnson as the best pitcher in the game during that period. Let's look at his numbers from his five best seasons:

1997: 17 wins, 8 losses; 1.90 ERA; 305 strikeouts
1998: 19 wins, 7 losses; 2.89 ERA; 251 strikeouts
1999: 23 wins, 4 losses; 2.07 ERA; 313 strikeouts
2000: 18 wins, 6 losses; 1.74 ERA; 284 strikeouts
2002: 20 wins, 4 losses; 2.26 ERA; 239 strikeouts

Martinez was the recipient of his league's Cy Young Award following the 1997, 1999, and 2000 seasons, and, with the possible exception of Roger Clemens in 1997, was the best pitcher in baseball in each of those years. He was clearly among the top five pitchers in the game in all five seasons.

In all, Martinez has won at least 16 games six times, has finished with an ERA under 3.00 ten times, twice allowing fewer than two runs per contest, and has struck out more than 200 batters nine times, twice topping the 300-mark. Martinez's career ERA of 2.91 is the lowest of any starting pitcher whose career began after 1980.

Should Martinez never pitch another game, his relatively low total of 214 victories might deter some members of the BBWAA from entering his name on their Hall of Fame ballots in his first year of eligibility. There is little doubt, though, that the majority of the writers will realize that the standard of excellence Martinez set for himself on the mound throughout his career earned him a first-ballot election to Cooperstown.

Tom Glavine

Lefthander Tom Glavine has never been the dominant pitcher that some of his contemporaries were through the years. He never possessed the overpowering fastball of Roger Clemens, the overwhelming fastball/slider combination of Randy Johnson, or either the great fastball or the superb curve of Pedro Martinez. And, for much of his career, he was overshadowed in Atlanta by his own teammate, Greg Maddux. But, while he may not have been a truly *great* pitcher, Glavine was, from 1991 to 2002, one of baseball's most consistent winners, and one of its top hurlers.

In his first 16 seasons with the Atlanta Braves, Glavine was a 20-game winner five times, and won at least 16 games three other times. He led the National League in wins five times, and in shutouts and complete games once each. He was named to the All-Star Team eight times, finished in the top ten in the league MVP voting once, and placed in the top five in the Cy Young balloting six times, winning the award twice. Glavine won the award for the first time in 1991 with a record of 20-11 and an ERA of 2.55. He won his second Cy Young in 1998, compiling a record of 20-6 and a 2.47 ERA. Glavine has also put together seasons in which he compiled records of 20-8, 22-6, and 21-9. In each of his 20-win seasons, Glavine was among the five best pitchers in baseball. Glavine has also posted an ERA below 3.00 six times. As of this writing, his career mark is 3.54, and his won-lost record is 305-203.

When Glavine's career is over and he eventually becomes eligible for induction into Cooperstown, there is little doubt that his 300 victories will prompt many members of the BBWAA to vote for him the first time his name appears on the ballot. If Glavine is not elected in his first year of eligibility, he most certainly will be voted in shortly thereafter.

Mariano Rivera

As of 2008, only five relief pitchers have been inducted into Cooperstown—Hoyt Wilhelm, Rollie Fingers, Dennis Eckersley, Bruce Sutter, and Goose Gossage. Unless someone such as Lee

Smith is inducted in the next few years, there is little doubt that Mariano Rivera will eventually become the sixth reliever to be enshrined in the Hall once his playing days are over. Over the course of his brilliant career, Rivera has established himself as the greatest closer in baseball history.

Rivera has been a dominant pitcher ever since he first served as set-up man to closer John Wetteland for the Yankees during New York's run to the 1996 world championship. After assuming Wetteland's role the following year, Rivera became the very best closer in the game. Over the past 12 seasons, he has been as close to automatic as anyone in baseball, finishing with at least 36 saves nine times during that period. He has reached 40 saves six different times, and has surpassed 50 on two separate occasions. Rivera has compiled an ERA under 2.00 eight times, and has finished with a mark over 3.00 only once (3.15 in 2007). Over the course of his career, he has surrendered only 800 hits in 1,024 innings of work, and his strikeout-to-walk ratio is better than 3 to 1.

Rivera has led American League relief pitchers in saves three times, has been selected to nine All-Star teams, has finished second in the Cy Young balloting once, and has placed third in the voting on three other occasions. He finished third in the balloting for the first time in 1996, when he compiled a record of 8-3, with a 2.09 ERA and 130 strikeouts in 108 innings pitched as a set-up man. He placed third in the balloting again in 1999, when he compiled a 4-3 record, with 45 saves and a 1.83 ERA, while surrendering only 43 hits in 69 innings of work. He finished third in the voting again in 2004, when he finished 4-2, with a league-leading 53 saves, and a 1.94 ERA. Rivera finished runner-up in the balloting in 2005, when he compiled a record of 7-4, with 43 saves and a 1.38 ERA, while allowing just 50 hits in 78 innings of work.

Rivera has not only been the best relief pitcher in baseball for most of his career, but has also been one of the greatest postseason pitchers in baseball history. In 76 playoff and World Series contests between 1996 and 2007, he compiled a won-lost record of 8-1 and an ERA of 0.77, while saving 34 games and allowing only 72 hits in 117 innings of work. Perhaps more than any other player, he was responsible for New York's successful playoff run that led to four world championships in five seasons between 1996 and 2000.

Rivera concluded the 2008 campaign with 482 career saves, placing him second on the all-time list. He also has posted a brilliant 2.29 ERA during his 14 big-league seasons. When Rivera eventually becomes eligible for induction to Cooperstown, it shouldn't take the BBWAA long to elect him. Indeed, he is likely to join Dennis Eckersley as only the second reliever to be inducted in his first year of eligibility.

Borderline Hall of Fame Candidates

There are several other active players in the latter stages of their careers who could be classified as borderline Hall of Fame candidates. This list of players includes:

Jim Thome
Todd Helton
Carlos Delgado
Omar Vizquel
Curt Schilling
John Smoltz
Trevor Hoffman

Jim Thome

While Fred McGriff fell seven home runs short of testing the theory that 500 home runs are no longer an automatic ticket to Cooperstown, Jim Thome may well be the first man to actually challenge whether or not that historical benchmark still applies. Heading into the 2009 campaign, Thome, one of baseball's purest sluggers over the past decade, has 541 home runs. Yet, when the greatest players of his generation are mentioned, Thome's name rarely comes up during the conversation.

Since Thome became a regular for the Cleveland Indians in his fifth year with the team in 1995, he has been one of baseball's top home run hitters and run-producers. Possessing tremendous power to all fields, as well as a keen batting eye that has enabled him to accumulate more than 100 walks nine different times, Thome has averaged 37 home runs and 102 RBIs in his 13 years as a full-time player. He has surpassed 30 homers 12 times, topping the 40-mark on six separate occasions. Thome has also driven in more than 100 runs nine times, and scored at least 100 runs eight times.

As a member of the Indians from 1996 to 2002, Thome surpassed 30 homers each year, knocked in and scored 100 runs six times each, collected more than 100 walks six times, and batted over .300 twice. His two best years were in 2001 and 2002. In the first of those campaigns, Thome hit 49 home runs, knocked in 124 runs, scored 101 others, batted .291, and drew 111 bases on balls. The following season, he hit a career-high 52 homers, drove in 118 runs, scored another 101, batted .304, and walked 122 times. Thome finished second in the league in home runs both seasons.

At the end of 2002, Thome signed a big free-agent contract with the Philadelphia Phillies. His first season with his new team was an extremely productive one in which he led the National League with 47 home runs, placed third in the circuit with a career-best 131 runs batted in, scored 111 runs, and finished fourth in the league MVP voting. Thome had another good year in 2004, hitting 42 homers and driving in 105 runs. However, he missed most of the 2005 season with a bad back, hitting only 7 home runs, driving in just 30 runs, and batting only .207 in just 193 at-bats. At the end of the year, Thome was traded to the Chicago White Sox, with whom he spent the last three seasons. Serving primarily as a designated hitter after spending the majority of his career as a first baseman, Thome combined for 111 home runs and 295 RBIs over the past three years in Chicago. Those 111 home runs are particularly significant because they moved Thome past the 500-home run mark. Here are his career statistics heading into the 2009 campaign:

AB	HITS	RUNS	2B	3B	HR	RBI	AVG	SB	OBP	SLG PCT
7,344	2,048	1,431	397	24	541	1,488	.279	19	.406	.560

Those are good numbers. In fact, most people would probably consider them good enough to get Thome elected to Cooperstown sometime during his eligibility period. However, I remain somewhat uncertain as to whether or not I share that opinion, since Thome's overall accomplishments, to this point, have not distinguished him enough from the other players of his era. In spite of the fact that he has surpassed the 40-homer mark five times during his career, Thome has led his league in that category only once, and has finished in the top three only two other times. He also has led the league in slugging percentage once, and in bases on balls three times, but has never finished first in any other major statistical category. Thome has never placed any higher than fourth in the league MVP balloting, and has made it into the top ten only four times. He has also been selected to the All-Star Team a total of five times, a relatively modest number for a potential Hall of Famer.

Taking everything into consideration, the feeling here is that Thome must improve significantly upon his current numbers before he can be considered a legitimate Hall of Famer. He must put together another two or three solid seasons, thereby increasing his home run total to a figure approximating 600. He must also add significantly to his RBI-total. Since Thome will turn 39 during the 2009 season, it remains somewhat questionable as to whether or not he will be able to accomplish these things. If he does not, he probably doesn't deserve to be inducted into Cooperstown.

Todd Helton

Colorado Rockies first baseman Todd Helton has been a full-time player in the major leagues since 1998. Helton was a truly exceptional player from 1999 to 2004, ranking among baseball's elite in each of those six seasons. In his first full season, he hit 25 home runs, knocked in 97 runs, and batted .315—all very respectable numbers. However, in each of the next six seasons, Helton was arguably among the ten best players in the game, hitting more than 30 homers, batting over .320, and scoring more than 100 runs each year, and knocking in over 100 runs in all but one of those seasons. He was perhaps among the top five players in baseball in both 2000 and 2001, and then again in 2003. In the first of those years, Helton hit 42 home runs and led the National League with 147 runs batted in, a .372 batting average, 59 doubles, 216 hits, and 405 total bases, while scoring 138 runs. He followed that up in 2001 by hitting 49 homers, driving in 146 runs, scoring 132 others, and batting .336. In 2003, Helton hit 33 home runs, drove in 117 runs, scored another 135, and batted .358.

In addition to his six seasons with at least 30 home runs and 100 runs scored, and his five seasons with more than 100 runs batted in, Helton has batted over .300 in all but one of his 11 full major league seasons, drawn more than 100 bases on balls five times, collected more than 200 hits twice, and compiled more than 50 doubles twice, accumulating as many as 49 on two other occasions. He has been a league leader in a major statistical category a total of seven times, and his career batting average of .328 places him third among active players. Helton has also been selected to five All-Star teams and has been awarded three Gold Gloves for his fine fielding at first base. Heading into 2009, these are his career statistics:

AB	HITS	RUNS	2B	3B	HR	RBI	AVG	SB	OBP	SLG PCT
5,962	1,957	1,143	471	31	310	1,116	.328	36	.428	.574

Those are not quite Hall of Fame numbers, but, since Helton will not turn 36 until late in the 2009 campaign, one would think he should be able to add to them significantly before his career is over. Yet, Helton's offensive productivity has dropped off dramatically the last four seasons. He has failed to hit more than 20 home runs, drive in more than 91 runs, score more than 94 times, or top the .320-mark in batting since 2004.

Furthermore, injuries limited Helton to only 83 games in 2008, a year in which he hit just 7 home runs, knocked in only 29 runs, and batted a career-low .264. Thus, it would seem that Helton's career is clearly on the decline. Another thing to consider is that, even though Helton compiled outstanding numbers between 1999 and 2004, he never finished any higher than fifth in the league MVP voting, placing in the top ten a total of only three times. There is little doubt that much of the blame for that last fact can be placed on the poor showings of Helton's Rockies team in most of those years. However, another contributing factor was undoubtedly the extent to which Helton's offensive numbers were aided by playing in Coors Field. In the end, that is something that is likely to work against Helton when he becomes eligible for the Hall of Fame, much as it will against his former teammate, Larry Walker. Therefore, Helton probably needs to put together four or five more exceptional seasons to have a legitimate chance of being elected to Cooperstown when his career is over—something it appears he is not likely to do.

Carlos Delgado

For much of his 16-year career, power-hitting first baseman Carlos Delgado has been among the most productive hitters in baseball. Since first becoming a full-time player with the Toronto Blue Jays in 1996, Delgado has failed to hit at least 25 home runs and drive in at least 90 runs just once. Indeed, over the past 13 seasons he has surpassed 30 homers 11 times, accumulating as many as 40 on three separate occasions. Delgado has also knocked in more than 100 runs nine times, topping 130 RBIs three different times. In addition, he has scored more than 100 runs five times and batted over .300 three times.

Delgado had his two best years in 2000 and 2003. In the first of those seasons, he hit 41 home runs, knocked in 137 runs, scored another 115, batted a career-high .344, and led the American League with 57 doubles. He finished fourth in the league MVP voting that year. In 2003, Delgado hit 42 homers, led the A.L. with 145 runs batted in, scored 117 runs, batted .302, and finished second in the MVP balloting.

However, other than leading the league in RBIs and doubles once each, Delgado has never topped his league in any other major offensive category. He also has finished in the top ten in the MVP balloting only two other times, aside from those 2000 and 2003 seasons, placing sixth in the N.L. voting in 2005 as a member of the Florida Marlins, and coming in ninth in 2008 after having a strong second half for the New York Mets. Furthermore, he has been selected to only two All-Star teams during his career, an extremely low number for a potential Hall of Famer. Delgado was among the 10 best players in the game in only those 2000 and 2003 seasons, and has never been thought of as being the best player at his position (Jason Giambi was the game's top first baseman in 2000; Albert Pujols was number one in 2003). Thus, while he is certainly a fine player, the degree to which Delgado has distinguished himself from the other players of his era is very much open to debate.

Another thing to consider is that Delgado has developed a reputation through the years as being a somewhat dispassionate player. The general perception held towards him is that he is not much of a leader, and that his offensive numbers hold more significance to him than does the success of his team. Whether or not that is entirely true is certainly debatable. However, one thing that is certain is that Delgado contributed greatly to the firing of New York Mets Manager Willie Randolph in 2008. Playing under Randolph during the season's first half, Delgado slumped terribly, often appearing lost at the plate, and not seeming to care much of the time. Yet, Delgado's performance improved dramatically during the final three months of the season, after Randolph was replaced at the helm by Jerry Manuel, someone with whom the first baseman had a much better relationship. In fact, Delgado's play improved so greatly that many onlookers believed his first-half performance clearly demonstrated his desire to play for another manager. Delgado finished the year with 38 home runs and 115 runs batted in. Therefore, it would seem that there may be a certain amount of truth to the allegations made against the slugging first baseman.

Nevertheless, Delgado's stat-line heading into 2009 is rather impressive:

AB	HITS	RUNS	2B	3B	HR	RBI	AVG	SB	OBP	SLG PCT
7,189	2,010	1,226	476	17	469	1,489	.280	14	.383	.546

Those are very good numbers, but Delgado probably needs to reach the 500-home run plateau to be considered a legitimate Hall of Fame candidate. He is likely to do so, since he will not turn 37 until midway through the 2009 campaign. Still, the feeling here is that, even if Delgado eventually surpasses 500 career home runs, he will probably fall just a bit short of being Hall of Fame worthy. He doesn't possess any intangible qualities that might further enhance his cause—he is a below-average fielder and baserunner, and, as was mentioned earlier, he has never been much of a team leader. More importantly, Delgado has not separated himself enough from the other players of his time to gain admittance to Cooperstown when his career is over.

Omar Vizquel

Had he come along 15 or 20 years earlier, in all likelihood Omar Vizquel would have been considered the premier shortstop of his time and a favorite to enter the Hall of Fame when his playing days were over. However, it was Vizquel's misfortune to enter the major leagues in 1989, at a time when two of the greatest shortstops in the history of the game, Cal Ripken Jr. and Ozzie Smith, were still in their prime. Vizquel spent his first five years in Seattle being largely overlooked in favor of both Ripken and Smith as the careers of the two men began to wind down. Later, after joining the Cleveland Indians in 1994, Vizquel spent most of his best years coming up short in comparisons to Alex Rodriguez, Derek Jeter, and Nomar Garciaparra, all of whom were considerably larger than the 5'9", 165-pound Venezuelan, and, therefore, possessed much more power at the plate. Thus, Vizquel has spent virtually his entire career being compared to some of the most talented men ever to play the position of shortstop.

Yet, through it all, Vizquel has remained the finest defensive shortstop in the game, and, quite possibly, the best in baseball history, aside from Ozzie Smith. From 1993 to 2001, Vizquel won nine consecutive Gold Glove Awards, and he captured two more after joining the San Francisco Giants in 2005. Vizquel's career .984 fielding percentage is actually considerably better than Smith's mark of .978. In 2000, he set a major league record for shortstops by committing only three errors in 647 total chances all year. In three full seasons between 2000 and 2002, he committed a total of just 17 errors.

Vizquel is a competent offensive player as well. His career batting average is .273, and he has batted over .290 five times. He has also scored more than 100 runs twice and stolen more than 30 bases four times. Vizquel had his finest season for the Indians in 1999, when he compiled a batting average of .333, with 112 runs scored, 191 hits, 36 doubles, and 42 stolen bases.

Vizquel's offensive numbers actually compare quite favorably to those posted by several other Hall of Fame shortstops. Let's look at his statistics alongside those of Luis Aparicio, another player who was known more for his great glove work than he was for his hitting:

PLAYER	AB	HITS	RUNS	2B	3B	HR	RBI	AVG	SB	OBP	SLG PCT
Omar Vizquel	9,745	2,657	1,361	426	72	77	892	.273	385	.338	.355
Luis Aparicio	10,230	2,677	1,335	394	92	83	791	.262	506	.313	.343

The two men are extremely close in most statistical categories, with Aparicio's only major advantage being his stolen base total. Vizquel, though, has driven in more runs in fewer at-bats, and has significantly higher on-base and slugging percentages. Certainly, it should be noted that Aparicio played during more of a pitcher's era. But, offensively, the difference between the two is negligible. And, although Aparicio was considered to be the finest defensive shortstop of his time, he certainly was no better than Vizquel. The biggest difference between the two is that, due to the greater level of competition that Vizquel has faced during his career, Aparicio received more recognition during his playing days for being among the best shortstops in baseball.

As a result of his bad timing, Vizquel has never been regarded as the best shortstop in his league, or even as one of the two or three best. He has been selected to only three All-Star teams, has never finished in the top ten in the league MVP voting, and has never come close to leading the league in any offensive category.

Omar Vizquel has been a fine player throughout his career. In fact, he is clearly better than at least three or four shortstops currently in the Hall of Fame. But, due to the era in which he has competed, and the fact that he has never been regarded as one of the very best shortstops in baseball, Vizquel is not likely to ever receive the support he will need to gain admittance to Cooperstown—something he probably doesn't quite deserve anyway.

Curt Schilling

Most people probably tend to think of Curt Schilling as a certain Hall of Famer. After all, from 2001 to 2004, he was one of baseball's most dominant pitchers, and, even before that, he had some truly outstanding seasons. However, the feeling here is that there is a need to take a closer look at Schilling's career before a plaque is constructed for him at Cooperstown.

In his first eight full seasons in the major leagues, as a member of the Philadelphia Phillies, Schilling was a good pitcher who had the misfortune of playing on predominantly poor teams. He was actually a *very* good pitcher in five of those years. In 1992, he finished only 14-11 but compiled an outstanding 2.35 earned run average. When the Phillies won the pennant the following year, his record improved to 16-7, but his ERA slipped to 4.02. Schilling was also very solid from 1997 to 1999, winning 47 games for weak Phillies teams those years, and striking out more than 300 batters twice. He had perhaps his finest season for the Phillies in 1997, compiling a record of 17-11, with a 2.97 ERA and a league-leading 319 strikeouts. Schilling was a fine pitcher in his years in Philadelphia, but, with the exception of one or two seasons, would have had a difficult time making anyone's list of baseball's top ten hurlers.

However, in 2001, as a member of the Arizona Diamondbacks, Schilling took his game to the next level. Experiencing something of a renaissance in Arizona, he became, along with teammate Randy Johnson, baseball's most dominant pitcher. That year, he finished 22-6, with a 2.98 ERA and 293 strikeouts, and was practically unhittable during the postseason. The following year, he finished 23-7, with a 3.23 ERA and 316 strikeouts. At the end of both seasons, he was named *The Sporting News* Pitcher of the Year. For those two seasons, Schilling was a truly great pitcher, one of the best in the game in quite some time.

Schilling was also extremely effective for the Diamondbacks during the first part of the 2003 campaign, before an injury forced him to miss the final two months of the season.. However, after becoming a free agent during the off-season, Schilling left Arizona to join the Boston Red Sox prior to the start of the 2004 campaign. With the Red Sox, Schilling had another fabulous year, compiling a record of 21-6 and an ERA of 3.26, while striking out 203 batters and leading Boston to its first World Championship in 86 years. Unfortunately, Schilling had a difficult time recovering from a foot injury he sustained late in the 2004 campaign and spent much of 2005 on the disabled list. When he returned to action, he was relatively ineffective much of the time, posting a record of only 8-8, with a 5.59 ERA. Healthy again in 2006, Schilling compiled a record of 15-7 and an ERA of 3.97. Schilling finally began succumbing to Father Time in 2007, when the 40-year-old won only nine of his 24 starts. He then missed the entire 2008 campaign with an injury to his pitching arm that may well bring an end to his major league career.

During his career, Schilling has led his league in wins, strikeouts, and innings pitched twice each, and in complete games four times. He has been selected to the All-Star Team six times, has finished in the top five in the Cy Young voting four times, placing second on three separate occasions, and has finished in the top ten in the MVP voting twice. Schilling has also been a tremendous big-game pitcher. In twelve postseason series, he has compiled a record of 10-2, with an ERA of 2.23, while striking out 120 batters and surrendering only 104 hits in 133 innings of work. In his seven World Series starts, Schilling has gone 3-1 with a 2.06 earned run average.

It would be difficult to disagree too strenuously with anyone who wished to initiate an argument on Schilling's behalf for his eventual induction into the Hall of Fame. However, it should be pointed out that he has won "only" 216 games—a relatively low number for a Hall of Fame pitcher. In fact, his career won-lost record stands at 216-146, and his earned run average is 3.46. Neither of those figures is particularly overwhelming. Furthermore, while Schilling was a truly great pitcher in 2001, 2002, and 2004, and an exceptional one in 1997, those are the only true Hall-of-Fame type seasons he has ever had. He had three other very good years for the Phillies, and another for the Red Sox, but was not among the very best pitchers in baseball in any of those campaigns. Therefore, even though the dominant image Schilling created of himself in the minds of most people in his years in Arizona, as well as his reputation for being an outstanding postseason performer will undoubtedly earn him a spot in Cooperstown when his playing days are over, the members of the BBWAA should take a step back and carefully consider Schilling's total body of work before they rush to enter his name on their ballots.

John Smoltz

Another pitcher who is likely to gain admittance to Cooperstown relatively early during his period of eligibility is John Smoltz, who has been one of baseball's best pitchers for much of the past 20 years.

Although overshadowed somewhat throughout much of his career by fellow Braves pitchers Greg Maddux and Tom Glavine, Smoltz has been one of the National League's most consistent winners over the last two decades. He has won at least 14 games ten times, leading the league in victories twice, and has also compiled an outstanding 3.26 earned run average. Smoltz has led all N.L. starters in strikeouts and innings pitched two times each, has been named to eight All-Star teams, has won a Cy Young Award, and has finished in the top five in the balloting two other times.

Smoltz had his best year for the Braves in 1996, when he captured N.L. Cy Young honors by finishing with a league-best 24-8 record, 276 strikeouts, and 254 innings pitched, while compiling an excellent 2.94 earned run average. He had another brilliant season in 1998, when he finished 17-3 with a 2.90 ERA despite missing more than a month of the campaign with arm problems. Over the course of his career, Smoltz has also established himself as one of the best big-game pitchers in the sport. In 24 postseason series, he has compiled a record of 15-4 and an exceptional 2.65 earned run average, while allowing only 168 hits in 207 innings of work.

Despite this body of work, the feeling here is that Smoltz should be viewed as a borderline Hall of Famer, rather than as an automatic selection when he eventually becomes eligible for induction. In 15 seasons as a full-time starter, he has won more than 15 games only three times, and, despite spending virtually his entire career with a contending team, he has won "only" 210 games—a relatively modest number for a Hall of Fame pitcher. Furthermore, much of the time, Smoltz was viewed as only the third best starter on his own team, behind both Greg Maddux and Tom Glavine. However, it must also be remembered that Smoltz's win total is somewhat misleading since he spent four seasons pitching out of the Braves' bullpen. In his three full years as a reliever, Smoltz saved a total of 144 games and established himself as one of the game's top closers, before being inserted back into the team's starting rotation in 2005. In addition, while he usually took a back-seat to Maddux and Glavine during the regular season, Smoltz generally surpassed both men in postseason play. He usually proved to be Atlanta's best pitcher in the playoffs and World Series.

All things considered, Smoltz's career won-lost record of 210-147 might make him something of a borderline Hall of Fame candidate. But, should the members of the BBWAA eventually choose to elect him, their decision would not be a bad one at all.

Trevor Hoffman

While others, such as Eric Gagne and Brad Lidge, were exceptional relievers for two or three seasons, the National League's dominant closer for most of the last 13 years has been Trevor Hoffman. In fact, with the exception of Mariano Rivera, Hoffman has been the best closer in the game since 1996.

Hoffman first assumed that role with the Padres in 1994, compiling 20 saves that year. He has surpassed 30 saves in all but one of the 14 subsequent seasons, topping the 40-mark on nine separate occasions. Hoffman had his finest season in 1998, when he led the league with a career-high 53 saves, while compiling a brilliant 1.48 earned run average, surrendering only 41 hits in 73 innings of work, and striking out 86 batters while walking only 21. He finished second in the Cy Young balloting that year, and, in helping San Diego to the N.L. pennant, also placed seventh in the league MVP voting. Two seasons later, Hoffman walked only 11 batters in 72 innings of work, while striking out 85. After another outstanding season in 2002, in which he saved 38 games in 41 save opportunities, Hoffman missed virtually all of the 2003 campaign due to injury. However, he returned in 2004 to save 41 games, and was extremely effective in each of the next three seasons as well, compiling 43, 46, and 42 saves, respectively. Although age finally began to catch up with Hoffman in 2008, he still managed to save 30 games for the 13th time in his career. In so doing, he increased his major league-leading all-time saves total to 554.

Trevor Hoffman has clearly been one of the finest relief pitchers in baseball history. In addition to leading his league in saves twice, he has finished second five other times. He has also pitched to an excellent 2.78 career ERA, and allowed only 762 hits in 988 innings of work, while striking out 1,055 batters. Hoffman has finished second in the Cy Young balloting twice, and has placed as high as sixth two other times. He also has finished in the top ten in the MVP voting twice and been named to six All-Star teams.

Nevertheless, it is difficult to think of Hoffman as a certain Hall of Famer when his playing days are over. Historically, the members of the BBWAA have been slow to recognize relief pitchers when they cast their ballots. It took Bruce Sutter 13 tries to finally get elected, and Goose Gossage finally gained admittance in his ninth year of eligibility. And both men were more dominant relievers than Hoffman. Neither closer collected nearly as many saves as Hoffman (Sutter had 300, Gossage had 310), but the game has changed significantly since Sutter and Gossage pitched during the 1970s and 1980s, and it would have been impossible for them to do so. Hoffman has led the N.L. in saves just twice. Sutter led the league a total of five times, and also finished in the top five on three other occasions. He also won the Cy Young Award in 1979, finished in the top five in the voting three other times, placed in the top ten in the league MVP balloting a total of five times, and was selected to six All-Star teams. Meanwhile, Gossage led his league in saves three times, and finished as high as third three other times. He also placed in the top five in the Cy Young balloting a total of four times, made it into the top ten in the league MVP voting twice, and was named to nine All-Star teams.

Furthermore, Hoffman has not pitched particularly well in big games. While his contemporary, Mariano Rivera, established himself as one of the greatest postseason pitchers in baseball history, Hoffman has a career record of only 1-2, with just four saves and an ERA of 3.46 in 12 playoff and World Series contests. He also hasn't fared particularly well in the All-Star Game. In six appearances, Hoffman has a record of 0-1 with no saves, and has allowed better than one run per-inning.

Therefore, while Hoffman's list of accomplishments is quite impressive, he should be viewed largely as a borderline Hall of Fame candidate. He certainly should have to wait at least as long as Sutter and Gossage did to be inducted into Cooperstown.

POTENTIAL HALL OF FAMERS

Our third group of Future Hall of Famers is comprised of those players who have performed at an extremely high level in the major leagues long enough (i.e. at least five seasons) to be projected as potential Hall of Fame candidates when their careers are eventually over. However, none of these men have yet accomplished enough to be considered certain inductees when their names are added to the eligible list several years from now.

Following is a list of these Potential Hall of Famers, and a brief summary of what they have accomplished thus far:

Albert Pujols
Ryan Howard

David Ortiz
Derek Jeter
Jimmy Rollins
Miguel Cabrera
David Wright
Eric Chavez
Scott Rolen
Chipper Jones
Vladimir Guerrero
Magglio Ordonez
Ichiro Suzuki
Johan Santana
Tim Hudson
Roy Halladay
Roy Oswalt

Albert Pujols

In his first eight major league seasons, the St. Louis Cardinals Albert Pujols has established himself as one of the game's most dominant hitters, and as perhaps the most likely *Potential Hall of Famer* on this list. In those eight seasons, Pujols has accomplished some truly amazing things.

Pujols' rookie season of 2001 drew comparisons to the debut seasons of baseball immortals Joe DiMaggio and Ted Williams. In his rookie campaign, Pujols hit 37 home runs, drove in 130 runs, scored another 112, and batted .329. (As a rookie in 1936, DiMaggio hit 29 homers, knocked in 125 runs, scored 132 others, and batted .323; in 1939, Williams hit 31 homers, drove in 145 runs, scored another 131, and batted .327). Over the next seven seasons, Pujols has proven that he was not a one-year wonder. Indeed, in 2005, he became the first player in major league history to hit more than 30 home runs, drive in more than 115 runs, score at least 100 others, and bat over .300 in each of his first five seasons. He surpassed each of those marks again in his sixth year.

While Pujols has been a superb player ever since he joined the Cardinals in 2001, he had perhaps his finest seasons from 2003 to

2006. In the first of those years, he hit 43 home runs, knocked in 124 runs, and led the National League with a .359 batting average, 137 runs scored, 212 hits, 51 doubles, and 394 total bases. In doing so, he finished second to Barry Bonds in the league MVP voting for the second consecutive season. In 2004, Pujols hit 46 homers, drove in 123 runs, batted .331, collected 51 doubles, led the league with 133 runs scored, and placed third in the N.L. MVP balloting.

Pujols finally came away with the MVP trophy in 2005 when he led the Cardinals to the division title by hitting 41 home runs, knocking in 117 runs, scoring 129 others, and batting .330. He followed that up in 2006 by placing among the league leaders with 49 home runs, 137 runs batted in, 119 runs scored, a .331 batting average, and a .431 on-base percentage, and leading the circuit with a .671 slugging percentage. Pujols finished second to Philadelphia's Ryan Howard in the league MVP voting and won the first Gold Glove Award of his career for his solid defensive work at first base. After having another solid season in 2007, Pujols performed brilliantly again in 2008, finishing among the league leaders with 37 home runs, 116 runs batted in, 44 doubles, 187 hits, a .357 batting average, and a .462 on-base percentage, and leading the circuit with a .653 slugging percentage. For his outstanding performance, Pujols was named N.L. MVP for the second time. In each of his eight big league seasons, Pujols has been among the five best players in the game, and the most dominant player at his position.

Pujols has placed in the top five in the MVP voting in seven of his eight years in the league, finishing ninth the other time. He has also been selected to seven All-Star teams. Although he will be only 29 when the 2009 season gets underway, Pujols already has 319 home runs, 977 runs batted in, 947 runs scored, and 1,531 hits. His .334 lifetime batting average is the highest among active players. Unless something dramatic happens in the next few years that adversely affects his performance, there is little doubt that Pujols will end up in Cooperstown when his playing days are over.

Ryan Howard

Yes, I know. Ryan Howard has been a full-time player in the major leagues for only three-and-a-half years as of this writing. But, ever since joining the Philadelphia Phillies midway through the 2005 campaign, the power-hitting first baseman has been arguably baseball's preeminent slugger.

Appearing in only 88 games during that 2005 season, Howard slugged 22 home runs and knocked in 63 runs, in just 312 official at-bats. That performance earned him N.L. Rookie of the Year honors at the end of the year. The 6'4", 240-pound Howard continued his onslaught on National League pitching in his first full major-league season the following year, leading the circuit with 58 home runs and 149 runs batted in, while also scoring 104 runs, batting .313, compiling an on-base percentage of .425, and finishing second in the league with a .659 slugging percentage. At the end of the year, Howard was named National League MVP and the Major League Player of the Year. Howard was somewhat less effective in 2007, batting only .268 and striking out a league-leading 199 times. But he also finished second in the league with 47 home runs and 136 runs batted in, helping the Phillies to the N.L. East title. Philadelphia repeated as Eastern Division champions in 2008, and Howard was once again a key contributor. Although he struck out another 199 times and saw his batting average fall to just .251, Howard led the league with 48 homers and 146 RBIs.

Howard has finished either first or second in the league in both home runs and RBIs in each of his three full seasons in the majors. He has also placed in the top five in the league MVP voting in each of those years. After the completion of the 2008 season, he had 177 home runs and 499 runs batted in to his credit, along with a career batting average of .279. Howard must accomplish a great deal more before his name can even be mentioned in connection with the Hall of Fame. And, as his career continues to progress, Howard's critics will undoubtedly point to his huge strikeout totals and the fact that he plays in a very good hitter's park in Philadelphia. But Howard has clearly established himself as one of the game's greatest sluggers in his first few seasons, and he will be only 29 years old at the start of the 2009 campaign. Thus, he most certainly deserves to have his name included on this list of Potential Hall of Famers.

David Ortiz

After spending his first six seasons as a part-time player with the Minnesota Twins, David Ortiz has developed into one of baseball's premier sluggers since joining the Boston Red Sox in 2003. From 2003 to 2007, Ortiz averaged 42 home runs and 128 runs batted in for Boston, while hitting over .300 three times.

In his six years with Minnesota, Ortiz combined for only 58 homers and 238 runs batted in. However, in his first year with the Red Sox, Big Papi hit 31 long balls and collected 101 RBIs. Over the next four years, the power-hitting first baseman/designated hitter developed into the American League's most dangerous hitter and outstanding clutch performer. In 2004, Ortiz finished second in the league with 41 home runs, 139 runs batted in, and a .603 slugging percentage. Then, he practically carried the Red Sox into the World Series with his tremendous clutch hitting during the American League playoffs. In Boston's three-game sweep of the Angels in the ALDS, Ortiz batted .545, with a home run and four RBIs. He was equally proficient against the Yankees in the ALCS, keying Boston's remarkable comeback from a three-games-to-none deficit by hitting three home runs, driving in 11 runs, and batting .387. Two of Ortiz's homers were walk-off game winners. Ortiz had exceptional seasons in each of the next three years as well. In 2005, he hit 47 home runs, scored 119 runs, and led the league with 148 runs batted in. He finished a close second to Alex Rodriguez in the MVP voting at the end of the year. In 2006, Ortiz led the American League with 54 homers and 137 runs batted in, and scored 115 runs. In 2007, Ortiz homered 35 times, drove in 117 runs, scored 116 others, and batted a career-high .332. A wrist injury caused Ortiz to miss 53 games this past season, limiting his offensive output to just 23 home runs and 89 runs batted in.

In all, Ortiz has topped 30 homers five times, hitting at least 40 on three separate occasions. He has also driven in more than 100 runs five times, and scored more than 100 runs, collected more than 40 doubles, and batted over .300 three times each. Ortiz has led the American League in a major statistical category six times, been selected to four All-Star teams, and finished in the top five in the league MVP voting five times. Heading into 2009, these are his career statistics:

AB	HITS	RUNS	2B	3B	HR	RBI	AVG	SB	OBP	SLG PCT
4,631	1,329	812	345	13	289	969	.287	10	.382	.554

Ortiz clearly has a lot of work to do before he can be considered a legitimate Hall of Fame candidate. His offensive numbers will have to be especially good since he spends the vast majority of his time serving as a designated hitter. But Ortiz has been such an outstanding offensive performer since he joined the Red Sox that the members of the BBWAA may well be able to overlook that last fact when his name is added to the eligible list several years from now. Still, Ortiz must continue to perform at an extremely high level for several more seasons in order to be seriously considered for induction. He will not turn 34 until the conclusion of the 2009 campaign, so he appears to have a significant amount of time left to compile the numbers he will need.

Derek Jeter

Derek Jeter differs somewhat from virtually every other player on this list of Potential Hall of Famers in that, even though it was my ultimate decision to include him here, he could have just as easily been grouped with those players who have already established themselves as borderline Hall of Fame candidates. Jeter's resume not only includes numerous appearances on the All-Star Team and several strong showings in the MVP balloting, but is further enhanced by the integral role he played on four World Championship teams. Furthermore, the impressive individual statistics Jeter has compiled during his career reveal only so much about him as a player. The Yankees shortstop possesses many intangible qualities that simply do not show up in the boxscores.

Jeter has been the Yankees starting shortstop since 1996, winning American League Rookie of the Year honors in his first season in pinstripes. The Yankees were World Champions in four of Jeter's first five years with the team, losing only three World Series games in the process. In fact, in his 13 seasons in New York, the Yankees have won six pennants and ten division titles, and have advanced into the postseason 12 times. There is little doubt that Jeter's presence in the Yankee lineup has had a great deal to do with that. Although he never finishes among the league leaders in home runs and runs batted in, Jeter is an outstanding offensive player who excels at virtually every other aspect of the game as well. He is an excellent baserunner, a solid fielder, an extremely intelligent and instinctive player, and an outstanding team leader. Those attributes have combined to make him arguably one of the sport's ten best all-around players for much of his career.

Jeter has batted over .300 in 10 of his 13 big league seasons. He has topped the 20-homer mark three times, collected more than 200 hits six times, stolen more than 30 bases three times, and scored more than 100 runs eleven times. He had his finest season in 1999, when he established career-highs in home runs (24), runs batted in (102), runs scored (134), hits (219), and batting average (.349). He had another exceptional year in 2006, when he knocked in 97 runs, scored another 118, batted .343, collected 214 hits, and stole a career-best 34 bases. Jeter finished runner-up in the league MVP voting that year, one of six times he has placed in the top ten in the balloting. He has led the American League in hits and runs scored once each, finished second in the batting race twice, and been selected to the All-Star Team a total of nine times. Jeter has also won three Gold Gloves and two Silver Sluggers. Always an outstanding big-game player, in 2000, Jeter became the first player in history to be named MVP of both the All-Star Game and the World Series in the same year. In 495 career post-season at-bats, covering 123 contests, Jeter has compiled a batting average of .309, with 17 home runs and 85 runs scored. Going into the 2009 season, here are his career numbers:

AB	HITS	RUNS	2B	3B	HR	RBI	AVG	SB	OBP	SLG PCT
8,025	2,535	1,467	411	57	206	1,002	.316	275	.387	.458

Jeter will turn 35 during the 2009 campaign and is currently on pace to accumulate well over 3,000 hits for his career. That would make him only the fourth shortstop in major league history to accomplish the feat (Honus Wagner, Cal Ripken Jr., and Robin Yount, who compiled many of his hits as a centerfielder, were the other three). However, considering all the other contributions Jeter makes to his team, he probably doesn't need to reach that milestone to be deemed a legitimate Hall of Famer. In all likelihood, many members of the BBWAA would vote for him even if he never played another game. Most certainly, another two or three solid seasons should virtually guarantee Jeter induction when his playing days are over.

Jimmy Rollins

One of major league baseball's finest all-around shortstops for much of the past decade has been the Philadelphia Phillies Jimmy Rollins. Although he hasn't received as much notoriety the last few years as his New York counterparts, Derek Jeter and Jose Reyes, Rollins has been as effective as either man, both in the field and at the bat. He has good power at the plate, hits for a fairly high batting average, has outstanding speed on the bases, and has excellent range and sure hands in the field.

Rollins took over as the Phillies starting shortstop in 2001. In his first full season, he hit 14 home runs, scored 97 runs, stole 46 bases, and batted .274. Rollins' performance slipped somewhat the next two seasons, although he remained a solid offensive player and a strong defender. But, in 2004, Rollins began a string of four consecutive years in which he was among the National League's most productive players. In each of those seasons, the leadoff hitter scored at least 115 runs, accumulated at least 190 base hits, and stole at least 30 bases. The 2006 and 2007 campaigns were Rollins' best. In the first of those years, he hit 25 home runs, drove in 83 runs, scored 127 others, batted .277, and stole 36 bases. In 2007, Rollins swiped another 41 bases and established new career-highs in home runs (30), runs batted in (94), batting average (.296), hits (212), runs scored (139), and triples (20), leading the league in the last two categories. He also won the first Gold Glove of his career, and was named the National League's Most Valuable Player for leading the Phillies to the Eastern Division title.

In all, Rollins has led the National League in triples four times, and in runs scored and stolen bases once each. He has been selected to three All-Star teams and has placed in the top ten in the league MVP voting twice. An exceptional defensive player, Rollins has not committed more than 14 errors in any of his eight years as a full-time shortstop. Generally considered to be the leader of the Phillies, both on and off the field, Rollins also possesses those intangible qualities statistics simply do not reveal. Nevertheless, here are his numbers heading into the 2009 season:

AB	HITS	RUNS	2B	3B	HR	RBI	AVG	SB	OBP	SLG PCT
5,269	1,461	845	307	90	125	544	.277	295	.333	.441

Rollins has a long way to go before his name can be mentioned in connection with the Hall of Fame. But he is only 30 years old as of this writing and appears to still have many outstanding seasons ahead of him. We will, therefore, have to see how the remainder of his career progresses.

Miguel Cabrera

Miguel Cabrera will not turn 26 until shortly after the 2009 campaign begins, and he has spent only five full seasons in the major leagues. But he has been such a productive player thus far that it would be impossible to exclude him from this list of Potential Hall of Famers. In each of his five full seasons, Cabrera has driven in well over 100 runs. He has also hit more than 30 home runs four times, scored more than 100 runs three times, and batted well over .300 three times, thereby establishing himself as one of baseball's best young players.

Splitting time between the outfield and third base after joining the Florida Marlins at midseason, Cabrera knocked in 62 runs in only 87 games in his rookie year of 2003. The following season, he made his first of four consecutive All-Star Game appearances, hitting 33 home runs, driving in 112 runs, scoring 101 others, and batting .294 for the Marlins. Cabrera improved upon those figures in 2005, hitting 33 homers and placing among the league leaders with 116 runs batted in, 106 runs scored, 198 hits, 43 doubles, and a .323 batting average. He placed fifth in the MVP voting at season's end. Shifted to third base full-time prior to the start of the 2006 campaign, Cabrera hit 26 home runs, knocked in 114 runs, scored 112 others, finished among the league leaders with 50 doubles and a .339 batting average, and placed fifth in the MVP voting once more. Cabrera posted outstanding numbers again in 2007, finishing the year with 34 home runs, 119 runs batted in, 91 runs scored, and a .320 batting average. Although he struggled somewhat during the first several weeks of the 2008 campaign after being traded to the Detroit Tigers during the offseason, Cabrera ended up leading the league with 37 homers, driving in 127 runs, and batting .292.

Still, Cabrera is not without his faults. He is a below-average fielder, having committed a total of 40 errors at third base for the Marlins during the 2006 and 2007 seasons. Spending the majority of his time at first base for Detroit this past season, he committed another 14 errors in the field. Furthermore, Cabrera has often been described as being somewhat lackadaisical in the field, and both his work ethic and dedication to the sport have frequently been questioned. Over the past few seasons, Cabrera's weight has ballooned to more than 250 pounds—up some 70 pounds from what it was when he first entered the league. These flaws appear to be the primary obstacles standing between Cabrera and an eventual place in Cooperstown. Perhaps the enigmatic slugger will eventually realize his full potential with the Tigers. Unlike the Marlins, Detroit has several veteran players capable of providing Cabrera with the leadership he apparently needs. If they are able to properly motivate him, there is no telling how good Cabrera might eventually become.

David Wright

Like Ryan Howard and Miguel Cabrera, David Wright has been performing at the major-league level for only a few seasons. However, since first becoming the New York Mets' starting third baseman midway through the 2004 campaign, Wright has been one of the National League's most productive hitters.

After batting .293 and hitting 14 home runs in 69 games as a rookie in 2004, Wright posted outstanding numbers in his first full season in New York the following year, hitting 27 homers, knocking in 102 runs, and batting .306. Following a similarly productive season in 2006, Wright had arguably his finest all-around year to-date in 2007. In leading the Mets to a close second-place finish in the N.L. East divisional race, the young third baseman hit 30 home runs, drove in 107 runs, scored another 113, accumulated 196 hits, batted .325, and stole 34 bases. Wright's outstanding performance earned him a fourth-place finish in the league MVP voting. He then established new career-highs in 2008, with 33 home runs, 124 runs batted in, and 115 runs scored.

In his four full seasons in New York, Wright has averaged 29 home runs, 112 runs batted in, and 106 runs scored. He has driven in more than 100 runs and batted over .300 each season. Wright has appeared in three All-Star games and has finished in the top ten in the league MVP balloting three times. While Wright's inclusion on this list of Potential Hall of Famers might seem a bit premature at this juncture, it must be remembered that he will be only 26 years old at the start of the 2009 season and still has most of his career ahead of him.

Eric Chavez

If he played almost any other position, Eric Chavez probably would not be included on this list of *Potential Hall of Famers*. Although he is a productive hitter and an outstanding fielder when he is healthy, Chavez has not truly distinguished himself from the other players of his era. But, due to the paucity of third basemen currently in Cooperstown, Chavez must be considered a possible candidate when his playing days are over.

Chavez is all that remains from the once-powerful Oakland Athletics infield that also included Jason Giambi and Miguel Tejada. After joining the Athletics two years earlier, Chavez became the team's regular third baseman in 2000. In his first full major league season, the lefthanded hitting slugger hit 26 home runs, drove in 86 runs, scored 89 others, and batted .277. In each of the following three seasons, prior to Alex Rodriguez being shifted to third base after he joined the Yankees in 2004, Chavez was the league's best all-around third baseman. In each of those years, he knocked in over 100 runs, hit at least 29 home runs, scored at least 87 runs, and batted at least .275. He had perhaps his finest season in 2001, when he hit 32 home runs, drove in 114 runs, scored another 91, and batted .288. He also established himself as the league's finest defensive third baseman that year, winning the first of his six consecutive Gold Gloves. In all, Chavez has surpassed 25 home runs six times, topping 30 on two separate occasions. He has also driven in more than 100 runs four times, scored at least 90 runs three times, and batted over .275 five times. As of this writing, here are his career statistics:

AB	HITS	RUNS	2B	3B	HR	RBI	AVG	SB	OBP	SLG PCT
4,642	1,247	720	273	20	229	776	.269	47	.346	.484

Chavez will be only 31 years old at the start of the 2009 season, so he figures to add to those numbers significantly. Furthermore, from 2001 to 2003, he was clearly the best all-around third baseman in the American League, and one of the two or three best in baseball. And, from 2001 to 2005, he was among the best players in the game at his position. Yet, other than leading the league with 95 walks in 2004, Chavez has never finished any higher than fourth in any major statistical category, and he has never placed any higher than 14th in the league MVP balloting. And, amazingly, Chavez has been selected to the All-Star Team only once. In addition, injuries have caused him to experience a significant drop-off in his offensive production the past three seasons. After missing almost a month of the 2006 campaign, Chavez appeared in a total of only 113 games the next two years.

In the three seasons since 2005, he has combined for only 39 home runs and 132 runs batted in, while posting batting averages of just .241, .240, and .247 in the process. At this point in his career, Chavez must be considered a long-shot to eventually gain admittance to Cooperstown.

Scott Rolen

Another player who has missed a significant amount of playing time is Scott Rolen. After having one of his best years in 2004, Rolen appeared in only 56 games the following season. Then, after having another solid 2006 campaign, Rolen missed almost two months of both the 2007 and 2008 seasons. Prior to that, though, he established himself as arguably the best all-around third baseman in baseball for most of a ten-year period. He has excellent power, is an extremely productive hitter, and is unquestionably the finest fielding third baseman in the game.

Rolen first came up with the Philadelphia Phillies in 1996, spending parts of seven seasons with the team before being dealt to St. Louis in 2002. He had his best year in Philadelphia in 1998, when he hit 31 home runs, knocked in 110 runs, scored 120 others, batted .290, and won the first of his seven Gold Gloves. He had another outstanding year for the Phillies in 2001, hitting 25 home runs, driving in 107 runs, scoring another 96, and batting .289. Splitting 2002 between the Phillies and Cardinals, Rolen hammered 31 homers, knocked in 110 runs, and scored 89 others. The following season, his first full one with the Cardinals, Rolen hit 28 homers, drove in 104 runs, scored another 98, batted .286, and finished second in the league with 49 doubles. Rolen had the finest year of his career for St. Louis in 2004, when he established career highs with 34 home runs, 124 runs batted in, and a .314 batting average, while also scoring 109 runs. At the end of the season, he finished fourth in the league MVP voting. After missing most of 2005 with a bad back, Rolen returned in 2006 to hit 22 homers, drive in 95 runs, score 94 others, and bat .296. Unfortunately, injuries caused him to miss a total of 97 games over the next two seasons, the second of which he spent with the

Toronto Blue Jays after being traded for fellow third baseman Troy Glaus. Rolen combined for only 19 home runs and 108 RBIs in 2007 and 2008, greatly diminishing his status as a future Hall of Famer.

Nevertheless, Rolen's resume is a rather impressive one. In all, he has topped the 25-homer mark seven times, surpassing 30 on three separate occasions. He has also driven in more than 100 runs five times, scored more than 100 runs twice, accumulated at least 45 doubles three times, and batted as high as .290 four times. Here are his career numbers:

AB	HITS	RUNS	2B	3B	HR	RBI	AVG	SB	OBP	SLG PCT
5,906	1,665	1,012	410	35	272	1,062	.282	109	.370	.501

Rolen will turn 34 shortly after the 2009 season gets underway, so, if he can remain healthy, there is still ample time for him to compile the kind of numbers that will make him a viable Hall of Fame candidate when his career is over. However, Rolen has yet to lead his league in any major statistical category, and he has finished in the top five a total of only five times. He also has placed in the top ten in the league MVP balloting only once. Still, Rolen has been selected to five All-Star teams, has already put together five Hall of Fame type seasons, and was the best third baseman in baseball in at least two of those years (2002: 31 HR, 110 RBIs, .266 AVG; and 2003: 28 HR, 104 RBIs, .286 AVG). He also vied for that honor with the Braves' Chipper Jones in 1998, and the Dodgers' Adrian Beltre in 2004. If he is able to string together another three or four solid seasons, Rolen will probably go down as the finest all-around third baseman of his era. Thus, his legacy is likely to be determined by whether or not he is able to remain healthy.

Chipper Jones

The Atlanta Braves Chipper Jones is someone who, like Derek Jeter, could just as easily be classified as someone who has already achieved borderline Hall of Fame status. In his 14 seasons with the Braves, Jones has already posted statistics that will undoubtedly prompt numerous members of the BBWAA to enter his name on their ballots when he eventually becomes eligible for induction. Nevertheless, I chose to include Jones here as a Potential Hall of Famer. Since he will not turn 37 until the 2009 campaign begins, Jones figures to compile the necessary numbers the next few seasons that should further enhance his chances of being inducted into Cooperstown when his playing days are over.

Jones became the Braves' regular third baseman in 1995, his first full season with the team. As a rookie, he hit 23 home runs and drove in 86 runs, while scoring another 87. The following year, Jones established himself as the best third baseman in the game, a title he held for the next six seasons, before moving to the outfield in 2002. In the six years from 1996 to 2001, Jones averaged 34 home runs, 109 runs batted in, and 114 runs scored. He topped the 30-homer mark and batted over .300 five times each during that stretch, and knocked in and scored more than 100 runs each season. Jones was particularly outstanding from 1998 to 2001. Here are his numbers from those four years:

1998: 34 HR, 107 RBIs, .313 average, 123 runs scored
1999: 45 HR, 110 RBIs, .319 average, 116 runs scored
2000: 36 HR, 111 RBIs, .311 average, 118 runs scored
2001: 38 HR, 102 RBIs, .330 average, 113 runs scored

Jones' exceptional performance in 1999 helped lead Atlanta to the National League pennant and earned him league MVP honors. Jones has finished in the top ten in the voting five other times. He also has been selected to six All-Star teams, and, although he has led the league in a major statistical category only twice, he has finished in the top five 14 other times. In all, Jones has surpassed 30 homers six times, driven in more than 100 runs nine times, scored more than 100 runs eight times, and batted over .300 ten times.

Jones was shifted to the outfield in 2002, where he had two more productive seasons, topping 25 homers, driving in better than 100 runs, and batting over .300 both years. He returned to his more natural position of third base in 2004 and subsequently suffered through three injury-plagued campaigns from 2004 to

2006. Yet, he remained a productive hitter, topping 20 homers in each of those years, while also driving in more than 85 runs and batting over .290 twice. Healthy again in 2007, Jones hit 29 home runs, knocked in 102 runs, scored 108 others, and finished second in the N.L. batting race with a mark of .337. He then led the league in hitting in 2008 with a batting average of .364. These are his career numbers heading into 2009:

AB	HITS	RUNS	2B	3B	HR	RBI	AVG	SB	OBP	SLG PCT
7,337	2,277	1,378	449	35	408	1,374	.310	138	.408	.548

As currently constituted, those figures may well be good enough to get Jones elected to the Hall of Fame, especially when one considers that he has hit more home runs as a third baseman than all but three men who ever played the position. His statistics are far superior to the numbers posted by several third basemen currently in Cooperstown, including Frank "Home Run" Baker, Jimmy Collins, Fred Lindstrom, and George Kell. Of course, it must be remembered that Baker and Collins competed during the Deadball Era. But, let's take a look at Jones' statistics alongside those of Lindstrom and Kell, both of whom played during excellent eras for hitters (Lindstrom played during the 1920s and 1930s; Kell competed during the 1940s and 1950s):

PLAYER	AB	HITS	RUNS	2B	3B	HR	RBI	AVG	SB	OBP	SLG PCT
Fred Lindstrom	5,611	1,747	895	301	81	103	779	.311	84	.351	.449
George Kell	6,702	2,054	881	385	50	78	870	.306	51	.368	.414
Chipper Jones	7,337	2,277	1,378	449	35	408	1,374	.310	138	.408	.548

Jones is clearly a much better offensive player than either Lindstrom or Kell. He has much more power than either man, is far superior as a run-producer, and hits for a comparable batting average while posting significantly higher on-base and slugging percentages. In fact, Jones is on pace to surpass all other third basemen in terms of total offensive productivity, with the exception of Mike Schmidt, Eddie Mathews, and George Brett. Therefore, it does not seem unreasonable to project Jones as a potential Hall of Fame candidate when he eventually becomes eligible for induction.

Vladimir Guerrero

Rightfielder Vladimir Guerrero is a general manager's dream, that rarest of baseball gems. He is a five-tool player—one that can hit, hit with power, run, field, and throw. Guerrero had "superstar" written all over him when he first joined the Montreal Expos as a 20-year old.

Shortly after Guerrero came up to the Expos, he began to impress everyone with his tremendous plate coverage, outstanding bat speed, and powerful throwing arm. He became Montreal's regular rightfielder midway through the 1997 campaign. In each of the next five seasons, Guerrero topped 30 home runs, 100 runs batted in, and 100 runs scored, while batting well over .300. His three best years with the Expos came in 1999, 2000, and 2002. In 1999, he hit 42 home runs, knocked in 131 runs, scored 102 others, and batted .316. The following year, he finished with 44 homers, 123 runs batted in, 101 runs scored, and a .345 batting average. In 2002, Guerrero came within one home run of joining the handful of players who have hit 40 home runs and stolen 40 bases in the same season. He hit 39 home runs, knocked in 111 runs, scored 106 others, stole 40 bases, and batted .336. A bad back limited Guerrero to just 112 games and 394 at-bats the following season. Yet, after returning from the disabled list, he still managed to hit 25 home runs, drive in 79 runs, and bat .330.

At the end of the 2003 season, Guerrero signed a free-agent deal with the Anaheim Angels, who, because of concerns about his back, were one of the few teams willing to take a chance on him. Guerrero rewarded their faith by hitting 39 home runs, driving in 126 runs, scoring another 124, batting .337, and collecting 206 hits, in leading the Angels to the A.L. West title and being named league MVP. He followed that up with outstanding performances in each of the next three seasons as well, averaging 31 home runs over that span, while knocking in more than 100 runs and batting well over .300 each year. Guerrero's offensive production fell off somewhat in 2008, a year in which he failed to drive in at least 100 runs for the first time in his 10 full seasons in the majors. But he still hit 27 home runs, knocked in 91 runs, and batted over

.300 for the twelfth consecutive year. In all, Guerrero has topped 30 homers eight times, driven in more than 100 runs nine times, scored more than 100 runs six times, collected at least 200 hits four times, and stolen more than 30 bases twice. He has led his league in runs scored once, and in hits once. He has been selected to eight All-Star teams and has finished in the top ten in the league MVP voting six times, making it into the top five on four separate occasions. Prior to the start of the 2009 season, these are his career numbers:

AB	HITS	RUNS	2B	3B	HR	RBI	AVG	SB	OBP	SLG PCT
6,617	2,136	1,126	404	43	392	1,268	.323	173	.389	.575

Guerrero will turn 33 shortly before the start of the 2009 campaign and appears to still have many outstanding seasons ahead of him. For most of his career, he has been one of the five best all-around players in the game. The only criticisms one might have of him are that he sometimes plays erratically in the field (he has committed 123 errors in his 12 seasons), and that he doesn't always hustle. In addition, he has spent increasingly more time at the DH spot the last two years. But Guerrero's tremendous talent and offensive production are more than enough to compensate for those shortcomings. Unless his earlier back problems resurface, Guerrero appears destined for Cooperstown.

Magglio Ordonez

One of baseball's most consistently productive offensive players for much of the past decade has been Magglio Ordonez. He has excellent power at the plate, hits for a high batting average, and is an outstanding run-producer.

Ordonez first joined the Chicago White Sox towards the end of the 1997 season. He took over as the club's starting rightfielder the following year, and, by 1999, established himself as the team's primary power threat, along with Frank Thomas. In the five seasons between 1999 and 2003, Ordonez averaged 32 home runs, 118 runs batted in, and 102 runs scored, while batting over .300 each year. His two best years in Chicago were 2000 and 2002. In the first of those campaigns, Ordonez hit 32 home runs, drove in 126 runs, scored 102 others, and batted .315. In 2002, he hit a career-high 38 homers, knocked in 135 runs, scored another 116, and batted .320.

However, after another extremely productive year in 2003, Ordonez needed surgery to repair a badly damaged knee that severely limited his playing time in 2004. After appearing in only 52 games for the White Sox that year, Ordonez signed on with the Detroit Tigers as a free agent at the conclusion of the campaign. Still recuperating from his earlier operation, Ordonez played in only 82 games for the Tigers in 2005. Thus, it appeared that any Hall of Fame aspirations Ordonez might have had earlier in his career had been shattered. But he returned to the Detroit lineup on a full-time basis the following year, hitting 24 home runs, driving in 104 runs, and batting .298. He followed that up with the greatest season of his career in 2007, hitting 28 home runs and establishing new career-highs with 139 runs batted in, 117 runs scored, 216 hits, and a league-leading 54 doubles and .363 batting average. Ordonez finished runner-up to Alex Rodriguez in the league MVP voting at the end of the year. The rightfielder had another solid year in 2008, hitting 21 homers, driving in 103 runs, and batting .317.

In all, Ordonez has topped 30 homers four times, 100 runs batted in seven times, 100 runs scored four times, and 40 doubles four times. He has also hit over .300 in nine of his eleven big league seasons, twice topping the .320-mark. Ordonez has been named to six All-Star teams, has placed in the top ten in the league MVP voting twice, and has led his league in a major statistical category twice, finishing as high as second on four other occasions. Heading into 2009, these are his career statistics:

AB	HITS	RUNS	2B	3B	HR	RBI	AVG	SB	OBP	SLG PCT
5,861	1,830	933	375	18	268	1,095	.312	88	.371	.520

Those are hardly Hall of Fame numbers, and, considering that Ordonez will be 35 at the start of the season, he may not be able to compile the totals necessary to convince the members of the

BBWAA to vote for him when he eventually becomes eligible for induction. Still, he continues to be an extremely productive hitter and may yet have another four or five outstanding years left in him. If he does, he has an outside chance of being elected when his playing days are over.

Ichiro Suzuki

The Seattle Mariners Ichiro Suzuki was hardly a typical major league rookie when he first joined the team in 2001. After all, the rightfielder previously starred in the Japanese professional leagues for several years. Indeed, as one of the greatest Japanese players ever, Ichiro is an icon in his native land. Thus, it should have come as a surprise to no one that, in his first big league season, Ichiro captured American League Rookie of the Year honors. The thing that did astound the American public, though, was the extent of Ichiro's talent. Not only was he an outstanding hitter, but he also possessed great running speed, a powerful throwing arm, and superb defensive skills in the outfield. Ichiro's overall ability enabled him to win the American League's Most Valuable Player Award in his first year in the league. As a rookie, he hit 8 home runs, knocked in 69 runs, scored 127 others, and led the league with a .350 batting average, 242 hits, and 56 stolen bases. He also won a Gold Glove Award for his excellent outfield play.

In each of the next seven seasons, Ichiro has continued to perform at an extremely high level, always finishing among the league leaders in batting average, hits, and stolen bases.

He had his greatest season in 2004, leading the league with a .372 batting average and 262 hits. Those 262 hits broke an 84 year-old record previously set by George Sisler (257) in 1920. Ichiro had another exceptional year in 2007, batting .351, scoring 111 runs, and leading the league with 238 hits. In his eight major league seasons, Ichiro has batted over .300, scored more than 100 runs, stolen more than 30 bases, and accumulated more than 200 hits each year. He has won two batting titles, has led the league in hits five times, has topped the circuit in stolen bases once, and has won a Gold Glove every year. He has also been selected to the All-

Star Team each year, and has finished in the top ten in the league MVP voting three times. After his first eight seasons, these are the numbers he has compiled:

AB	HITS	RUNS	2B	3B	HR	RBI	AVG	SB	OBP	SLG PCT
5,460	1,805	885	197	64	73	469	.331	315	.377	.430

Ichiro's .331 career batting average is the second-highest among active players, and he has more hits after his first eight seasons than any player in baseball history. However, since he will be 35 at the start of the 2009 campaign, there is a possibility he will never reach 3,000 safeties for his career. Nevertheless, Ichiro's status as one of the era's greatest hitters and finest all-around players practically guarantees him a place in Cooperstown when his career is over. Prior to 2007, the only stumbling block appeared to be whether or not Suzuki wished to continue playing baseball in the United States once his contract with Seattle expired at the end of the season. But, after he signed an extension with the Mariners early in the year, it became clear that Ichiro will eventually meet the ten-year minimum requirement to be eligible for induction to the Hall of Fame.

Johan Santana

Major league baseball's best pitcher since the turn of the century has been lefthander Johan Santana. In his five years as a full-time starter, Santana has been named *The Sporting News* Pitcher of the Year twice, has won two Cy Young Awards, and has placed in the top five in the voting three other times.

Santana first arrived in the big leagues with the Minnesota Twins in 2000, pitching mostly out of the bullpen his first three years with the team. He earned a regular spot in Minnesota's starting rotation midway through the 2003 campaign, compiling a record of 12-3 in his 18 starts, and striking out 169 batters in 158 innings of work. The following year, Santana developed into the American League's best pitcher, finishing 20-6, with a league-leading 2.61 earned run average and 265 strikeouts. At season's end, he was awarded his first Cy Young trophy and also placed sixth in the league MVP balloting. Santana had another outstanding season in 2005, going 16-7 with a 2.87 ERA, and leading the league with 238 strikeouts. He followed that up with a brilliant 2006 campaign in which he captured the pitcher's triple crown by leading all American League hurlers in wins (19), earned run average (2.77), and strikeouts (245). Santana won his second Cy Young that year and also placed seventh in the MVP voting. His performance fell off a bit in 2007 (he finished only 15-13), but he still managed to place among the league leaders in earned run average (3.33) and strikeouts (235). At the end of the season, Santana was dealt to the New York Mets, for whom he pitched brilliantly in 2008.

Santana finished the year with a record of 16-7, and would have easily won 20 games had New York's shaky bullpen not betrayed him on numerous occasions, squandering leads he left to its members during the final two innings. In addition to his outstanding won-lost record, Santana led all N.L. hurlers with a 2.53 ERA and 234 innings pitched, and also finished second in the circuit with 206 strikeouts.

In his five full seasons as a starter, Santana has led the league in wins once, earned run average three times, strikeouts three times, and innings pitched twice. In addition to his two Cy Young Awards, Santana has won a Gold Glove and has been named to three All-Star teams. Heading into 2009, he has a career record of 109-51, with an ERA of 3.11 and 1,587 strikeouts in 1,543 innings pitched. Having allowed opposing hitters only 1,274 base hits, he has an excellent hits-to-innings pitched ratio. He also has an outstanding strikeouts-to-walks ratio of almost four-to-one.

Santana will turn 30 shortly before the 2009 season begins. He, therefore, should still have many fine years ahead of him. Although he must accomplish a great deal more before his name can be linked to the Hall of Fame, Santana appears to be well on his way to doing just that.

Tim Hudson

Upon his arrival in the big leagues with the Oakland Athletics in 1999, righthander Tim Hudson was an instant success, compiling a record of 11-2 with a 3.23 ERA as a rookie. Although Hudson's ERA was a mediocre 4.14 in his sophomore campaign, he finished 20-6, making him the American League's winningest pitcher, and enabling him to finish second in the Cy Young balloting. Hudson was also extremely effective in each of the next three seasons. In 2001, he finished 18-9, with a 3.37 earned run average. In 2002, he was 15-9, with an ERA of 2.98. In 2003, he finished 16-7, with a 2.70 ERA. In both 2004 and 2005, Hudson's total number of starts was reduced somewhat due to a slight soreness he experienced in his pitching arm. Yet, he still managed to finish a combined 26-15, with an ERA just over 3.50 both years. Pitching more regularly in 2006, Hudson won 13 games for the Braves, who acquired him in a trade with Oakland the previous year. He had his best year in Atlanta in 2007, finishing 16-10, with a 3.33 ERA.

Through 2008, Hudson has compiled an outstanding won-lost record of 146-77, with a very respectable 3.48 ERA. He has led his league in wins once, and in shutouts twice. He has been selected to the All-Star Team twice, and has finished in the top ten in the Cy Young balloting three times, placing in the top five on two occasions. Hudson is a fine pitcher, and he will be only 33 years old at the start of the 2009 season. If he is able to put together another five or six solid seasons and raise his win total to something approaching 250, Hudson has a chance to be elected to Cooperstown when his career is over.

Roy Halladay

One of baseball's best pitchers from 2002 to 2008 has been righthander Roy Halladay of the Toronto Blue Jays. For much of that time, he has rivaled Johan Santana as the American League's best pitcher, consistently placing among the circuit's leaders in wins, earned run average, innings pitched, and complete games.

Halladay first joined the Blue Jays at the end of the 1998 campaign, finally becoming a regular member of the team's starting rotation in 2002. In his first full year as a starter, Halladay compiled a record of 19-7, with an outstanding 2.93 ERA and a league-leading 239 innings pitched. He was even better in 2003, leading all American League pitchers with a record of 22-7, 266 innings pitched, and nine complete games, and also finishing among the leaders with 204 strikeouts and a 3.25 earned run average. For his outstanding performance, Halladay was presented with the Cy Young Award at season's end, and was also named *The Sporting News* Pitcher of the Year.

Injuries limited Halladay to a total of only 40 starts the next two seasons, when he combined for just 20 victories. Yet, he remained an extremely effective pitcher, particularly in 2005, when he compiled a record of 12-4 and an exceptional 2.41 ERA, before being placed on the disabled list at midseason. Healthy again in 2006, Halladay won 16 games in each of the next two seasons, before having his finest all-around year in 2008. Halladay finished 20-11, with a 2.78 earned run average, 206 strikeouts, and a league-leading nine complete games and 246 innings pitched. During his career, Halladay has compiled an outstanding 131-66 record, while pitching to a very respectable 3.52 ERA.

Halladay has won at least 16 games in each of his five years as a full-time starter, and has compiled an earned run average below 3.25 in four of those seasons. He has led the American League in wins once, in shutouts twice, in innings pitched three times, and in complete games four times. He has been selected to five All-Star teams, and, in addition to winning the Cy Young Award once, has finished in the top five in the voting three other times. Halladay will turn 32 early in the 2009 campaign, so, if he can remain healthy, he has plenty of time to compile the sort of numbers that will make him a viable Hall of Fame candidate.

Roy Oswalt

The National League's finest pitcher since 2001 has been Houston Astros righthander Roy Oswalt. Over the past eight years, Oswalt has consistently finished among the league leaders in wins, winning percentage, earned run average, and innings pitched, while also faring extremely well in the Cy Young balloting.

Oswalt became a regular member of the Astros starting staff early in the 2001 campaign, finishing the regular season with an outstanding 14-3 record and 2.73 earned run average. The following year, Oswalt placed among the league leaders in wins (19), earned run average (3.01), innings pitched (233), and strikeouts (208), to earn a fourth-place finish in the league's Cy Young voting. After another solid season in 2003, Oswalt had perhaps his two best years in 2004 and 2005. In the first of those campaigns, he finished 20-10 to lead all National League pitchers in victories. He also placed among the league leaders in innings pitched (237) and strikeouts (206). In 2005, Oswalt compiled a record of 20-12, with an outstanding 2.94 ERA in 242 innings of work. Although poor run-support limited him to 15 victories in 2006, Oswalt led all N.L. starters with a 2.98 earned run average. He won another 14 games in 2007, again placing among the league leaders in earned run average (3.18) and innings pitched (212). In 2008, Oswalt finished 17-10 and threw another 209 innings.

In his eight major league seasons, Oswalt has won at least 15 games five times, compiled an ERA below 3.00 four times, struck out more than 200 batters twice, and thrown more than 200 innings six times. He has led the National League in wins and earned run average once each, and has finished in the top five in a major statistical category a total of 15 times. Oswalt has placed in the top five in the Cy Young balloting five times and has been selected to three All-Star teams. His career won-lost record is 129-64, and he has posted an outstanding 3.13 ERA over his eight seasons.

Oswalt will not turn 32 until late in the 2009 campaign. He, therefore, appears to have an excellent chance of establishing himself as a legitimate Hall of Fame candidate before his playing days are over.

STEROIDS

The hypocrisy that major league baseball has come to represent was further manifested by the manner in which it chose to virtually ignore the growing problem of steroid abuse. One can only speculate as to when the use of performance-enhancing drugs began to become a serious problem in the sport. One retired player confessed that he began experimenting with them as early as the late-1970s. In all likelihood, though, they started to become far more prevalent about a decade later, during the latter portion of the 1980s.

In a television interview conducted shortly after the 2005 Congressional hearing on steroids was held, Fay Vincent, the commissioner of baseball from September 13, 1989 to September 7, 1992, said that, looking back, he probably could have put forth more of a concerted effort to wage a battle against the use of performance-enhancing drugs in the sport. But he added that, at that particular time, his administration was more concerned with fighting the more widespread problem of substance abuse. And his record in that area is something of which Mr. Vincent should certainly be extremely proud. It was during his administration that pitcher Steve Howe was suspended, and later reinstated, three different times for violating baseball's anti-drug policy. Thus, the specter of Vincent as baseball commissioner clearly struck fear into the hearts of any potential violators.

However, the use of steroids became far more widespread during the administration of the equally inept Bud Selig. During Selig's reign, offensive numbers increased dramatically, leaving fans of the sport to wonder if the vast majority of players used some form of performance-enhancing drug. The intent here is not to discredit the hitters of the "steroid era." There were several other factors that contributed to the increase in offensive production during this period. Hitters began gravitating towards lighter bats to increase their bat speed, thereby creating greater hitting power. They also adopted a different approach to hitting, one that sacrificed contact for power. Continuous expansion in the majors resulted in the gradual dilution of pitching talent. Pitchers grew increasingly fearful of pitching inside to opposing batters. And hitters simply became bigger and stronger than those from prior generations.

But, consider the following:

- From 1966 to 1994, only two men—George Foster (1977) and Cecil Fielder (1990) hit as many as 50 home runs in a season.

- Between 1995 and 2002, the 50-homer plateau was reached 18 times, with at least one player hitting 50 home runs in every one of those seasons. Four players reached the 50-homer mark in both 1998 and 2001.
- Four players reached the 50-homer plateau multiple times during this period: Sammy Sosa—four times; Mark McGwire—four times; Ken Griffey Jr.—two times; and Alex Rodriguez—two times). Six players reached the 50-homer mark once: Albert Belle, Brady Anderson, Greg Vaughn, Barry Bonds, Luis Gonzalez, Jim Thome.

Only an extremely naïve person would believe that none of these ten players were aided by steroids when they accomplished what so few players before them were able to do. Of course, it would be equally foolish to presume that hitters were the only ones using performance-enhancing drugs. There is little doubt that a certain percentage of pitchers experimented with them as well. But, the fact is that, with offensive productivity increasing so dramatically, it became increasingly difficult to determine if the offensive numbers a player compiled corresponded more to his natural ability, dedication, and hard work, or, rather, to his willingness to aid his performance by some artificial means.

That is something that troubled true fans of the sport everywhere. Meanwhile, the baseball hierarchy did nothing to alleviate their concerns. While every other major sport previously adopted an anti-steroid policy, major league baseball failed to even address the issue. Concerned only with keeping the turnstiles in motion, the Commissioner's office yielded more to the wishes of the "casual" fan, who, it assumed, preferred to see balls constantly flying out of ballparks. Thus, it completely ignored a problem it knew existed in its sport for a long time.

Finally, the Commissioner's office was forced to address the issue on March 17, 2005. Following the release of Jose Canseco's controversial *Juiced: Wild Times, Rampant 'Roids, Smash Hits, and How Baseball Got Big*, Bud Selig, several members of his office, and a select group of major league players were subpoenaed to appear before a Congressional hearing on steroids. Among the active and retired major league players in attendance were Canseco, Mark McGwire, Sammy Sosa, and Rafael Palmeiro. The members of Congress in attendance actually accomplished very little that day. For the most part, they fawned all over the sluggers, who they identified as "personal heroes" of theirs, thanking them for appearing at the hearings, and failing to mention that the players really had no choice in the matter. And the questions they asked could hardly be described as penetrating.

But one thing that clearly came across was the arrogance and duplicity of the players in attendance, something that will be discussed in detail later in this section. They clearly had something to hide, and, at the same time, felt that they were beyond reproach. Indeed, while his testimony appeared to be somewhat inconsistent at times, Canseco was the only individual who gave direct answers to the questions that were posed to him.

In the end, nothing was said at the hearings that restored anyone's faith in the players in question. Sosa and, in particular, McGwire, came out looking very bad. Thus, an even darker cloud was cast upon the career accomplishments of those players whose names had been previously mentioned in connection with the use of performance-enhancing drugs. In his book, Canseco identified McGwire, Palmeiro, and Ivan Rodriguez as players he injected with steroids while they were teammates in Oakland and Texas. Since then, Barry Bonds and Gary Sheffield were both identified as steroid-users in the book *Game of Shadows.* Roger Clemens was accused of using performance-enhancing drugs by his former close friend and personal trainer, Brian McNamee, in the *Mitchell Report.* Alex Rodriguez was identified as being one of 104 players who tested positive for performance-enhancing drugs during Major League Baseball's testing conducted in 2003. And most people believe Sammy Sosa to be a user as well.

These eight men comprise our final group of Potential Hall of Famers—those whose names have been linked to the use of performance-enhancing drugs.

The cases of these eight players must be handled most delicately because, with the exception of Palmeiro and Alex Rodriguez, none of them have ever been *proven* guilty of using steroids. And, even in the cases of Palmeiro and A-Rod, there is no way of knowing with any degree of certainty the degree to which they used them during their careers. The feeling here is that all eight men likely used some form of performance-enhancing drug at some time. I will attempt to add credibility to my argument by examining the career of each man at various stages. This should enable me to properly identify a specific point in each player's career at which his performance improved dramatically.

However, the identification of a player as a steroid-user should not, at least in my opinion, eliminate him from Hall of Fame consideration when his playing days are over. While I find such actions to be most unsavory and completely reprehensible, it must be remembered that baseball did not place any sort of official restraints upon the use of performance-enhancing drugs until 2004. Therefore, any player that used steroids prior to the start of that season did not break any specific rules of the game; at least none that the Commissioner's office found punishable. Any such player may have been dishonest with himself, his teammates, and his opponents. And he certainly cheated the fans of the sport. But he did nothing to contradict baseball law from a practical perspective, and the Commissioner's office was equally culpable.

Thus, the feeling here is that, when reviewing the Hall of Fame credentials of these eight men, the determining factor should ultimately be the degree to which their performances may have been aided by the use of steroids. If any of these players previously carved out Hall of Fame careers for themselves prior to using performance-enhancing drugs, they should be considered viable candidates when their names are added to the eligible list. If not, they should not be admitted to Cooperstown, no matter how impressive their statistics were.

Potential Hall of Famers Linked to Performance-Enhancing Drugs:

Mark McGwire
Rafael Palmeiro
Ivan Rodriguez
Roger Clemens
Sammy Sosa
Gary Sheffield
Barry Bonds
Alex Rodriguez

Mark McGwire

When Mark McGwire retired in 2001, most people tended to think of him as a certain first-ballot Hall of Fame inductee. As one of the greatest sluggers in baseball history, he finished his career fifth on the all-time home run list (he has since slipped to seventh), with 583, and with the highest home run-to-at-bat ratio in the history of the game. Along with Sammy Sosa, he is one of only two players to top the 50-homer mark in four straight seasons, accomplishing the feat each year from 1996 to 1999. McGwire also hit at least 30 home runs in a season seven other times, knocked in more than 100 runs seven times, scored more than 100 runs three times, and batted over .300 twice. He led his league in home runs four times, in runs batted in once, in bases on balls and on-base percentage twice each, and in slugging percentage four times. McGwire was a 12-time All-Star, and he finished in the top ten in the league MVP voting a total of five times, placing in the top five on three separate occasions.

Yet, in spite of all his accomplishments and the tremendous popularity he always enjoyed with fans and the media, the feeling here is that Mark McGwire was, and always will be, one of the most overrated, over-hyped players in the history of baseball. His selection to the All-Century Team, along with Lou Gehrig at first base, was a complete travesty (Jimmie Foxx should have been the other first baseman selected). McGwire was, for much of his career, a totally one-dimensional player who never would have been able to achieve the things he did without the aid of artificial stimulants. Let's take a closer look.

McGwire had outstanding home run power from the time he first entered the major leagues in 1987. As a rookie with the Oakland Athletics that year, the lanky but powerful McGwire established a new rookie record by hitting 49 home runs. He also drove in 118 runs and batted .289 for the A's. However, while he remained a productive hitter the next few seasons, the 1987 campaign was easily the best of his early years in Oakland.

Over the next four years, these are the figures McGwire posted:

1988: 32 HR, 99 RBIs, .260 AVG, 87 RUNS
1989: 33 HR, 95 RBIs, .231 AVG, 74 RUNS
1990: 39 HR, 108 RBIs, .235 AVG, 87 RUNS
1991: 22 HR, 75 RBIs, .201 AVG, 62 RUNS

Those are decent power numbers, but McGwire clearly left a lot to be desired in every other area. Nevertheless, an instant fan favorite after his outstanding rookie season, he was voted onto the All-Star Team by the fans in every one of those years, even though there were far more deserving first basemen each season. In fact, with the possible exception of the 1987 campaign, at no point during that five-year stretch could a legitimate case be made for McGwire being even among the top two first basemen in the American League (at different times, Don Mattingly, Wally Joyner, Fred McGriff, Cecil Fielder, Frank Thomas, and Rafael Palmeiro were all better).

McGwire had his second-best season in 1992, hitting 42 home runs, driving in 104 runs, batting .268, and making his sixth consecutive All-Star team. But, he would have been ranked well behind the even more productive Frank Thomas that year (Thomas knocked in 115 runs and batted .323 for the White Sox). McGwire then suffered through injury-riddled seasons in both 1993 and 1994, appearing in a total of only 74 games.

Thus, McGwire was an extremely productive hitter over the first half of his career. He was a healthy, full-time player in six of his first eight major league seasons. In five of those years, he topped the 30-homer mark, surpassing 40 on two occasions. He also drove in more than 100 runs three times and was selected to the All-Star Team in each of his six full seasons.

Yet, McGwire batted over .250 in only three of those seasons, and his lifetime batting average stood at only .249. He failed to score as many as 100 runs in a season even once, and he walked 100 times only once. McGwire led the American League in a major statistical category only twice and finished in the top ten in the league MVP balloting only twice, making it into the top five just once. Although McGwire was voted onto six All-Star teams by the fans, he was truly deserving of only two or three of those selections. Furthermore, in no single season, up to that point, was he generally considered to be the best first baseman in the American League.

During the first half of his career, McGwire gradually added approximately 30-35 pounds of muscle onto his frame. However, when he returned to the A's in 1995 after missing most of the previous season, he appeared significantly larger. McGwire ended up sustaining a season-ending injury once more but, in only 104 games and 317 at-bats that year, hit 39 home runs and drove in 90 runs. The following season, a healthy McGwire returned to hit 52 home runs, knock in 113 runs, score 104 runs, walk 116 times, and bat a career-high .312.

It was the following year, though, in 1997, that *The Legend of Mark McGwire* truly began. Splitting his season between the Athletics and Cardinals, McGwire hit a major league leading 58 home runs, drove in 123 runs, and batted .274. He was even more dominant in 1998 and 1999. In the first of those years, McGwire established a new major league single-season home run record, shattering Roger Maris' existing mark of 61, by hitting 70 of his own. He also knocked in 147 runs, scored another 130, walked 162 times, batted .299, and finished second to Sammy Sosa in the league MVP voting. In 1999, McGwire again led the majors in homers, this time with 65. He also knocked in 147 runs for the second consecutive year, scored 118 times, drew 133 bases on balls, and batted .278. That was McGwire's last great year, however, since injuries relegated him to part-time status in each of the next two seasons, before eventually forcing him into retirement.

McGwire ended his career with 583 home runs, 1,414 runs batted in, 1,167 runs scored, and a .263 batting average. But, a look at the statistics he posted during the first and second halves of his career is most revealing:

	AB	HITS	RUNS	HR	RBI	AVG
Pre-1995	3,342	834	546	238	657	.249
Post-1995	2,845	792	621	345	757	.278

McGwire was clearly far more effective after he returned from the injuries that kept him out of the Oakland lineup for most of the 1993 and 1994 seasons. Over the remainder of his career, he compiled 500 fewer official at-bats. Yet, he hit 107 more home runs, knocked in 100 more runs, scored 75 more runs, and collected only 42 fewer hits. He also batted almost 30 points higher, thereby enabling himself to raise his career average to a respectable .263. Prior to 1995, McGwire averaged a home run every 14 times at-bat. After 1995, that ratio changed to one home run every 8.2 times at-bat. It was also during the latter period that McGwire won three of his four home run titles, led his league in runs batted in for the only time, and finished first in on-base percentage for the only two times. He batted over .300 for the only two times in his career, and scored over 100 runs for the only three times. He finished in the top ten in the league MVP balloting three times after 1995, and was truly among the game's most dominant players only from 1996 to 1999. He was the best first baseman in baseball in only 1998 and 1999.

Some might suggest that the improvement McGwire displayed during the second half of his career was simply part of his maturation into more of a complete hitter. Others might argue that it merely coincided with the offensive explosion that occurred throughout baseball as a whole at the time. While there may be a certain amount of truth to both arguments, the feeling here is that there were other factors that contributed far more to McGwire's increased productivity. All one needs to do is to reflect on his physical development into a man of gargantuan-like proportions. During his playing days, McGwire was known to leave bottles of human-growth hormones displayed openly in his locker for all to see. True, those were not steroids, but they certainly provided him with an unfair advantage.

Furthermore, McGwire's evasive responses at the Congressional hearings held on March 17, 2005 as much as convicted him of using steroids. At those hearings, a relatively lean and frail-looking McGwire repeatedly responded to any references made to his playing days by saying, "I'm not here to talk about the past...I only want to look ahead to the future."

Yes, Mr. McGwire, with that very statement you incriminated yourself. You were a good player, but you were never the player the American public and the national media made you out to be. Had you not artificially enhanced your performance, you wouldn't even be considered a borderline Hall of Fame candidate. You do *not* deserve to have your name associated with the all-time greats of the game, and you do *not* belong in the Hall of Fame.

The members of the BBWAA seem to agree, since fewer than 25 percent of them entered McGwire's name on their ballot for the third consecutive year in 2009.

Rafael Palmeiro

In 2005, Rafael Palmeiro became only the fourth player in major league history to hit more than 500 home runs and compile more than 3,000 hits, joining the select group of Hank Aaron, Willie Mays, and Eddie Murray. In doing so, he apparently further solidified his status as a future Hall of Famer. At the same time, he made this individual look like a complete fool, since I had previously contended, against popular opinion, that Palmeiro was nothing more than a borderline candidate. Even during the previous few seasons, as Palmeiro drew inexorably closer to 500 home runs—and even after he eventually passed that milestone—I continued to stubbornly maintain that he was not a truly great player, and, therefore, should not be viewed as an obvious Hall of Fame selection no matter how many home runs he went on to hit. I based my opinion on a number of factors.

Most importantly, I felt that it was necessary to judge Palmeiro within the context of his own era. Viewing him in that manner indicated to me that, in spite of his excellent numbers, he never truly distinguished himself as a dominant player. Despite leading his league in hits, doubles, and runs scored one time each, he never finished first in either home runs, runs batted in, or batting average. He finished in the top ten in the league MVP voting only three times, placing no higher than fifth in 1999. He was selected to the All-Star team only four times, a relatively low number for a potential Hall of Famer. In addition, he was never recognized as the best first baseman in the game, and was the American League's top player at that position only twice, in 1998 and 1999. Finally, I believed it was important to consider that Palmeiro was always fortunate enough to play in excellent hitters' ballparks, whether it be Chicago's Wrigley Field, Baltimore's Camden Yards, or the Ballpark at Arlington, in Texas.

However, when Palmeiro reached the 3,000-hit plateau in 2005, I was forced to concede. The arguments on his behalf became too great. By the end of the season, he was ninth on the all-time home run list, with 569. He had also compiled 1,835 runs batted in, 1,663 runs scored, 3,020 hits, 585 doubles, and a .288 lifetime batting average. He had topped 30 homers 10 times, surpassing 40 on four separate occasions. He had driven in more than 100 runs ten times, including nine straight years at one point. He had also scored more than 100 runs four times, batted over .300 six times, and won three Gold Gloves. The numbers were just too overwhelming to ignore.

But it was also during the 2005 season that Palmeiro tested positive for steroids. Ironically, just a few months earlier, after being implicated by former teammate Jose Canseco in the latter's book, Palmeiro was the one player at the Congressional hearings to emphatically state his innocence. Looking directly at the members of Congress, and pointing his fingers at them resolutely, Palmeiro said with great conviction, "I have never used steroids...period."

Perhaps Palmeiro was stupid enough to think he would never get caught. Perhaps he was arrogant enough not to care. Maybe he even believed that, if he was caught, the American public would be naïve enough to think that injecting steroids into his system was something he hadn't been doing for years. In all likelihood, there are some people gullible enough to believe that. Nevertheless, all available evidence seems to indicate that the numbers Palmeiro compiled during his career were aided considerably by the use of performance-enhancing drugs. Let's examine the facts:

Palmeiro began his major league career with the Chicago Cubs in 1986. After seeing limited duty his first two seasons, he became a full-time player in 1988. In his only year as a regular in the Chicago starting lineup, Palmeiro batted .307, with only 8 home runs and 53 runs batted in. In 1989, he joined the Texas Rangers, with whom he spent the next five seasons. In his first four years with the team, Palmeiro was a solid, line-drive hitter who showed only occasional glimpses of power. From 1989 to 1992, he batted over .300 twice, scored more than 100 runs once, collected more than 200 hits once, and compiled more than 40 doubles once. However, he never hit more than 26 home runs, totaling as many as 15 only one other time. He also never knocked in more than 89 runs. In 1993, though, Palmeiro experienced a power-surge for the first time in his career. That season, he hit 37 home runs, drove in 105 runs, scored another 124, and batted .295. Coincidentally, Palmeiro's teammate on the Rangers that year was Jose Canseco, who spent his first full year with the team after being dealt to Texas for Ruben Sierra during the latter stages of the previous campaign.

Palmeiro was traded to Baltimore in 1994 and put up solid numbers during that strike-shortened season. But, over the next nine seasons, splitting his time between Baltimore and Texas, Palmeiro compiled power numbers he seemed completely incapable of earlier in his career. Over that nine-year stretch, he never hit fewer than 38 home runs, surpassing 40 four different times. He also knocked in more than 100 runs in each of those years, compiling at least 120 RBIs on four separate occasions. His two most productive years were with the Rangers in 1999 and 2001. In the first of those years, he hit 47 home runs, knocked in 148 runs, and batted .324. In 2001, he again hit 47 homers, while driving in 123 runs and batting .273.

Those are numbers that, in all likelihood, Palmeiro never would have even approached without the aid of some artificial stimulant. Not only is there Canseco's accusation, as well as the above evidence to support that theory, but there is also the fact that he tested positive for steroids in 2005. Yet, only a few months earlier, Palmeiro had sat in front of the members of Congress, looked into their faces, pointed his finger at them, and told each and every one of them, "I have never used steroids...period."

If the rules that theoretically govern the Hall of Fame elections actually do mean anything to the members of the BBWAA, it is inconceivable that any of them could even think of writing Palmeiro's name onto their ballot. If "integrity" and "character" are indeed qualities that a Hall of Fame candidate should possess, how could they consider electing someone who not only made a mockery of the sport, but also of the United States Congress? Yes, many other players of questionable integrity and character have been admitted to Cooperstown. But they did not perjure themselves before Congress. And they also compiled their statistics legitimately.

Unfortunately, there will undoubtedly be several members of the BBWAA who take a far more liberal approach towards Palmeiro. Many of the writers probably developed an excellent working relationship with him over the years. As a result, they will likely be much more forgiving, and Palmeiro may well end up in Cooperstown. Indeed, in that aforementioned television interview with Fay "Reinstatement" Vincent, the former Commissioner was asked about Palmeiro's situation, and the possibility of him eventually being elected to Cooperstown. In response, Vincent said that he believed that, in time "…everything would blow over and Raffy would get in." I suppose one could not have expected anything else from him. One can only hope, though, that not everyone is as forgiving as Vincent, and that the majority of the voters are far more concerned with the integrity of the game.

Ivan Rodriguez

In his book, Jose Canseco claimed that he injected Ivan Rodriguez with steroids when the two men were teammates in Texas. This came as a bit of a surprise to me because, of all the players whose names had previously been linked to the use of performance-enhancing drugs, I thought Rodriguez the least likely candidate to have actually been guilty of using them. Although he was always solidly built, Rodriguez was never overly muscular. And, with the exception of three or four seasons in the middle of his career, he never really compiled any particularly impressive power numbers on offense. I had always taken Rodriguez's career at face value, never questioning in the least his on-field achievements. And those achievements made him, with the possible exception of Mike Piazza, the best catcher in the game for more than a decade.

Rodriguez first came up with the Texas Rangers in 1991, becoming a regular the following season. Although he hit only 8 home runs, knocked in just 37 runs, and batted only .260 in his first full season, Rodriguez made the All-Star Team and won the first of his ten consecutive Gold Glove Awards. He had solid seasons in each of the next six years, batting over .300 four times, hitting more than 20 homers twice, driving in more than 85 runs twice, scoring more than 100 runs once, and making the All-Star Team each year. His best season was in 1998, when he hit 21 home runs, knocked in 91 runs, batted .321, and scored 88 runs.

Rodriguez dramatically increased his offensive productivity in 1999, when he established new career-highs in home runs (35), runs batted in (113), runs scored (116), and stolen bases (25), batted .332, and was named the American League's Most Valuable Player. A season-ending injury limited Rodriguez to only 91 games the following year. Yet, he still managed to hit 27 home runs, drive in 83 runs, and bat .347. Although his playing time and offensive productivity were similarly reduced by injuries in each of the next two years, Rodriguez batted over .300 each season, and combined for a total of 44 home runs in only 217 games. In 2003, he signed on as a free agent with the Florida Marlins and ended up leading them to a World Series victory over the New York Yankees. From there, he moved on to Detroit, where he spent four-plus seasons before being traded to the Yankees during the second half of the 2008 campaign.

In all, Rodriguez has hit more than 20 homers five times, batted over .300 ten times, and scored more than 100 runs twice. He has been selected to 14 All-Star teams, has won 13 Gold Gloves, and has finished in the top ten in the league MVP voting a total of four times. Here are his career numbers heading into 2009:

AB	HITS	RUNS	2B	3B	HR	RBI	AVG	SB	OBP	SLG PCT
8,645	2,605	1,253	524	48	295	1,217	.301	124	.339	.475

Those might appear to be only borderline Hall of Fame type numbers to many, and add to that the fact that Rodriguez has never led his league in any major statistical category, placing in the top five a total of only four times. But consider the following:

1. Rodriguez's 2,605 hits are the most by any catcher in major league history.
2. Rodriguez's 1,253 runs scored and 124 stolen bases are the second-highest totals ever compiled by a major league catcher, placing him behind only Carlton Fisk in both categories.
3. Rodriguez's 524 doubles are the most by any catcher in major league history.

Furthermore, it must be remembered that, as good as Rodriguez was offensively, his greatest strength has always been his defense. Over the years, not very many catchers have even been mentioned in the same breath as Johnny Bench. However, Rodriguez's fielding has actually been compared quite favorably to Bench's by many baseball experts. His 13 Gold Glove Awards are a testament to his defensive excellence, and his mere presence behind home plate often intimidates opposing baserunners. Rodriguez's defensive skills made him easily the American League's best all-around catcher for most of his career, and, with the possible exception of Mike Piazza, his generation's best all-around receiver.

Yet, there remains that cloud of suspicion hanging over Rodriguez as a result of the allegations made against him regarding his use of steroids. Did he, in fact, use them, and, if so, to what extent did they enhance his performance? Since Rodriguez never tested positive for steroids, there is no way of knowing for sure. Nevertheless, the feeling here is that the accusations made against him by Jose Canseco in his book were true. Regardless of what one's personal feelings might be towards Canseco, he seems to have described numerous events quite accurately in his work. And, if he did lie about anything, why haven't any of the players he lied about sued him for defamation of character?

In addition, Rodriguez's offensive numbers tend to support Canseco's claim. After failing to hit more than 21 home runs in any of his first six full seasons, Rodriguez suddenly slugged 35 home runs and drove in a career-high 113 runs in 1999. Over the next three seasons, he combined for 71 home runs in only 310 games. Canseco's contention is further supported by Rodriguez's performance since 2005. After the Congressional hearings were held prior to the start of the season, a svelte Rodriguez reported to Detroit Tigers training camp some 25 pounds lighter than he was at the conclusion of 2004. He has totaled only 45 home runs in the four seasons since, covering a total of 509 games. Yet he has remained a solid hitter, posting batting averages of .276, .300, .281, and .276 the last four years.

Thus, the evidence seems to strongly suggest that Rodriguez did indeed use steroids, although he likely used them for only four or five seasons. We will, therefore, work under the assumption that some of his offensive numbers cannot be taken at face value. Still, there is the defensive brilliance Rodriguez displayed behind the plate throughout his career. He was a great receiver from his earliest days in the major leagues, and there is no way of knowing if any performance-enhancing drugs he may have taken further added to his defensive skills. Would they have affected his quickness behind the plate, or his ability to throw runners out on the basepaths? That is open to much conjecture.

Taking all these factors into consideration, the feeling here is that Ivan Rodriguez should be deemed a worthy Hall of Famer when his playing days are over. Although his performance was likely aided a few seasons by the use of steroids, he earlier established himself as one of the two greatest catchers of his generation, and as arguably the finest defensive receiver ever. His 13 Gold Gloves are proof of his defensive brilliance, and he won seven of those prior to 1999, the year his offensive power numbers took a quantum leap. He also appeared in seven All-Star games prior to that, and was already considered to be the American League's best catcher. The members of the BBWAA should consider those points when Rodriguez eventually becomes eligible for induction.

Roger Clemens

Roger Clemens has often been referred to as the greatest pitcher of his era. Some have even called him the greatest pitcher in baseball history. Clemens' supporters point to his record seven Cy Young Awards, his 354 career victories, and his 4,672 career strikeouts. They argue that those 354 wins are the ninth highest total ever compiled in the major leagues, and, aside from Warren Spahn's 363 victories and Greg Maddux's 355, the most accumulated by any pitcher whose career began after 1920. In addition, Clemens' 4,672 strikeouts place him third on the all-time list, behind only Nolan Ryan and Randy Johnson.

Clemens was a truly great pitcher for much of his 24-year major league career that began in 1984 with the Boston Red Sox. He had his first great season for Boston in 1986, after becoming a regular member of the team's starting rotation for the first time at the start of the year. Clemens finished 24-4, with 238 strikeouts and a league-leading 2.48 earned run average to capture both A.L. MVP and Cy Young honors. He was brilliant again the following season, compiling a record of 20-9, with 256 strikeouts and a 2.97 ERA. Clemens was awarded his second straight Cy Young at the end of the season.

Clemens pitched extremely well in both 1988 and 1989, before having arguably his best year for the Red Sox in 1990. Although he finished second in the A.L. Cy Young balloting to Oakland's Bob Welch, Clemens compiled a record of 21-6, with 209 strikeouts and a league-leading 1.93 earned run average. He captured his third Cy Young Award the following season, finishing 18-10 for Boston and leading the league with 241 strikeouts and a 2.62 ERA. However, after pitching exceptionally well in 1992, Clemens was much less effective the next few seasons, prompting the Red Sox to allow him to leave via free agency prior to the start of the 1997 campaign.

After signing on with the Toronto Blue Jays, Clemens had two of his finest seasons in 1997 and 1998, capturing the pitcher's version of the triple crown both years. In 1997, he finished 21-7, with 292 strikeouts and a 2.05 ERA. The following year, he went 20-6, with 271 strikeouts and a 2.65 earned run average. Clemens won the Cy Young Award both times. At the end of 1998, he was dealt to the Yankees, for whom he pitched the next five seasons. Although somewhat less effective in his time in New York, Clemens pitched well enough to capture his sixth Cy Young Award in 2001, going 20-3, with 213 strikeouts and a 3.51 ERA. After announcing his retirement at the conclusion of the 2003 season, Clemens decided to pitch for his hometown Houston Astros, with whom he spent the next three years, before rejoining the Yankees for one final season in 2007. In his first year in Houston, Clemens, at the age of 42, won his record seventh Cy Young Award, compiling a record of 18-4, with 218 strikeouts and a 2.98 ERA.

Clemens ended his career with a won-lost record of 354-184 and an outstanding 3.12 earned run average. He led his league in wins four times, earned run average seven times, strikeouts five times, shutouts six times, complete games three times, and innings pitched twice. He won at least 20 games six times and accumulated at least 17 victories six other times. He also struck out more than 200 batters twelve times and compiled an earned run average below 3.00 twelve times, allowing the opposition fewer than two runs per game on two separate occasions. Clemens was a member of 11 All-Star teams and, in addition to winning the Cy Young Award seven times, placed in the top five in the voting three other times. He also finished in the top ten in the MVP balloting six times.

The resume of Roger Clemens is certainly an impressive one, prompting virtually everyone to think of him as a certain first-ballot Hall of Famer upon his retirement. However, Clemens' situation became far more complex in December of 2007 when his name was included on a list of current and former major league players that allegedly used performance-enhancing drugs during their careers. In an investigation conducted by former United States Senator George Mitchell, Clemens' former close friend and personal trainer Brian McNamee claimed he injected the pitcher with steroids and provided him with human growth hormones several times while he was a member of the Toronto Blue Jays and New York Yankees. Clemens vehemently denied the accusations, claiming they were lies, strongly defending the integrity of his accomplishments, and crediting much of his success to his intense workout regimen.

But one has to wonder what McNamee had to gain by making false statements about someone who was once so close to him. In addition, McNamee's testimony was given a great deal of credibility by another player he worked with in New York, Andy Pettitte, who admitted that McNamee's claim that he provided Pettitte with HGH on at least two separate occasions to help him recuperate from injuries was accurate. Furthermore, Pettitte later testified under oath that Clemens discussed with him the advantages of using HGH when the two were teammates in New York. Pettitte's testimony was perhaps more damaging to Clemens than McNamee's since the latter has a somewhat sordid background. Meanwhile, prior to his admitted use of HGH, Pettitte was always viewed as a model citizen.

While Clemens has steadfastly continued to proclaim his innocence, the feeling here is that he is indeed guilty as charged. Although his amazing ability to pitch extremely well into his mid-forties drew tremendous admiration from baseball enthusiasts everywhere, an examination of the progression of his career would seem to indicate that he received artificial assistance along the way.

Clemens pitched exceptionally well for Boston from 1986 to 1992, winning at least 17 games in each of those seasons, and topping 20 victories three times during that stretch. He also allowed fewer than three runs per game in six of those seven years, while striking out more than 200 batters each season and winning three Cy Young Awards. However, his performance began to slip in 1993, one of three consecutive seasons in which injuries forced him to miss several starts. Between 1993 and 1995, Clemens compiled a record of only 30-26, failed to strike out more than 168 batters in any single season, and compiled an ERA below 4.00 only once. After finishing just 10-13 in 1996, despite striking out 257 batters and pitching to a respectable 3.63 ERA, Clemens was allowed to leave Boston by Red Sox management, who believed that the 34-year-old power pitcher's best days were behind him.

Angered by the lack of interest shown him by the Boston front office, Clemens approached the 1997 campaign with a burning desire to prove he still had several good years left. In his first year in Toronto, Clemens re-established himself as baseball's best pitcher, capturing his fourth Cy Young Award by leading A.L. starters in virtually every statistical category. However, Clemens got off to a slow start in 1998, compiling a record of only 6-6 in his first 12 decisions.

It was right around that time that Brian McNamee claims he provided Clemens with performance-enhancing drugs for the first time. Clemens finished the season with 14 consecutive victories, to go 20-6 for the year, lead the league again in both strikeouts and ERA, and capture the Cy Young Award for the fifth time. McNamee followed Clemens to New York after the pitcher joined the Yankees in 1999 and claims he injected him with steroids during the latter stages of the 2000 campaign. Clemens was only average during the regular season that year, going 13-8 with a 3.70 ERA. But, after being hit hard by Oakland in the ALDS, Clemens was simply magnificent against Seattle in the ALCS and the Mets in the World

Series. In his lone start against the Mariners, Clemens pitched one of the most dominant games in postseason history, allowing only one hit and striking out 15 batters in a complete game shutout. He was almost as good against the Mets in the World Series, allowing only two hits and striking out nine in eight shutout innings. The following season, a 39-year-old Clemens went 20-3 for New York to win the sixth Cy Young Award of his career. After spending two more years with the Yankees, Clemens joined the Houston Astros in 2004 and proceeded to win his seventh Cy Young Award, at the age of 42, by going 18-4, with 218 strikeouts and a 2.98 earned run average. Although he finished only 13-8 the following season, Clemens was arguably more effective than he was in 2004, compiling a brilliant 1.87 ERA.

It could be argued that Clemens' resurgence after he left Boston at the conclusion of the 1996 campaign was spurred on by his desire to prove Red Sox management wrong. It could also be argued that the outstanding numbers he posted as a member of the Houston Astros were compiled pitching in a weaker league, against inferior lineups. It is also true that Clemens did indeed employ an extremely rigorous exercise routine to stay in top shape. But it is also a fact that his frame grew significantly larger and thicker during the second half of his career, and that much of the success he experienced during that period seemed to coincide with the injections that Brian McNamee claimed he administered to Clemens. Furthermore, it does not seem natural that a pitcher well into his forties would lose very little velocity off his fastball, and would continue to perform at an extremely high level.

Thus, the inevitable conclusion is that Roger Clemens did indeed artificially enhance his performance during the latter stages of his career. The question that follows, then, is whether or not he accomplished enough on his own to be voted into Cooperstown when he eventually becomes eligible for induction. Some members of the BBWAA have already gone on record as saying they will not enter his name on their ballots a few years from now. However, the feeling here is that, despite his duplicity and dishonesty, Clemens deserves to be elected to Cooperstown. Prior to 1998, the year he supposedly used performance-enhancing drugs for the first time, Clemens had already compiled a career record of 213-118, won four Cy Young Awards, been named league MVP once, been selected to six All-Star teams, and led his league in a major statistical category a total of 23 times. While it is extremely doubtful that Clemens would have been able to pitch as well as he did during the second half of his career without the assistance of artificial stimulants, he was a truly dominant pitcher even before he ever debased himself by injecting foreign substances into his system. The baseball writers should consider that fact when Clemens' name is eventually added to the list of eligible players.

Sammy Sosa

In my first published work, *A Team For The Ages: Baseball's All-Time All-Star Team*, I selected the greatest players at each position in the history of the game. First, I named the five greatest players at each position during the first half of the 20th century. Then, I did the same for the period extending from 1951 to 2003. Finally, I named an All-Time Team. When selecting my All-Time Team, I had Sammy Sosa fifth among rightfielders. In naming the team representing the period from 1951 to 2003, I placed Sosa third on the list of rightfielders, behind only Frank Robinson and Roberto Clemente, and just ahead of Tony Gwynn and Reggie Jackson. If I was to make my selections again, Sosa wouldn't fare nearly as well in the rankings. Since that time, several things have transpired that have caused me to view the slugging outfielder in a very different light.

For one thing, it has become quite apparent that Sosa simply was not a winning player. He was never willing to make the sacrifices necessary to make his team better, and he was always concerned only with his own statistics. He demonstrated that a few years ago when Chicago Cubs Manager Don Baylor suggested to Sosa that he work a little harder to improve his all-around game in order to help the team. He proposed that Sosa lose some of his bulk, cut down a little on his swing, and put forth more of an effort to be a good baserunner and defensive outfielder. Sosa responded by exhibiting the dark side that lay beneath the big, broad smile he always displayed to the general public. Demonstrating the depth of his selfishness, Sosa expressed his anger by chastising his manager in the newspapers, telling the media that Baylor made him feel unappreciated and disrespected. Eventually, Baylor was dismissed from his managerial position.

Sosa further demonstrated his self-absorption in his final year in Chicago. With the Cubs vying for a wild-card spot in the playoffs in 2004, Sosa was in the midst of a terrible second-half slump. Yet, when his manager attempted to drop him to fifth in the Chicago batting order, Sosa once again complained to the press, calling the action a show of "disrespect" to him.

Furthermore, Sosa was never a particularly good all-around player. He was never much of an outfielder, and he was only a good baserunner early in his career. After bulking up considerably early in his tenure with the Cubs, Sosa became a liability, both in the field and on the basepaths. He also was not very selective at the plate, compiling huge strikeout totals while drawing relatively few bases on balls. During his career, Sosa struck out at least 150 times in six different seasons. Meanwhile, he accumulated more than 80 walks only three times.

Yet, all the negatives notwithstanding, it is extremely difficult to overlook the prolific offensive numbers Sosa posted during his career, especially the ones he compiled between 1998 and 2001. Here are his statistics from those four seasons:

1998: 66 HR, 158 RBIs, .308 AVG, 134 RUNS, .647 SLG PCT
1999: 63 HR, 141 RBIs, .288 AVG, 114 RUNS, .635 SLG PCT
2000: 50 HR, 138 RBIs, .320 AVG, 106 RUNS, .634 SLG PCT
2001: 64 HR, 160 RBIs, .328 AVG, 146 RUNS, .737 SLG PCT

The 243 home runs Sosa hit during that four-year stretch represent the second highest total in baseball history (Mark McGwire hit 245 homers between 1996 and 1999). He was named the National League's Most Valuable Player in 1998, and also finished second in the balloting in 2001. In all, Sosa topped the 40-homer mark seven times, reaching 30 on four other occasions.

He also knocked in more than 100 runs nine times, scored more than 100 runs five times, and batted over .300 four times. Upon his retirement at the conclusion of the 2007 campaign, these were his career numbers:

AB	HITS	RUNS	2B	3B	HR	RBI	AVG	SB	OBP	SLG PCT
8,813	2,408	1,475	379	45	609	1,667	.273	234	.344	.534

Those 609 home runs place Sosa sixth on the all-time list. He also was a league-leader in a major statistical category a total of seven times, was selected to seven All-Star teams, and finished in the top ten in the league MVP voting seven different times. Furthermore, between 1998 and 2001, he was most certainly considered to be one of the elite players in the game. Thus, Sosa clearly has the necessary qualifications of a desirable Hall of Fame candidate.

However, there is one additional factor that must be considered. When I made my selections for my All-Time All-Star Team, I had reservations about including Sosa. Even though major league baseball had yet to institute any kind of formal investigative procedure, there was already widespread speculation as to which players might be involved with the use of performance-enhancing drugs. And Sosa's name was at the top of everyone's list. Although I chose to give him the benefit of the doubt when formulating the rankings for my book, I was extremely suspicious of Sosa, very much doubting the integrity of his offensive numbers. The progression of Sosa's career, as well as the development of his physique, both contributed greatly to my skepticism. Let's take a closer look at both.

When Sosa first entered the major leagues as a member of the Texas Rangers in 1989, he was a relatively thin 20-year old, with good running speed and only marginal home run power. He was traded to the Chicago White Sox later that year, and spent the next two seasons with the Sox, playing as a regular in one of them. In that season, Sosa hit 15 home runs, drove in 70 runs, scored 72 others, batted only .233, and struck out 150 times. Prior to the start of the 1992 campaign, the 23-year-old Sosa was dealt to the crosstown Cubs, for whom he appeared in only 67 games. In 262 at-bats, he hit only 8 home runs, drove in 25 runs, and batted .260. In 1993, a more physically mature 24-year-old Sosa became a regular in the Cubs starting lineup, hitting 33 home runs, knocking in 93 runs, scoring 92 others, batting .261, and stealing 36 bases. Over the next three seasons, Sosa continued to develop into more of a complete offensive player. In the strike-shortened 1994 campaign, he hit 25 home runs, drove in 70 runs, batted .300, and stole 22 bases. In 1995, he hit 36 home runs, knocked in 119 runs, batted .268, and stole 34 bases. In 1996, he hit 40 homers, drove in 100 runs, batted .273, and stole 18 bases. Sosa had another productive year in 1997, hitting 36 home runs, knocking in 119 runs, batting .251, and stealing 22 bases. It was in the following season, though, that he began his amazing run.

However, it was a few years earlier, during the mid-90s, that Sosa began adding a great deal of bulk to his frame. Indeed, he eventually developed a massive physique that was much larger than the one he carried just a few years earlier. Was this merely the result of advanced weight training, or was he perhaps using some form of performance-enhancing drug? Sosa would have us believe the former, especially since he did not test positive for steroids after baseball instituted its testing policy in 2005. But everything about the man suggests he used steroids to create additional body mass and greatly enhance his performance. After all, anyone who would cork his bat to get an edge would likely cheat in any number of other ways.

Furthermore, Sosa's evasiveness at the Congressional hearings, as well as the utter disdain he displayed for the entire proceedings, indicated that he must have something to hide. He schemingly had his opening statement read by his attorney, claiming in a prepared statement that he didn't wish to address the members of Congress directly since he was concerned that his poor English might cause his words to be misinterpreted. However, anyone familiar with Sosa knows that he speaks the English language quite well. He certainly never had any problems promoting himself to the media, or expressing his disdain for his managers to the press. Then, every time the members of Congress posed a question to Sosa, he responded by stating, "I agree with what Mark (McGwire) just said." Well, Sammy, that might have meant something, except for the fact that Mark never said anything. All McGwire kept reiterating was that he wasn't there to talk about the past.

Thus, we are left with someone who, based purely on statistics, deserves to be enshrined in Cooperstown, yet whose suspected use of steroids will undoubtedly place a huge question mark in the minds of most voters when he eventually becomes eligible for induction. Still, there will be those who consider this a no-brainer. They will say, "How could you even think about keeping someone out who has accomplished the things that Sosa has?" Since Sosa never tested positive for steroids he is likely to be elected to the Hall of Fame some time during his period of eligibility. That will be the politically correct thing to do, and most of the writers will probably not have the courage to do anything else. They will not have it in them to exclude from their ballots someone who compiled the kind of numbers Sosa did during his career. And they will not have the courage to ignore someone who is so revered throughout the Latino community. Hopefully, though, there will be others who feel as I do. They will have too many concerns about the legitimacy of Sosa's accomplishments to view him as a worthy Hall of Famer, and they will choose not to vote for him.

Gary Sheffield

For much of his 21-year career, spent with seven different teams, Gary Sheffield has been among the most productive and feared hitters in baseball. He has established a reputation as an outstanding clutch hitter, the kind that his teammates always want to see at the plate when the game is on the line. And his violent swing strikes fear into the hearts of opposing pitchers around the majors.

Sheffield began his major league career in 1988, as a shortstop with the Milwaukee Brewers. After being shifted to third base in 1990, he spent two more years in Milwaukee before joining the San Diego Padres in 1992. Sheffield had his breakout season with the Padres that year, hitting 33 home runs, driving in 100 runs, leading the National League with a .330 batting average, finishing third in the league MVP voting, and being named *The Sporting News* Player of the Year. The following year, Sheffield was traded to the Florida Marlins, who converted him into an outfielder. With Florida in 1996, Sheffield had another tremendous year, hitting 42 home runs, driving in 120 runs, scoring 118 others, batting .314, and walking a career-high 142 times. After winning the World Series in 1997, the Marlins decided to break up the nucleus of their team. As part of the fire sale, Sheffield was dealt to the Dodgers during the middle of the following season.

Sheffield spent the 1999-2001 campaigns in Los Angeles, averaging 38 home runs, 103 runs batted in, and 102 runs scored, and batting well over .300 each season. However, after squabbling with team management about the terms of his contract, he was traded to the Braves prior to the start of the 2002 campaign. Sheffield had two extremely productive seasons in Atlanta, having perhaps the finest all-around season of his career in 2003. That year, he hit 39 home runs, drove in a career-high 132 runs, scored a career-best 126 others, batted .330, and finished third in the league MVP voting. At the end of the season, he elected to join the Yankees via free agency in the hope that he might win another world championship with them. Over the next two seasons, Sheffield demonstrated that the change in leagues had virtually no effect on him. In 2004, he hit 36 home runs, knocked in 121 runs, scored another 117, batted .290, and finished runner-up in the league MVP balloting. In 2005, he hit 34 homers, drove in 123 runs, scored 104 others, and batted .291. However, Sheffield missed most of the 2006 campaign with an injury, and was subsequently dealt to the Detroit Tigers at the end of the year. With Detroit in 2007, Sheffield hit 25 home runs, knocked in 75 runs, and scored 107 others, despite missing more than a month with an injured hand. The 39-year-old Sheffield finally succumbed to Father Time in 2008, batting just .225, hitting only 19 home runs, and driving in just 57 runs in 114 games for the Tigers.

In all, Sheffield has hit more than 30 homers and driven in more than 100 runs eight times each, batted over .300 nine times, scored more than 100 runs seven times, and drawn more than 100 bases on balls four times. He has been named to nine All-Star teams, and has finished in the top ten in the league MVP voting six times, making it into the top five on three occasions. At the conclusion of the 2008 campaign, these were Sheffield's career statistics:

AB	HITS	RUNS	2B	3B	HR	RBI	AVG	SB	OBP	SLG PCT
8,949	2,615	1,592	454	25	499	1,633	.292	251	.394	.516

Those numbers would appear to make Sheffield a strong candidate for Hall of Fame honors when he eventually becomes eligible for induction, and his numerous All-Star Game appearances and consistently strong showing in the MVP balloting further enhance the strength of his candidacy. His credentials should receive an additional boost when he surpasses 500 home runs in the 2009 campaign.

Yet, there are other factors that must be considered when evaluating Sheffield's Hall of Fame credentials. For one thing, aside from winning the batting title in 1992, he has led his league in a major statistical category only one other time (on-base percentage in 1996). On the other hand, it should be pointed out that he has placed in the league's top five a total of 21 times during his career.

Something else to consider is the fact that Sheffield has been a poor postseason performer throughout most of his career. After batting .307 for the Braves during the 2002 regular season, Sheffield had only one hit in 16 times at bat during the playoffs, for a meager .062 batting average. After hitting 39 home runs, driving in 132 runs, and hitting .330 for Atlanta the following year, Sheffield batted just .143 in the playoffs. With the Yankees in 2004, Sheffield batted just .222 in the ALDS against the Minnesota Twins. He then got off to a hot start against Boston in the League Championship Series, but faltered badly as New York collapsed, losing the final four games to the Red Sox. In 2006, Sheffield had only one hit in 12 at-bats against Detroit in the ALDS, then berated Joe Torre to the press after his manager failed to enter his name on the lineup card for the final game. In 161 career post-season at-bats, Sheffield has only six home runs, 19 runs batted in, and a .248 batting average.

Nevertheless, Sheffield's lack of production during the postseason should not, by itself, keep him out of the Hall of Fame when he becomes eligible for induction. In Ted Williams' only World Series appearance, he had just 5 hits in 25 at-bats, for an uncharacteristic .200 batting average, with no home runs and only one run batted in. In four World Series appearances with the Cardinals, Stan Musial batted only .256, with just one home run and eight runs batted in. And, in three World Series with the Tigers, Ty Cobb batted just .262, with no home runs and nine runs batted in. Therefore, the ability to excel in the postseason has never been a prerequisite for being admitted into Cooperstown.

However, two other factors are much more likely to adversely affect Sheffield's chances of eventually being inducted. The first is rooted in the slugging outfielder's reputation for being a self-promoting malcontent who is concerned only about himself, and who, sooner or later, wears out his welcome wherever he goes. It is certainly true that not everyone agrees with that assessment. In fact, when Sheffield left Atlanta at the end of the 2003 season, Braves Manager Bobby Cox spoke glowingly of him, stating that the Yankees were getting someone who was both a good player and a good man in the clubhouse in Sheffield. Yet, Sheffield's time in Los Angeles and New York both ended in acrimony, with the outfielder criticizing the front office and manager of both teams.

Far more damaging to Sheffield's chances, though, is the speculation that he used steroids to greatly improve his performance. While the outfielder was long-rumored to be using some form of performance-enhancing drug, *San Francisco Chronicle* reporters Mark Fainaru-Wada and Lance Williams pointed a direct finger at him in their 2004 book entitled *Game of Shadows*. The aforementioned work, the result of 15 months of relentless investigation by the authors, broke the story of

BALCO, a tiny nutritional supplement company that, according to sworn testimony, supplied elite athletes with banned drugs. The book provided the names of specific athletes who were involved, identifying, among others, Sheffield and his former close friend Barry Bonds.

One particular incident that was mentioned in the book described the manner in which Bonds referred Sheffield to his close friend and personal trainer, Greg Anderson, when Sheffield was playing for the Braves. In the midst of a horrendous slump, Sheffield sought out Bonds for advice. According to the book, Bonds suggested he contact Anderson, who subsequently supplied him with steroids that enabled Sheffield to go on a hitting tear shortly thereafter.

There are those who might doubt the credibility of the book's contents. But it is difficult to question the accuracy of a work that so precisely describes the details of events steeped in so much subterfuge. And certainly none of the parties mentioned in the work have filed lawsuits against either Fainaru-Wada or Williams. Furthermore, an examination of the careers of both Bonds and Sheffield greatly supports the contentions made by the book's authors.

In Sheffield's case, the outfielder has had what could be classified as eight true Hall-of-Fame type seasons. The first two came relatively early in his career, with the Padres in 1992, and with the Marlins in 1996. However, those were the only two dominant years he had in his first eleven in the major leagues. In the six full seasons he played during that period, Sheffield averaged 25 home runs and 86 runs batted in. Sheffield's six other exceptional seasons occurred between 1999 and 2005, after he turned 30. Over that seven-year stretch, he averaged 35 home runs and 110 runs batted in. He had his three most productive years in 2003, 2004, and 2005, between the ages of 34 and 36. Therefore, while some might attempt to attribute the increase in offensive productivity Sheffield experienced rather late in his career to other factors, the logical assumption is that the accusations made against him in *Game of Shadows* are true. That being the case, it would be impossible to endorse the selection of Sheffield to the Hall of Fame when his playing days are over.

Barry Bonds

The Hall of Fame credentials of Barry Bonds are undeniable. He ended his career with 762 home runs, the most in major league history. He also is first all-time in walks (2,558), third in runs scored (2,227), fourth in runs batted in (1,996), ranks high on the list in on-base percentage (.444) and slugging percentage (.607), had a .298 lifetime batting average, and stole 514 bases in his 22 major league seasons. Bonds holds the single-season records for most home runs (73), bases on balls (232), highest on-base percentage (.609), and highest slugging percentage (.863). He was the first player ever to hit more than 400 home runs and steal more than 400 bases. He later became the first man to surpass 500 homers and 500 steals, and he eventually became the only member of the 700/500 club. Bonds is the only player in baseball history to win seven Most Valuable Player Awards. He also finished in the top five in the voting five other times.

Bonds was selected to 14 All-Star teams and won eight Gold Glove Awards. He hit more than 30 homers 14 times, drove in more than 100 runs 12 times, scored more than 100 runs 12 times, batted over .300 on 11 separate occasions, and stole more than 30 bases nine times. He led his league in home runs twice, in runs batted in and runs scored one time each, in batting average twice, in on-base percentage ten times, and in slugging percentage seven times. Bonds is generally recognized as the finest player of his generation, and as one of the greatest players in the history of the game.

The only thing that most people question about Bonds is the legitimacy of many of his accomplishments, and the authenticity of the offensive numbers he compiled during the latter stages of his career. Bonds was an exceptional all-around player his first 13 big-league seasons, winning three Most Valuable Player Awards and eight Gold Gloves. However, after adding some 20 pounds of muscle to his frame prior to the start of the 1999 campaign, Bonds became far more dominant than he ever was before. He greatly increased his offensive production in 1999 and 2000, then became arguably the most dominant hitter in baseball history in 2001, at the age of 36. That is something that goes against the very laws of nature. No matter how well-conditioned an athlete may be, it is a simple fact that, after he reaches his mid-30s, his reflexes and, in the case of a baseball player, his bat-speed, begin to slow down. With Bonds, though, the opposite occurred.

Let's take a look at his numbers to create a clearer picture:

- Over his first ten major league seasons, from 1986 to 1995, Bonds hit more than 40 home runs in a season only once (46 in 1993). He also surpassed 30 homers four other times. Over that same period, he knocked in more than 100 runs five times and batted over .300 four times.
- From 1996 to 2000, Bonds topped 30 homers each season, surpassing 40 home runs on three separate occasions. He peaked at 49 in 2000.
- In 2001, at age 36, Bonds established a new single-season major league record by hitting 73 home runs—*24* more than he hit in any previous season. He also established a new single-season record for highest slugging percentage (.863), while knocking in a career-high 137 runs.
- Bonds followed that up in 2002 by hitting 46 home runs in only 403 at-bats (he walked 198 times). He also batted a career-high .370, to win the first batting title of his career at age 37.
- In 2003, Bonds hit 45 home runs in only 390 at-bats, while batting .341 and capturing his third consecutive Most Valuable Player Award.
- In 2004, at age 39, Bonds hit 45 home runs in only 373 at-bats, while batting a league-leading .362. He also established new all-time single-season records for most walks (232) and highest on-base percentage (.609). At season's end, Bonds was awarded his record seventh MVP trophy.

Furthermore, consider the following:

- The tremendous amount of bulk that Bonds gradually added to his frame over the course of his career, particularly during the off-season preceding the 1999 campaign (he reported to spring training that year with an additional 20 pounds of muscle on his frame). Also, the huge increase in the size of his head since his earliest days in the league.
- The fact that his personal trainer was his boyhood friend Greg Anderson, who not only has a checkered past, but, who, in October of 2005, was sentenced to three months in prison for money laundering and steroids distribution.
- The fact that it was Anderson who introduced Bonds to Victor Conte, a known steroid-supplier, at the end of the 2000 season. In 2001, Bonds reported to spring an additional 18 pounds heavier, solid as a rock—and a better hitter than he ever was before.
- The fact that Bonds' use of steroids is described, in detail, in *Game of Shadows*.

These facts are difficult to ignore and detract greatly from many of Bonds' career accomplishments. For that reason, those members of the media who began referring to Bonds as "the greatest player in baseball history" at the conclusion of the 2001 campaign, and have continued to do so ever since, really need to be a bit more responsible with the statements they make to the public. Not only are they failing to consider all the facts, but they have obviously forgotten just how far Bonds rose in stature in just a few short years. Apparently none of them remember that they said nary a word when Bonds was not included on the All-Century Team that was announced just prior to the turn of the century. They didn't say anything at the time because, while Bonds was an exceptional player prior to 2000, he simply wasn't the Superman he later became.

Still, even totally disregarding everything Barry Bonds accomplished after 2000, he has to be considered a legitimate Hall of Famer. Prior to the start of the 2000 season, he already had

445 home runs, 1,299 runs batted in, 1,455 runs scored, 2,010 hits, and 460 stolen bases. He already won three Most Valuable Player Awards and finished in the top five in the voting another four times. He also was selected to eight All-Star teams and won eight Gold Glove Awards. Therefore, in spite of the arrogance, condescension, and lack of integrity Bonds displayed throughout his career, he deserves to be voted into Cooperstown when his name is eventually added to the list of eligible players.

As for how Bonds' records should be viewed, that is up to the discretion of the individual. My own personal feeling is that, until someone else comes along to shatter the record, Hank Aaron will remain major league baseball's All-Time Home Run Champion, just as Roger Maris continues to remain its single-season record holder.

Alex Rodriguez

The man who most people considered to be the player most likely to restore the integrity of baseball's all-time home run record was Alex Rodriguez. The third baseman for the New York Yankees ended the 2008 campaign with 553 home runs and, at age 33, appears to have an excellent chance of surpassing Barry Bonds' total of 762. More than just a great home-run hitter, A-Rod's 1,606 runs batted in have also put him in position to seriously challenge Hank Aaron's existing RBI record of 2,297, and his 1,605 runs scored have him on pace to eventually surpass Rickey Henderson's career record of 2,295. With 2,404 hits, Rodriguez also seems likely to join the exclusive 3,000 hits club before he retires. Furthermore, Rodriguez's brilliance has not been limited to the offensive end of the game throughout his major league career. Before moving over to play third base after joining the Yankees prior to the start of the 2004 season, A-Rod won two Gold Gloves as a shortstop.

Indeed, his unique blend of power, speed, and fielding ability has prompted many baseball experts to view Rodriguez as arguably the finest all-around player of his era, and as one of the greatest players in baseball history.

Rodriguez's skills began to surface shortly after he joined the Seattle Mariners as an 18-year-old at the end of the 1994 season. He became the Mariners' starting shortstop two years later and hit 36 home runs, drove in 123 runs, led the league with 141 runs scored and a .358 batting average, and finished second in the A.L. MVP voting in just his first full season in the big leagues. At the end of the campaign, Rodriguez was named *The Sporting News* Player of the Year. After another solid season the following year, Rodriguez became a member of the elite 40-40 club in 1998, hitting 42 home runs and stealing 46 bases for the Mariners. He also knocked in 124 runs, scored another 123, collected 213 hits, and batted .310 for Seattle that year.

The 1998 season was just the first of six consecutive years in which Rodriguez surpassed the 40-homer mark, making him only the second player in the history of the game to achieve that feat (Babe Ruth was the other). In two of those seasons, Rodriguez surpassed 50 homers, hitting 52 long balls in 2001, and another 57 in 2002, both for Texas. After joining the Yankees in 2004, Rodriguez won his second Most Valuable Player Award the following season, hitting 48 home runs, driving in 130 runs, scoring 124 others, and batting .321. He captured his third MVP trophy at the conclusion of the 2007 campaign for leading the major leagues with 54 homers, 156 runs batted in, and 143 runs scored, while batting .314.

In all, Rodriguez has topped 40 homers in eight of his 13 full seasons in the major leagues, surpassing 30 on three other occasions. He has also driven in more than 100 runs 12 times, batted over .300 nine times, and scored more than 100 runs each season. In scoring more than 100 runs for the 13th consecutive season in 2008, Rodriguez became the first player to do so since Lou Gehrig. In addition to his batting title, Rodriguez has led the league in home runs five times, runs batted in twice, runs scored five times, hits once, and doubles once.

Needless to say, Rodriguez's many achievements appeared to make him a future certain first-ballot Hall of Famer heading into the 2009 season, even if he were never to play another game. However, his situation became far more muddled in early February of that year after it was discovered that he was one of 104 players who tested positive for performance-enhancing drugs in a 2003 survey testing conducted by Major League Baseball. It later surfaced that Rodriguez was found guilty of using testosterone and an anabolic steroid known by the brand name Primobolan. Testosterone can be taken legally with an appropriate medical prescription, but Primobolan is not an approved prescription drug in the United States, nor was it in 2003. According to steroid experts, the latter substance improves strength and maintains lean muscle with minimal bulk development. It also is known to have relatively few side effects.

Thus, the "clean" image that Alex Rodriguez always attempted to present of himself to fans and the media alike suddenly became tarnished, and the hopes of baseball purists everywhere that the all-time home-run record would be legitimized once more were dashed. Rodriguez quickly tried to minimize, at least to some degree, the negative perception he knew most people would subsequently hold towards him by admitting during a television interview conducted two days after his name was leaked to the press that he used performance-enhancing drugs from 2001-03. A-Rod attempted to explain his actions by claiming that they were prompted by his desire to prove he was worthy of the exorbitant contract he signed with the Texas Rangers prior to the start of the 2001 season. He stated in his TV interview: "When I arrived in Texas in 2001, I felt an enormous amount of pressure. I felt like I had all the weight of the world on top of me and I needed to perform, and perform at a high level every day."

Rodriguez accepted full culpability for his actions, claiming he was "young, stupid, and naïve" at the time, and also stating that he didn't use performance-enhancing drugs prior to 2001, and that he hasn't used them since 2003.

If Rodriguez's words are true, the feeling here is that he must still be deemed a worthy Hall of Fame candidate when his playing days are over. After all, he was a great player in his five full seasons in Seattle before he joined the Rangers, and he has subsequently been a great player in his five years in New York. Here is a breakdown of his per-season averages with all three teams:

TEAM	YEARS	HITS	RUNS	2B	3B	HR	RBI	AVG	SB
SEATTLE	1996-2000	184	122	38	2	37	115	.315	25
TEXAS	2001-2003	190	127	30	3	52	132	.305	15
NEW YORK	2004-2008	174	119	28	1	42	123	.303	21

Although Rodriguez averaged several more home runs per-season in Texas, his overall numbers in both Seattle and New York are quite comparable to the figures he compiled with the Rangers. And at least part of the home-run discrepancy could probably be attributed to the fact that the Ballpark at Arlington has always been a great park for home-run hitters. Furthermore, as Rodriguez has steadfastly maintained, he had arguably his two finest all-around seasons in Seattle (1996) and New York (2007).

Nevertheless, one must seriously doubt the sincerity of anything Rodriguez says. There are just too many inconsistencies in his words. In an interview conducted with CBS's *60 Minutes* in December of 2007, Rodriguez answered "No" when he was asked if he had ever used steroids, human growth hormone, or any other performance-enhancing substance. He even said that he had never even considered using them.

Rodriguez later said during his 2009 admission to ESPN television, "...to be quite honest, I don't know exactly what substance I was guilty of using." Yet he directly contradicted those words just one week later during a press conference held at the New York Yankees spring training facility. In his address to the media, Rodriguez not only provided the name of the performance-enhancing drug he used, but also discussed the frequency with which he took it.

Thus, one must question the veracity of Rodriguez's claims, including those that state he used performance-enhancing drugs only from 2001-2003. He stated that his actions those three years were prompted by his desire to succeed under the enormous amount of pressure he felt after signing his contract with the Rangers. But Rodriguez left Texas in 2004 to play in New York—the media capital of the world—for the most famous franchise in sports. Are we to believe that he felt less pressure after joining his new team? Furthermore, three major league players revealed to *Sports Illustrated* that Gene Orza, the chief operating officer of the players' union, tipped off Rodriguez in early September of 2004 that he would be drug-tested later that month. And, who is to say that, despite his claims to the contrary, Rodriguez has not been using the undetectable HGH ever since?

Alex Rodriguez has nine years remaining on his contract with the New York Yankees, and it will presumably be some 15 years before he becomes eligible for induction into the Hall of Fame. Perhaps during that time more information will surface that will enable us to better understand the degree to which Rodriguez used performance-enhancing drugs over the course of his career. Perhaps a test for HGH will be developed in the next year or two that will allow us to be completely certain that the numbers Rodriguez compiles each season are legitimate. And quite possibly the names of the other 103 players who tested positive will be revealed, altering our view of several of the other men included on this list of Future Hall of Famers. But, because of his involvement with steroids, Rodriguez can never be considered the *true* home-run champion, no matter how many homers he goes on to hit.

As for his status as a potential Hall-of-Famer, my first inclination is to say that Rodriguez probably should be inducted into Cooperstown when his playing days are over. However, it would probably be best to withhold judgment on that issue until we know more of the facts, and until Rodriguez actually does become eligible.

SUMMARY

Throughout this book, an attempt has been made to accurately identify those players who truly belong in the Baseball Hall of Fame, and those who do not. Along the way, many opinions were expressed that some will agree with, and others probably will not. Behind every player evaluation and every opinion expressed, though, was a sincere effort to bring to the forefront the chagrin that many baseball fans feel over the manner in which the quality of a once great American institution has degenerated over the years. Even though induction into the Hall of Fame is still considered to be the greatest honor a baseball player can hope to attain, in truth, it has lost some of its luster. Due to the lack of integrity shown by many of those involved in the selection process, and an overall lowering of the standards, many former players have been admitted who, based on the criteria used in this book, were clearly undeserving. In addition, there are several other players with superior Hall of Fame credentials who have yet to be elected for one reason or another.

There are currently 228 members of the Hall of Fame who were elected primarily as players. The evaluations conducted here indicate that 148 of those players were clearly deserving of election, while another 49 men possessed borderline credentials. That leaves 31 others who truly never should have been admitted. Their presence in the Hall of Fame is either the result of voter bias, peer pressure from other committee members, or just plain poor judgment, and serves as a constant reminder that the Hall's standards are not what they should be. Ever since that first group of 21 players from the turn of the last century was elected in 1945 and 1946, the Hall's standards have not been what they once were.

Unfortunately, we cannot go back in time and undo the mistakes that were made in the past. The players who don't truly belong are in, and will remain in. Nothing can be done to change that. However, what we can do is prevent the same type of mistakes from being made in the future. Earlier errors in judgment should not be further propagated. Taking this approach may allow us to restore, at least to some degree, much of the integrity the Hall of Fame has lost over the years.

As this book has suggested throughout, far too many borderline candidates have already been elected to Cooperstown The feeling here is that the members of both the BBWAA and the Veterans Committee should refrain from electing such candidates in the future. However, those involved with the selection process have chosen to ignore several other players whose qualifications are far more impressive than many of those whose names they entered on their ballots.

Following is a list, in no particular order, of the 25 most-deserving players yet to be inducted:

1) Gil Hodges
2) Don Mattingly
3) Steve Garvey
4) Keith Hernandez
5) Cecil Cooper
6) Vern Stephens
7) Ken Boyer
8) Ron Santo
9) Graig Nettles
10) Stan Hack
11) Joe Torre
12) Ted Simmons
13) Thurman Munson
14) Bob Elliott
15) Bob Johnson
16) Tony Oliva
17) Dale Murphy
18) Andre Dawson
19) Tim Raines
20) Dave Parker
21) Jack Morris
22) Jim Kaat
23) Tommy John
24) Luis Tiant
25) Bob Caruthers

Most of these men are not likely to be elected to Cooperstown in the future, and most of them shouldn't be. However, as I noted earlier, they are more deserving than several players who have already been inducted. If the ten most-deserving players on this list could somehow replace the ten least-deserving members currently in the Hall of Fame, the substitutions would look something like this:

Players In	**Players Out**
Ron Santo	Rick Ferrell
Ken Boyer	Roger Bresnahan
Gil Hodges	Ray Schalk
Andre Dawson	Bill Mazeroski
Vern Stephens	Joe Tinker
Joe Torre (as player/manager)	Johnny Evers
Ted Simmons	Tommy McCarthy
Luis Tiant	Harry Hooper
Bob Caruthers	Rube Marquard
Tim Raines	Eppa Rixey

Of course, such a displacement is impossible, and the names *Hooper*, *Marquard*, *Tinker*, and *McCarthy* will forever be intermingled with *Ruth*, *Grove*, *Wagner*, and *Mays*. The Hall of Fame will always have to live with the shame and embarrassment caused by such an inequity.

GLOSSARY

Abbreviations and Statistical Terms

AB. At-bats. The number of times a player comes to the plate to try to get on base. It does not include those times when a walk was issued, the player hit a sacrifice fly to score a runner, or the player advanced a baserunner via a sacrifice bunt.

AVG. Batting average. The number of hits divided by the number of at-bats.

Bases on balls. Better known as walks. A free trip to first base as a penalty to the pitcher when he fails to get the ball over the plate four times during an at-bat.

CG. Complete games pitched.

ERA. Earned run average. The number of earned runs a pitcher gives up, per nine innings. This does not include runs that scored as a result of errors made in the field and is calculated by dividing the number of runs given up, by the number of innings pitched, and multiplying the result by 9.

GS. Games started by a pitcher.

HITS. Base hits. Awarded when a runner safely reaches at least first base upon a batted ball, if no error is recorded.

HR. Home runs. Fair ball hit over the fence, or one hit to a spot that allows the batter to circle the bases before the ball is returned to home plate, if no error is recorded.

IP. Innings pitched.

L. Losses.

OBP. On-base percentage. Hits plus walks plus hit-by-pitches, divided by plate appearance.

PCT. Winning percentage. A pitcher's number of wins divided by his number of total decisions (that is, wins plus losses).

RBI. Runs batted in. Awarded to the batter when a runner scores upon a safely batted ball, a sacrifice or a walk.

RUNS. Runs scored by a player.

SB. Stolen bases.

SLG PCT. Slugging percentage. The number of total bases earned by all singles, doubles, triples and home runs, divided by the total number of at-bats.

SO. Strikeouts.

3B. Three-base hits. Triples.

2B. Two-base hits. Doubles.

W. Wins.

BIBLIOGRAPHY

BOOKS

DeMarco, Tony, et al., *The Sporting News Selects 50 Greatest Sluggers*. The Sporting News, a division of Times Mirror Magazines, Inc., St. Louis, Mo., 2000.

Dewey, Donald, and Acocella, Nicholas, *The Biographical History of Baseball*. Carroll & Graf, Inc., New York, 1995.

Honig, Donald, *Baseball When the Grass Was Real*. Coward, McCann and Geoghegan, Inc., New York, 1975.

James, Bill, *Whatever Happened to the Hall of Fame?* Simon and Schuster, New York, 1994.

Langford, Walter M., *Legends of Baseball*. Diamond Communications, Inc., Indiana, 1987.

Nemec, David, et al., *Players of Cooperstown—Baseball's Hall of Fame*. Publications International, Ltd., Lincolnwood, Il., 1994.

Okrent, Daniel, and Lewine, Harris, eds., with David Nemec, *The Ultimate Baseball Book*. Houghton Mifflin Co. / A Hiltown Book, Boston, Mass., 1988.

Ritter, Lawrence, *The Glory of Their Times*. Random House, New York, 1985.

Shalin, Mike, and Neil Shalin, *Out by a Step: The 100 Best Players Not in the Baseball Hall of Fame*. Diamond Communications, Inc., Indiana, 2002.

Thorn, John, and Palmer, Pete, eds., with Michael Gershman, *Total Baseball*. HarperCollins Pub., Inc., New York, 1993.

VIDEOS

New York Yankees: The Movie. Magic Video Publishing Company, 1987.

The Sporting News' 100 Greatest Baseball Players. National Broadcasting Co., 1999.

INTERNET WEBSITES

The Ballplayers, online at BaseballLibrary.com (http://www.baseballlibrary.com/baseballlibrary/ballplayers).

Historical Stats, online at MLB.com (http://www.mlb.com/stats_historical/individual_stats_player).

History, online at BaseballHallofFame.org (http://www.baseballhalloffame.org/about/history)

Lists, online at BaseballHallofFame.org (http://www.baseballhalloffame.org/hofers_and_honorees/lists)

Negro Leagues Profiles, online at MLB.com (http://www.mlb.com/history/negro_leagues_profile).

Rules, online at BaseballHallofFame.org (http://www.baseballhalloffame.org/hofers_and_honorees/rules)

The Players, online at Baseball-Almanac.com (http://www.baseball-almanac.com/players).

The Players, online at Baseballink.com (http://www.baseballink.com/baseballink/players).

The Players, online at Baseball-Reference.com (http://www.baseball-reference.com/players).

Voting, online at BaseballHallofFame.org (http://www.baseballhalloffame.org/history/hof_voting)

INDEX

A

B

C

D

E

F

G

H

I

J

K

L

M

N

O

P

Q

R

S

T

V

W

Y